The way we handle mental health and mental illness in our society is neither fair nor effective. We have dumped so much of it onto the criminal justice system, which isn't any good for people who need treatment; it also puts police and correctional officers in impossible situations where they are bound to fail, sometimes tragically. Professor Bratina and the other contributors to this book do a fine job of dissecting the current situation and describing solutions that would greatly improve the terrible mess our negligence has created.

—**Gary Cordner,** *Professor Emeritus, Kutztown University*

FORENSIC MENTAL HEALTH

Forensic Mental Health: Framing Integrated Solutions describes a criminal justice–mental health nexus that touches every population—juvenile and adult male and female offenders, probationers and parolees, the aging adult prison population, and victims of crime. In the United States today, the criminal justice system functions as a mental health provider, but at great cost to society. The author summarizes the historical roots of this crisis and provides an overview of mental illness and symptoms, using graphics to illustrate the most prevalent disorders encountered by police and other first responders. Bratina demonstrates in detail how the Sequential Intercept Model (SIM) supports integration of the U.S. healthcare and justice systems to offer more positive outcomes for offenders with mental illness.

This book takes a multidisciplinary approach, addressing social work, psychology, counseling, and special education, and covers developments such as case law related to the right to treatment and trauma-informed care. Designed for advanced undergraduates, this text also serves as a training resource for practitioners working with the many affected justice-involved individuals with mental illness, including juveniles, veterans, and substance abusers.

Michele P. Bratina is an Assistant Professor in the Criminal Justice Department at West Chester University in West Chester, Pennsylvania. Previously, she was the Forensic and Children's Mental Health Coordinator for the Florida Department of Children and Families in the 19th Judicial Circuit—a role that inspired this book. She is First Vice President of the Northeastern Association of Criminal Justice Sciences (NEACJS) Academy of Criminal Justice Sciences and holds the position of Executive Counselor for the Academy of Criminal Justice Sciences (ACJS) Juvenile Justice Section. Her research interests and publications revolve around issues related to human exploitation, criminological theory, race, social structure, ethnicity and crime, and forensic mental health. She has published her work in the *Journal of Ethnicity in Criminal Justice* and in the *International Journal of Police Science and Management*.

FORENSIC MENTAL HEALTH

Framing Integrated Solutions

MICHELE P. BRATINA

Routledge
Taylor & Francis Group

NEW YORK AND LONDON

First published 2017
by Routledge
711 Third Avenue, New York, NY 10017

and by Routledge
2 Park Square, Milton Park, Abingdon, Oxon, OX14 4RN

Routledge is an imprint of the Taylor & Francis Group, an informa business

Library of Congress Cataloging-in-Publication Data
Names: Bratina, Michele P., 1972– author.
Title: Forensic mental health : framing integrated solutions / Michele P. Bratina.
Description: New York, NY : Routledge, 2017.
Identifiers: LCCN 2016054629 | ISBN 9781138935389 (hbk) |
    ISBN 9781138935396 (pbk) | ISBN 9781315677460 (ebk)
Subjects: LCSH: Forensic psychiatry—Methods. | People with mental disabilities
    and crime—United States. | Mentally ill offenders—Care—United States.
Classification: LCC RA1151 .B73 2017 | DDC 614/.15—dc23
LC record available at https://lccn.loc.gov/2016054629

ISBN: 978-1-138-93538-9 (hbk)
ISBN: 978-1-138-93539-6 (pbk)
ISBN: 978-1-315-67746-0 (ebk)

Typeset in Bembo
by Apex CoVantage, LLC

Visit the eResource: www.routledge.com/cw/9781138935396

For my dad, Vito William Bracciodieta.
Your encouragement and love will last forever.

CONTENTS

PREFACE

The criminal justice–mental health nexus is a profound topic in that it touches on every population in the field of criminal justice—juvenile and adult male and female offenders, probationers and parolees, sexually violent predators, the aging adult prison population, and victims of crime and serious abuse. Through a multifaceted approach to learning and understanding the crime–mental health relationship, readers will be able to more effectively gauge the issues presented and the various ways in which they might become positive change agents in the field.

Prior to my career in academia, I had the fortunate experience of working for the Florida Department of Children and Families (DCF), Judicial Circuit 19, Substance Abuse and Mental Health Program Office (SAMH). I did not realize it at the time, but Dr. George Woodley, program administrator and all-around amazing human, had the keen ability to predict my future when he hired me in the summer of 2010. In the position of "Forensic and Children's Mental Health Coordinator," I was quickly forced to navigate multiple systems of care, as I was responsible for the direct oversight of contracted programs that provided an array of substance abuse and mental health services to children, adolescents, and adults—many of whom were justice-involved. During that time, I witnessed a substantial amount of trauma and abuse and the resistance of service providers who were unable or unwilling to venture across systems to make change; however, I also observed glimpses of great healing and progress and the development of partnerships between people and agencies in places where I would least expect it.

Unfortunately, due to threats of restructuring and the elimination of many SAMH positions, including my own, I left SAMH to accept a tenure-track faculty position back in Pennsylvania. At about the same time, I accepted a temporary contracted position as a "systems integrator." The meetings I facilitated involved individuals from multiple systems of care, including juvenile justice and criminal justice systems and child welfare, substance abuse, education, and several others—and we were engaging in information sharing beyond anything I had experienced before. So much of this text comes from that perspective. The original idea for the book, and the motivation necessary for its development and fruition, can be attributed to the traumatized children who suffer from want of true love and compassion; the stigmatized mental health court clients who proudly express their progress to an intimidating, yet relatable, judge; and the frustrations observed between educators, providers, and police who, from across a conference table, manage together to find solutions to the continued criminalization of mental illness.

The scope of this book is broad because it approaches the subject matter from a multidisciplinary perspective, including relevant concepts and issues in the fields of social work, psychology, counseling, and special education. The reader will benefit from getting the latest developments in areas such as prisoner rights to treatment and juvenile justice—particularly, more recent developments pertaining to the *school-to-prison pipeline* and *trauma-informed care*. Instructors will benefit from having access to pedagogical tools and activities that corroborate with the major sections of the book. Furthermore, each chapter ends with a list of key concepts/acronyms (italicized throughout the chapter) and a list of discussion questions so that the instructor can assess and students can apply what they have learned throughout the course.

The progression and current state of systems of care as they relate to mental health and co-occurring substance abuse deserve much discussion so that students interested in forensic mental health studies can formulate an accurate perception of the importance of the model in practice.

Structure of the Text

The bulk of the text is designed as a conceptual "walk through" the justice system; however, in contrast with typical criminal justice–related texts, the discussion at each level is based on key diversion points and offers suggestions and solutions for positive systematic changes. Using the *Sequential Intercept Model* (SIM) as a guide (discussed in more detail in Chapter 3), the chapters attempt to fuse practical and academic knowledge to present an accurate vision of forensic mental health.

Before delving into the core intercept points as identified in Chapters 5–9, some essential background factors must be identified and clarified further for the reader. Chapter 1 provides a glimpse as to what is meant by "mental illness" and its general prevalence rates. The chapter also introduces the concept of forensic mental health and outlines key differences inherent between the mental health and justice systems in the context of the "language" spoken and challenges encountered by each. The purpose for leading the rest of the text with this section is to understand some of the conflict that has historically bounded individuals to an independent philosophy that does not allow or support change. In this way, the reader quickly begins to understand that most failed systems lead to multiple encounters with the same population of individuals.

Chapter 2 traces the historical treatment of persons with mental illness in the United States, with some comparative information from places outside the United States. Most importantly, the chapter introduces the idea of stigmatization and provides a context for the transformation in which society has criminalized mental illness. The Sequential Intercept Model is presented to the reader in Chapter 3, along with supporting literature, with a description for the remaining structure of the book.

In Chapter 4, Dr. Ford Brooks delineates mental health and co-occurring substance abuse from a more clinical perspective. This is the perfect backdrop for our structural model, as the information provided foreshadows the probable reasons why the initial interception with the justice system happens in the first place. Chapters 5 through 9 provide concepts, literature, research, and case examples for each of the key diversion points for justice-involved offenders. Though following along with the SIM map, the reader will soon notice that the material in these chapters is presented in a format that is similar to the more traditional criminal justice textbook—policing, courts, corrections—in that particular order.

The final chapter synthesizes research and practice to illustrate the salience of systems integration and interagency collaboration. Several key initiatives that have been successful in terms of diversion are presented and discussed, including the trauma-informed care (TIC) movement.

Several pedagogical tools are provided that can be used alongside the text to bridge theory and practice, including varied classroom activities and experiential learning projects, questions for discussion, and mini-research assignments using existing data sources. The tools are designed to provide learners with opportunities to further develop their knowledge and ability to critically analyze the issues presented, but also, to increase their opportunities to practice collaboration and, in some cases, cross-disciplinary approaches in responding to issues that affect multiple systems. The ultimate goal of these activities is to allow learners the opportunity to read firsthand accounts of the nature of the work involved so that they might enhance their skill at decision making, and further explore the required academic preparation for varied human service–related occupations they may not have considered before now.

Pedagogical Tools

Embedded in Chapter 3 is an illustration of the Sequential Intercept Model for reference when navigating through the text, as well as for use with activities requiring learners to identify and discuss various diversion points. Spotlight features that may include tables/figures and photos pertaining to particular programs, agencies, and case studies are provided throughout the chapters; also, in selected chapters, there is a section that presents featured practitioners and their perspectives on a number of pertinent issues discussed in the text. These "Practitioner's Corner" sections are designed to give students/readers some insight on careers in the field that may involve the divergence of criminal justice and mental health. Other pedagogical tools include "Thinking Critically" and "Fast Fact" text boxes throughout the chapters that present key issues for discussion and other critical thinking activities. There is also a glossary of key terms at the end of each chapter.

Ancillaries

Chapters outline specific challenges presented by this population for police, probation, parole, and other actors; students are provided the chance to apply what they have learned to "real-world" scenarios that are provided for each chapter. Along with these case studies are possible questions to enhance learning in and out of the classroom (e.g., take-home writing assignments). Sample exams and other thought-provoking in-class activities are also available.

A webliography is also provided corresponding with chapter content that links to relevant educational videos, including seminars, monologues, panel presentations, and two PBS/Frontline documentaries, *The New Asylums* and *The Released*, and other media content (particularly news sources) are provided as supplemental learning resources.

CONTRIBUTORS

Taylor P. Andrews, Esq.
Andrews & Johnson
Carlisle, PA 17013

Taylor P. Andrews is a 1968 graduate of Bucknell University and a 1972 graduate of the Dickinson School of Law, now of Penn State University. He served as Chief Public Defender of Cumberland County, Pennsylvania, from 1976 through 2010. From September 1998 until September 2000 he also was Special Counsel to the Treatment Advocacy Center in Arlington, Virginia. The Treatment Advocacy Center is a nonprofit organization originally founded from within the National Alliance for the Mentally Ill. Its mission is to reduce or eliminate barriers to effective treatment for individuals with serious mental illness. Mr. Andrews chaired the Criminal Law Section of the Pennsylvania Bar Association from 1990 until 1997. He was a director of the Public Defender Association of Pennsylvania (PDAPA) from 1977 through 2010, and he served as president from 1989 until 1991. Mr. Andrews has been active with NAMI (National Alliance on Mental Illness) at the state and local level since 1992. He was president of the NAMI PA Cumberland/Perry Counties affiliate organization from 1997 through 2003, from 2004 to 2006, and again, from 2014 to 2015. From November 2000 to November 2001 he was president of the state organization, NAMI PA. Since 1994 Mr. Andrews has worked within his professional associations to increase understanding of serious mental illness.

**Ford Brooks, EdD, Licensed Professional Counselor (LPC),
Nationally Certified Counselor (NCC), Certified Alcohol and
Drug Counselor (CADC)**
Professor
Shippensburg University
Department of Counseling and College Student Personnel
Shippensburg, Pennsylvania

Ford Brooks is a professor of counselor education in the Department of Counseling and College Student Personnel at Shippensburg University, Shippensburg, Pennsylvania. He holds a doctorate in counseling from The College of William and Mary and a master's degree in rehabilitation counseling from Virginia Commonwealth University-Medical College of Virginia, with a specific focus in alcohol and drug counseling.

He has been a counselor educator for 19 years and prior to that worked as a counselor for 14 years in addiction treatment. He most recently was the counselor in residence through the National Board for Certified Counselors, where he worked for three months in Thimphu, Bhutan, as a clinician in the psychiatric ward.

Cymantha Bryce, MS
Resident Advocate for the Treasure Coast Forensic Treatment Center
Certified CIT Coordinator for Florida Judicial Circuit Nineteen
Indiantown, Florida

Cymantha Bryce is the resident advocate for a 225 bed, all-male forensic treatment center located in Central Florida. Cymantha Bryce graduated from the University of South Florida with a BA in Interdisciplinary Science with a concentration in Psychology and Criminal Justice. Cymantha received her MS from Walden University in Forensic Psychology. Cymantha has worked in the mental health, substance abuse, law enforcement, and forensic fields since 1995.

Kelly M. Carrero, PhD, BCBA
Assistant Professor
Psychology, Counseling, and Special Education Department
Texas A&M University – Commerce
Dallas, Texas

Dr. Kelly M. Carrero is an Assistant Professor in the Department of Psychology, Counseling, & Special Education at Texas A&M University – Commerce. She earned her doctorate in special education with an emphasis in behavioral disorders at the University of North Texas. Prior to entering academia, Dr. Carrero served children identified with exceptionalities and behavioral concerns in a variety of settings. Her research projects serve as a vehicle for positive social change and advocacy for children identified with exceptionalities and challenging behaviors (including autism spectrum disorders).

Meghan Kozlowski, BA
University of Maryland, College Park

Meghan Kozlowski is a Criminology and Criminal Justice PhD student at the University of Maryland, College Park. She is a 2014 graduate of Shippensburg University of Pennsylvania, holding a Bachelor of Arts degree in Psychology and Criminal Justice. Meghan's research interests include the intersection of mental health and criminal justice, corrections, evidence-based assessment, suicide risk assessment, and program evaluation. She is experienced in federally funded research initiatives, primarily the National Institute of Justice Comprehensive School Safety Initiative, evaluating an Emotional and Behavioral Health model to promoting school safety with the University of Maryland, Baltimore. In addition to research, Meghan has clinical experience working with persons with mental illness, both in community and correctional settings.

Charlene Lane, PhD, LCSW-R
Assistant Professor
Department of Social-Work and Gerontology
Shippensburg University
Shippensburg, Pennsylvania

Charlene Lane is a Licensed Clinical Social Worker with over 19 years of clinical experience. Dr. Lane obtained a BA degree in Psychology from York College (CUNY), a master's in Clinical Social Work from New York University, and a PhD from Adelphi University (all in New York). Dr. Lane's research interest focuses on older adults aging in their respective communities. She recently partnered with her colleague, Dr. Michele P. Bratina, and conducted research on the lived experiences of individuals 55 and older who are growing old in four prisons in Central Pennsylvania. Dr. Lane plans to continue to investigate the experiences of older adults in their respective communities with specific emphasis on the impact of their mental health issues and aging.

Justin M. Lensbower, MS, LPC
Health Services Administrator, Primecare Medical, Inc.
Director of Mental Health Services
Franklin County Jail
Chambersburg, Pennsylvania

Justin has direct oversight of the medical and mental health contract for the medical department at Franklin County Jail in Chambersburg, Pennsylvania. He conducts suicide and risk assessments, advises the jail administration on how to manage those with high mental health needs, monitors and coordinates psychiatric medication for the inmates, and conducts the sexual offender group treatment program. He also supervises employees who are pursuing an LPC and students working at the jail who are enrolled in the clinical master's in counseling internship program at Shippensburg University.

James Ruiz, PhD
Professor Emeritus of Criminal Justice
School of Public Affairs
Penn State Harrisburg
Middletown, Pennsylvania

James (Jim) Ruiz received his PhD from the College of Criminal Justice at Sam Houston State University, Master of Arts in Criminal Justice from the University of Louisiana at Monroe, and his Bachelor of Arts and Associates of Arts in Criminal Justice from Minot State University. His previous teaching experience includes serving as an instructor at The University of Louisiana at Lafayette, Teaching Fellow at Sam Houston State University, and Assistant Professor at Westfield State College. He began his career in criminal justice as a police officer with the New Orleans Police Department in 1967 serving in the Patrol, Communications, and Mounted Divisions, as well as the Emergency Services Section and National Crime Information Center (N.C.I.C.). He retired in 1985. Some of his publications have appeared in *Police Quarterly, American Journal of Police, Journal of Police and Criminal Psychology, Criminal Justice Ethics, International Journal of Public Administration, International Journal of Police Science and Management, The Critical Criminologist, Police Forum,* and *Texas Law Enforcement Management and Administrative Statistics Program Bulletin.* He is the author of *The Black Hood of the Ku Klux Klan* and co-author of *The Handbook of Police Administration.* His research interests include police administration and supervision, ethics in policing, police interaction with persons with mental illness, use of force, canine deployment, and the Ku Klux Klan.

Cori Seilhamer, MS, LCC
Mental Health Program Specialist
CIT Coordinator
Franklin/Fulton County Mental Health/Intellectual Disabilities/Early Intervention
Chambersburg, Pennsylvania

Cori Seilhamer completed her BS in Public Service from The Pennsylvania State University in 1994. After working in the human service field for eight years, she decided to begin a master's program at Shippensburg University. In order to foster her progressing career goals, she chose the community counseling track. Cori continued to work full time and be the mother of three children. Her family was her priority, so her college pursuit took eight years.

Since graduating in 2011, Cori has found a passion for disaster response services. She has served in disaster recovery centers during times of flooding. She has also assisted the local community victims and assisted families and neighborhoods during times of fire and missing persons. But it was during her field placements in the Franklin County Jail that her interest in developing a relationship between the mental health and the criminal justice systems took vision. Her drive to assist her community has resulted in her pursuit to create the South Central Crisis Intervention Team (CIT) in Franklin County. Currently, there are over 40 members of local law enforcement and first responders working with the mental health community to try and divert persons living with a mental illness into treatment/support instead of the criminal justice system.

Brian D. Stubbs
Certified Peer Specialist
Published Author
Founder of Decide 2 Evolve

Brian D. Stubbs is a certified peer specialist, mental illness and trauma liberation advocate, educator and speaker. He is the author of *A Mental Health Survival Guide: How to Manage the Severities of Multi-Mental Health Diagnosis*, an Amazon #1 bestseller across three categories. It is a memoir of his severe struggles associated with coping with a psychiatric comorbidity (the co-occurrence of two or more mental health diagnoses) and is full of documented skills, tools, and tips he developed as an action plan to cope and manage. Brian is also founder of Decide 2 Evolve, which is an agency promoting chronic illness recovery (www.decide2evolve.com).

Leah Vail, MA
Vice President of Forensic Services
Meridian Behavioral Healthcare
Gainesville, Florida

Leah Vail is the Forensic Program Director for a large, community mental health organization. After graduating New Mexico State University, Leah Vail worked in the field providing direct social services to clients. In 2006 she became a part of a public safety collaborative resulting in funding for a comprehensive forensic jail and state hospital diversion team. Ms. Vail has worked in community forensic mental health ever since. She directed the creation of and leads one of the strongest all-inclusive forensic mental health and substance abuse programs in the country. By developing and teaching seminars, obtaining grants, and advocating in speaking engagements nationwide she has made significant contributions to the field. In 2014 she was named Florida Administrator of the Year for community mental health and substance abuse treatment.

Sarah Zucca, MS, LPC, CADC
Mental Health/Substance Abuse Counselor
Mock Mays Associates
Carlisle, Pennsylvania

Sarah Zucca graduated from The Pennsylvania State University with a BA in Psychology and received her master's degree in Mental Health Counseling from Shippensburg University. She is a licensed professional counselor and a certified drug and alcohol counselor. She has worked in a variety of settings to include a juvenile detention center and a psychiatric private practice in Winchester, Virginia. At the detention center she provided intake services to newly admitted juveniles; individual, group, and family therapy; and case management to the residents who needed to be linked to services in the community upon release. She currently works at a private practice in Carlisle, Pennsylvania, providing individual and family therapy to clients with mental health and substance abuse needs.

ACKNOWLEDGMENTS

I thank my mentor and friend, Dr. Alida V. Merlo, for her guidance, encouragement, and support throughout this process. Her belief in my ability to do great things is inspiring and tremendously appreciated. My dear friends and experts in their respective fields (special education, social work, and counseling), Drs. Kelly M. Carrero, Charlene Lane, Calli Lewis, and Ms. Cori Seilhamer —thank you for your input, knowledge, and generosity, especially while reviewing my work in those final hours. This book has been strengthened by contributions made by Dr. Ford Brooks and Ms. Meghan Kozlowski. I thank them for their commitment to addressing the intersections of mental health and criminal justice, and the overrepresentation of persons with serious mental illness in jails and prisons. Thank you, Quentin Helsel, for your motivating words regarding my influence, and your efforts to springboard this project through the use of imagery. Also, I am grateful to all of the practitioner-contributors who work tirelessly in the field, and who continue to show compassion and kindness, even in the most difficult of circumstances. Their wisdom and experiences enhanced the text.

In addition, I would like to most gratefully acknowledge the multidisciplinary team of staff, providers, and administrators who I met professionally at the Florida Department of Children and Families, Substance Abuse and Mental Health Program Office, Judicial Circuit 19. Without you and your incredible faith in the possibility for change, I would not have been inspired to write this book. A special thank you to Dr. George Woodley, our very interesting and wise leader, for mentoring me in my early career, and for demonstrating the true meaning of trauma-informed care. He sparked and guided my interest in mental health and the system's response.

To the incredible team at Routledge-Taylor & Francis, Pamela Chester, Ellen Boyne, and Eve Strillacci—thank you for fostering the development of an idea, for giving me the chance to express myself, and for your support, editorial skills, and "virtual hugs." I would also like to extend my sincere appreciation to Francesca Hearn, Kevin Kelsey, Lisa McCoy, and all of the remaining staff involved in the production of this manuscript.

Most importantly, I would like to thank my family for their constant love and support throughout my life. To my parents—Vito and Fran—thank you for always seeing the butterfly I strive to become. I cannot imagine any more love than that which you have shared with me. I am grateful for my brother, Charles, who broadens my perspective, helping me to see multiple truths. A heartfelt "thank you" to my sister, Gia, who is my muse and constant wing-woman. It's only looking up from here, my dear sister. Finally, a special thank you to my daughter, Sophia. She generously sacrificed her time with mommy so that this idea could come to fruition. You are my sunshine and I will forever and always "lava" you.

CHAPTER 1 An Overview of the Mental Health–Criminal Justice Nexus

"The more hopeless you were, the further away they hid you."
—*Sylvia Plath, The Bell Jar*

Armed with what was believed to be an arsenal of weapons and two canisters of tear gas, James Egan Holmes, a 24-year-old honors graduate in neuroscience from UC Riverside and former PhD student at the University of Colorado, entered a local multiplex in Aurora, Colorado, on July 21, 2012 (see Figure 1.1), and opened fire on random individuals as they watched the midnight premier of *The Dark Knight Rises*. Holmes had purchased a ticket for the film and entered the theater as a "regular" patron. Shortly after the film began, however, he left through the exit door only to return moments later donned in protective gear from head to toe and a long black coat and sporting neon orange–colored hair. Allegedly referring to himself as "The Joker" to his soon-to-be victims, Holmes released the gas and then killed 12 and wounded dozens of movie-goers before being arrested in the theater parking lot. Initially, the incident was depicted by some media outlets as an act of domestic terrorism and Holmes as a terrorist (Holden, 2012; Sidhu, 2012). As the case unfolded in the media, Holmes's mental health history came under the microscope, and disturbing images of him, with unkempt hair and with his eyes seemingly bulging, were splattered about the news and social media. Holmes was presented to the public as a violent and crazed madman whose actions might have been the result of an untreated (or undertreated) mental illness (Healy & Turkewitz, 2015). Reports of his previous engagement in counseling sessions with multiple therapists emerged, as did a letter he supposedly mailed to a psychiatrist with whom he was acquainted at the University of Colorado directly before the shooting; both were supportive of his more recent portrayal. Holmes eventually pled not guilty by reason of insanity, but was found guilty and sentenced to life imprisonment in July 2015.

Figure 1.1
Aurora, Colorado. Location of the Movie Theater Shooting
Source: http://creativecommons.org/licenses/by-sa/3.0, via Wikimedia Commons

Introduction

Just as in similar cases before and after this, including shootings perpetrated by:

- Seung-Hui Cho (Virginia Tech, 2007)

- Jared Loughner (Tucson, Arizona, shooting involving Congresswoman Gabby Giffords, 2011)

- Adam Lanza (Sandy Hook Elementary School, 2012)

- Aaron Alexis (Washington Navy Yard, 2013)

- Elliot Rodger (near University of California, Santa Barbara, 2014)

- Dylann Roof (Charleston church shooting, 2015)

Holmes' actions were received by the public as those of a crazed lunatic who should be feared and isolated from the rest of society, if not executed. The violence is unacceptable, and the random nature of the offenses has cast a *stigma* on mental illness that, in effect, contributes to a phenomenon that has been referred to as the *criminalization of mental illness* (Fisher, Silver, & Wolff, 2006; Slate, Buffington-Vollum, & Johnson, 2013).

THINKING CRITICALLY

What do you want to be when you "grow up"? Chances are that many of you will encounter persons with mental illness who are experiencing crisis situations in the course of your work. In your ideal occupation, how will you navigate encounters with PwMI in crisis? Consider beliefs you have about mental illness or PwMI in general; how might these affect your response in the field?

The media tales, however, are not confined to persons with mental illness as *perpetrators* of violence; in fact, a great number of stories that have emerged in recent years involve the actions of criminal justice officials who have invoked negative attention related to the justice system's treatment of *persons with mental illness (PwMI)* in its custody. Whether violence and victimization are perpetrated by or against PwMI, the intersections of mental health and criminal justice have become one of society's major social problems to contend with. Throughout the past decade, all three primary justice-involved agencies—policing, courts, and corrections—have been implicated (Beck & Maruschak, 2001; DeMatteo, LaDuke, Locklair, & Heilbrum, 2013; Hartford, Carey, & Mendonca, 2006; Heilbrum, DeMatteo, Strohmaier, & Galloway, 2015; National Alliance on Mental Illness, 2013). Consequently, challenges are presented for police, probation, parole officers, and a variety of additional corrections officials in terms of addressing the prevailing stigmatization of all parties involved and in coming up with methods to more effectively manage the increasing populations of juveniles and adults with serious behavioral and mental health issues who have violated the law (DeMatteo, et al., 2013; Griffin, et al., 2015). Unfortunately, however, there has been a significant gap in the amount of training criminal justice officials are exposed to in relation to understanding forensic mental health and in responding to stigmatized groups such as PwMI (Applebaum, Hickey, & Packer, 2001; Brandt, 2012; Deane, Steadman, Borum, Veysey, & Morrissey, 1999; Lamb, Weinberger, & DeCuir, 2002). Given these challenges, students who are interested in pursuing careers in the criminal or juvenile justice fields and, more generally, in human services–oriented positions, would certainly benefit from the opportunity to develop a basic understanding of mental illness and the extent to which they will encounter PwMI during the course of their work. Furthermore, for the sake of future policy implications, students also must learn the various intersections of mental illness and criminal justice and how they can become positive change agents at numerous points in the justice process.

Identifying the Population of Interest

This book centers on presenting issues and possible solutions as they relate to *forensic mental health*. Contrary to student expectations, forensic simply means pertaining to and about the law. Forensic mental health, then, would refer to mental health issues as they pertain to the law. A broad definition that has been so eloquently offered by Mullen (2000) refers to forensic mental health as an "area of specialisation that, in the criminal sphere, involves the assessment and *treatment* of those who are both mentally disordered and whose behaviour has led, or could lead, to offending" (p. 307, original emphasis). For many people who hear this concept for the first time, it takes on a connotation related to forensic science and forensic psychology—particularly as it pertains to the profiling aspect that drives students to seek careers in crime scene investigations (CSI) or for positions in which they would be working in forensic crime labs. Thus, although the aforementioned positions (CSI and crime lab technician) may involve interrelated areas of study and are certainly worth pursuing, forensic mental health as presented in this text is less about the development of psychological profiles and more about systematic responses to persons with mental illness who have violated the law. In this way, forensic mental health *services* refer to services available or received by justice-involved persons who have mental health issues. (As will be discussed later, under the law, the issues must cause serious functional impairment in order to qualify for services.) In the following sections, the concepts of mental health and mental illness are briefly defined and discussed, including the fundamental facts about prevalence and representation in the justice system. It is this author's intention to provide a basic understanding of justice-involved individuals with mental health issues and, at the same time, dispel some of the myths related to this population.

In this book, persons with mental illness who may or may not be justice-involved (accused of or charged with a criminal offense) are referred to in a few different ways, depending on the context of the discussion; this may include persons with mental illness (PwMI), persons with serious mental illness (SMI) or with *severe and persistent mental illness* (SPMI), consumers (of mental health, substance abuse, and other services), and patients (in forensic hospitals or other treatment-based facilities).

Mental Health: An Introduction to Disorders, Prevalence, and Common Terminology

Defining Mental Illness

Mental illness can be described as the presence of a mental, behavioral, or emotional disorder that has been diagnosed by a licensed clinician, excluding intellectual and developmental disabilities (e.g., autism) and disorders primarily related to substance abuse (Substance Abuse and Mental Health Services Administration [SAMHSA], 2013). Additional dimensions accounted for when making a diagnosis of mental illness include the duration and intensity of symptoms, both of which must meet criteria set forth by the *Diagnostic and Statistical Manual of Mental Disorders* (American Psychological Association [APA], 2013). This manual, more commonly known as the *DSM*, is used by various doctors and mental health practitioners as a guide for diagnosing mental disorders. The DSM is published by the APA and has been printed in five iterations, with the fifth being the most recent, published in 2013. First and foremost, it is important to understand that the concept "mental illness" is often used in an all-encompassing way in order to simplify an otherwise extremely varied, complex group of conditions experienced by individuals from all cultural and socioeconomic backgrounds. Furthermore, the terms mental illness, mental health, behavioral health, and emotional behavioral health may be used interchangeably—though their unique applications will be introduced where appropriate throughout this text. A more advanced discussion of mental illness and substance abuse, which are frequently *co-occurring* (occurring together) (National Alliance on Mental Illness [NAMI], 2013), is presented later in Chapter 4, including detailed information about diagnoses and medications. As a general definition for the purposes of this book, mental illness refers to a mental health-related diagnosis that is serious enough to affect an individual's overall well-being and daily life, including in matters of physical health, but particularly with regard to their ability to function at work, in school, and in interpersonal relationships.

Mental Health Diagnoses

The most common mental health diagnoses in the United States are those related to anxiety, depression, attention deficit/hyperactivity, mood (bipolar and related disorders), conduct and impulse control, obsessive-compulsive behavior, thought disorders such as schizophrenia and other psychotic disorders, and disorders related to stressors and trauma, such as post-traumatic stress disorder or PTSD (SAMHSA, 2015). The following sidebar provides brief descriptions of these disorders.

Overview of Primary Mental Health Disorders

Anxiety: Excessive worry or fear that is difficult to control, thereby negatively affecting ability to function in daily life—affects 18 percent of the U.S. population

Major depression: Hopelessness, sad, empty, and irritable mood and cognitive and somatic changes negatively affecting daily living—affects about 7 percent of adults

Attention deficit/hyperactivity: Consistent patterns of inattention and hyperactivity and impulsive behaviors, most commonly diagnosed among children—affects 8 percent of children ages 3 to 7 years, 9 percent of children ages 13 to 18 years, and 2.5 percent of adults

Mood disorders: Dramatic shifts in mood, cycling between periods of extreme highs (intense happiness, impulsivity, irritability) and lows (intense hopelessness and sadness/sorrow)—affects 3 percent of the U.S. adult population

Conduct and impulse control: Low self-control over emotions and behaviors, leading to conduct that may violate social and legal norms—oppositional-defiant disorder (ODD) affects about 3 percent of children; conduct disorder (CD) affects about 9 percent of children and youth

Obsessive-compulsive: Presence of persistent thoughts, urges, or images, sometimes requiring repetitive behaviors that interrupt daily activities—1.2 percent prevalence rate over a 12-month period

Thought disorders: Abnormalities experienced in one or more of the following five domains: disorganized thinking, disorganized motor behavior, delusions, hallucinations, and negative symptoms (e.g., lack of emotion)—affects about 1 percent of U.S. adults

Stressors and trauma: Feelings of extreme anxiety and stress following exposure to a traumatic event; PTSD is the most common—affects about 7.7 million people in the United States, with a higher proportion of women

Source: SAMHSA (2016); http://www.samhsa.gov/disorders/mental

Collectively, anxiety disorders are the most commonly experienced by Americans, followed by mood disorders, such as those falling under the bipolar spectrum (National Institute of Health [NIH], 2013). It is important to note that, regardless of the diagnosis, related symptoms and methods of treatment affect people in different ways. For example, some diagnoses, such as schizophrenia, may symptomatically become more serious or debilitative in some individuals—to the point where symptoms seriously affect the degree to which the individual functions in daily life; for others, symptoms could be quite manageable. Also, modes of treatment, including medication management, may produce varying effects across participants, improving symptoms for some, but not for others (Mental Health Conditions, 2015). In various ways, then, mental illness can be viewed as falling along a continuum, with least serious on one side and most serious on the other. As will be presented and discussed in more detail throughout the remainder of the text, one's ability to effectively cope and function with mental illness in the community is critical and becomes a salient factor in understanding maladaptive behaviors, which may lead to disorderly conduct by definition under the criminal law.

Serious Mental Illness

Another concept found in the literature related to mental health and forensic involvement is that of *serious mental illness (SMI)*. A SMI is one that produces a particular level of chronicity in symptoms so that one's daily functioning is significantly impaired or inhibited (Cocozza & Skowyra, 2000; Jones, Macias, Barreira, Fisher, Hargreaves, & Harding, 2004). For instance, schizophrenia, which is symptomatically linked to hallucinations and delusional thinking, is categorized as an SMI due to the significant impairment experienced by a large majority of those who have the illness. In the context of justice-involved PwMI, SMI commonly involves a primary diagnosis of schizophrenia, schizoaffective disorder, bipolar disorder, or, depending on the impairment in functioning, major depression (Substance Abuse and Mental Health Services Administration [SAMH], 2013). As will be especially noted throughout this book, the population of PwMI who most often encounter the criminal justice system in some capacity are adults with SMI (Slate, et al., 2013). Nevertheless, there is no reason to presume that adults and juveniles with less serious or debilitating symptoms of mental illness are immune from entering our nation's detention centers, jails, and prisons.

FAST FACT

It has been suggested that roughly half of America's adult population will suffer from a mental disorder at some point in their lifetime (Sickel, Seacat, & Nabors, 2014).

Prevalence of Mental Illness

Estimates suggest that approximately 450 million people worldwide have suffered with mental health or behavioral disorders at some point in their lifetime (World Health Organization [WHO], 2015). In the United States alone, national prevalence data indicate that approximately one in every four persons in the general population will be diagnosed with some kind of mental illness during their lifetime, with 14 being the average age of onset for most mental health disorders (NAMI, 2013). The National Institute of Mental Health (NIMH) has reported lifetime prevalence rates for mental illness among adults and children using data derived from the National Survey of Drug Use and Health (NSDUH) (SAMHSA, 2013). Some statistics are presented in the following box.

According to survey results from 2013, an estimated 43.8 million Americans aged 18 or older reported having any mental illness (AMI) that year—the equivalent of about 19 percent of all U.S. adults. In terms of SMI, data for the same year indicated that an estimated 10 million adults, or 4.1 percent of the adult U.S. population, reported having an SMI that same year. For both SMI and AMI, the highest prevalence rates were found among females and American Indian/Alaska Natives and also among individuals who were between the ages of 26 and 49 (SAMHSA, 2013).

As defined in the DSM, major depressive episode (MDE) is when a person experiences a depressed mood and a majority of depression symptoms, including a lack of interest and pleasure in performing daily activities. For youth ages 12 to 17, SAMHSA reported on those who had past-year (2012–2013) MDE. Estimates suggested that there were 2.6 million youths, or 10.7 percent, who

---

continued

met the diagnostic criteria. Statistics also indicated that there was a greater proportion of females with MDE (16.2 vs. 5.3 percent), and a larger proportion of the total MDE group (33.2 percent) had indicated past-year use of illicit drugs compared to their counterparts without MDE (15.1 percent). With respect to children between the ages of 13 and 18, data estimates from 2012 suggest that the lifetime prevalence rate for any disorder that year was 46.3 percent; for severe mental health disorders, the rate was 21.4 percent. Among this population, females and males were equally distributed, although there were statistically significant differences in prevalence rates found between age and race categories. For younger children, ages 8 to 15, data from the National Health and Nutrition Examination Survey (NHANES) that year showed a 13 percent prevalence rate for *emotional and behavioral disorders (EBDs)* over the prior year for this group—the most commonly diagnosed disorder being attention deficit/hyperactivity disorder (ADHD), which reportedly affected about 9 percent of children in this age group (SAMHSA, 2013).

Cross-national comparisons in prevalence rates have also been examined, and differentials have been observed between the United States and other countries. In fact, according to data derived from a survey sponsored by WHO, the United States shares the lead spot with New Zealand in its prevalence rates for depression, anxiety, mood disorders, and disorders related to impulsivity and substance use among individuals who self-reported specific indicators during the reporting period of 2002–2005 (7.7 percent and 10.9 percent, respectively) (Countries Compared by Health, 2016). Figure 1.2 provides a snapshot of comparative data on the prevalence of bipolar disorder.

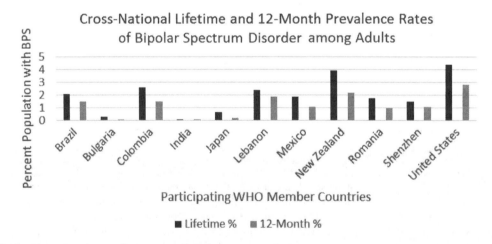

Figure 1.2

Comparative Mental Health Statistics

Source: Findings taken and adapted from Merikangas, et al. (2012); Raw data originally derived from World Health Organization

Although the primary focus of this book relates to mental health and the administration of justice in the United States, it is instructive to understand the prevalence of mental illness and access to treatment worldwide and how comparative systematic responses could potentially inform policy in our country. Such issues will be presented throughout the remainder of the book where information is available to report.

PRACTITIONER'S CORNER 1.1

When Mental Health and Criminal Justice Meet, Part One: Treating Offenders Who Are Also Victims

Contributor: Charlene Lane, PhD, LCSW-R

A female inmate sentenced for life at an all-female prison in Central Pennsylvania exemplifies the struggle between mental health needs and criminal justice responses. "Jane," the 77-year-old inmate, admitted receiving the best mental healthcare in prison. Jane disclosed that while growing up she was always the "odd ball"—at times hearing voices and acting out violently. She remembered getting into trouble as a teen, being truant, and accumulating a history of arrests. As a young adult, Jane's poor decision-making ability led her to involvement with a notorious drug dealer who encouraged her to commit a heinous violent crime. The irony of Jane's story is that being incarcerated has led to effective treatment and management of her mental health issues. This reality leads one to ask the question: Is Jane truly a criminal or a mentally ill individual who committed a criminal act due to symptoms related to the nature of her illness? What, then, is the true operational definition of "criminal"? Is it "criminal" to accept the criminalization of mental health issues?

Jane's story is one of many. In the course of our research, which examined the lived experiences of inmates 55 and older who are aging in place in prison, many of the respondents were like Jane—they had admitted exhibiting mental health issues (sometimes undiagnosed) prior to incarceration. There were inmates whose poor impulse control, sense of paranoia, and noncompliance with medication management ultimately lead to behaviors resulting in incarceration.

In an era where there is a growing number of individuals who are introduced to the criminal justice system secondary to an underlying psychiatric diagnosis, it is imperative that criminal justice practitioners are cognizant of the intersectionality between criminal justice and mental health.

Historically, criminal justice practitioners have been remiss when it comes to effectively identifying the signs of mental health illness. Mental health certification should be required as part of the criminal justice curriculum; all future practitioners should become mental health trained and certified in crisis intervention prior to graduation.

In particular, criminal justice practitioners should be trained on the deescalation of a crisis, identification of the manifestation of psychiatric illnesses, and the utilization of less-than-lethal weapons as opposed to "shooting to kill." Individuals with psychiatric illnesses can present as being extremely volatile and aggressive; they may demonstrate poor judgment and may have little or no apparent respect for those in authority. Hence, the reason for criminal justice practitioners being dually trained and equipped to address the mental health as well as the criminal aspect of the individuals who they serve.

Intersections of Criminal Justice and Mental Health: Forensic/Justice-Involved PwMI

Cases like that of the Aurora movie theater shooting presented at the beginning of the chapter demonstrate what some have referred to as preventable tragedies (Treatment Advocacy Center, 2015) or the consequences of failed information sharing between mental health and justice systems. But, are incidents like those in Aurora and elsewhere truly preventable with more effective training, education, and communication? Is it possible to seamlessly communicate potential danger—or simply an individual's potential for violence? Are criminal justice actors and mental health providers even speaking the same language?

PwMI Incarcerated

By comparison to the statistics noted earlier, the number of PwMI who are justice-involved (in adult and juvenile justice systems) in the United States is substantial. Depending on the data source, estimates show up to 20 percent of jail inmates and 24 percent of state prison inmates report recent histories of having a diagnosable mental health condition, figures that are higher than the general population, and may even be conservative estimates (NAMI, 2013). In fact, depending on the way in which mental illness is defined, higher rates have been found. For example, in their study of federal, state, and jail correctional populations, James and Glaze (2006) collected data derived from offender mental health history information and clinical interviews. Their conceptualization of "mental illness" not only included recent history, but also current symptoms experienced. As a result, their findings indicated that rates of mental illness were 64 percent in jails and 56 percent and 45 percent in state and federal prisons, respectively. Statistics on mental illness in correctional settings are revisited in Chapter 6 specifically and elsewhere throughout the book.

In terms of gender and incarcerated persons, findings suggest that despite their overwhelming representation in correctional populations, males are less likely than females to report mental illness (e.g., 6 percent vs. 11 percent, respectively; Maruschak, 2004). There are also race and ethnicity differentials in the data reported, in which findings indicate that the proportion of Caucasian inmates who report having any mental health issues is significantly larger than that of their African American and Hispanic/Latino counterparts (using reported symptoms and recent mental health history: 61 percent, 51 percent, and 44 percent, respectively; James & Glaze, 2006). Reasons for these differentials should also be considered and explored moving forward; perhaps lower rates of reporting mental illness reflect the same reasons why persons of color fail to report other social problems (including crime) to those in authority positions, such as mistrust, fear, and embarrassment due to large-scale systematic discrimination and the resulting effects of internalized racism (Smedley, 2012). James and Glaze (2006) also found age differences—in particular, that younger inmates (ages 24 or younger) were more likely to report mental illness, though there is a significant gap in the literature related to age with respect to forensic-specific populations (Brandt, 2012).

Mental Health and Co-occurring Substance Abuse

It is further estimated that about one-third of PwMI who are incarcerated (or about 72 percent) also have co-occurring substance abuse disorders (Ditton, 1999), and that suicide in correctional institutions is a significant social problem—most profoundly among inmates who have been diagnosed with severe and persistent mental illness (SPMI) (Hayes, 2012). The reasons for such a high prevalence of co-occurring substance abuse and suicidal ideation among adult correctional populations are plentiful. While largely centering on *deinstitutionalization*[1] and stigma, it may also be related to the conditions of confinement, which arguably exacerbate—perhaps even trigger—underlying psychosis for some individuals. These are salient issues in the literature and practice and will be explored in great detail in the remaining chapters of this book.

Justice-Involved PwMI in the Community

Additional data have been collected with regard to individuals under correctional supervision in the community. For example, in addition to the study of inmates, Ditton (1999) examined the prevalence of mental illness among adult probationers, and for the purposes of her data collection, individuals were identified as having mental illness if they were currently experiencing an emotional or mental health condition or had ever been admitted to a state hospital or other treatment program overnight. Whereas inmates were much more likely to report an overnight hospital stay than probationers, her findings revealed that 16 percent of probationers (or over 500,000) self-reported having a mental disorder under this definition. It should also be noted that rates of homelessness and prior sexual and physical trauma or victimization were also found to be significantly higher among offenders (probationers and inmates) with mental illness in her nationally representative sample—a finding that has emerged in other research reports (Hawthorne, Folsom, Sommerfeld, Lanouette, Lewis, Aarons, Conklin, Solorzano, Lindamer, & Jeste, 2012; McGuire & Rosenheck, 2004; NAMI, 2010), particularly when related to female offenders (DeHart, Lynch, Belknap, Dass-Brailsford, & Green, 2014; Gunter, Chibnall, Antoniak, McCormick, & Black, 2012; Wolff, Frueh, Shi, & Schumann, 2012).

Juveniles and Behavioral Health Issues

The juvenile justice system does not fare better in terms of its reception of juveniles who are dealing with behavioral health issues. Mental illnesses experienced by juveniles can include depression, anxiety disorders, post-traumatic stress disorder (PTSD), suicidal tendencies, mood disorders, conduct disorder, and substance use disorder (Riley, 2014). Although it is rare, schizophrenia can also occur in certain juvenile populations as an early-onset form of illness. At any given point it is estimated that at least 90,000 juveniles reside within correctional facilities in the United States (Burriss, Breland-Noble, Webster, & Soto, 2011; Nelson, Jolivette, Leone, & Mathur, 2010). Research has indicated that approximately 70 percent of justice-involved juveniles placed in residential facilities have been diagnosed with one or more psychiatric disorders, and at least 20 percent with a severe and persistent mental illness (NAMI, 2013; Shufelt & Cocozza, 2006; Teplin, Abram, McClelland, Mericle, Duncan, & Washburn, 2006). For example, in their study of adolescents placed in residential facilities in Cook County, Illinois, Teplin and colleagues (2006) found that 60 percent of males and 70 percent of females had received at least one psychiatric diagnosis, excluding conduct disorder. Moreover, researchers have also concluded that an abundance of youth possess multiple diagnoses, referred to as *comorbidities* (Cocozza & Skowyra, 2000; Teplin, et al., 2006). In particular, as many as 65 percent of juveniles experience comorbid issues (such as drug addiction) that are unlikely to be addressed adequately through treatment plans (Kapp, Petr, Robbins, & Choi, 2013; Riley, 2014). Like adults with mental illness under correctional supervision, addiction can be generated by the detention environment or co-occurring as part of the mental illness that the juvenile suffers from. Regarding youth under supervision in the community, recent risk assessment tools being utilized at case entry have identified that 50 percent of youth present at intake have an underlying psychiatric diagnosis (Shufelt & Cocozza, 2006).

THINKING CRITICALLY

The rate of mental illness among inmates is estimated to be two to three times higher than in the general community. Most studies estimate that approximately 10 to 15 percent of the nearly 6 million offenders in U.S. jails and prisons and on probation and parole have a diagnosable mental illness. What do you think might explain this phenomenon?

Service Utilization/Treatment Engagement

For many individuals in both community and correctional settings, behavioral health treatment is one of the primary pieces in the recovery process and may include medication management, counseling or therapy, substance abuse services, case management, and a host of other educational and therapeutic interventions (Lamb & Weinberger, 1998; NAMI, 2015). Depending on funding and the resources available in the locale, the treatment needs of PwMI are sometimes met by what has been perceived as barely adequate programs and planning. This holds true whether we are talking about community-based care, state hospitals, or secure juvenile or adult placement. It is important to realize that gaps in available and adequate services may be due to a number of unavoidable barriers, including the high cost of care, lack of communication between providers and agencies, training deficiencies, and lack of structured programs, to name a few (Burriss, et al., 2011; Kapp, et al., 2013). There is also the high likelihood that individuals with mental health issues will not actively seek out services due to symptoms that are characteristic of their illness, personal financial barriers or restrictions, or because they do not have the knowledge as to available services (Hartford, Carey, Mendonca, 2006; Slate, et al., 2013). Lack of treatment engagement may also be greatly attributed to reasons related to fear of stigma and ridicule. Specific reasons for not seeking mental health services have been provided by adults surveyed about their perceived unmet past-year mental health care needs (2012–2013); some of the most frequently occurring responses have included the previous factors and the fear of being committed and having to take medication (SAMHSA, 2014).

General Population Data

Data have been collected to determine the extent to which PwMI are utilizing available treatment services for both substance abuse and mental health. As provided by SAMHSA (2014), utilization is defined differently depending on the ages of the consumers receiving services. For adults (18 years of age or older), mental health service utilization is related to the receipt of treatment or counseling for any problem with emotions, nerves, or mental health that was not related to substance abuse; treatment may be rendered in any inpatient or outpatient setting and may or may not involve the use of prescription medication. For youth ages 12 to 17, mental health service utilization involves treatment or counseling for any emotional or behavioral problem, with services rendered in any of the following settings:

(a) the *specialty mental health setting* (inpatient or outpatient care); (b) the *education setting* (talked with a school social worker, psychologist, or counselor about an emotional or behavioral problem; participated in a program for students with emotional or behavioral problems while in a regular school; or attended a school for students with emotional or behavioral problems); (c) the *general medical setting* (pediatrician or family physician care for emotional or behavioral problems); (d) the *juvenile justice setting* (received services for an emotional or behavioral problem in a detention center, prison, or jail); or (e) the *child welfare setting* (foster care or therapeutic foster care).

(SAMHSA, 2014, p. 41)

According to results of the 2013 National Survey on Drug Use and Health (NSDUH), the number of adults who received treatment or counseling for past-year (2012–2013) mental health issues was 34.6 million; comparatively, for adolescents with past-year MDE, the percentage who received treatment or counseling was 38.1— increasing to 45.0 percent for those who had a "severe impairment" (SAMHSA, 2014). For a more detailed look at the treatment landscape, additional utilization data among adults from 2012–2013 are presented in Figures 1.3 and 1.4.

The utilization of mental health services varied among adults in 2013. Adults who used mental health services the year under evaluation were more likely to have serious mental illness and engage in outpatient treatment and least likely to be hospitalized in an inpatient facility. There were also utilization differences by gender, with females being more likely to engage in services, regardless of type.

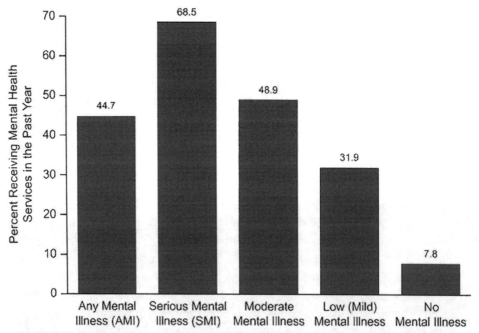

Figure 1.3

Receipt of Mental Health Services among Adults Aged 18 or Older by Level of Mental Illness: 2013

Source: SAMHSA (2014)

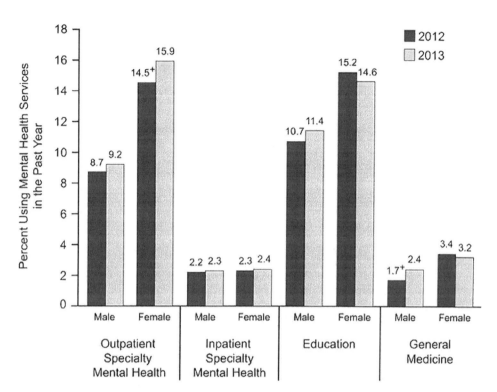

Figure 1.4

Receipt of Mental Health Services among Adults Aged 18 or Older by Gender and Level of Care (2012–2013)

Source: SAMHSA (2014)

Among youth (12 to 17 years old), gender differentials were also observed. Particularly, in 2013, 15.9 percent of females versus 9.2 percent of males had engaged in outpatient mental health services, 14.6 versus 11.4 percent engaged in education services, and 3.2 versus 2.4 percent used general medical-based services (Figure 1.5).

Correctional Data

Data derived from a survey of adult state and federal community and confinement-based correctional facilities in the United States in 2000 indicated that an estimated 191,000 of the inmates surveyed had self-reported some form of mental illness as of midyear. Among the 191,000, 1 in every 8 was receiving some kind of mental health services. The data were further broken down by type of treatment, and reports

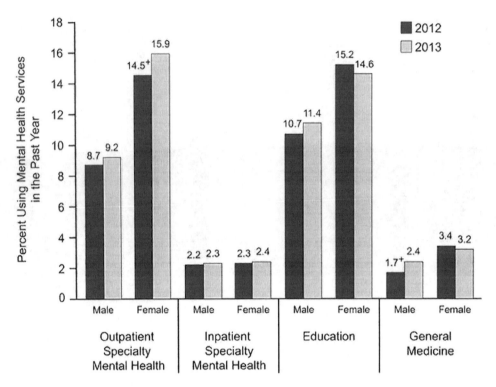

Figure 1.5

Past Year Mental Health Service Use among Youths Aged 12 to 17 by Gender: 2012 and 2013
Source: SAMHSA (2014)

indicated that a total of 1.6 percent of inmates across reporting institutions (n = 17,354) had received 24-hour mental health care, 12.8 percent (n = 137,385) received therapy or counseling, and 9.7 percent (n = 105,336) had received psychotropic medication for their mental health–related illness, compared with 5 percent of the nonincarcerated population of PwMI (Beck & Maruschak, 2001).

For a variety of reasons, mental health programming and related reentry services have not been prioritized in jail and prison settings; therefore, issues such as a high incidence of mental health disorders and significant histories of trauma that far surpass that of their nonincarcerated counterparts has further taxed resources that were already sparse. Moreover, research suggests that offenders with mental illness are quite difficult to treat (Morgan, Flora, Kroner, Mills, Varghese, & Steffan, 2012), if not resistant to treatment overall (Lamb & Weinberger, 1998). Based on this resistance, and coupled with unique criminal histories that indicate the potential for violence

(James & Glaze, 2006; Lamb & Weinberger, 1998), mental health providers are often reluctant to treat them to begin with (Lamb, Weinberger, & Gross, 1999). As a result, a growing number of justice-involved persons with mental illness needing treatment have not been able to obtain it to the extent necessary—an outcome that reflects the noninstitutionalized population experience (Sickel, et al., 2014). In contrast to offending populations without mental illness, the lack of engagement for this group is sometimes related to collateral consequences of their incarceration or other involvement in the criminal justice system, such as the loss of Medicare, Medicaid, or disability benefits (NAMI, 2010). Because research indicates that inmates who have mental health problems are likely to spend an average of four months longer incarcerated than those without (James & Glaze, 2006), the urgency of treatment becomes more imminent.

Unless reentry services are implemented during one's period of incarceration and treatment services are received soon after release (within two weeks), the same individuals who may have been stabilized while inside the institutional setting may quickly decompensate in the community, thereby becoming at risk for repeated encounters with justice and other systems of care (e.g., public welfare). Varying trajectories are examined in more detail later in the book.

Competing Interests? Challenges in Managing Justice-Involved PwMI

The most primary obstacle between the mental health and criminal justice systems may be a historical resistance to share ideas and to collaborate (Applebaum, Hickey, & Packer, 2001; Deane, et al., 1999; Lamb, et al., 2002). The reasons for this are plentiful, though may revolve around unique philosophies held by each system and the profound language barrier as a result. For example, although police officers are oftentimes regarded as "street psychiatrists," they would most likely prefer a distinct separation between their role and that played by social workers, particularly in terms of their responses to potentially violent situations. This preference indicates an understandable resistance to any direction that requires them to drop their "guard" during a crisis encounter—particularly those involving persons whose behaviors are viewed as exceptionally unpredictable or unstable (Lamb, et al., 2002). However, when phrased in a way that recognizes the possibility of dangerousness and the need for officer (and citizen) safety, new approaches and techniques become more palatable to individual officers and other law enforcement officials. It is at those moments when collaboration is made possible and change can be accomplished. For the purposes of facilitating productive collaboration among students who are reading this book, it is essential to compare and contrast key differences and similarities between the mental health and justice systems.

PRACTITIONER'S CORNER 1.2

Where Mental Health and Criminal Justice Meets, Part Two: What a Criminal Justice Practitioner Needs to Know about Mental Health

Contributor: Leah Vail, MA, Vice President of Forensic Services

The following contribution by Ms. Vail is based on a real case scenario involving one of her clients—a female we will refer to as "Pam."

Pam lives in Alachua County with her brother and loves to collect dolls and socialize with her family. She also provides respite care for her elderly father by helping her sister in Union County. Her family and friends value her sense of humor, sweet disposition, and caring nature. However, Pam also has schizophrenia, which can change her behaviors; when untreated, she can become violent. Pam became very ill in 2010, which resulted in an altercation with the neighbor, and law enforcement was called. Fortunately, the responding officers were *Crisis Intervention Team* trained and recognized that Pam was ill. The incident still resulted in Pam crawling underneath her mobile home and refusing to come out. Due to their specialized training, the officers were able to talk her into coming out and being peacefully taken into custody without incident. However, she eventually was sentenced to probation related to felony charges. She was well known at Meridian, given her history of three state hospital admissions and over 20 *CSU* admissions. When released from the jail, Pam worked with a forensic specialist to attain the reinstatement of benefits, financial management, advocacy with the legal system (probation/court), and medication management and to become involved in activities of daily living.

Next, Ms. Vail provides some helpful advice for those who are interested in careers in forensic mental health.

Surviving the Profession

Balancing the needs of the client, their family, the many facets of the criminal justice system, and other stakeholders can be very stressful. That stress is a prime reason for the high turnover rate in the profession.

At times the stress will build, and to survive in the field, the practitioner needs to find ways to relieve it. I have found the following to be helpful:

- Keep things in perspective. Frequently remind yourself that there will be many disappointments and that you have only a limited control of your client's behavior and the resolution of their cases.
- Find distractions in your personal life. Socializing with friends, a hobby, and working out on a regular basis are good stress relievers. Use your vacation days and enjoy life outside of work.
- Finally, share your feelings and concerns with coworkers and family. Many mental health organizations offer counseling for their employees to counter the stress; don't be afraid to take advantage of it.

continued

Author's Note: Crisis Intervention Team (CIT) training is a specialized police-based response designed to more effectively resolve police encounters with citizens experiencing mental health–related crisis. CIT is discussed in more detail in Chapter 5 of the text. A "CSU" is a Crisis Stabilization Unit; this is a facility (perhaps a hospital emergency room) in which persons (children and adults) are evaluated and treated for acute mental health crises. Once found to be clinically stable, the individual may be evaluated for further placement (commitment/incarceration) or discharge back to the community.

Take-Home Message

As briefly discussed here and presented in more detail in later chapters, the numbers of justice-involved persons who struggle with mental health conditions and trauma, whether preexisting or induced by incarceration, are staggering. As stated, there are a number of reasons for the overrepresentation of PwMI across the system, but the primary origin has been attributed to a decrease in available inpatient psychiatric beds in state-run hospitals and the rapidly shrinking community mental health services (NAMI, 2010). In short, persons with SMI are no longer able to access necessary treatment and services. As a result, they may begin a cycle of cross-systems encounters as they struggle with lack of adequate care, homelessness, trauma and PTSD, substance abuse, periods of incarceration or other criminal justice supervision, and continued crisis events—all leading to their own criminalization. Unfortunately, the communities in which these individuals live are carrying the burden in terms of financial consequences: the estimated cost of incarceration for one year in a state or federal prison is approximately $23,000 for typical inmates; in comparison, the cost of inmates with SMI increases anywhere from $50,000 to slightly over $100,000, depending on the jurisdiction and available services (Torrey, Zdanowicz, Kennard, Lamb, Eslinger, Biasotti, & Fuller, 2014).

QUESTIONS FOR CLASSROOM DISCUSSION

1. What do you think of when you hear the term "mental illness"? What beliefs have you been taught about mental disorders? Can you distinguish between myths and facts? How?
2. What personal experiences have you had with persons with mental disorders? What is that person's relationship to you, and how did their mental disorder affect you?
3. What are your feelings about the label—or stigma—associated with having a mental disorder? Do you think those feelings will have any impact on your professional work? If so, what is the impact?
4. Using your responses to questions 1–3, describe in detail what you think could be the potential benefits and challenges for mental health and criminal justice professionals when working together in the field.

KEY TERMS & ACRONYMS

- Comorbidities
- Co-occurring
- Criminalization of mental illness
- Crisis Stabilization Unit (CSU)
- Crisis Intervention Team (CIT)

- Deinstitutionalization
- Diagnostic Statistical Manual (DSM)
- Emotional and behavioral disorders (EBDs)
- Forensic mental health

- Persons with mental illness (PwMI)
- Serious mental illness (SMI)
- Severe and persistent mental illness (SPMI)
- Stigma

Note

1. Beginning in the 1960s, a large-scale treatment philosophy shift had the effect of redirecting tens of thousands of persons with serious mental illness from state hospitals back into community settings where they were expected to receive community-based care.

Bibliography

American Psychiatric Association. (2013). *Diagnostic and Statistical Manual of Mental Disorders* (5th Ed.). Arlington, VA: American Psychiatric Association.

Appelbaum, K. L., Hickey, J. M., & Packer, I. (2001). The Role of Correctional Officers in Multidisciplinary Mental Health Care in Prisons. *Psychiatric Services, 52,* 1343–1347.

Beck, A. J., & Maruschak, L. M. (2001). *Mental Health Treatment in State Prisons, 2000.* Washington, DC: US Department of Justice, Office of Justice Programs, Bureau of Justice Statistics.

Brandt, A. L. S. (2012). Treatment of Persons with Mental Illness in the Criminal Justice System: A Literature Review. *Journal of Offender Rehabilitation, 51*(8), 541–558.

Burriss, F. A., Breland-Nobel, A. M., Webster, J. L., & Soto, J. A. (2011). Juvenile Mental Health Courts for Adjudicated Youth: Role Implications for Child and Adolescent Psychiatric Mental Health Nurses. *Journal of Child and Adolescent Psychiatric Nursing, 24*(2), 114–121.

Cocozza, J. J., & Skowyra, K. R. (2000). Youth with Mental Health Disorders: Issues and Emerging Responses. *Juvenile Justice, 7*(1), 3–13.

Countries Compared by Health. Mental Health. Prevalence of Mental Health Problems. 12-Month Prevalence. International Statistics at NationMaster.com, OECD Country Statistical Profiles 2009. Aggregates compiled by NationMaster. Retrieved from http://www.nationmaster.com/country-info/stats/Health/Mental-health/Prevalence-of-mental-health-problems/12-month-prevalence

Deane, M. W., Steadman, H. J., Borum, R., Veysey, B. M., & Morrissey, J. P. (1999). Emerging Partnerships between Mental Health and Law Enforcement. *Psychiatric Services, 50*(1), 99–101.

DeHart, D., Lynch, S., Belknap, J., Dass-Brailsford, P., & Green, B. (2014). Life History Models of Female Offending the Roles of Serious Mental Illness and Trauma in Women's Pathways to Jail. *Psychology of Women Quarterly, 38*(1), 138–151.

DeMatteo, D., LaDuke, C., Locklair, B. R., & Heilbrum, K. (2013). Community-Based Alternatives for Justice-Involved Individuals with Severe Mental Illness: Diversion, Problem-Solving Courts, and Reentry. *Journal of Criminal Justice, 41,* 64–71.

Ditton, P. M. (1999). *Special Report: Mental Health and Treatment of Inmates and Probationers.* Washington, DC: US Department of Justice, Bureau of Justice Statistics.

Fisher, W. H., Silver, E., & Wolff, N. (2006). Beyond Criminalization: Toward a Criminologically Informed Framework for Mental Health Policy and Services Research. *Administration and Policy in Mental Health and Mental Health Services Research, 33*(5), 544–557.

Fuller, D. A., Lamb, R. H., Biasotti, M., & Snook, J. (December, 2015). *Overlooked in the Undercounted: The Role of Mental Illness in Fatal Law Enforcement Encounters.* Treatment Advocacy Center. Retrieved from TACReports.org/overlooked-undercounted.

Griffin, P. A., Heilbrun, K. Mulvey, E. P., DeMatteo, D., & Schubert, C. A. (2015). *Sequential Intercept Model and Criminal Justice: Promoting Community Alternatives for Individuals with Serious Mental Illness.* New York, NY: Oxford University Press.

Gunter, T. D., Chibnall, J. T., Antoniak, S. K., McCormick, B., & Black, D. W. (2012). Relative Contributions of Gender and Traumatic Life Experience to the Prediction of Mental Disorders in a Sample of Incarcerated Offenders. *Behavioral Sciences & the Law, 30*(5), 615–630.

Hartford, K., Carey, R., & Mendonca, J. (2006). Pre-Arrest Diversion of People with Mental Illness: Literature Review and International Survey. *Behavioral Sciences & the Law, 24,* 845–856.

Hawthorne, W. B., Folsom, D. P., Sommerfeld, D. H., Lanouette, N. M., Lewis, M., Aarons, G. A., Conklin, R. M., Solorzano, E., Lindamer, L. A., & Jeste, D. V. (2012). Incarceration among Adults Who Are in the Public Mental Health System: Rates, Risk Factors, and Short-Term Outcomes. *Psychiatric Services, 63*(1), 26–32.

Hayes, L. M. (2012). National Study of Jail Suicide 20 Years Later. *Journal of Correctional Health Care, 18*(3), 233–245.

Healy, J., & Turkewitz, J. (July 16, 2015). Guilty Verdict for James Holmes in Aurora Attack. *The New York Times.* Retrieved from http://www.nytimes.com.

Heibrun, K., DeMatteo, D., Strohmaier, H., & Galloway, M. (2015). The Movement toward Community-Based Alternatives to Criminal Justice Involvement and Incarceration for People with Severe Mental Illness. In Griffin, P. A., Heilbrun, K., Mulvey, E. P., DeMatteo, D., & Schubert, C. A., *The Sequential Intercept Model and Criminal Justice: Promoting Community Alternatives for Individuals with Serious Mental Illness* (pp. 1–20). New York, NY: Oxford University Press.

Holden, W. C. (July 20, 2012). Gunman Shoots 70, Kills 20 at Batman Premiere. Retrieved from http://kdvr.com/2012/07/20/dark-night-in-aurora-gunman-shoots-71-kills-12-at-batman-premiere/.

James, D. J., & Glaze, L. E. (2006). *Mental Health Problems of Prison and Jail Inmates* (pp. 1–16). Washington, DC: Bureau of Justice Statistics Special Report.

Jones, D. R., Macias, C., Barreira, P. J., Fisher, W. H., Hargreaves, W. A., & Harding, C. M. (2004). Prevalence, Severity, and Co-Occurrence of Chronic Physical Health Problems of Persons with Serious Mental Illness. *Psychiatric Services (Washington, D.C.), 55*(11), 1250–1257. doi:10.1176/appi.ps.55.11.1250.

Kapp, S. A., Petr, C. G., Robbins, M. L., & Choi, J. J. (2013). Collaboration between Community Mental Health and Juvenile Justice Systems: Barriers and Facilitators. *Child and Adolescent Social Work Journal, 30*(6), 505–517.

Lamb, H. R., & Weinberger, L. E. (1998). Persons with Severe Mental Illness in Jails and Prisons: A Review. *Psychiatric Services, 49*(4), 483–492.

Lamb, H. R., Weinberger, L. E., & DeCuir Jr., W. J. (2002). The Police and Mental Health. *Psychiatric Services, 53*(10), 1266–1271.

Lamb, H. R., Weinberger, L. E., & Gross, B. H. (1999). Community Treatment of Severely Mentally Ill Offenders under the Jurisdiction of the Criminal Justice System: A Review. *Psychiatric Services, 50*(7), 907–913.

Maruschak, L. M. (2004). HIV in Prisons and Jails, 2002. *Bureau of Justice Statistics Bulletin*, 1–11.

McGuire, J. F., & Rosenheck, R. A. (2004). Criminal History as a Prognostic Indicator in the Treatment of Homeless People with Severe Mental Illness. *Psychiatric Services*, *55*(1), 42–48.

Merikangas, K. R., Jin, R., He, J. P., Kessler, R. C., Lee, S., Sampson, N. A., . . . & Ladea, M. (2011). Prevalence and Correlates of Bipolar Spectrum Disorder in the World Mental Health Survey Initiative. *Arch Gen Psychiatry*, *68*(3), 241–251. doi:10.1001/archgenpsychiatry.2011.12.

Merikangas, K. R., & McClair, V. L. (2012). Epidemiology of Substance Use Disorders. *Human Genetics*, *131*(6), 779–789.

Morgan, R. D., Flora, D. B., Kroner, D. G., Mills, J. F., Varghese, F., & Steffan, J. S. (2012). Treating Offenders with Mental Illness: A Research Synthesis. *Law and Human Behavior*, *36*(1), 37.

National Alliance on Mental Illness (NAMI). (2010). *Election 2010: People with Mental Illness Don't belong behind Bars; Are Candidates Addressing the Facts?* Retrieved from http://www.nami.org/Press-Media/Press-Releases/2010/Election-2010-People-with- Mental-Illness-Don-t-Bel#sthash.G7ID0Cms.dpuf.

National Alliance on Mental Illness (NAMI). (2013). *Mental Illness Facts and Numbers.* Retrieved from https://www2.nami.org/factsheets/mentalillness_factsheet.pdf.

National Alliance on Mental Illness (NAMI). (2015). *Mental Health Conditions.* Retrieved from https://www.nami.org/Learn-More/Mental-Health-Conditions.

Nelson, C. M., Jolivette, K., Leone, P. E., & Mathur, S. R. (2010). Meeting the Needs of at Risk and Adjudicated Youth with Behavioral Challenges: The Promise of Juvenile Justice. *Behavioral Disorders*, *36*(1), 70–80.

Shufelt, J. L., & Cocozza, J. J. (2006). *Youth with Mental Health Disorders in the Juvenile Justice System: Results from a Multi-State Prevalence Study* (pp. 1–6). Delmar, NY: National Center for Mental Health and Juvenile Justice.

Sickel, A. E., Seacat, J. D., & Nabors, N. A. (2014). Mental health stigma update: A review of consequences. *Advances in Mental Health*, *12*(3), 202–215.

Sidhu, D. S. (2012, July 24). Call the Colorado shootings what they were: Terrorism. *The Baltimore Sun.* Retrieved from http://www.baltimoresun.com.

Slate, R. M., Buffington-Vollum, J. K., & Johnson, W. W. (2013). *The Criminalization of Mental Illness: Crisis and Opportunity for the Justice System* (2nd Ed.). Durham, NC: Carolina Academic Press.

Smedley, B. D. (2012). The Lived Experience of Race and Its Health Consequences. *American Journal of Public Health*, *102*(5), 933–935.

Substance Abuse and Mental Health Services Administration. (2013). *Behavioral Health, United States, 2012.* HHS Publication No. (SMA) 13–4797. Rockville, MD: Substance Abuse and Mental Health Services Administration.

Substance Abuse and Mental Health Services Administration. (2014). *Results from the 2013 National Survey on Drug Use and Health: Mental Health Findings,* NSDUH Series H-49, HHS Publication No. (SMA) 14–4887. Rockville, MD: Substance Abuse and Mental Health Services Administration.

Substance Abuse and Mental Health Services Administration, Center for Behavioral Health Statistics and Quality. (September 4, 2014). *The NSDUH Report: Substance Use and Mental Health Estimates from the 2013 National Survey on Drug Use and Health: Overview of Findings.* Rockville, MD: Substance Abuse and Mental Health Services Administration.

Teplin, L. A., Abram, K. M., McClelland, G. M., Dulcan, M. K., & Mericle, A. A. (2002). Psychiatric Disorders in Youth in Juvenile Detention. *Archives of General Psychiatry*, *59*(12), 1133–1143.

Torrey, E. F., Zdanowicz, M. T., Kennard, A. D., Lamb, R. H., Eslinger, D. F., Biasotti, M. C., & Fuller, D. A. (2014). *The Treatment of Persons with Mental Illness in Prisons and Jails: A State Survey*. Arlington, VA: Treatment Advocacy Center.

United States Department of Health and Human Services, Substance Abuse and Mental Health Services Administration, Center for Behavioral Health Statistics and Quality. (2011). *National Survey on Drug Use and Health* (ICPSR34481-v3). Ann Arbor, MI: Inter-University Consortium for Political Research, doi: http://doi.org/10.3886/ICPSR34481.v3.

Wolff, N., Frueh, B. C., Shi, J., & Schumann, B. E. (2012). Effectiveness of Cognitive–Behavioral Trauma Treatment for Incarcerated Women with Mental Illnesses and Substance Abuse Disorders. *Journal of Anxiety Disorders, 26*(7), 703–710.

World Health Organization. World Health Report. (2001). *Mental Disorders Effect One in Four People: Treatment Available But Not Being Used*. Retrieved from http://www.who.int/whr/2001/media_centre/press_release/en/.

CHAPTER 2 Historical Responses to Mental Illness

"Man is not made better by being degraded; he is seldom restrained from crime by harsh measures, except the principle of fear predominates in his character; and then he is never made radically better for its influence."

—Dorothea Dix (American philanthropist and
social reformer, 1802–1887)

Advancements in Psychosurgery

Dr. Walter Freeman, a neuropathologist, and Dr. James Watts, a neurosurgeon, were best known for developing and perfecting a procedure called a *leucotomy or bilateral prefrontal lobotomy* (Figure 2.1), a type of psychosurgery used on chronic and seriously mentally ill psychiatric patients from the 1940s through the 1970s (mostly inflicted with schizophrenia; Stone, 2001). It is estimated that about 60,000 individuals in Europe and the United States were lobotomized between the 20-year period of 1936 to 1956 (Raz, 2008). The procedure, as popularized by Dr. Freeman in the United States, was presented as relatively simple. The patient received nothing more than either local anesthesia or sedation, sometimes accompanied by electric convulsive shock therapy, or ECT, and there were only two primary instruments used to perform the surgery—a rubber mallet and a modified ice pick (New, n.d.). Much to the horror and chagrin of his colleagues, Freeman reportedly performed the procedure without gloves or other sterilization tools. Most often, the patients were still awake during the procedure (Getz, 2009). The criteria necessary for a patient to be eligible for the surgery was not at all complicated; rather, it involved observed symptoms of severe anxiety, depression, or psychosis and a recommendation, usually initiated by family, but supported by the treating physician. Freeman had personally performed close to 4,000 lobotomies by the 1950s, at which time several psychotropic medications had been introduced to the market and approved by the Food and Drug Administration (FDA). Medication, which

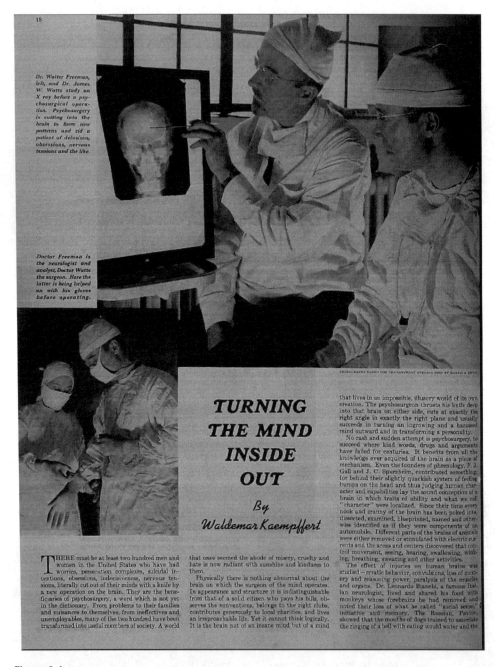

Figure 2.1

Leucotomy or Bilateral Prefrontal Lobotomy

Source: Article text by Waldemar Kaempffert; photography by Harris A. Ewing (*Saturday Evening Post*, May 24, 1941, pages 18–19). [Public domain] via Wikimedia Commons

was preferable and the least intrusive means to treat mental illness, seemed to alleviate the need for the continued use of psychosurgery, and lobotomies were dismissed as the primary and vogue method of treatment. Although the procedure was largely disfavored and its results were no longer viewed in a positive way, lobotomies were still being performed, though minimally, in the United States and elsewhere.

Introduction

Mental illness has long been stigmatized and misunderstood both on cross-national and cross-cultural fronts. Societal views of persons who suffer with mental and behavioral health issues all across the spectrum have been relatively negative and speckled with erroneous beliefs that relate having mental health issues with maladaptive behaviors—particularly violence and crime (Hinshaw & Stier, 2008; Slate, et al., 2013). Given such views, it is understandable why treatment for mental illness, especially in the early nineteenth and twentieth centuries, had been formulated to punish or even eradicate those who suffered from it. From institutionalization and barbaric forms of psychosurgery to the eugenics movement and sterilization, the United States has a dark history of cruel and unusual punishment toward persons with mental illness (Diamond, 1961).

As indicated throughout world history, the distinction between behaviors deemed "normal" and "abnormal" has been determined in large part by those members of society having the most (political) power. Consequently, depending on cultural norms of the mainstream (powerful members of society), such definitions change from time to time and from place to place (Sellin, 1938). This process or phenomenon can be referred to as *cultural relativism* (Pollis, 1996). Those who have the misfortune of falling out of acceptability as defined by the mainstream are stigmatized and oftentimes ostracized by the larger society. Sadly, PwMI represent one of many stigmatized groups who, across time, have been ascribed to a larger group of social deviants, including heretics or witches, addicts, vagrants, immigrants, sex offenders, or other social outcasts (Abrego, 2011; Hinshaw & Stier, 2008; Tewksbury, 2005).

The following sections retrace the steps of societal responses to mental illness across time. Interestingly, approaches to mental health treatment throughout the eras can be reduced to three concise themes: supernatural, *somatagenic*, and *psychogenic* (Farreras, 2015). Furthermore, submerged in the themes are a number of dichotomous relationships; for example, the rights of PwMI versus the responsibility of the state to keep the community safe *from* PwMI; stigma versus compassion; confinement versus communal living; spiritual versus biological origins of mental illness; moral treatment versus punishment; and patient versus criminal. Moreover, these thematic "opposites" are also cyclical in nature. In response to political and public sentiment regarding mental health and treatment; developments in psychiatry, psychology, and medicine; and strong advocacy by highly influential individuals and groups, transformations in law and practice have occurred throughout the course of time.

Societal Responses to Mental Illness: Thematic Eras

Demons, Spirits, and Possession (5000 to 400 BCE)

The earliest accounts of mental illness and responding treatments were recorded throughout ancient civilization; in particular, as early as 5000 BCE, among Neolithic and Mesopotamian civilizations (Foerschner, 2010). A substantial influence throughout most of this early history was religion or spirituality. During ancient times, persons so afflicted with mental disease were viewed as immoral creatures who were most likely possessed by demons (Spanos, 1978). Commonly held beliefs were based upon perceptions that such individuals had sorcerous attributes, and therefore, they were subjected to a displeasing response (e.g., punishment) by the gods (Faria, 2013; Shorter, 1997; Spanos, 1978).

A SNAPSHOT IN COMPARATIVE HISTORY: THE RELATIONSHIP BETWEEN STIGMA AND MENTAL HEALTH TREATMENT APPROACHES

Supernatural beliefs about mental illness continue to exist around various parts of the world and within various cultures. For example, due to its association with otherworldly and potentially evil and deviant influences (e.g., masturbation), the stigma attached to mental illness is so profound that PwMI and their family members in places like China, Greece, Morocco, Lebanon, and the United Arab Emirates are likely to immediately seek out traditional healers and pharmaceutical treatment. Unfortunately, many also find it easier to hide their afflictions from family members and self-medicate until they eventually become so disruptive to society that they are incarcerated (Foerschner, 2010).

Individuals so afflicted were shunned by society and subjected to harsh "cleansing rituals" and moral punishments that were oftentimes referred to by those inflicting them as a form of saving grace (Shatkin, n.d.; Shorter, 1997). The responding cure for disease of the mind revolved around techniques designed to cast away any evil spirits from their bodies. Such attempts included exorcisms, incantations, and other spiritually induced cleansing rituals (Neugebauer, 1979). Individuals were also subjected to painful surgical-like techniques that were primitive by their very nature and not medically safe. For example, a process known as *trephination* (see Figure 2.2) was commonly used for centuries as a cure for not just mental disease or a defect (presumed to be the result

Neolithic trephining. Making a hole in the skull to let the devils out.

Figure 2.2

Illustration of Neolithic Trephination

Source: Behind the doctor/Logan Clendening. Wellcome Library, London [CC BY 4.0 (http://creativecommons.org/licenses/by/4.0)] via Wikimedia Commons

of demonic influence), but also for conditions such as migraines, skull fractures, and epilepsy (Faria, 2013). This ancient practice involved the use of a primitive stone tool to remove sections of the skull in order to release any evil spirits that were hindering an individual's ability to function as a rational and faithful member of society. It should be noted that other more intrusive responses were used in the name of religion or spirituality, including the use of barbaric forms of punishment as a means to obtain submission (Foerschner, 2010).

Among ancient Hebrews and Persians, defying God's will (sinning) was viewed as the ultimate source of mental disease, and only through prayer and spiritual rituals was one able to be healed (Shorter, 1997). Ancient Egyptians were also heavily influenced by deity and in the belief that the trespass thereof was the primary source of mental ill-ness (Foerschner, 2010). Treatment became centered on primitive forms of psychosur-gery performed by priest-doctors—particularly the continued use of trephination, but also other procedures such as vaginal fumigation for "wandering uterus," or what was eventually referred to as hysteria among women (now "conversion disorder"). Aside from these surgical methods, the Egyptians were progressive in that they advanced the notion that recreation would alleviate mental distress, and therefore, they promoted involvement in activities such as music, dancing, and participation in the arts to achieve some level of spiritual balance or normalcy (Foerschner, 2010).

A visual depiction of mental health treatment in the form of a chronological timeline can be found online at http://www.pbs.org/wgbh/amex/nash/timeline/. Students are encouraged to reference it as they read through the chapter, as it more clearly illustrates underlying perceptions of mental illness and key treatment approaches from each historical era.

Early Medical Model (400 BCE to Middle Ages)

The sources of psychopathology continued to remain immersed in superstition and spirituality until sometime between the fifth and third centuries BCE. Early writings indicate that in 400 BCE, Hippocrates, a Greek physician, dismissed the long-held belief that mental illness was the result of sin and evil trepidation. Rather, he argued, it is a natural response to organically borne pathology in the brain of a human being (Foerschner, 2010). This is not to say that treatment approaches had been substantially altered forever; in fact, there is some evidence that trephination and other psychosurgical measures are still being practiced in some cultures today (Gross, 1999).

Given advancements made by Hippocrates and other medical writers during the classical antiquity period, mental illness was treated as a form or type of medical ill-ness. In terms of early treatment approaches, there was an exceptional focus on body chemistry and the understanding that there were four primary fluids (humors) of the body: blood, phlegm, bile, and black bile. If any of these were to become imbalanced, the body chemistry would be interrupted, and therefore, an individual's physical health (including brain function) would become dysfunctional (Foerschner, 2010). Prescribed treatments were designed to return the body to its proper balance, and thus included procedures such as purging with laxatives and other concoctions designed to induce vomiting, as well as bloodletting or bleeding (otherwise known as phlebotomy)—which, for some, involved the use of leeches or processes such as "cupping" or "tapping" (Foerschner, 2010; Shatkin, n.d.).

The gyrating chair was a spinning apparatus designed to restore equilibrium and increase blood flow to the brain. A more detailed description of the chair and other methods of stabilization and treatment used in the early asylum, including photos, can be found at http://americanasylums. weebly.com/treatments.html.

The Middle Ages: Dungeons and a Return to Demonology

In the period extending from about 1200 CE through the late seventeenth century, persons with mental illness were responded to somewhat differently depending on the region in which they lived (Foerschner, 2010). For example, PwMI in Eastern societies were mostly living freely in their communities-villages as long as they were not considered dangerous. In parts of Western Europe, philosophies regarding superstition and mysticism prevailed, and persons who were considered mentally afflicted were in some societies treated as witches who were inhabited by demons. In certain cultures, PwMI who were unable to care for themselves were cared for and treated by religious orders, but caregiving functions were in most places almost always the responsibility of families (Foerschner, 2010) (See the text box on page 28 for cultural differences in caregiving).

Given inadequacies in at-home care and, at the extreme end, gross mistreatment of PwMI by family members and other caregivers, institutionalization in *asylums* became the popular or preferred option, and persons with chronic mental illness were lodged in cottages and hospitals with intentions of receiving humane care by professional persons who could provide more sophisticated treatment. The first European facility specifically for people with mental illness was established in Valencia, Spain, in 1407 ("Timeline: Treatments for Mental Illness," 2007).

Period of Enlightenment (Late 1600s to 1840)

FAST FACT: THE EARLY ASYLUMS

Patients were shackled to the walls of a cold, dark cell (see Figure 2.3). Naked and starving, they would be standing in their own feces and urine and perhaps some remnants of scattered straw that

---

continued

was originally designed to act as bedding or to provide warmth to the cell. They might also be wearing iron cuffs and collars to restrict their movement—just enough so that they could eat, but not enough that they could sleep in any other position except for standing (Shorter, 1997).

Conditions and Treatment Methods at the Asylum

At the beginning of the Enlightenment era, mental disorders were not considered legitimate illnesses; rather, persons so afflicted were merely a disturbance to the community. PwMI were frequently abandoned once committed to an asylum because there was not consistency on how to treat them. The clergy played a huge role in treating patients, but was only available to those who could afford to send him to the patient

VERSCHEIDEN WIJZEN VAN PIJNIGINGE, BIJ DE INQUISITIE GEBRUIKELIJK.

Figure 2.3
Eighteenth-Century Dungeon
Source: Author unknown [Public domain], via Wikimedia Commons

(Foerschner, 2010). Asylums were formed in order to hold the swelling population of PwMI; they were used to lift the burden from family members who often neglected to provide proper care. Unfortunately, reports indicated that a large majority of individuals who were employed at the asylums were untrained and sometimes accused of mistreating the patients under their care (Shorter, 1997). In the 1600s, Europeans began to move PwMI out of asylums and into more punitive prison environments. Persons identified as insane started to be treated inhumanely, chained to walls, or kept in dungeons where they were deprived for days, months, and even years of social interaction, nutrition, sleep, and light.

In terms of treatment during this period, an emphasis on *phrenology* (brain size, structure, and functions; see Figure 2.4) and *physiognomy* (form or features of the

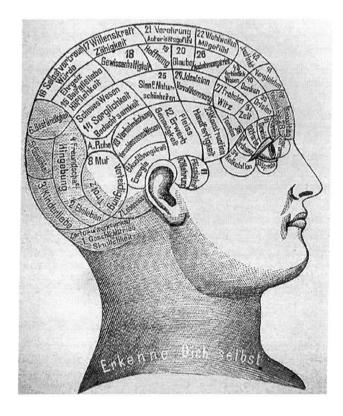

Figure 2.4

Phrenology

Source: Scan by de: Benutzer: Summi edited by "Wolfgang" [Public domain] via Wikimedia Commons

body—particularly facial expressions) to explain psychopathy was evident, and studies evolving around biological predictors of behavior were popular (e.g., Gall in the 1790s; Carlson, 1958; Collins, 1999). Consequently, given the emphasis on *determinism*, treatment modalities of the past had continued such as purging and bloodletting. More innovative practices were also introduced in prisons and other places where PwMI were confined, including the "gyrating chair," strait jackets, and the use of physical restraints, which are straps that, when tightened, restrict a person's movement (Foerschner, 2010).

For many, particularly females, their illness was viewed by early European psychiatrists as hysteria, a condition that caused somatic symptoms, including blindness and paralysis, with no apparent medical explanation. In fact, a considerable debate ensued from early eighteenth century through the middle of the nineteenth century with respect to whether this condition was psychosomatic or neurological. Innovative treatment philosophies were introduced, including a procedure introduced by Franz Anton Mesmer. The procedure, referred to as *mesmerism*, was based in the perception that hysteria was the result of the imbalance of the body's magnetic fluid, and treatment involved the use of animal magnetism to restore balance. This practice was eventually replaced with the use of hypnosis, which was supported by a psychogenic explanation for mental illness (particularly hysteria) (Farreras, 2015).

A Shifting Philosophy

During the late 1700s, a concern about the harsh methods of mental health treatment grew in Europe and in the original American colonies, which led to occasional reforms. In 1793 Phillippe Pinel instituted what was coined *moral treatment* (traitement moral) of persons with mental illness when he took over the Bicêtre insane asylum and removed patients from dungeons ("Timeline: Treatments for Mental Illness," 2007). Moral treatment required more humane procedures, as it was presumed that a cure was attainable, specifically for individuals without chronic disabilities. Places of confinement began to provide more acceptable living quarters and adequate and safe medical care. The new philosophy was carried over into the United States by early crusader Benjamin Rush (Floyd, 2015).

Despite developments in Europe during the period, mental health treatment in early nineteenth-century America was relatively nonexistent, and PwMI continued to be housed in prisons and jails, almshouses (shelters for the poor), or at home with families who could not properly care for them (Shorter, 1997). Americans reverted back to physiology and the notion that insanity was the result of physical impairment within particular sections of the brain (Neugebauer, 1979). Consequently, treatment practices such as bloodletting were still being used because advancements in medicine and practice had not yet been made readily available. The moral treatment movement continued, however, and both scientific and lay communities began to analyze the role of the environment in maladaptive behaviors and proposed that improvements in the conditions may result in a cure for those minimally afflicted (Foerschner, 2010).

Persons in charge of early asylums were referred to as superintendents. These individuals were active in their respective communities, and although well educated, their educational backgrounds were not necessarily in the practice of medicine or in understanding human behaviors. The institutions in which they worked were oftentimes located in rural environments—a calculated practice so that patients were far removed from family influences and their previous home environments (Foerschner, 2010; Neugebauer, 1979). The mission of asylums under the moral treatment philosophy was to keep patients engaged through healthy living, which included exercise, religious practice, work, and education. Medications were not regularly dispensed or ingested, and PwMI were to be viewed by all as unfortunate, not evil, beings.

FAST FACT: THE ORIGIN OF "BEDLAM"

Saint Mary of Bethlehem was a monastery in London, England, that was transformed into one of the most infamous asylums that began admitting patients in 1547. Patients who were chronically mentally ill were often put on public display to be ridiculed for amusement purposes, and those who were only mildly afflicted were subjected to panhandling for charity. Due to its reputation for the abuse and severe mistreatment of patients, the facility became known as "Bedlam," a derogatory descriptor that continues to be referenced today (Figure 2.5) (Foerschner, 2010).

Inferior Genetics

Given the conditions of asylums and other issues that riddled the institutional setting such as a shortage of qualified administration and staff, restrictions in funding, and extreme overcrowding, this method of treatment was soon replaced. By the mid-1800s, mental illness was becoming ascribed to heredity; the idea was that families viewed as genetically inferior would produce offspring who bore the same weak family vices (e.g., alcoholism and masturbation) and therefore, would be at a higher risk for madness (Hinshaw & Stier, 2008; Neugebauer, 1979). With this influence of *Social Darwinism*, patients who were referred to quite often as imbeciles, idiots, or the feeble-minded were subjected to a number of deplorable "treatment" methods, including the use of strong drugs to subdue them (e.g., chloroform) or sterilization. This period of

Drawn by Tho.H.Shepherd.   Engraved by J.Tingle.

NEW BETHLEM HOSPITAL, ST. GEORGE'S FIELDS.

Figure 2.5

Bethlem Hospital, acquired from antique print shop. The print is described as a "steel engraving from 1828" and is a print from a book

Source: https://upload.wikimedia.org/wikipedia/en/b/b7/BethlemSteelEngraving1828.png

American history was characterized by a *eugenics* movement to eliminate entire groups of people, including PwMI (Floyd, 2015).

During the mid-to-late nineteenth century, asylums became dumping grounds for persons with mental problems; however, because of the overcrowded conditions, lack of treatment options, and funding deficits, many PwMI—particularly those with a history of violence—were housed instead in jails and prisons (Floyd, 2015; Foerschner, 2010; Slate, et al., 2013). Prison staff often left them unclothed without running water and little food, and many were housed alongside violent criminals. PwMI were chained to the walls of jail or prison dungeons, resulting in a gruesome display of torment and punishment (Shorter, 1997). In attempts to "cure" their illnesses, doctors would employ treatments such as *electroconvulsive or shock therapy (ECT)*. When doctors started to realize that their treatments were not working, they would just leave the person to wither away, oftentimes in worse shape than before treatment commenced (Foerschner, 2010).

Advocacy Movement

During her tour of the East Cambridge jail in Cambridge, Massachusetts, in 1841, retired teacher and renowned human rights crusader Dorothea Dix discovered that the female inmates with whom she was charged with teaching had not violated any laws, but rather, were mentally ill. Of particular concern to Ms. Dix was the negligence and willful mistreatment by those who were considered caregivers. Dix wrote on her observations, describing conditions that both female and male inmates with mental illness had endured—which included filthy and foul-smelling living quarters, the use of chains or other apparatus to secure them to the walls, severe injuries resulting from lashing and other beatings, and self-inflicted (untreated) mutilation (Dix, 1843, as cited in *The History of Mental Retardation*, n.d.). Over a 40-year period after her initial observations, she continued to advocate on behalf of PwMI and succeeded in driving the establishment of 32 state hospitals as asylums (Figure 2.6).

CRUSADERS FOR THE MORAL TREATMENT OF PWMI

Dorothea Dix was a key advocate of the humane treatment of persons with mental illness during the mid-to-late nineteenth century. Although her work had a huge influence on the development of state-run institutions to house and treat PwMI, there were other influential figures at the time whose work contributed toward improved treatment and confinement of persons under supervision by the state—including prisoners and those afflicted with chronic mental illness. During an 1871 visit to America, British writer and reformer Charles Dickens had the opportunity to tour the Eastern State Penitentiary in Philadelphia. The following is an excerpt of his original observations with respect to the conditions of solitary confinement.

> *My firm convictions, that independent of the mental anguish it occasions—an anguish so acute and so tremendous, that all imagination of it must fall far short of the reality—it wears the mind into a morbid state, which renders it unfit for the rough contact and busy action of the world. It is my fixed opinion that those who have undergone this punishment, must pass into society again morally unhealthy and diseased. There are many instances on record, of men who have chosen, or have been condemned, to lives of perfect solitude, but I scarcely remember one, even among sages of strong and vigorous intellect, where its effect has not become apparent, in some disordered train of thought, or some gloomy hallucination. What monstrous phantoms, bed of despondency and doubt, and born and reared in solitude, have stalked upon the earth, making creation ugly, and darkening the face of Heaven! Suicides are rare among these prisoners: are almost, indeed, unknown. But no argument in favour of the system, can reasonably be deduced from this circumstance, although it is very often urged. All men who have made diseases of the mind their study, know perfectly well that such extreme depression and despair as will change the whole character, and beat down all its powers of elasticity and self-resistance, may be at work within a man, and yet stop short of self-destruction. This is a common case.*
>
> *(Dickens, 1866)*

Figure 2.6

Portrait of Dorothea Lynde Dix

Source: Bier, C. (2008, July 7). Dorothea Lynde Dix. Retrieved August 8, 2015, from https: //commons.wikimedia.org/wiki/Dorothea_Dix#/media/File:Dix-Dorothea-LOC.jpg

State mental hospitals became very popular throughout the late nineteenth century and into the early-to-mid-twentieth century; consequently, they also became very crowded. By the 1880s, superintendents were largely replaced with neurologists who sought control of the asylums (Floyd, 2015). Although neurologists made some positive contributions, stories emerged in the news regarding exaggerated conditions of patient abuse. Original reports of a low staff–patient ratio and humane treatment were replaced by images of overwhelmed staff and the warehousing of humans, which led to the development of oversight commissions and, ultimately, the reexamination of hospitalization as an effective tool for treatment. As a result, interested parties began to consider the development of community-based treatment options. Other developments at the turn of the century included advancements in medical education and research on psychopathology and insanity as an individual topic for study. Asylums were now referred to as hospitals as an early approach to reduce stigma associated with mental illness (Floyd, 2015). Advancements such as these, however, were not able to overcome the persistent view that PwMI were genetically inferior, and so stigmatization and eugenics-based "treatment" approaches persisted into the twentieth century. At about the same time that the United States was the recipient of significant European immigration waves into its cities, Americans became acquainted with the influence of the unconscious mind (Floyd, 2015).

An Era of Psychoanalysis (Late 1800s to Mid-1900s)

In previous eras, theories of mental illness had remained grounded in superstition and spiritual forces or in somatogenic explanations for functional impairment in physicality due to illness, genetic inheritance, or some level of brain damage or imbalance. As advancements in research on the human psyche and behavior continued, and with the emergence of psychoanalytic theories and scholars such as Sigmund Freud and Carl Jung, psychogenic theories for mental illness became more commonly advanced (Foerschner, 2010); this group of theories focused on traumatic or stressful experiences, maladaptive learned associations and cognitions, or distorted perceptions.

FAST FACT

As discussed in the opening paragraph of the chapter, Dr. Walter Freeman had lobotomized close to 4,000 individuals during the course of his career. A 2008 documentary about Freeman was aired on PBS as part of the American Experience series and is titled "The Lobotomist." The documentary included footage of Freeman performing a lobotomy on one of his female candidates. Students can find the documentary in whole and part on youtube.com. Warning: Parts of the video are somewhat disturbing.

Although private psychotherapy sessions were being conducted, most people with psychosis at this time were still receiving custodial care in institutions (Faria, 2013). Unfortunately, conditions in some mental health institutions were still inhumane. In fact, as in previous times, people were writing and publishing on their experiences as patients. For example, in 1908 Clifford Beers, a former patient, published his autobiography titled *A Mind that Found Itself*, where he described his own dehumanizing experiences in a Connecticut mental institution (Morrissey & Goldman, 1986; Parry, 2010). Under the leadership of Beers, the *mental health hygiene movement* began, and publicly available accounts of mistreatment of patients generated calls for reform—calls that were answered by the development of a National Committee for Mental Hygiene, an education and advocacy group that later became the National Mental Health Association or MHA (Parry, 2010).

Available treatments for chronic mental illness during the early-to-mid-twentieth century included an experimental mix of psychoanalysis, medication, and more progressive forms of psychosurgery (Foerschner, 2010; Morrissey & Goldman, 1986). Specific approaches included highly-potent drugs, ECT, and insulin-induced comas. Surgery, particularly the *prefrontal lobotomy*, was commonly used to treat people with schizophrenia (Faria, 2013; "Timeline: Treatments for Mental Illness," 2007). In fact, Dr. Walter Freeman (discussed in the introduction of the chapter) was considered a pioneer in this method for use in the United States, having performed close to 4,000 lobotomies over the course of his career, which was at its high point in the 1940s (Faria, 2013).

Due to continued publicity surrounding mental health reform, President Harry Truman signed the National Mental Health Act in 1946. The act established the National Institute of Mental Health (1949) and created accountability and redirected oversight of state mental health institutions from the state to the federal government (National Institutes of Health [NIH], 2013). Also during this period, advancements were being made with regard to drug therapy for chronic mental health issues (e.g., the 1949 advancement of lithium by Australian psychiatrist, J.F.J. Cade, to treat psychosis and, later, bipolar disorder; "Timeline: Treatments for Mental Illness," 2007).

The Dawn of a New "Error": Drug Therapy and Deinstitutionalization (1940s to Mid-1980s)

As observed in the previous section, mental health (and corresponding treatment) in the first half of the twentieth century was influenced by theories that emphasized psychosomatic origins of mental illness, and therefore, the need for psychogenic-based therapeutic interventions. For many, this involved a mix of services they could receive in the community, including individualized therapy sessions, family or group counseling, and medication management. For a small proportion of the population with mental illness, therapeutic intervention continued to involve secure placement or confinement and the use of painfully intrusive techniques (e.g., shock therapy) and surgical interventions (e.g., lobotomy) (Shorter, 1997). A variety of different styles or approaches to therapy were being introduced and practiced in an office as opposed to a hospital setting. In contrast with previous eras, all shared the same resounding philosophy: an alliance between the patient and therapist that reflected privacy concerns, humanizing responses to treatment, and a mutual respect.

The Advent of Drugs and Community-Based Care

Despite the changing philosophy, many PwMI continued to be hospitalized due to their chronic or unexplainable conditions (Goldman & Morrissey, 1985). For example, in post–World War II United States, state and private hospitals for PwMI were at their fullest capacities due to the relative ease of commitment procedures. In the 1950s, the first antipsychotic drug, chlorpromazine (Thorazine), was introduced for treatment of psychosis, and due to its overwhelming effectiveness, was routinely viewed as a cure for chronic mental illness (Slate, et al., 2013). Over the next few decades, the advent of this and other antipsychotic drugs such as haloperidol had the effect of dramatically reducing the state hospital populations in favor of community-based treatment and drug therapy. Soon after Thorazine became available in the United States in 1955, a process or phenomenon of rapid **deinstitutionalization** occurred (Faria, 2013). As an illustration of this point, in 1955 there were 560,000 patients in state psychiatric hospitals in the United States; by comparison, in 1980, this number had dropped to 130,000. Consequently, in addition to the creation of new problems such as serious side effects of the medication, society was faced with a new problem: the infiltration of thousands of chronically mentally ill individuals into the community.

Antipsychiatry and Skepticism

Fueled by these and other developments, the entire field of psychiatry became vulnerable to discrimination, as lay persons began to question the state's role in the institutionalization of what seemed like a great majority of poor and powerless sects of society. Moreover, there was now a resounding skepticism as to the meaning of insanity and whether this was more of a socially constructed condition caused by society itself (Morrissey & Goldman, 1985). Consequently, the 1960s witnessed an antipsychiatry movement, led most prominently by counterculture writers such as R.D. Laing and Michel Foucault. Additional supporters of the movement included psychiatrist Thomas Szasz, who published *The Myth of Mental Illness*, and sociologist Erving Goffman who, in his 1961 book, *Asylums*, argued that institutionalization over long periods of time produces symptoms of psychosis, thereby perpetuating the need for further institution-alization and isolation from society ("Timeline: Treatments for Mental Illness," 2007). Also at this time was the release of the film adaption of Ken Kesey's novel, *One Flew over the Cuckoo's Nest*, which became very influential in terms of informing public per-ceptions of the perils in institutional settings.

In conjunction with the counterculture response to psychiatry and a wave of human rights movements at the time (including the rights of persons with disabilities), national politics reflected a liberal view that certainly supported the movement in progress (Slate, et al., 2013). President John F. Kennedy openly disclosed the disability of his sister, Rosemary (see Figure 2.7), and advocated extensively for persons with mental health and developmental disabilities (Berkowitz, 1980; Mason, Menolascino, & Galvin, 1976). The philosophy on mental health treatment was changing again, and the new approach was to provide local care for "the emotionally disturbed" at the neigh-borhood level to avoid hospitalization, thereby saving money and providing what were perceived to be more effective alternatives (Morrissey & Goldman, 1986). In 1963, the Community Mental Health Centers Construction Act was passed, which provided federal money to develop a network of community mental health centers. Unfortu-nately, this legislation occurred after mass deinstitutionalization was well underway, and therefore, the resources were quickly depleted.

Public support for community-based treatment was lacking as well, as PwMI were often viewed by the general public as dangerous, dirty, and unpredictable (Corrigan & Watson, 2002). Such stigmatizing views led to what has been referred to as a *not in my backyard (NIMBY) mentality*. In some cases, members of the public have fought to keep services such as supportive housing for previously hospitalized persons with chronic mental illness out of their neighborhoods ("Housing First: A Special Report," National Public Radio [NPR], 2002). The mass deinstitutionalization of the 1960s and 1970s led to multiple social consequences that were presumably unanticipated, includ-ing substantial homelessness and *transinstitutionalization*, or repetitive encounters across multiple systems of care (e.g., public welfare, dependency/foster care, criminal justice, and substance abuse and mental health) (Goldman & Morrissey, 1985; Morrissey & Goldman, 1986).

Amidst social and human rights–related reforms, a number of legislative changes regarding commitment procedures had been implemented during the 1970s that toughened the criteria for involuntary commitment, incorporating language that reflects what has been referred to as a "dangerousness standard"; these new require-ments had the effect of further stigmatizing PwMI as violent and dangerous individuals—ultimately restricting people who were truly ill from getting the help they needed (Hinshaw & Stier, 2008). In addition to changes with regard to com-mitment criteria, further advocacy, training, and research groups surfaced throughout

Figure 2.7

The Kennedy Family at Hyannis Port, 1931

L-R: Robert Kennedy, John F. Kennedy, Eunice Kennedy, Jean Kennedy (on lap of) Joseph P. Kennedy Sr., Rose Fitzgerald Kennedy (behind) Patricia Kennedy, Kathleen Kennedy, Joseph P. Kennedy Jr. (behind) Rosemary Kennedy. Dog in foreground is "Buddy."

Source: Photograph by Richard Sears in the John F. Kennedy Presidential Library and Museum, Boston [Public domain] via Wikimedia Commons

the next decade or so. For example, in 1979, the National Alliance on Mental Illness (NAMI) was founded—a prominent advocacy group that provides research for people with serious psychiatric illness and support for PwMI and their families ("Timeline: Treatments for Mental Illness," 2007). Further developments during the course of the next two decades included the introduction of a new generation of antipsychotic drugs, such as clozapine, used to treat the symptoms of schizophrenia ("Mental Health Medications," 2015). New-generation drugs appeared to be more effective and had fewer side effects.

The Present Condition: Criminalization of Mental Illness (Mid–1980s to?)

When the deinstitutionalization movement began, it was meant—in theory—to have people move from mental institutions into community healthcare establishments and to be immersed into towns and neighborhoods where they would get services, accommodations, and housing. Furthermore, newer- generation psychotropic drugs were keeping symptoms in check for chronically ill PwMI, and therefore, making it possible for them to function in daily activities. Over a 17-year period following Kennedy's call for the development community mental health centers (CMHCs), the federal government spent in excess of 20 billion dollars to build outpatient clinics that would replace long-term hospitals (Faria, 2013). At the same time, the number of allocated patient beds in state and federal institutions for persons with mental illness had rapidly declined from close to 500,000 in 1970 to well below 100,000 (Torrey, et al., 2008). As the funding and resources for treatment and services become depleted, many PwMI are unable to obtain the necessary resources to provide for themselves. This may lead to a number of maladaptive outcomes, including homelessness, rapid decompensation, self-medication, a state of crisis, and the criminalization of PwMI who become incarcerated in local prisons for typically inconsequential crimes (e.g., disturbing the peace or vagrancy) (Faria, 2013). Figures 2.8 and 2.9 illustrate this trend.

Institutional census estimates have indicated that on any given day, there are approximately 283,000 persons with severe mental illnesses who are incarcerated in state and federal jails and prisons in the United States. By comparison, the proportion of persons with serious mental illness who are in public psychiatric hospitals is estimated to be 70,000–30 percent of whom are forensic clients, meaning those who are court involved ("The Criminalization of People," n.d.). At present time, about 50 percent of American adults (9 million) and almost three-quarters of jail inmates suffer from a mental disorder during their lifetime, most often co-occurring with substance abuse (SAMHSA, 2013). Co-occurring mental health and substance abuse disorders are exceptionally high among persons who are homeless (23 percent lifetime prevalence rate), many of whom are returning veterans—a point that will be discussed in more detail later in the book. Consequently, it has been suggested that incarceration is replacing mental health treatment, and as a result, the criminal justice system has now been referred to as the de facto mental health system. Advocates for PwMI find these facts to be appalling and continue to fight in an effort for the provision of adequate mental healthcare in prison.

The treatment, or lack thereof, available to justice-involved PwMI who are incarcerated comprises a huge area of research. Due to symptoms of their illness and other distinct factors that set them apart from inmates in the general population, the horrors of imprisonment are felt more profoundly by this class of offenders—particularly in jail and during the first two weeks of detainment. Oftentimes, inmates with mental health

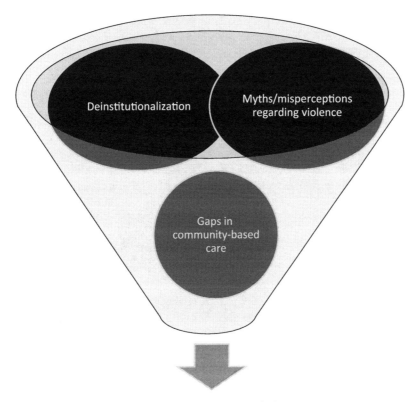

Restrictions on getting help

Figure 2.8
Restrictions on Getting Help
Source: Author

and intellectual disabilities are also targets for cruelty, such as physical and sexual abuse by other inmates. Their strange behaviors can cause them to be punished more often, mostly resulting in solitary confinement, which only causes their condition to deterio-rate further (Satel, 2003). There have been legal developments in the area of treatment, and precedent has been set with regard to a number of pressing issues related to com-petency and mental health; these developments are summarized in Chapters 6 and 7.

However promising these and other legal developments, the fact still remains that most justice-involved PwMI are not accessing treatment while incarcerated for both individual and systematic reasons (Slate, et al., 2013). And despite the watchful eye of the courts, mental health understaffing still persists throughout most correctional facil-ities. Furthermore, the general public remains quite fearful of who they perceive as "the mentally ill" and may express little sympathy for them (Byrne, 2000).

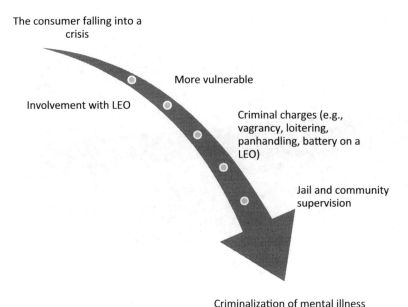

The consumer falling into a crisis

More vulnerable

Involvement with LEO

Criminal charges (e.g., vagrancy, loitering, panhandling, battery on a LEO)

Jail and community supervision

Criminalization of mental illness

Figure 2.9

The Criminalization of Mental Illness

Source: Author

Students: Please keep in mind that the person must be discussed separately from the disorder (i.e., "a person diagnosed with bipolar disorder" rather than "a bipolar"). In the field, this is referred to as "person-first" language. Challenge yourself as you move through the materials and discuss them with friends, co-workers, and classmates. Are you using person-first language in your interactions?

It is presumed that most persons, if asked, would not be in favor of incarceration as a viable answer to the housing or treatment needs of PwMI. Unfortunately, however, that is exactly what happens. In fact, a concept that will be returned to later in the text is that of "mercy bookings"—this refers to police making the decision to arrest PwMI in crisis merely because they know that is the only way the individual will gain access to care. Some advocates believe that these conditions persist because of the stigma that is attached to and surrounds mental illness. Despite efforts to raise awareness and education with regard to the common occurrence of mental health problems among U.S. adults and youth, persistent stigma makes getting help difficult for many people.

Put mental illness aside for a moment. In other times and places multiple persons or groups of persons have been singled out and mistreated by members of society. Can you think of specific examples of stigmatized groups and the ways in which they were outcast or mistreated? What were the motives of those who were doing the stigmatizing?

Take-Home Message

The historical responses to mental illness have revolved around three primary philosophies regarding the origins of psychological issues: (a) supernatural theories that attribute mental illness to evil possession by demonic influences, the displeasure of gods, lunar or planetary events, curses, and, most profoundly, sinfulness; (b) somatogenic theories, which identify physical dysfunction or disability as a result of illness, genetic inheritance, brain damage, or imbalance of bodily fluids; and, (c) psychogenic theories, which focus on individual experiences that were traumatizing or stressful, maladaptive or dysfunctional cognitive development or learning, or distorted perceptions. The treatments subscribed to PwMI are largely determined on the favored etiological advancement and have historically ranged between drug treatment therapy and trephination and lobotomy. As illustrated by the narrative here, all of these explanations coexist across time and place; moreover, the corresponding treatment approaches may recycle, despite previous controversy and ineffectiveness, as we have seen recently in the mass incarceration of PwMI for nonserious offenses. Although the road to progression has been plagued with unbridled discretion at times, the objective has become the institution of moral treatment of persons with mental illness, and new, more humane, strategies continue to emerge.

The growing number of justice-involved offenders incarcerated in the United States is cause for great concern. Prison conditions are not the only obstacles met in the incarceration of PwMI. This population is also challenged by the scant resources available to them concerning counseling or treatment. Progressive states have already experimented with the creation of mental health courts to determine whether such a creation will meet the needs of mentally ill offenders (Kondo, 2003, p. 257). Such innovations have been referred to as *therapeutic jurisprudence*, a concept that will be revisited later in the text. The main focus is on treating mentally ill offenders with fairness, compassion, dignity, and respect. It is suggested that such measures will more positively affect the outcome of mental health treatment.

REFLECTIVE PRACTICE

Imagine being a prisoner with untreated (nonmedicated) serious mental illness in the early nineteenth century. You are a first-time offender who has now been charged with vagrancy. You arrive at the jail in a state of paranoia and confusion, and after a traumatizing cavity search and being stripped of your belongings, you are pushed into an overcrowded jail cell that is filthy, damp, and freezing (there is no heat in the winter). With the exception of an occasional ray of sunshine that makes its way through a tiny window at the end of the row of cells, there is barely any light. The cells are mere holes in the solemn concrete architecture of the prison; they are dangerous as constructed and

continued

offer no ventilation. There are slots in the steel doors where stale and sometimes moldy bread and water are pushed through. When you have "misbehaved" according to the guards, you are placed in an isolation cell in the "dungeon," which provides complete darkness and a stench that resembles what you imagine the worst of hell would smell like. In isolation, prisoners have no mattresses to sleep upon (only the hard, cold, filthy, and sometimes feces- and urine-flooded floors), given the possibility that harm to self or others could be caused with the springs. If you are considered ill enough to warrant a trip to the prison hospital, there you will find incompetent doctors who lack the essential resources to provide you with adequate care. In fact, it is quite possible that you will perish due to self-inflicted harm or inadequate medical treatment. Should you be lucky enough to survive to complete your sentence, you will be turned out without resources, treatment for your illness, or hope.

QUESTIONS FOR CLASSROOM DISCUSSION

1. Identify and discuss specific beliefs or events in history that exemplify each of these etiological theories of mental illness: supernatural, somatagenic, or psychogenic (e.g., hysteria, humorism, witch hunts, asylums).
2. What do you view as the most restrictive form of treatment for mental illness during the course of history? On what criteria did you base your selection?
3. Research the concept "dual stigmatization"; what does this refer to? What implications does this have with regard to the population of PwMI who are incarcerated? Can you think of any other traits or characteristics that might create additional levels of stigmatization for these individuals?

KEY TERMS & ACRONYMS

- Asylum
- Cultural relativism
- Deinstitutionalization
- Determinism
- Electroconvulsive "shock" therapy (ECT)
- Eugenics

- Leucotomy or bilateral prefrontal lobotomy
- Mental health
- Mesmerism
- Moral treatment
- NIMBY (not in my backyard) mentality
- Phrenology

- Physiognomy
- Psychogenic
- Social Darwinism
- Somatagenic
- Therapeutic jurisprudence
- Transinstitutionalization
- Trephination

Bibliography

Abrego, L. J. (2011). Legal Consciousness of Undocumented Latinos: Fear and Stigma as Barriers to Claims-Making for First-and 1.5-Generation Immigrants. *Law & Society review, 45*(2), 337–370.

Adejumo, A., & Adejumo, P. (2005). Time to Act against Medical Collusion in Punitive Amputations. *British Medical Journal, 330,* 1275–1277.

Berkowitz, E. D. (1980). The Politics of Mental Retardation during the Kennedy Administration. *Social Science Quarterly, 61*(1), 128–143.

Biascotti, M. C., & Torrey, E. F. (December, 2011). *The Impact of Mental Illness on Law Enforcement Resources.* Arlington, VA: Treatment Advocacy Center.

Brandt, A. L. S. (2012). Treatment of Persons with Mental Illness in the Criminal Justice System: A Literature Review. *Journal of Offender Rehabilitation, 51*(8), 541–558.

Byrne, P. (2000). Stigma of Mental Illness and Ways of Diminishing It. *Advances in Psychiatric Treatment, 6*(1), 65–72.

Carlson, H. B. (1958). Characteristics of an acute confusional state in college students. *American Journal of Psychiatry, 114*(10), 900–909.

Collins, F. S. (1999). Medical and societal consequences of the Human Genome Project. *New England Journal of Medicine, 341*(1), 28–37.

Corrigan, P. W., & Watson, A. C. (2002). Understanding the Impact of Stigma on People with Mental Illness. *World Psychiatry, 1*(1), 16–20.

Daniel, A. E. (2007). Care of the Mentally Ill in Prisons: Challenges and Solutions. *Journal of the American Academy of Psychiatry and the Law, 35*, 406–410.

Deane, M. W., Steadman, H. J., Borum, R., Veysey, B. M., & Morrissey, J. P. (1999). Emerging Partnerships between Mental Health and Law Enforcement. *Psychiatric Services, 50*(1), 99–101.

Diamond, B. L. (1961). Criminal Responsibility of the Mentally Ill. *Stanford Law Review, 14*, 59–86.

Dickens, C. (1842). Except from American Notes. Retrieved from http://law.jrank.org/pages/12336/Dickens-Charles-Excerpt-from-American-Notes.html.

Dickens, C. (1866). Pictures from Italy and American Notes (Vol. 17). Chapman & Hall.

Dix, D. L. (1843). The History of Mental Retardation, Collected Papers. *Memorial to the Legislature of Massachusetts.* Retrieved July 28, 2015 from Disability History Museum. http://www.disabilitymuseum.org/dhm/lib/detail.html?id=737&page=all.

Dudley, R. G. (2015). *Childhood Trauma and Its Effects: Implications for Police: New Perspectives in Policing Bulletin.* Washington, DC: U.S. Department of Justice, National Institute of Justice.

Faria, M. A. (2013). Violence, Mental Illness, and the Brain—A Brief History of Psychosurgery: Part 1—From Trephination to Lobotomy. *Surgical Neurology International, 4*, 49. doi:10.4103/2152–7806.110146.

Farreras, I. G. (2017). History of mental illness. In R. Biswas-Diener & E. Diener (Eds), *Noba textbook series: Psychology.* Champaign, IL: DEF publishers. DOI: nobaproject.com.

Floyd, B. (June 26, 2015). *From Quackery to Bacteriology: The Emergence of Modern Medicine in 19th Century America: An Exhibition.* [19th Century American Culture]. Mental Health. Toledo, OH: University of Toledo Library Archives. Retrieved from http://www.utoledo.edu/library/canaday/exhibits/quackery/quack5.html.

Foerschner, A. M. (2010). The History of Mental Illness: From 'Skull Drills' to 'Happy Pills'. *Student Pulse, 2*(09). Retrieved from http://www.studentpulse.com/a?id=283.

Freeman, W. (1949). Transorbital Lobotomy. *American Journal of Psychiatry, 105*(10), 734–740.

Fuller, D. A., Lamb, H. R., Biasotti, M., & Snook, J. (December, 2015). *Overlooked in the Undercounted: The Role of Mental Illness in Fatal Law Enforcement Encounters.* Treatment Advocacy Center. Retrieved from TACReports.org/overlooked-undercounted.

Gall, F. J. (1791). *Philosophisch-Medizinische Untersuchungen über Natur und Kunst im kranken und gesunden Zustande des Menschen.* Rudolph Gräffer.

Getz, M. (2009). The Ice Pick of Oblivion: Moniz, Freeman, and the Development of Psychosurgery. *TRAMES, 2*, 128–152.

Goldman, H. H., & Morrissey, J. P. (1985). The Alchemy of Mental Health Policy: Homelessness and the Fourth Cycle of Reform. *American Journal of Public Health, 75*(7), 727–731.

Gross, C. G. (1999). A Hole in the Head. *The Neuroscientist, 5*(4), 263–269.

Hartford, K., Carey, R., & Mendonca, J. (2006). Pre-Arrest Diversion of People with Mental Illness: Literature Review and International Survey. *Behavioral Sciences & the Law, 24*, 845–856.

Hinshaw, S. P., & Stier, A. (2008). Stigma as Related to Mental Disorders. *Annu. Rev. Clin. Psychol., 4*, 367–393.

Housing First: A Special Report [Special Report]. (2002). *National Public Radio News [NPR]*. Retrieved from http://www.npr.org/news/specials/housingfirst/resources/index.html.

IG Ferraras. (2016, August 18). History of mental illness [Web log post]. Retrieved from http://nobaproject.com/modules/history-of-mental-illness.

Lamb, R. H., & Weinberger, L. E. (2014). Decarceration of U.S. Jails and Prisons: Where Will Persons with Serious Mental Illness Go? *Journal of the American Academy of Psychiatry and the Law, 42*, 489–494.

Kondo, L. (2003). Advocacy of the establishment of mental health specialty courts in the provision of therapeutic justice for mentally ill offenders. *American Journal of Criminal Law, 28*, 255–336.

Lamb, R. H., Weinberger, L. E., Gross, B. H. (1999). Community Treatment of Severely Mentally Ill Offenders under the Jurisdiction of the Criminal Justice System: A Review. *Psychiatric Services, 50*(7), 907–913.

Lamberti, J. S., Weisman, R., & Faden, D. I. (2004). Forensic Assertive Community Treatment: Preventing Incarceration of Adults with Severe Mental Illness. *Psychiatric Services, 5*(11), 1285–1293.

Lange, S., Rehm, J., & Popova, S. (2011). The Effectiveness of Criminal Justice Diversion Initiatives in North America: A Systematic Literature Review. *International Journal of Forensic Mental Health, 10*, 200–214.

Mason, B. G., Menolascino, F. J., & Galvin, L. (1976). Mental Health-the Right to Treatment for Mentally Retarded Citizens: An Evolving Legal and Scientific Interface. *Creighton L. Rev., 10*, 124.

National Alliance on Mental Illness. (n.d.). *The Criminalization of People with Mental Illness*. Retrieved from the National Alliance on Mental Illness, http://www2.nami.org/Content/ContentGroups/Policy/WhereWeStand/The_Criminalization_of_People_with_Mental_Illness___WHERE_WE_STAND.htm.

National Alliance on Mental Illness. (n.d.). *Mental Health Medications*. Retrieved from the National Alliance on Mental Illness, https://www.nami.org/Learn-More/Treatment/Mental-Health-Medications.

National Institute of Mental Health. (December 7, 2002). Retrieved from http://www.nimh.nih.gov. Read more: http://www.faqs.org/espionage/Ne-Ns/NIMH-National-Institute-of-Mental-Health.html#ixzz3h4hALsby.

Neugebauer, R. (1979). Medieval and Early Modern Theories of Mental Illness. *Arch Gen Psychiatry, 36*(4). doi:10.1001/archpsyc.1979.01780040119013.

New, W. S. (n.d.). Transorbital lobotomy. In Encyclopedia. Retrieved from http://www.statemaster.com.

Parry, M. (2010). From a Patient's Perspective: Clifford Whittingham Beers' Work to Reform Mental Health Services. *American Journal of Public Health, 100*(12), 2356.

Pollis, A. (1996). Cultural Relativism Revisited: Through a State Prism. *Human Rights Quarterly, 18*(2), 316–344.

Raz, M. (2008). Between the Ego and the Icepick: Psychosurgery, Psychoanalysis, and Psychiatric Discourse. *Bulletin of the History of Medicine, 82*(2), 387–420. The Johns Hopkins University Press. Retrieved July 22, 2015, from Project MUSE database.

Satel, S. (2003). Out of the Asylum, into the Cell. *New York Times*, A-29.

Sellin, T. (1938). Culture Conflict and Crime. *American Journal of Sociology, 44*(1), 97–103.

Shatkin, J. P. (n.d.). *The History of Mental Health Treatment [PowerPoint slides]*. Retrieved from aacap.org.

Shorter, E. (1997). The Birth of Psychiatry. In E. Shorter (Ed.), *A History of Psychiatry: From the Era of the Asylum to the Age of Prozac* (pp. 1–8). New York, NY: John Wiley & Sons, Inc.

Slate, R. M., Buffington-Vollum, J. K., & Johnson, W. W. (2013). *The Criminalization of Mental Illness: Crisis and Opportunity for the Justice System* (2nd Ed.). Durham, NC: Carolina Academic Press.

Spanos, N. P. (1978). Witchcraft in Histories of Psychiatry: A Critical Analysis and an Alternative Conceptualization. *Psychological Bulletin, 85*(2), 417–439. doi:10.1037/0033–2909.85.2.417.

Stone, J. (2001). Dr. Gottlieb Burchardt: The Pioneer of Psychosurgery. *Journal of the History of the Neurosciences, 10*(1), 79–92.

Timeline: Treatments for Mental Illness. (2007). *American Experience—A Brilliant Madness: Timeline. 1992–2002*. PBS. 6 Nov. 2007.

Torrey, E. F., Entsminger, K., Geller, J., Stanley, J., & Jaffe, D. J. (2008). *The Shortage of Public Hospital Beds for Mentally Ill Persons: A Report of the Treatment Advocacy Center*. Arlington, VA: Treatment Advocacy Center.

Wallace, C., Mullen, P. E., & Burgess, P. (2004). Criminal Offending in Schizophrenia Over a 25-Year Period Marked by Deinstitutionalization and Increasing Prevalence of Comorbid Substance Use Disorders. *American Journal of Psychiatry, 161*(4), 716–727.

CHAPTER 3 The Sequential Intercept Model

"Unfortunately, we force people to break the law in order to get any kind of mental health treatment."

—Pete Earley, author

Introduction

The information contained in Chapter 2 is instructive: the deinstitutionalization movement has reshaped the treatment landscape and distinct challenges that persons with chronic mental illness confront in their lives. Historically, appropriate and supportive treatment has often been inaccessible for a variety of reasons, including gaps in health insurance, restricted housing and/or means of transportation, a general lack of insight as to one's illness (referred to as *anosognosia*), and fear or concern of stigma (Lamb, Weinberger, & Gross, 2004; Morrissey & Goldman, 1986; Munetz & Griffin, 2006; Slate, Buffington-Vollum, & Johnson, 2013). Moreover, due to symptoms directly or indirectly related to their illnesses, some individuals tend to engage in behaviors that may bring them to the attention of public safety officials (Lamb, Weinberger, & Gross, 2004; Morrissey & Goldman, 1986). Many PwMI who are left untreated for whatever reason(s) find themselves recycling through multiple systems of care in an ongoing spiral that garners them the title of "frequent flyers." For individuals with chronic mental illness, survival behaviors such as pan handling, public urination, and theft of basic necessities (food, clothing, etc.) may place them directly under correctional supervision (Slate, et al., 2013). For an overwhelming number of justice-involved PwMI, however, diversion to substance abuse and mental health programs would likely yield a reduction in costs and recidivism, improvement in overall health, the opportunity for a better quality of life for the individual, and improvement in the functioning of society (Lamb, Weinberger, & Gross, 2004).

MENTAL HEALTH IN THE NEWS: THE CASE OF JEROME MURDOUGH

Jerome Murdough, a 54-year-old former Marine, had been cold and looking for shelter one chilly Harlem night in 2014. Murdough was back in the United States for about three years—he had returned from serving at least one tour in Japan and now found himself periodically homeless and living in local shelters, finding warmth at hospitals, and generally roaming the city streets. Murdough had been diagnosed with schizophrenia and bipolar disorder and had been sporadically living with his 75-year-old mother and other family members, including a sister. He was not stable in terms of his medication management and was now actively psychotic and abusing alcohol, according to family members. During his bouts with homelessness and substance abuse, Murdough built a criminal record that contained several criminal convictions for nonviolent offenses such as trespassing, public consumption of alcohol, and minor drug charges. That night in Harlem, Murdough was picked up and charged with trespassing when police found him curled up in a stairwell so he could keep warm as he slept; he was arraigned and after not being able to post the bail, which was set at 2,500 dollars, he was sent to Rikers Island Jail where he was held for one week before discovered dead in his cell. At the time of his detainment, Murdough was taking psychotropic medications, and due to his mental state, was eventually placed in an isolated cell that had a malfunctioning heating system on the mental observation unit where he was supposed to be subjected to 15-minute suicide checks by correctional staff (see Figure 3.1 for an example of an isolation cell). It was not until four hours after being placed in the cell that Murdough was found slumped over and dead—his body temperature at the time he was discovered was 100 degrees. The medical examiner ruled the death accidental and the cause of death hyperthermia due to his exposure to intense heat coupled with heat sensitivity due to his medications (Branch, 2015; Mencimer, 2014).

Why Diversion?

Approximately 14 million bookings occur in U.S. jails annually. Of these admissions, it is estimated that approximately 1,100,000 include persons with serious mental illness ("SMI," see Chapter 1). About 72 percent of persons booked also meet the criteria for co-occurring substance abuse disorders (Center for Mental Health Services [CMHS] National GAINS Center, 2007). These numbers are concerning for two primary reasons: the proportion of PwMI who are being arrested and the strain on resources that have traditionally *not* revolved around treatment options or rehabilitative goals, but rather, punishment. In fact, best available estimates reveal that it costs 60 percent more to incarcerate individuals with SMI than to incarcerate an inmate without mental illness (Slate, Buffington-Vollum, & Johnson, 2013). Along with community reintegration concerns, budgeting issues have encouraged the justice and mental health systems to generate an improved model for minimizing the appearances of PwMI in the criminal justice system. The solutions revolve around diverting them to appropriate systems of care.

Anosognosia, meaning "unawareness of illness," is a common symptom observed in people with serious mental illness. People who suffer with anosognosia lack insight as to their condition, and therefore, even in the face of evidence to the contrary, do not believe they are ill. What kinds of problems do you think this symptom might present in the context of one's ability to function in the community, a hospital, or a jail setting?

Source: Andrews (2003)

Before going any further, it is essential to briefly discuss what *diversion* actually means in the context of this book. There is a distinction in the concept, depending on whether it is being used in a traditional criminal justice context or a mental health context (Steadman, Morris, & Dennis, 1995). For many criminal justice officials, diversion refers to a point in a case when an offender eschews criminal liability in exchange for participation in some kind of community-based program. In short, upon a formal agreement, charges are not filed or are subsequently dropped. Alternatively, in the mental health arena, diversion is more likely to refer to alternative forms of supervision (voluntary or involuntary) that abandon criminal sanctions for those that are treatment oriented and prevent further penetration into the criminal justice system (*What is jail diversion*, n.d.). In line with the goals of this text, diversion refers to alternatives to criminal sanctions that are made available for PwMI who come into contact with the law in some context (Hartford, Carey, & Mendonca, 2006). Alternatives may be voluntary or court ordered and may or may not involve continuous supervision by justice personnel (juvenile or adult, community based or institutional). Closely corroborating with the primary structural diversion points in the traditional criminal justice flowchart (see Figure 3.2), such alternatives are ideally available at each interception from pre-arrest/ booking to re-entry from a correctional facility.

The reality, however, is that human services, which includes mental health and substance abuse treatment, have become significantly underfunded and overutilized (Honberg, Diehl, Kimball, Gruttadaro, & Fitzpatric, 2011; Johnson, Oliff, & Williams, 2011). Thus, as a by-product of deinstitutionalization and philosophical shifts from treatment to punishment, a large majority of PwMI have entered the criminal justice system *by way of the underlying symptoms of illnesses which were not properly treated for a myriad of reasons*. In fact, a significant proportion of offenders are frequent "cross-over" clients in multiple systems of care (including criminal justice, mental health, public welfare, and substance abuse). To improve the systematic response to this population, there was a need for the development of a conceptualized model of diversion points by which to provide opportunities for treatment and prevent individuals from further penetration into the system of criminal justice. As a result of ongoing discussion

Figure 3.1

A View of One of the Antisuicide Cells in Maximum Security of the Old Montana Prison

Source: By Tanankyo (own work). [Public domain] via Wikimedia Commons

and collaboration, the Sequential Intercept Model (SIM) was generated (Munetz & Griffin, 2006).

Mental Illness and the Criminal Justice System: An Integrative Framework

The SIM is a conceptual mapping tool that was developed by Munetz and Griffin in 2006. One of its most basic functions is to provide a foundation by which key stakeholders in forensic mental health services could conceptualize the system of care in any given jurisdiction. Through the process of identifying gaps in services and available resources, the SIM provides a framework that communities can use to create and organize strategies for those with mental illnesses who have become involved with the law (Griffin, Heilbrun, Mulvey, DeMatteo, & Schubert, 2015). In its original form, the

What is the sequence of events in the criminal justice system?

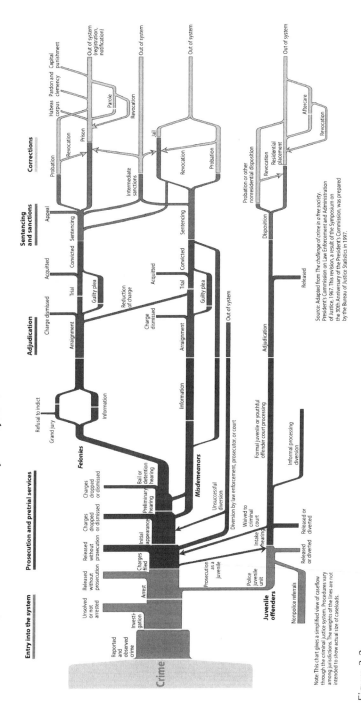

Figure 3.2

Criminal Justice System Flowchart

Source: Bureau of Justice Statistics (2016)

model has five different intercept points and three different graphic depictions—a vertical funnel, a linear flowchart, and a cyclical process (Griffin, et al., 2015). In November of 2016, Policy Research Associates (PRA) announced an expansion of the model to include a sixth intercept point—intercept "0", which represents early intervention efforts in the community in terms of treatment and other service engagement (Vincent-Roller, 2016). Given that the expanded model has only recently been released, and that diversion strategies pre-arrest/pre-booking have historically been subsumed under Intercept One, the original model, with five intercept points, forms the basis for this text.

Depending on the jurisdiction and its resources, each intercept point offers different programs and service linkages that can be utilized to prevent deeper penetration into the criminal justice system. Since the model's inception, dozens of communities around the United States have participated in "systems mapping" workshops or activities, whereby select individuals from various agencies gather together for approximately a day and a half to collaborate in the creation of a systems "map." The map provides a series of steps and respective agencies that justice-involved PwMI might encounter and identifies any particular diversion programs that are offered in that jurisdiction, or the lack thereof, at each intercept point. Examples of jurisdictions that have participated in the activity, available information, and links to access more detailed information are provided in Figure 3.3.

More about Systems Mapping: A Collaborative Framework

Systems mapping workshops are grant funded through the *Substance Abuse and Mental Health Services Administration* (SAMHSA) *GAINS center for Behavioral Health and Justice Transformation* (commonly referred to as the "GAINS" Center). The GAINS Center, which is operated by Policy Research Associates (PRA), is nationally recognized for the collection and dissemination of data that relate to PwMI who are justice-involved—particularly in terms of the overall access to services that address mental health and co-occurring substance abuse disorders. GAINS staff provide trainings and technical support to assist in systems integration and collaboration at all levels throughout individual jurisdictions (GAINS Center, 2016). The outcome of SIM mapping workshops is typically an effective navigation through multiple and diverse systems of care. Participants are guided to produce a "living" document that indicates the gaps in services at each specific inception—with the overarching goals of the workshop to include collaboration, information sharing, and support for funding requests.

It should be noted that there have been innovations with regard to the use of the SIM as a mapping tool in other settings. For example, it has been utilized to assist first responders and other systems personnel on how to more effectively handle a crisis

March 2015

SIM Workshop held in Springfield, Massachusetts. Workshop covered Hampden County & was held in Commissioner's Hearing Room at the Hampden County Hall of Justice.

-45 people participated including: Springfield Police Dept., Holyoke Police Dept., Westfield Police Dept., Hampden County Sheriff's Dept.

-Also in attendance: court staff, probation, local treatment providers, persons w/ lived experience, prosecutors, defense attorneys & bar advocates.

Source: SAMHSA's GAINS Center Facilitates SIM Workshop in Springfield, MA. (2015, March 1). Retrieved July 29, 2015, from http://gainscenter.samhsa.gov/eNews/march15.html#third

January 2015

Cochise County, Arizona

Duval County, Florida

Missoula County, Montana

Santa Fe County, New Mexico

Milwaukee County, Wisconsin

Source: SAMHSA'S GAINS Center Selects Five Communities for Sequential Intercept Mapping Workshops Focusing on Early Diversion. (2015). Retrieved July 29, 2015, from http://gainscenter.samhsa.gov/eNews/january15.html#third

December 2014

SIM Report: Los Angeles County, California

Source: Davis, H. (2014, December 1). Policy Research Associates, Inc. Completes Sequential Intercept Mapping Report for Los Angeles County, Inspires Criminal Justice Reform. Retrieved July 29, 2015, from http://www.prainc.com/la-sim-2014/

August 2014

Duchess County, New York

-40 representatives from law enforcement, corrections, mental health services and community organizations

Source: GAINS Staff Develops SIM Mapping for Duchess County. (2014, August 1). Retrieved July 29, 2015, from http://gainscenter.samhsa.gov/eNews/august14.html#fourth

July 2014

GAINS Staffers had created SIM Mapping for New York City's Mayor's Task Force on Behavioral Health & Criminal Justice System.

-created to "identify resources, gap & priorities in each of NYC's five boroughs"

Source: GAINS Staff Develops SIM Mapping for NYC Task Force. (2014, July 1). Retrieved July 29, 2015, from http://gainscenter.samhsa.gov/eNews/july14.html#third

October of 2013

Sandusky County, Ohio held SIM Workshop.

On page 19, list of participants. Link: http://www.neomed.edu/academics/criminal-justice-coordinating-center-of-excellence/pdfs/sequential-intercept-mapping/CJCCoEwebsiteSanduskyCountyFinalSIMReport.pdf

Source: Sequential Intercept Mapping Final Report. (2013, October 1). Retrieved July 29, 2015, from http://www.neomed.edu/academics/criminal-justice-coordinating-center-of-excellence/pdfs/sequential-intercept-mapping/CJCCoEwebsiteSanduskyCountyFinalSIMReport.pdf

Figure 3.3

Examples of Sequential Intercept Mapping around the United States

situation involving veterans and how to subsequently link them with support services in the community. The model has also been used in various communities to identify gaps in the provision of services and more effective responses to juvenile justice issues. SIM has also been successfully used to facilitate workshops on college campuses and in tribal communities (Rogers, 2015). More recently, the SIM has provided the structure needed to incorporate *trauma-informed care (TIC)*, and workshops have been facilitated among criminal justice personnel—a point that will be revisited later in this book (Rogers, 2015).

Key Diversion Points

To effectively divert adults with serious behavioral health problems from involvement in the justice system, it is necessary to identify the population early and accurately. Further, proper treatment plans must be developed and other measures designed to engage them in an array of services tailored to meet their needs. The process of identification should be accomplished using evidence-based screening and assessment tools, and dispositional outcomes should be based on careful (and thorough) evaluation by mental health professionals and the collaboration between parties of interest who are involved in any particular case (e.g., judges, attorneys, probation, and community-based service providers) (Steadman, Morris, & Dennis, 1995).

The SIM, as originally proposed in 2006, outlines five potential "intercept" points in which personnel in multiple systems and at multiple points of processing could potentially divert PwMI away from further justice involvement (Figure 3.4). In short, in its linear form, it is a familiar structure that can be compared with the traditional criminal justice linear "flowchart" presented earlier, which is often presented to students of criminal justice in introductory courses in college. Similar to the SIM, the flowchart illustrates the horizontal nature of the criminal justice process from beginning to end and the various vertical points at which offenders can be filtered out of the system. One difference, however, is that it reflects the criminal justice–specific definition of diversion (discussed earlier) in which charges can be dismissed for a number of reasons such as a lack of evidence or upon agreement to commit to a community-based sanction. By comparison, although the SIM illustrates a similar "filtering out" of the system, the difference is that diversion for offenders is either voluntary or involuntary and PwMI are rerouted into alternative systems of care that may be more appropriate and effective in terms of combating recidivism and improving their general well-being. The ultimate goal is not to eschew accountability for offenders who have mental illness or to disregard the criminal intent to commit the crimes for which they are charged; rather, it is to reduce the criminalization of mental illness and prevent further penetration into the criminal justice system for those persons with mental illness who have engaged in behaviors that are largely the result of the absence of proper treatment (Munetz & Griffin, 2006).

Note by the illustration that the SIM is anchored at both ends by "community"; this point is essential in understanding the uniqueness of the model as it applies to PwMI in that the journey through the justice process is wholly dependent on available, accessible, and effective community resources. Because the extent of available resources will be different depending on the locale in which services are rendered, it is preferable to present this information in more general terms, and this is accomplished in the succeeding chapter. Moreover, each intercept point contained in the structural model is presented and discussed in more detail, and supporting research highlighted, in subsequent chapters. A summary of the original model is provided next.

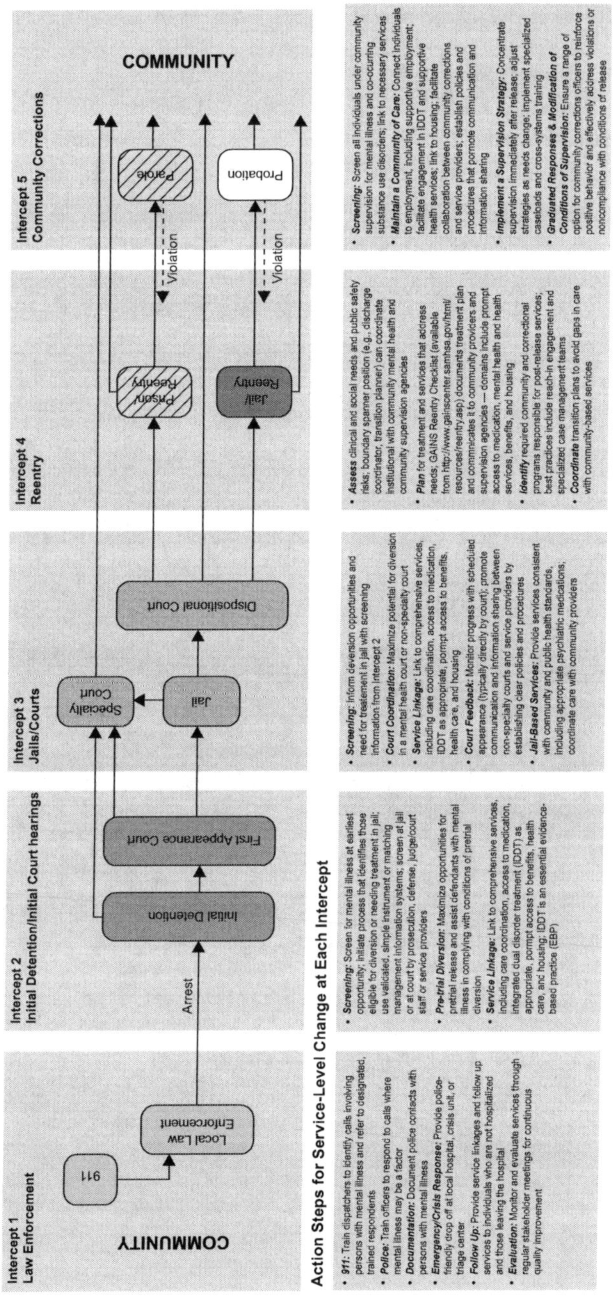

Intercept 1 — Law Enforcement

COMMUNITY

911 → Local Law Enforcement

Intercept 2 — Initial Detention/Initial Court hearings

Arrest

Initial Detention → First Appearance Court

Intercept 3 — Jails/Courts

Jail → Specialty Court → Dispositional Court

Intercept 4 — Reentry

Prison Reentry / Jail Reentry

Intercept 5 — Community Corrections

Parole
Probation

Violation

COMMUNITY

Action Steps for Service-Level Change at Each Intercept

Intercept 1
- **911:** Train dispatchers to identify calls involving persons with mental illness and refer to designated, trained respondents
- **Police:** Train officers to respond to calls where mental illness may be a factor
- **Documentation:** Document police contacts with persons with mental illness
- **Emergency/Crisis Response:** Provide police-friendly drop off at local hospital, crisis unit, or triage center
- **Follow Up:** Provide service linkages and follow up services to individuals who are not hospitalized and those leaving the hospital
- **Evaluation:** Monitor and evaluate services through regular stakeholder meetings for continuous quality improvement

Intercept 2
- **Screening:** Screen for mental illness at earliest opportunity; initiate process that identifies those eligible for diversion or needing treatment in jail; use validated, simple instrument or matching management information systems; screen at jail or at court by prosecution, defense, judge/court staff or service providers
- **Pretrial Diversion:** Maximize opportunities for pretrial release and assist defendants with mental illness in complying with conditions of pretrial diversion
- **Service Linkage:** Link to comprehensive services, including care coordination, access to medication, integrated dual disorder treatment (IDDT) as appropriate, prompt access to benefits, health care, and housing; IDDT is an essential evidence-based practice (EBP)

Intercept 3
- **Screening:** Inform diversion opportunities and need for treatment in jail with screening information from Intercept 2
- **Court Coordination:** Maximize potential for diversion in a mental health court or non-specialty court
- **Service Linkage:** Link to comprehensive services, including care coordination, access to medication, IDDT as appropriate, prompt access to benefits, health care, and housing
- **Court Feedback:** Monitor progress with scheduled appearance (typically directly by court); promote communication and information sharing between non-specialty courts and service providers by establishing clear policies and procedures
- **Jail-Based Services:** Provide services consistent with community and public health standards, including appropriate psychiatric medications; coordinate care with community providers

Intercept 4
- **Assess** clinical and social needs and public safety risks; boundary spanner position (e.g., discharge coordinator, transition planner) can coordinate institutional with community mental health and community supervision agencies
- **Plan** for treatment and services that address needs; GAINS Reentry Checklist (available from http://www.gainscenter.samhsa.gov/html/resources/reentry.asp) documents treatment plan and communicates it to community providers and supervision agencies — domains include prompt access to medication, mental health and health services, benefits, and housing
- **Identify** required community and correctional programs responsible for post-release services; best practices include reach-in engagement and specialized case management teams
- **Coordinate** transition plans to avoid gaps in care with community-based services

Intercept 5
- **Screening:** Screen all individuals under community supervision for mental illness and co-occurring substance use disorders; link to necessary services
- **Maintain a Community of Care:** Connect individuals to employment, including supportive employment; facilitate engagement in IDDT and supportive health services; link to housing; facilitate collaboration between community corrections and service providers; establish policies and procedures that promote communication and information sharing
- **Implement a Supervision Strategy:** Concentrate supervision immediately after release; adjust strategies as needs change; implement specialized caseloads and cross-systems training
- **Graduated Responses & Modification of Conditions of Supervision:** Ensure a range of option for community corrections officers to reinforce positive behavior and effectively address violations or noncompliance with conditions of release

Figure 3.4

The Sequential Intercept Model—Linear Version

Source: SAMHSA's GAINS Center for Behavioral Health and Justice Transformation. (2013). Developing a comprehensive plan for behavioral health and criminal justice collaboration: The Sequential Intercept Model (3rd Ed.) Delmar, NY: Author

Intercept One: Law Enforcement/Emergency Services (Pre-Booking)

As previously discussed, in some communities, there are significant gaps in community-based services available and accessible for PwMI, including access to transportation, adequate housing, medication, therapy, case management, meaningful daily activities, and crisis services (Slate, et al., 2013). Early intervention in the form of community supports and consumer engagement in services needed would produce the desired response; that is, the prevention of a behavioral health crisis (as discussed earlier, more recently introduced as "Intercept 0"). *Decompensation* refers to stress or strain that results in behavioral or psychological imbalance; the source of the stress is based largely on restrictions to access any of the aforementioned services and may directly (or indirectly) place PwMI at risk for contact with law enforcement officials (Lamb & Weinberger, 2014). Consequently, the first diversion opportunity in the original SIM occurs when the police or other emergency first responders encounter some sort of crisis situation in the community (see Figure 3.5 for an example of a potential crisis situation).

Historically, law enforcement agencies have not provided specialized training for officers on how to deal with and process mental health crises beyond a minimal number

Figure 3.5

Mental Illness

Source: By Alex Proimos from Sydney, Australia (Mental illness). [CC BY 2.0 (http://creative commons.org/licenses/by/2.0)] via Wikimedia Commons

of hours received at their academy training (Deane, Steadman, Borum, Veysey, & Morrissey, 1999; Lamb, Weinberger, & DeCuir, 2002; Lew, Pham, Morrison, 2014). With an increasing proportion of encounters between police and PwMI, specialized policing responses (SPRs) have been designed and implemented by law enforcement agencies in the United States and abroad to provide pre-booking diversion options that may more effectively address any underlying issues and/or needs related to this particular population. Examples of these programs can be broadly placed under three categories: (a) crisis intervention teams (CITs), (b) co-responder teams, and (c) follow-up teams[1] (Reuland & Yasuhara, 2015). Each of these is briefly explained next, with more detail provided in Chapter 5.

In response to several high-profile crisis situations in which PwMI, police officers, or both were injured, or even killed in the encounter, communities have rallied in support of the development of CITs. First implemented in Memphis, Tennessee, these programs give officers specialized mental health training and send them out to respond to any call that may involve a behavioral health crisis. Research on the CIT model has generally shown improved safety for the officer and community (primarily measured through decreased use-of-force encounters), a decrease in the number of arrests and an increase in the number of referrals by law enforcement to mental healthcare for those in need, and decriminalization of those with mental illness, measured by assessing pre- and post-perceptions of officer-trainees with regard to their views of mental illness and PwMI (Browning, Hasselt, Tucker, & Vecchi, 2011). The success of this approach relies heavily on collaborative and positive partnerships between law enforcement and mental health practitioners (Reuland, Schwarzfeld, & Draper, 2009)—a point discussed in more detail in Chapters 5 and 10.

Depending on the jurisdiction and its available resources, the co-responder model might be the most effective SPR to employ in a crisis situation. Under this model, police officers team up with clinical mental health professionals to respond to the scene of a crisis situation involving a PwMI. The police role is typically to secure the environment and the person(s) involved, whereas the mental health professionals provide consultation as to mental health–related issues and assist with determining the types of services that are needed in any given situation. The most popular example of this type of SPR is referred to as a Mobile Crisis Team or Unit. Again, depending on the resources, the team may provide follow-up services to the clients in an attempt to gauge continuity of care and the provision of services (Reuland, et al., 2009; Reuland & Yasuhara, 2015).

Last, follow-up teams are also employed in some jurisdictions to respond to PwMI who have multiple encounters with law enforcement—particularly to establish breaks in services and to generate individualized plans to reconnect. Teams consist of police officers who are specially trained; these officers work closely alongside mental health practitioners to develop and enrich community partnerships (Reuland & Yasuhara, 2015). SPRs are presented in more detail in Chapter 5, whereas specific models are spotlighted and related empirical work is discussed.

Stop and Think: *What might be some of the general issues that PwMI must contend with that lead to justice involvement at Intercept One?*

Access to. . .
. . . Treatment and medication
. . . Housing
. . . ??

Intercept Two: Initial Hearings and Detention (Post-Arrest)

For some offenders with mental illness, the circumstances under which they encounter law enforcement do not allow for diversion, but rather, lead to arrest and booking at a local jail or detention center (juveniles). Although the booking process itself can produce a substantially traumatic response, the initial detainment period—typically, the first two weeks of confinement—is capable of severe impairment, including victimization, exacerbated symptoms and decompensation, induced psychosis, and self-harm—from self-mutilation to suicidal ideation and completion (Heilbrun, DeMatteo, Brooks-Holliday, & Griffin, 2015; Slate, et al., 2013). Fortunately, the first appearance in court provides another opportunity to divert low-level offenders. Post-arrest diversion procedures are available prior to the preliminary hearing and before the defendant-client enters a plea (Heilbrun, et al., 2015). Courts may establish pre-trial services divisions, directly hire mental health professionals, or develop relationships with outside organizations to assess offenders and advise judges with regard to the disposition of the case. In this case, mental health workers advise the court about the possible presence of mental illness, issues of competency (discussed in later chapters), and options for assessment and treatment (DeMatteo, LaDuke, Locklair, & Heilbrun, 2013; Heilbrun, et al., 2015; Griffin, Munetz, Bonfine, & Kemp, 2015). Individuals are also screened for services should they participate in mental health or other treatment courts (see Intercept Three later). Intercept Two post-arrest/booking diversion programs and related empirical findings are further presented and discussed in Chapter 6.

Intercept Three: Jails and Courts (Post-Conviction)

To address the needs of PwMI who have committed more serious misdemeanors or felonies and have not been diverted at Intercept Two, a number of jurisdictions have developed mental health or other specialized courts (e.g., veterans' courts) that focus on problem solving and treatment rather than punishment (Griffin, Steadman, & Petrila, 2002). Specialized courts are based on the therapeutic jurisprudence model of treatment, collaboration, and wrap-around services, which stands in stark contrast to the adversarial nature of the traditional court system in the United States. Practices in mental health court, such as conditional release and forensic case management, also allow opportunities for PwMI to remain in the community setting as long as they are meeting the conditions of an individualized program (Liu & Redlich, 2015; Slate, et al., 2013). Specialty court clients are still subject to sanctions, however, should they fail to engage in any aspects of the program as prescribed by the collaborative "treatment team"; sanctions may include periods of detention and hospitalization. Through the use of treatment courts, the state is able to save money, provide community-based therapy, and allow defendants who were once incarcerated to remain in their home environments with minimal supervision. Once "clients" (as they are often referred to by the treatment team) have made it through the program successfully, there is typically a graduation ceremony in the courtroom, and, depending on a number of factors, charges may be subsequently dismissed (Liu & Redlich, 2015). Juvenile mental health courts (JMHCs) are also being implemented in states such as California, Georgia, and Texas (SAMHSA, 2015). Intercept Three and related research are expanded upon in Chapter 7.

Intercept Four: Reentry

Primarily due to the serious nature of the offense, sometimes a PwMI penetrates further into the traditional justice system and is convicted and sentenced to a period of incarceration in a jail or prison; in some cases, a defendant may even be committed to a forensic or state hospital directly from detainment. Regardless of the type of supervision or confinement, the point when offenders are preparing to return to their communities represents another opportunity to connect them with services. Depending on available resources and the receptiveness of administration, a number of programs are designed to provide inmates with skills to succeed upon their release and beyond (Griffin, et al., 2015). Programs may be accessible within the institution or post-release in a community mental health setting, and typically revolve around issues such as substance abuse and the development of coping skills or cognitive-based interventions, life skills such as shopping or cooking, and gaining access to human capital, such as job skills and education (e.g., high school diploma and courses for college credit) (Osher & King, 2015). Some of the programs are faith based or have distinct religious components.

As a result of time served and participation in counseling or programming, many justice-involved PwMI have made significant improvements in coping, medication management, and behaviors, and have become genuinely prepared to reenter society again. Others have not had the mental capacity during most of their detainment and may require intensive case management or participation in an assertive or forensic assertive community treatment team (ACT or FACT, discussed later in the text) upon release (DeMatteo, et al., 2012).

To facilitate a more effective transition to the community setting, some departments of corrections have created reentry specialist positions and encouraged the use of *boundary spanners*—a concept that refers to a liaison who works on behalf of forensic clients to coordinate mental health, judicial, and law enforcement involvement and expectations (Steadman, Morris, & Dennis, 1995). Such developments have translated into improved outcomes in terms of successful reintegration, particularly when accompanied by procedures designed to encourage (or require) reentry planning for transitional care immediately after an inmate is booked into the facility. To this point, a model known as the *APIC Model for Transition Planning* is instructive; APIC stands for assess, plan, identify, and coordinate (Osher & King, 2015). The model and its four goals are expanded upon and evaluated in Chapter 8.

SUCCESSFUL DIVERSION PRACTICES AT INTERCEPT FOUR: INMATE AFTERCARE IN FLORIDA

Florida provides a good example of a state that attempts to regulate reentry practices. In particular, in a *memorandum of understanding* (MOU) between the state Departments of Children and Families and Corrections (DCF & DOC, respectively), an agreement was made that requires a re-entry coordinator (DOC) to maintain contact with a point person (DCF) related to the provision of aftercare services for inmates with serious mental health and substance abuse needs in the county in which the inmate will be released (CF Operating Procedure No. 155-47, 2009). This partnership centers on the scheduling of initial appointments with local providers for a date within the two-week period after the inmate is released from the facility.

Intercept Five: Community Corrections and Community Support Services

Due to the nature of the prison or jail environment and the limited access to treatment services during their stay, a significant proportion of inmates with SMI are at a high risk for encountering multiple systems of care, and ultimately, coming to the attention of criminal justice personnel again at some point after their release (Lovell, Gagliardi, & Peterson, 2002). Consequently, specialized parole and probation programs have been implemented in a number of jurisdictions in an attempt to ensure that former inmates get the treatment they need and stay out of jail. Unfortunately, offenders with mental illness—particularly those with SMI—may not have the ability to comprehend the expectations as to their behavior and may unintentionally violate probation and parole due to such competency-related misunderstandings. For this reason, specialized training programs have also been offered to community corrections personnel to address the signs and symptoms of mental illness (e.g., CIT, discussed in Chapter 5). Furthermore, the engagement of boundary spanners has also improved the communications between clients and their community supervision staff.

THINKING CRITICALLY: SUICIDE IN JAILS AND PRISONS

Earlier, you read the story of Mr. Jerome Murdough, a seriously mentally ill Marine who died in his Rikers Island Jail cell due to a malfunctioning heating system and a lack of observation on the part of the correctional staff. Rikers has unfortunately seen its fair share of tragedy with regard to PwMI under its watch. During the same year as the Murdough death, another inmate died after sexually mutilating himself; he had been left alone in his cell for seven days. Further, months after these cases, Rikers was the site for another a high-profile case involving the suicide of a man by the name of Fabian Cruz. Cruz, who was 35, had been ordered to be moved to a specialized unit for observation, but when he refused to go, staff simply ignored protocol and returned him to his regular cell; shortly thereafter, he hanged himself (Associated Press, 2015).

Suicide is the third leading cause of death in U.S. prisons and the second highest in jails (Daniel, 2007). The suicide rate has ranged from 18 to 40 per 100,000 during the past three decades in prisons. Pre-trial detainees have a suicide attempt rate of about 7.5, and sentenced prisoners have a rate of almost six times the rate of males at home; also pretrial inmates who commit suicide in custody are generally men who are between the ages of 20 and 25 who are unmarried and first-time offenders who have been arrested for minor, usually substance-related, offenses (Daigle, Daniel, Dear, Frottier, Hayes, Kerkhof, Konrad, Liebling, Sarchiapone, 2007 p.114).

Have you ever experienced the loss of someone who has committed suicide? Or maybe you have encountered friends or loved ones who have expressed suicidal ideation? Maybe you have felt your own feelings of despair. How might some of these feelings of helplessness and hopelessness be exacerbated behind jail or prison walls?

Last, and possibly the most important factor at this place in the SIM, is collaboration and shared knowledge of community resources (Slate, et al., 2013). As previously stated, in addition to the intersection of mental health and criminal justice systems, a number of other systems share the same clients, including, but not limited to, public welfare, veterans' affairs/services, substance abuse, and foster care or dependency. The development of strong partnerships between various stakeholders whose services are interconnected in a number of ways allows forensic-based case managers, re-entry coordinators, or other boundary spanners to make appropriate referrals to community providers (for example, mental health, drug and alcohol, juvenile justice, etc.). Collaboration among all parties can ensure proper services are being implemented, save resources and funding, and provide for the implementation of on-going evaluations (Kaffenberger & O'Rorke-Trigiani, 2013). These are the subject matter discussed in Chapter 9 of this text.

Research on the SIM

At this point in time, the SIM has been most effectively used as a structural guide to understanding the path through forensic mental health and the potential for diversion at each stage in the justice process from encounters with police to community corrections. In this context, it has also been used as an organization tool for multisystemic mapping activities throughout the nation. Unfortunately, mapping activities have not netted any empirical data or support thus far. For this reason, the SIM has also been introduced as a descriptive (theoretical) model to identify primary research questions at each stage so that researchers could pursue empirical analyses (Heilbrun, Mulvey, DeMatteo, Schubert, Filone, & Griffin, 2015). Although research associated with Intercepts One and Three has been examined in some detail (e.g., CIT and specialty court outcomes), other intercepts have had minimal attention in this regard. Of the existing literature, a number of strengths and limitations are considered and addressed in each successive chapter of this text.

PRACTITIONER'S CORNER 3.1

How SIM Differs from Traditional Treatment Models

Contributors: Cori Seilhamer, MS, NCC, and Justin M. Lensbower, MS, LPC

Police are alerted from a man that his sister, Ellen, was sitting on the porch at a local restaurant with a suitcase for more than an hour and refusing to come home. The restaurant offered her water while the police contacted the mental health delegate who dispatched to talk with her. Ellen had walked away from home because she believed her family was poisoning her and she had no intention of returning. The delegate was able to secure an emergency appointment with Ellen's outpatient counselor, who was able to assess her mental status and get her emergency mental health treatment instead of loitering charges from the criminal justice system.

When a community implements the SIM, it creates opportunities for historically separate disciplines to collaborate in an effort to afford treatment to those in need rather than incarceration as the solution. This relationship is helpful for individuals who need services and for law enforcement, as it provides additional supports and resources as solutions. This is most effective when each participant strives to understand the other and communicates often with each other in an effort to reduce resistance toward potentially competing interests.

With declining budgets and a struggling economy, sharing of resources and collaboration becomes even more important for public services. Law enforcement through 911 call centers are becoming increasingly utilized strategies for accessing the mental health system due to these obstacles. For this reason, it is important that dispatchers are included in the collaborative relationships through the SIM.

Author's Note: A "mental health delegate" is an individual who works for the area (county, state, or region) mental health services office; this person has been designated, most likely statutorily, as the key decision maker in terms of contract oversight and allocation of resources, but also, in making discretionary decisions pertaining to the emergency evaluation and treatment of persons in their jurisdiction who are in crisis.

Take-Home Message

Persons with mental illness should not be involved in the criminal justice system at a rate higher than offenders without mental illness (Munetz & Griffin, 2006). Even though critical intercept points have been identified and diversion strategies at each point have been found to be effective to some extent, the SIM as a model of transformation is useless when practitioners lack insight into the signs and symptoms of mental illness. Consequently, proper training becomes key. Additionally, other strategies have been recommended to local governments as a means to support ongoing transformational change; these include the provision of funding incentives, the removal of barriers to services (financial and other restrictions on access), the provision of educational resources related to mental health and substance abuse disorders, changes in legislation and practice so to assist local mental health systems to develop the capacity to acquire data to identify and implement best practices, and the promotion of cross-systems collaboration and information sharing (Vail & Santangelo, n.d.).

Despite a positive public response to diversionary efforts, it is quite possible that PwMI do not wish to undergo mental health and/or substance abuse treatment and, in fact, may willingly seek placement in the justice system. In that case, constitutional and other legal protections must be enforced throughout the process as long as there is no reason to believe public safety risks are present. As will be discussed in more detail later in the text, should a person with mental illness show a risk for injury to self or others, a legally prescribed and qualified entity may move toward an order for psychiatric evaluation, and possibly *commitment*, for a designated period. State laws are instructive as to commitment procedures, and certain criteria, must be met.

Now that the structure for the remainder of the book has been introduced, we will begin our journey through the forensic mental health system, keeping in mind that for many, the system is not linear but rather cyclical in nature. Similar to those who enter the criminal justice system who do not have mental illness, the revolving door phenomena can unfortunately serve to perpetuate a continued life of recidivism and trauma for all who are involved. The following chapter provides the reader with an introductory discussion on mental health and co-occurring substance use disorders (symptoms, diagnoses, and treatment) and outlines a systematic approach to the needs of persons with serious mental illness through the identification of an "ideal" system of care and the most common gaps in services.

QUESTIONS FOR CLASSROOM DISCUSSION

1. In small groups, create outlines in which the group will identify and discuss some of the problems presented at Intercepts One and Two. After about 10 minutes, open up a class discussion regarding proposed solutions and barriers to them.

2. In your opinion, what do you view as the most important intercept point in the SIM? On what criteria did you base your selection?
3. The SIM has been utilized in various communities and referred to as a "tool for transformation." It is suggested that the most successful transformations have occurred because of positive and continuous systems collaborations. In the jurisdiction in which you live/work, what agencies and key stakeholders do you think should be involved in SIM mapping workshops and/or systems integration meetings pertaining to justice-involved PwMI?

KEY TERMS & ACRONYMS

- Anosognosia
- Boundary spanners
- Containment
- Decompensation
- Diversion

- GAINS Center for Behavioral Health and Justice Transformation
- Mental health delegate
- Memorandum of understanding

- Substance Abuse and Mental Health Services Administration (SAMHSA)
- Trauma-informed care (TIC)

Note

1. Law enforcement agencies that have developed SPRs have made significant changes in policies and procedures, which have greatly affected traditional policing practices. In addition, a multitude of mental health–based specialized responses have been implemented successfully at the jurisdiction level solely by mental health agencies; however, for the purposes of this text, only programs involving police are referenced.

Bibliography

Andrews, T. (2003). *Mental Health Procedures and Criminal Law*. Notes presented at the meeting of the Pennsylvania Bar Institute, Montour County, PA.

Associated Press. (January 2, 2015). Rikers Island Inmate Dies After Suicide Watch Ignored. *New York Post*. Retrieved from http://nypost.com/2015/01/02/rikers-island-inmate-dies-after-suicide-watch-ignored/.

Branch, C. (January 6, 2015). Tragic Deaths Shed Light On Brutality at Rikers. *The Huffington Post*. Retrieved from http://www.huffingtonpost.com/2015/01/05/rikers-island-brutality_n_6419632.html.

Browning, S. L., Van Hasselt, V. B., Tucker, A. S., & Vecchi, G. M. (2011). Dealing with Individuals Who have Mental Illness: The Crisis Intervention Team (CIT) in Law Enforcement. *The British Journal of Forensic Practice*, 13(4), 235–243.

Burriss, F. A., Breland-Nobel, A. M., Webster, J. L., & Soto, J. A. (2011). Juvenile Mental Health Courts for Adjudicated Youth: Role Implications for Child and Adolescent Psychiatric Mental Health Nurses. *Journal of Child and Adolescent Psychiatric Nursing*, 24(2), 114–121.

CMHS National GAINS Center. (2007). *Practical Advice on Jail Diversion: Ten Years of Learnings on Jail Diversion from the CMHS National GAINS Center.* Delmar, NY: Author.

Daigle, M. S., Daniel, A. E., Dear, G. E., Frottier, P., Hayes, L. M., Kerkhof, A., ... & Sarchiapone, M. (2007). Preventing suicide in prisons, part II: international comparisons of suicide prevention services in correctional facilities. *Crisis, 28*(3), 122–130.

Daniel, A. E. (2007). Care of the mentally ill in prisons: Challenges and solutions. *Journal of the American Academy of Psychiatry and the Law Online, 35*(4), 406–410.

Davis, H. (December 1, 2014). Policy Research Associates, Inc. Completes Sequential Intercept Mapping Report for Los Angeles County, Inspires Criminal Justice Reform. Retrieved July 29, 2015 from http://www.prainc.com/la-sim-2014/.

Deane, M. W., Steadman, H. J., Borum, R., Veysey, B. M., & Morrissey, J. P. (1999). Emerging Partnerships between Mental Health and Law Enforcement. *Psychiatric Services, 50*(1), 99–101.

DeMatteo, D., LaDuke, C., Locklair, B. R., & Heilbrum, K. (2013). Community-Based Alternatives for Justice-Involved Individuals with Severe Mental Illness: Diversion, Problem-Solving Courts, and Reentry. *Journal of Criminal Justice, 41*, 64–71.

GAINS Center for Behavioral Health and Justice Transformation. (2016, January 7). Retrieved January 3, 2017, from http://gainscenter.samhsa.gov/eNews/august14.html#fourth.

GAINS Staff Develops SIM Mapping for Duchess County. (August 1, 2014). Retrieved July 29, 2015 from http://gainscenter.samhsa.gov/eNews/august14.html#fourth.

GAINS Staff Develops SIM Mapping for NYC Task Force. (July 1, 2014). Retrieved July 29, 2015 from http://gainscenter.samhsa.gov/eNews/july14.html#third.

Griffin, P. A., Heilbrun, K., Mulvey, E. P., DeMatteo, D., & Schubert, C. A. (2015). *Sequential Intercept Model and Criminal Justice: Promoting Community Alternatives for Individuals with Serious Mental Illness.* New York, NY: Oxford University Press.

Griffin, P. A., Munetz, M., Bonfine, N., & Kemp, K. (2015). Development of the Sequential Intercept Model. In Griffin, P. A., Heilbrun, K., Mulvey, E. P., DeMatteo, D., & Schubert, C. A. (Eds.). *The Sequential Intercept Model and Criminal Justice* (pp. 21–39). New York, NY: Oxford University Press.

Griffin, P. A., Steadman, H. J., Petrila, J. (2002). The Use of Criminal Charges and Sanctions in Mental Health Courts. *Psychiatric Services, 53*(10), 1285–1289.

Hartford, K., Carey, R., & Mendonca, J. (2006). Pre-Arrest Diversion of People with Mental Illness: Literature Review and International Survey. *Behavioral Sciences & the Law, 24*, 845–856. doi: 10.1002/bsl.738.

Heilbrun, K., DeMatteo, D., Brooks-Holliday, S., & Griffin, P. A. (2015). Initial Detention and Initial Hearings. In Griffin, P. A., Heilbrun, K., Mulvey, E. P., DeMatteo, D., & Schubert, C. A. (Eds.). *The Sequential Intercept Model and Criminal Justice* (pp. 57–77). New York, NY: Oxford University Press.

Heilbrun, K., Mulvey, E. P., DeMatteo, D., Schubert, C. A., Filone, S., & Griffin, P. A. (2015). The Sequential Intercept Model: Current Status, Future Directions. In Griffin, P. A., Heilbrun, K., Mulvey, E. P., DeMatteo, D., & Schubert, C. A. (Eds.), *The Sequential Intercept Model and Criminal Justice* (pp. 276–284). New York, NY: Oxford University Press.

Heretick, D. M. L., & Russell, J. A. (2013). The Impact of Juvenile Mental Health Court on Recidivism among Youth. *Journal of Juvenile Justice, 3*(1), 1–14.

Honberg, R., Diehl, S., Kimball, A., Gruttadaro, D., & Fitzpatric, M. (March, 2011). *State Mental Health Cuts: A National Crisis.* NAMI. Retrieved from https://www.nami.org/getattachment/About-NAMI/Publications/Reports/NAMIStateBudgetCrisis2011.pdf.

Johnson, N., Oliff, P., & Williams, E. (February, 2011). *An Update on Stat Budget Cuts: At Least 46 States Have Imposed Cuts That Hurt Vulnerable Residents and Cause Job Loss.* Washington, DC: Center on Budget and Policy Priorities.

Kaffenberger, C., & O'Rorke-Trigiani, J. (2013). Addressing Student Mental Health Needs by Providing Direct and Indirect Services and Building Alliances in the Community. *Professional School Counseling, 16*(5), 323–332.

Lamb, H. R., & Weinberger, L. E. (2014). Decarceration of U.S. Jails and Prisons: Where Will Persons with Serious Mental Illness Go? *Journal of the American Academy of Psychiatry and the Law, 42,* 489–494.

Lamb, H. R., Weinberger, L. E., & DeCuir Jr., W. J. (2002). The Police and Mental Health. *Psychiatric Services, 53*(10), 1266–1271.

Lamb, H. R., Weinberger, L. E., & Gross, B. H. (2004). Mentally Ill Persons in the Criminal Justice System: Some Perspectives. *Psychiatric Quarterly, 75*(2), 107–126.

Lew, P., Pham, J., & Morrison, L. (August, 2014). *An Ounce of Prevention: Law Enforcement Training and Mental Health Crisis Intervention* (Publication #CM51.01). Sacramento, CA: Disability Rights California.

Liu, S., & Redlich, A. D. (2015). Intercept 3: Jails and Courts. In Griffin, P. A., Heilbrun, K., Mulvey, E. P., DeMatteo, D., & Schubert, C. A. (Eds.), *The Sequential Intercept Model and Criminal Justice* (pp. 78–94). New York, NY: Oxford University Press.

Lovell, D., Gagliardi, G. J., & Peterson, P. D. (2002). Recidivism and Use of Services among Persons with Mental Illness after Release from Prison. *Psychiatric Services, 53*(10), 1290–1296.

Mencimer, S. (April 8, 2014). There Are 10 Times More Mentally Ill People Behind Bars than in State Hospitals. *Mother Jones.* Retrieved from: http://www.motherjones.com/mojo/2014/04/record-numbers-mentally-ill-prisons-and-jails.

Munetz, M. R., & Griffin, P. A. (2006). Use of the Sequential Intercept Model as an Approach to Decriminalization of People with Serious Mental Illness. *Psychiatric Services, 57*(4), 544–549.

Osher, F., & King, C. (2015). Intercept 4: Reentry from Jails and Prisons. In Griffin, P. A., Heilbrun, K., Mulvey, E. P., DeMatteo, D., & Schubert, C. A. (Eds.), *The Sequential Intercept Model and Criminal Justice* (pp. 95–117). New York, NY: Oxford University Press.

Policy Research Associates (2010). Final Report: Multnomah County, Oregon, Sequential Intercept Mapping & Taking Action for Change. Retrieved from https://multco.us/file/35510/download.

Reuland, M., Schwarzfeld, M., & Draper, L. (2009). *Law Enforcement Reponses to People with Mental Illnesses: A Guide to Research Informed Policy and Practice.* New York, NY: Council of State Governments Justice Center.

Reuland, M., & Yasuhara, K. (2015). Law Enforcement and Emergency Services. In Griffin, P. A., Heilbrun, K., Mulvey, E. P., DeMatteo, D., & Schubert, C. A. (Eds.), *The Sequential Intercept Model and Criminal Justice* (pp. 40–56). New York, NY: Oxford University Press.

Rogers, D. (2015). Sequential Intercept Model. *Policy Research Associates.* Retreived from http://www.prainc.com/incorporating-trauma-informed-care-into-the-sequential-intercept-model/.

SAMHSA's GAINS Center Awards Training Opportunities to 16 Communities Nationwide. (November, 2012). Retrieved July 29, 2015 from http://gainscenter.samhsa.gov/enews/may-2012c.html.

SAMHSA's GAINS Center Facilitates SIM Workshop in Springfield, MA. (2015, March 1). Retrieved July 29, 2015 from http://gainscenter.samhsa.gov/eNews/march15.html#third.

SAMHSA's GAINS Center Selects Five Communities for Sequential Intercept Mapping Workshops Focusing on Early Diversion. (2015). Retrieved July 29, 2015 from http://gainscenter.samhsa.gov/eNews/january15.html#third.

Sequential Intercept Mapping Final Report. (October 1, 2013). Retrieved July 29, 2015 from http://www.neomed.edu/academics/criminal-justice-coordinating-center-of-excellence/pdfs/sequential intercept-mapping/CJCCoEwebsiteSanduskyCountyFinalSIMReport.pdf.

Slate, R. M., Buffington-Vollum, J. K., & Johnson, W. W. (2013). *The Criminalization of Mental Illness: Crisis and Opportunity for the Justice System* (2nd Ed.). Durham, NC: Carolina Academic Press.

State of Florida Department of Children and Families. (2009). *Mental Health/Substance Abuse* (CF Operating Procedures No. 155–47). Tallahassee, FL.

Steadman, H. J., Morris, S. M., & Dennis, D. L. (1995). The Diversion of Mentally Ill Persons from Jails to Community-Based Services: A Profile of Programs. *American Journal of Public Health, 85*(12), 1630–1635.

Substance Abuse and Mental Health Services Administration. (n.d). *What Is Jail Diversion?* Rockville, MD: SAMHSA Gains Center for Behavioral Health and Justice transformation. Retrieved from http://gainscenter.samhsa.gov/topical_resources/jail.asp.

Vail, L., & Santangelo, J. (n.d.). The Sequential Intercept Model [PowerPoint slides]. Retrieved from http://static1.1.sqspcdn.com/static/f/1176392/19498158/1342644696663/Sequential+Inter cept+Model+Vail.ppt?token=IzZYsMNBcts8wMpEBdbC3Lw4V6c%3D.

Vincent-Roller, N. (2016, November 23). Introducing "intercept 0". [Web log post]. Retrieved January 10, 2017, from https://www.prainc.com.

CHAPTER 4 Foundations of Mental Health and Substance Abuse

Ford Brooks, EdD, LPC, NCC, CADC

Community Mental Health Act

In October 1963, President John F. Kennedy signed legislation that initiated the Community Mental Health Act (Figure 4.1). This landmark legislative proposal initiated the provision of mental health services in community counseling centers and authorized federal grants for the construction and development of these centers, which provide inpatient, partial, outpatient, and emergency care. The most substantial effect of the act is that it has helped those warehoused in state hospitals and institutions to return to the community (deinstitutionalization, discussed in Chapter 1) (National Council for Behavioral Health, 2015). In particular, this was accomplished through the creation of community services boards in the 1960s and early 1970s, where catchment areas spanned 50 to 60 miles and provided all mental health and substance abuse services to consumers in that area (see Chapter 2 for a discussion of community mental health centers, or CMHCs). The emphasis was to keep consumers of services out of the state inpatient psychiatric facilities and to integrate them into community outpatient care. This was done primarily from a therapeutic standpoint as well as a financial/budgetary perspective. Sadly, Kennedy died one month after the legislation was signed. Although his vision of a community-based care model has persisted over time, the funding has significantly diminished. Ironically, the three largest community mental health providers today are jails: Cook County Jail, Illinois; Los Angeles County Jail; and Rikers Island, New York (Slate, Buffington-Vollum, & Johnson, 2013).

Figure 4.1

President John F. Kennedy signs the Mental Retardation Facilities and Community Mental Health Center Construction Act. Looking on are Senator George A. Smathers (left) and Representative Paul G. Rogers (right), both of Florida. Cabinet Room, White House, Washington, D.C.

Source: John F. Kennedy Presidential Library and Museum. Retrieved at http://www.jfklibrary. org/Asset-Viewer/Archives/JFKWHP-AR8215-B.aspx

Introduction

Since the passage of the Community Mental Health Act, many changes have occurred in mental health and substance abuse treatment, as well as the integration of treatment services in correctional facilities; this is evidenced in Chapter 2, which provides an in-depth discussion of the historical progression of mental health treatment in the United States and, to some extent, abroad. The present chapter is focused on the following areas, which are important in mental health/substance abuse treatment in the criminal justice system: First, are the changes to the *Diagnostic and Statistical Manual of Mental Disorders, fifth edition (DSM-5)*. This iteration of the DSM has substantially changed the diagnostic assessment of substance use and the use of multi-axis diagnosis. Additionally, the signs and symptoms of mental health and substance use disorders with consumers and how to assess and refer individuals without increasing mental health symptoms is explored. Also presented is the understanding of persistent mental illness and how this affects the justice system, including a general understanding of ways in which to assess and refer; and finally, an exploration of the medications that can be used with a variety of disorders and the importance of a team approach with criminal justice, mental health, and psychiatry is also discussed. Although the subject of child and adolescent behavioral/mental health and substance abuse is an important area of study in our analysis of the system of care, the depth of information and discussion is best reserved for a single work. Of significance for this book is the developmental aspects of adolescents, the impact of substance use on development, and how co-occurring disorders will affect treatment; these topics are introduced at the end of the chapter. Various case studies are incorporated throughout to provide the reader with meaningful illustration.

Author's Note: I'm writing this chapter from the perspective of a counselor who worked extensively with the criminal justice system, spent a majority of time as an addiction treatment provider, and who supervised and instructed probation and parole officers as well as detention home staff. Although I support aspects of the chapter with current literature and changes in the DSM, it is mainly a chapter on understanding more clearly how substance abuse and mental health issues significantly affect the work of criminal justice providers and the interface with the mental health system.

As a fledgling counselor in the mid-1980s, I worked with probation and parole officers (state and federal) with clients who mainly were in legal trouble due to their substance use/addiction. Many, if not all, of the probation and parole officers I worked with had degrees in social work. Today, most officers have degrees in criminal justice with some education in mental health and treatment services as part of their curriculum.

We begin our discussion with the first step in the process by which many justice-involved PwMI enter the forensic mental health system of care—with an *assessment*. Before navigating through the assessment process, which will include an introduction to myriad practitioner-based terms and concepts, it may be instructive to begin with a case study. The following is the story of John.

John is a 23-year-old sergeant in the Army National Guard. Three years after entering basic training, he was deployed and in combat over a period of time in which he was exposed to profound traumatic events. Although John was seen by military physicians overseas for lethargic behavior, severe sluggishness, and reports (by superiors) of possible substance abuse (alcohol and pain pills), he was uncompromising and would not discuss any issues that would lead to an evaluation of any matters pertaining to mental health and/or substance abuse. John spent the first month back in the States with family but eventually, within two years, left his parents' house and became homeless. While on the streets, he had been in and out of hospitals for alcohol poisoning and injuries sustained while intoxicated. On July 4, John encountered police during a fireworks display. According to witnesses, John was rolling around under the bleachers at a softball stadium, trying to pull onlookers to the ground with him while exclaiming "take cover!" to the crowd. By the time officers arrived, John was sitting still on the bottom row of the bleachers and appeared to be shivering and confused. When they attempted to calm him down, he began swinging and eventually struck one of the officers. He was restrained and taken to jail for assault. During the intake process at the jail, John was flagged as a possible suicide risk; given this risk, John was initially placed on suicide watch and moved to a segregated housing unit at the jail. After a week in jail, it became obvious that John's problems were worsening (e.g., insomnia, irritability, depression, and occasional nightmares). In fact, staff had been alerted to a recent conversation he had with a correctional counselor that indicated continued suicidal ideation. The counselor scheduled an appointment for John to be screened and assessed for community-based mental health services, including counseling, medication management, and case management.

Comprehensive Assessment

An assessment is initiated by a clinical professional who engages in a determination of the client's mental health and/or substance abuse treatment needs. A critical aspect of an assessment begins with the reasons why individuals are presenting for assessment and the events leading up to it. The assessment is a process conducted at the first session and continues over the course of subsequent sessions for diagnosis determination and treatment planning. In a prison setting, the assessment may occur after transfer or within a week or two of incarceration. The precipitating event typically is a crisis point for the client that dictates some intervention, whether that be treatment, arrest, or incarceration. The precipitating event could be a robbery initiated after running out of money for the purchase of drugs or, as in John's case, an initially nonthreatening encounter with law enforcement that escalated quickly due to the presence of *triggers* or other precipitating factors. It is important for the individual completing the assessment to ask for specifics as much as possible and to create a timeline or history with respect to mental health and substance use. The comprehensive assessment highlights and outlines patterns in the person's life that result in repetitive behaviors such as crime, alcohol/drugs, or both. According to Erickson, "Assessment is ongoing; it occurs throughout therapy" (as cited in Geary, 2001, p. 1).

Essential Assessment Components

Medical

The actual assessment document needs to include a substantial medical evaluation of general symptoms and conditions of the client's overall health. Medical review questions, including blood pressure rates, history of mental illness, and cancer (to name a few), are to be asked at the beginning of this process in order to understand medical issues that may or may not stem from the mental illness or substance use disorders. Further, the case may require more specific questioning of withdrawal symptoms after a time of cessation from the drug and symptoms that may appear which would affect the treatment and recommendation process; examples of symptoms include shakiness, insomnia, and increased depression; seizures in the past; and rapid heartbeat (tachycardia). Also included in this would be current illnesses and medication use—current and a history thereof. The method of drug ingestion is important so to evaluate the need for medical examination (i.e., intravenous use and resultant abscesses). Having an examination by a physician is important in comprehensive treatment planning. A drug screen upon entrance into a correctional facility will provide information on whether the inmate was using drugs, and if so, what kind.

Psychiatric

Exploring a history of psychiatric treatment, both inpatient and outpatient, is crucial along with psychotropic medications that have been utilized with and without success. In particular, the assessment should contain record of current medications used—dosage, frequency, and administration. Furthermore, the client should be asked about symptoms of psychiatric disorders in the following areas: lonely/depressed, difficulty relaxing, nightmares, auditory noises, white flashes in the corner of eyes, memory problems, the presence of paranoid or manic behavior, *anhedonia* (loss of capacity to experience pleasure; Definition of anhedonia, 2016), changes in mood, and suicidal and homicidal thoughts and attempts. According to Brooks and McHenry (2015), suicide assessment, particularly with those who have a substance abuse history, is essential on a regular basis. Suicide is the leading cause of preventable deaths in U.S. jails (Way, et al.,

2005). It has also been found that suicide rates in correctional facilities are three to nine times higher than individuals outside of the system (Hall & Garbor, 2004; Mumola, 2005; Tataro & Lester, 2005; Tripodi & Bender, 2007). Cox (2003) found that 86 percent of inmates who die by suicide have a history of self-injurious behavior. Offenders are more likely to have preexisting conditions such as psychological disorders, substance use disorders, and impulsive and aggressive tendencies (Tripodi and Bender, 2007). Those at most risk for suicide attempts tend to be white, newly incarcerated or sentenced, have longer sentences given, or have inmate relational problems (Tripodi & Bender, 2007). Suicide in a jail setting, including screening and assessment thereof, is discussed in more detail in Chapter 6 of the text.

Assessment instruments such as the *Minnesota Multiphasic Personality Inventory (MMPI)* and the *Beck Depression Scale*, as well as projective tests such as the *Thematic Apperception Test (TAT)* or the *Rorschach Inkblot Test*, can be utilized during the assessment process. Unfortunately, cost and time are involved in administering instruments, so those instruments that take less time tend to be administered in jail settings due to the brevity of incarceration. In prison, inmates have extended periods of incarceration and the clinician will have more time to administer lengthy psychological tests.

Substance Use History

A comprehensive review of the client's alcohol and drug history should be conducted, including the age of first use, last use and current/past frequency, and amounts. The drug categories to be assessed include alcohol, amphetamine, cannabis, cocaine, sedatives, hallucinogens, inhalants, opioids, nicotine, and steroids. Exploring what the drug(s) of preference are and if the individual has used with others or alone is key. A review of the individual's relapse history is also important for treatment recommendations and focus (Gorski, 1989). If the client has been in treatment more than once, has made attempts to remain clean and sober with difficulty for any substantial period of time, or has a relapse history, all of this information should be documented, as it will be of great help during the assessment.

In 1970, the *CAGE* was introduced by Ewing and Rouse. The acronym helps with the assessment of substance use issues: **C:** have you ever felt a need to *cut down* on your drinking? **A:** have you ever felt *annoyed* by someone criticizing your drinking? **G:** have you ever felt *guilty* about your drinking? **E:** have you ever had an *eye opener* or drank to steady your nerves in the morning? This assessment with others such as the *Substance Abuse Subtle Screening Inventory (SASSI)* and *Michigan Alcoholism Screening Test (MAST)* are used in the process of determining if a substance use problem exists. The SASSI-3 is the most recent iteration of this assessment, is brief, has been extensively researched and utilized, takes less than 15 minutes to complete, and is used extensively as a substance abuse inventory.

FROM THEORY TO PRACTICE: THE CASE OF JEFF

Jeff works as a claims adjuster for a rather large insurance company. On most evenings after work he stops at the local pub to drink his usual three shots and two beers before he goes home. Over the past few years, Jeff's alcohol intake has increased, and his wife has been concerned about this. He is well known in the community, but over the past three years has been less involved in activities. On this particular night, Jeff drives home after having consumed six shots of liquor and four beers and hits another car head on, killing the driver of the other car.

Jeff is arrested for drunk driving and vehicular manslaughter and is sent to the local jail for booking. This is his second DUI in seven years, and he has had no previous treatment. Jeff has also had two suicide attempts in the past three years after his brother died of cancer. On one occasion, he cut himself on the wrist and came very close to dying. He is on antidepressants; however, his alcohol use negates the effect of the medication on his depression.

Assessment Process

Jeff would be considered a high risk for suicide due to his depressive history, history of suicide attempts, his increasing use of alcohol, and this subsequent crime under the influence that took the life of another person, plus the traumatic nature of the crime. Ideally, the clinician working in the jail would want to administer the SASSI-3, complete a suicide assessment, and have the client placed on regular suicide checks for the first 72 hours to observe his behavior for suicide risk. The clinician would likely refer Jeff to the staff psychiatrist for medication evaluation. In addition, it would be recommended that a clinician meet with the client individually to review the results of the SASSI and to refer the client to a substance abuse group in the jail should it exist. The combination of suicide assessment, medication evaluation, evaluation of his alcohol use, and the use of therapy would address his co-occurring issues and prepare him for ongoing help and treatment following his incarceration.

In addition to the SASSI-3, which is an instrument, is the new iteration of the DSM-5, which, as mentioned, provides consistent language, allowing for a common understanding among practitioners. A DSM-5 diagnosis is also required for insurance reimbursement; therefore, it is essential to be familiar with DSM-5 criteria for the diagnosis of mental health and substance abuse disorders.

Mental Health Disorders

The top-presenting serious mental health disorders in both jail and prison settings are mania or manic episode, bipolar disorder, major depression, and psychotic disorders, notwithstanding the diagnosis of substance use disorder. In fact, almost 75 percent of all incarcerated inmates (both state and federal) were dependent or abusing alcohol/drugs prior to their offense (Bureau of Justice Statistics, 2006). Anxiety and post-traumatic stress disorder (PTSD) are also prevalent diagnoses among justice-involved persons with mental illness, and the sufferer may not have developed any symptoms until post-detention or incarceration. Symptomology related to each disorder is presented in some detail next.

Key Symptoms of Mania

Manic episodes consist of a distinct period of mood elevation and irritability for at least a week. Within this behavior are symptoms of *grandiosity*, inflated esteem, sleep disturbance and needing less sleep, cognitive disorganization, racing thoughts, distraction, and goal focus, as well as involvement in pleasurable activities with high possibility for painful consequences. Three of these symptoms need to be present to meet the diagnostic criteria (APA, 2013).

With a manic episode, the behavior will affect the functioning of the person socially and vocationally and may require hospitalization in order to attain stabilization. The difficulty for law enforcement here is in differentiating this behavior and someone under the influence of drugs or alcohol. The way in which to rule that out would be with a drug/alcohol screening test. PCP, cocaine, and methamphetamine use can mimic manic behavior. A thorough psychiatric history will need to be conducted in order to rule that out for treatment purposes.

Key Symptoms of Bipolar Disorder

According to the DSM-5, more than 90 percent of individuals who experience a single manic episode will continue to have episodes in the future; furthermore, 60 to 70 percent of manic episodes occur immediately before or after a major depressive episode. Multiple iterations of the disorder are included in the diagnostic manual: bipolar I and II with variations of mixed, hypomanic, and unspecified (APA, 2013). Depending on the point in time when law enforcement is in contact with the individual, behavioral observations may reflect a swing in mood from severely depressed and suicidal to having grandiose ideas, minimal sleep, and agitation. Those working in jails and prisons will be able to monitor and assess more clearly; those working in the community may need repeated contact in order to determine the proper type of diagnosis.

Key Symptoms of Major Depression

Individuals with major depressive disorder or major depression may be suicidal; severely depressed; and experience anhedonia, a lack of motivation, reduced appetite, and difficulty with sleeping. Sleep is either episodic or constant and disrupts the regular sleep cycle of clients. Sadness and tearful moments can also be a part of the depression. Fits of anger and out-of-control rage can also be part of depression when emotions are suppressed and the addition of alcohol or drugs is in the equation. There may also be diminished emotional expression and a decrease in self-motivated activities. An individual with a very *flat affect*, or a lack of expression of any emotion, and a decrease in activities, can sit for lengthy periods of time without much movement (Figure 4.2) (APA, 2013). Based on the research, it appears that incarceration can lead to some mood-related psychiatric disorders, such as major depression, and have significant implications for post-release from prison and ongoing parole compliance. It also seems clear that inmates may come into prison with depressive (ASA, 2013). The Federal Bureau of Prisons has a clinical practice guideline outlining the diagnosis and treatment of depression; this publication would be recommended to readers for additional information on treatment of depression (Federal Bureau of Prisons, 2014).

Key Symptoms of Psychotic Disorders

Delusions

A delusion is a symptom of psychosis that refers to a person having fixed beliefs that conflict significantly with the present experience. Persecutory delusions occur

Figure 4.2
Depicting Depression
Source: Alexa DeFrancesco (2016)

when an individual believes that one is going to be harmed or harassed by a person or group. Referential delusions occur when the individual believes that signs, cues, and environmental movements are all being directed at them. For example, the coffee shop gave out a cup without a top, which means someone is watching them from above. Grandiose delusions are such that the person believes he or she has exceptional abilities, fame, or wealth, none of which are accurate. Erotomania delusions are when the individual believes a person is in love with them when in fact they are not. Examples include those who stalk celebrities because they feel as though they have a special relationship and are admired by the celebrity.

Hallucinations

A hallucination is characterized by an occurrence of a sensory perception (taste, smell, hearing, touch, sight) without any type of external stimulus. Hearing voices or auditory hallucinations are most common with this disorder. This can also be drug and alcohol induced as well.

Disorganized Speech

The officer may encounter a PwMI who is talking incoherently and appears disconnected from thought to thought; this is referred to as disorganized speech or "word salad" (Slate, et al., 2013). A grossly disorganized individual may go from bouts of child-like laughter to irritability and agitation in short amounts of time, unrelated to any type of substance use (APA, 2013).

These disorders can significantly affect social and interpersonal relationships of the person who suffers with them and the community. Evaluation, stabilization, and medication are important in the treatment. For community law enforcement, these consumers may be very challenging and will oftentimes become well known to officers. As a result, the officers become community contacts that can facilitate hospitalization and initiate harm prevention through referrals. For instance, in the community where I worked as a counselor, many of the consumers who suffered from psychotic disorders were noncompliant with their medications, and the result would be very bizarre behavior and concern for their well-being and that of others. What officers did was to work with our community mental health services and the local emergency room to help stabilize these consumers. Usually the officers were called due to safety issues. The officers acted as community points of contact and worked as team members within the mental health and medical community community to divert, rather than incarcerate, consumers.

INTEGERATION IN PRACTICE: THE CASE OF E. B.

Three months ago, Mr. E.B. was released from the county jail but didn't make it to the lobby of Behavioral Healthcare until two weeks ago. He was escorted to treatment by a long-term friend who insisted he come in. Actually, she would not let him leave until I saw him. Apparently, she had picked him up off the street, where he had been wandering around homeless and heavily drinking alcohol. She was worried about his safety. He was embarrassed but wanted treatment and remembered an encouraging conversation with a Behavioral Healthcare staff member in the jail about the forensic program. I talked to E.B. and developed a plan for him to enter detox first and then transition to the forensic program. While in my office, we made arrangements for him to enter detox. Two days later he called and reported that he was admitted to detox. Three days later he made it a point to visit me and report that he made it through detox but thought it would be better for him to go into residential substance abuse treatment for aftercare. He stated, "I am so grateful for all the caring individuals who helped me through my crisis" (Vail, 2015).

Key Symptoms of Anxiety Disorders and Post-Traumatic Stress Disorder

Law enforcement will observe anxiousness, extreme anxiety, panic, and impairment in social functioning with those suffering from an anxiety disorder. Panic disorders are included in this category and may have no significant origin but can be quite disabling. The observer could see agitation, rapid movements, fearful expressions, and avoidant behavior (APA, 2013).

PTSD presents symptoms including intrusive recollections of the traumatic event, dreams of the event, acting or feeling as if the trauma were recurring, intense distress at exposure to internal or external cues or triggers, and physiological reactivity. The person may also experience difficulty in recalling the event, feelings of detachment and restricted affect, as well as difficulty with sleeping, anger outbursts, hypervigilance, and difficulty concentrating. About 3.6 percent of U.S. adults ages 18 to 54 (5.2 million people) have PTSD during the course of a given year. About 30 percent of the men and women who have spent time in war zones experience PTSD. One million war veterans developed PTSD after serving in Vietnam. PTSD has also been detected among veterans of the Persian Gulf War, with some estimates running as high as 8 percent (Smith, 2014).

Daniel (2008) reported a high rate of veterans' contact with the criminal justice system, where 40 percent of veterans who suffer from PTSD are noted to have committed a violent crime since their completion of military service. In numbers this would be close to 120,000 criminal acts by veterans suffering from PTSD. One significant study examined prosecutors' willingness to offer treatment options to veterans with PTSD instead of criminal charges (Wilson, Brodsky, Neal, & Cramer, 2011). The research indicated how prosecutors were generally willing to extend treatment options over criminal charges, thus illustrating some effort to address the national crisis. PTSD, veterans, and veterans' court are discussed again later in Chapters 5, 7, and 10.

Severe and Persistent Mental Illness

There is a high likelihood that those suffering with persistent mental illness who are adults have been a part of the community mental health system for years, sometimes decades, and are often referred to by practitioners as "frequent flyers." As stated before, clients with persistent/chronic mental illnesses affect the system in that substantial needs are required to be addressed, which typically start with medication evaluation. Common with clients who suffer with SPMI are bouts in jail and time spent in outpatient or inpatient care, along with emergency room visits and housing needs. The legal system for many becomes the community "family," whereby legal authorities act as surrogate parents, and therefore, provide parameters, structure, and attention in the form of probation guidelines, incarceration, and parole requirements. The expectation is that the local community provides the treatment services; however, in contemporary times, the care and structure, if not provided by mental health program staff, are provided by those in corrections or law enforcement.

As will be referenced throughout the remainder of this text, due to stigma, structural changes in the mental healthcare system, and a significant lack of resources in many communities across the nation, the criminal justice system has become the de facto mental health system. Officers of the court, law enforcement, emergency responders, and probation/parole officers, both for adults and adolescents, will need continued training in assessment of signs, knowledge of referral resources, and a basic understanding of the therapeutic process and how that may be playing out with respect to the commission of a crime or displays of irrational behavior in the community.

Substance Use Disorders

Effective alcohol and drug intake forms contain questions that parallel the symptoms found in the DSM-5, making the assessment of substance use disorders helpful for counselors. As with mental health assessment, the alcohol and drug assessment data provided by clients, as well as information from other referral sources (e.g., hospital, probation), potentially provide important ancillary information for criminal justice practitioners as they make their preliminary diagnoses. The more information they have from family members, referral sources, hospitals, and prior therapy or treatment providers, the better likelihood of developing an effective treatment plan. As with any assessment procedure, successful understanding is facilitated through the use of multiple methods over time.

The newest DSM iteration has brought about a different way of examining substance use—thus, the new category: substance use disorders. The change in the DSM-5 eliminates the use of abuse and dependency as categories but rather lays out the use of substances in a continuum whereby the severity of the use disorder is connected to the number of symptoms, present from mild to severe, as found in the accompanying box. The *DSM-IV-TR* had two major categories: substance abuse and substance dependence. The DSM-5 views the path of nonuse to addiction as a process, whereby not all who use alcohol or drugs are dependent and each individual may experience a variety of symptoms. The abuse category from the DSM-IV-TR would be equivalent to a mild substance use disorder diagnosis; however, those considered in the dependency category would be in the DSM-5 category of severe symptoms.

Because of this reconfiguration of symptoms and the continuum outlined, interventions and referrals for resources, education, prevention, and treatment will be altered to fit the appropriate level of severity.

UPDATED DSM: INFORMATION AND DIAGNOSIS

The following highlights the changes in the newest iteration of the DSM that views substance use as a continuum rather than categories of abuse and dependence:

- Substance-related disorders was renamed substance-related and addictive disorders in the DSM-5.
- This category now includes both substance-related and nonsubstance addictions (gambling)—a substantial shift in this category.
- Cannabis withdrawal was added, whereas caffeine withdrawal is under further study.
- Criteria for early and sustained remission were changed in the DSM-5 to 3 to 12 months and 12+ months and allow for cravings.
- No longer are there categories of substance abuse and dependence. They were merged into a single category of substance use disorders (SUDs).
- Tolerance and withdrawal were eliminated as symptoms required for substance use disorder. Only when a client/patient is being prescribed medication that has known addictive properties do these terms apply.
- The term "dependence" now is limited to physiological dependence and is often a normal response to certain types of medications.
- The new "craving" diagnostic criterion was added.
- "Legal problems" was eliminated as a diagnostic criterion.

The DSM-5 provides criteria for each drug category (e.g., stimulants, hallucinogens, sedative-hypnotics) and contains information that helps counselors diagnose more specifically. So instead of "chemical dependency," a client can be diagnosed as having alcohol, cocaine, and/or cannabis use disorder. Because of the length of each drug category in the DSM-5, it is strongly recommend for practitioners to read the new DSM-5 section on substance-related and addictive disorders for additional information.

Presenting Symptoms for Law Enforcement to Observe

Author's Note: I remember when I first started as a counselor in Petersburg, Virginia, how integral the police department and probation and parole officers were with my clients. As counselors at the agency, we were charged with evaluating clients for medical and detoxification services. Willing participants went with the family members, but those unwilling and those in danger to self were assessed for a temporary detention order (TDO), which included involvement with the district magistrate and the sheriff's department.

For probation and parole officers, the symptoms of drug and alcohol use and withdrawal vary with their probationers. Overall, intoxication with most drugs and alcohol can result in significant impairment, erratic behavior, anxiousness, depression, and in some cases, aggression. Auditory and visual hallucinations can be found with significant use of drugs and alcohol as well as during withdrawal. For example, stimulant withdrawal can mimic schizophrenia, anxiety and depression, bipolar disorder, and panic and generalized anxiety. It will be important to assess, if possible, the amount and method of ingestion so as to determine appropriate contact with mental health professionals. The following provides a list of common substance abuse–related symptoms that officers may encounter in the field.

Alcohol Intoxication

Smell of alcohol, belligerent, slurring words, passing out, aggressive, emotional instability, vomiting, unsteady gait, stupor, or memory problems.

Alcohol Withdrawal

Increase in blood pressure, sweating, tremors in hands, nausea or vomiting, hallucinations or illusions (tactile or auditory), agitation, seizures, and anxiety

Cannabis Intoxication

Dry mouth, tachycardia, increased appetite, red glassy eyes, slow motor response

Cannabis Withdrawal

Irritability, aggression and anxiety, difficulty sleeping, restless, depressed mood, possible sweating/fever/chills/headache

Those individuals who are intoxicated or withdrawing from sedative, hypnotic, and anxiolytic drugs may mimic alcohol intoxication. Anxiety disorders or symptoms of anxiety can present in withdrawal of this category.

Phencyclidine can present as schizophrenia, depression, and anxiety during its use and withdrawal.

DSM-5 Criteria for Diagnosis of Substance Use Disorder

The DSM-5 (2013) describes substance use disorders as a maladaptive pattern of substance use, which leads to clinically significant impairment or distress, as manifested by two of the following criteria occurring within the same 12-month period:

CRITERIA 1–4 (IMPAIRED CONTROL)

1. Substance is taken in larger amounts or over a longer period than intended.
2. A persistent desire or unsuccessful efforts to cut down use.
3. Disproportionate time is spent obtaining, using, or recovering from substance.
4. Craving—an intense desire or urge for the drug. This is more likely in environment where using previously occurred.

CRITERIA 5–7 (SOCIAL IMPAIRMENT)

5. Inability to fulfill major role obligations at work, school, or home.
6. Continued use despite social or interpersonal problems.
7. Priority shift—social, occupational, or recreational activities are given up.

CRITERIA 8–9 (RISKY USE)

8. Recurrent substance use in situations in which it is physically hazardous.
9. Continued use despite known psychological or physical problems.

CRITERIA 10–11 (PHARMACOLOGICAL)

10. Tolerance (exceptions for prescribed medication).
11. Withdrawal (exceptions for prescribed medication).

Severity and Specifiers

The range of severity is from mild to severe and is based on the number of criteria endorsed as the result of an evaluation. A mild substance use disorder is suggested when two to three symptoms are present. Moderate is suggested by four to five symptoms, and severe by six or more. To further clarify the diagnosis, the following specifiers are considered.

COURSE SPECIFIERS

- Early remission
- Sustained remission-maintenance therapy
- In a controlled environment

THINKING CRITICALLY

The provision of food, shelter, and structure, and the facilitation of mental health assessment and medication management seem to take place in the jails now more than in the community. The decision by President Obama to release nonviolent offenders with mainly alcohol and drug charges has left, and will continue to leave many individuals in the community in need of mental health and substance abuse services. *How do you propose we respond to this issue?*

Co-occurring Disorders

Over 70 percent of incarcerated individuals have a co-occurring disorder of mental illness and substance use (Cloud & Davis, 2013). Two structures affect these clients: incarceration and those on probation and parole. As referenced earlier, those who have been candidates for inpatient psychiatric treatment find themselves committing crimes and subsequently obtaining treatment from the local jail or regional prison. Those incarcerated may have the option of counseling and medication evaluation for mental health disorders, and in a growing number of facilities, there are separate tiers to address substance use disorders as well as mental health issues.

The challenge in treating those with co-occurring disorders is accurate diagnosis and appropriate treatment planning and recommendations. As an outpatient alcohol and drug counselor, I worked with a significant number of clients on probation and parole. All of the probation and parole officers I worked with at the time had their degrees in helping services and not in corrections. Our work together was a team effort between the client and the probation/parole officer, where I would do the initial evaluation and diagnosis and then work with the client and the probation officer on treatment recommendations as well as medication evaluation. Most, if not all, of the clients I worked with were addicted to drugs and/or alcohol; however, I did see clients who had a persistent mental illness and who also drank or used drugs but were not addicted. In those cases it was important to educate clients on medication compliance and the impact drinking alcohol would have on their lives. The concept of *self-medicating* can be applied here; it refers to when the client is compensating for the painful emotions with alcohol or drugs, without consideration of the interaction or effects these will have with psychotropic medications used in their treatment regimen (Figure 4.3).

Figure 4.3
Depicting Self-Medicating as a Coping Mechanism
Source: Alexa DeFrancesco (2016)

Self-Medication Hypothesis (Khantzian, 1985): A theory of addiction based on the idea that people use substances, such as alcohol and drugs, to cope with or mask underlying emotions or trauma that has not been properly treated.

Assessment of Co-occurring Disorders

Most detention facilities or jails/prisons have programs in place to provide treatment. Programs typically include group counseling sessions and a thorough assessment of mental health and substance use issues, which is of significant importance in order to recommend appropriate treatment options.

Criminal justice professionals need to be knowledgeable of both mental health and substance use disorder symptomatology so as to tease out the presenting issues. Historically, mental health counselors conducted mental health work, and substance abuse counselors conducted alcohol and drug counseling; the philosophy was that the two should never meet. Over the years, however, a concerted and progressive effort to bring those two areas of counseling together has been initiated. That said, today someone can be assessed for significant mental impairment and at the same time be assessed for significant alcohol and drug use.

As previously discussed, serious mental disorders that are found in jails/prisons are as follows: major depression, mania and bipolar disorder, and psychotic disorders (Bureau of Justice and Statistics, 2006). These disorders, compounded with substantial use of alcohol and drugs, significantly affect life choices and may result in incarceration. In fact, the rate of serious mental illness is two to six times higher among incarcerated populations than it is in the general population (Cloud & Davis, 2013). Further, the number of inmates who commit crimes under the influence is significant; likewise, the number of inmates who report unmedicated mental health issues is also significant. Sadly, these are the very same individuals 25 and 30 years ago who were being treated in state psychiatric facilities, which stabilized them for community involvement. Estimates of the cost of inpatient psychiatric care in 2008 were 9.7 billion dollars (Piper, 2011); by contrast, estimates for incarceration in 2010, as reported by 40 states, revealed the cost to be 39 billion dollars a year—5.4 billion more than states' aggregate corrections spending (Henrichson & Delany, 2012). Based on these estimates, it appears that providing mental health treatment is less expensive than incarcerating individuals with mental illness.

Much has been written about work with adults and incarceration, but significant focus and attention in terms of mental health and substance use disorders must also be placed with adolescents and the juvenile population. In particular, there is a growing body of evidence that suggests the proportion of juvenile offenders with mental health and substance abuse issues surpasses that of adults and that there are additional challenges and needs to consider in terms of analysis. Consequently, it is important to discuss this population independently.

Working with Juveniles

In my career, I've taught graduate courses to juvenile probation officers (JPOs) and supervised counselors in juvenile detention facilities. The amount of work and responsibility found with adolescent work is significant, particularly within the juvenile justice system. The developmental issues, trauma, socioeconomic status, and use of drugs and alcohol are salient. At-risk juveniles have a significant grouping of issues, making it very challenging for rehabilitation, where in reality a great deal of it is *habilitation*.

When working with juveniles, those providing service have to contend with the family system more and attend to the alignment with family structure. For many juveniles, *social learning* as well as *genetic loading* factor into the behavior that finds them incarcerated or under probationary supervision. The implications of traumatic events are discussed again later in the final chapter of this text. When working with families, the identified client to which the family engages in treatment or therapy is many times the one involved in the criminal justice system via getting into trouble at school or other legal problems. In adolescence, we also understand the developmental process that unfolds into the early 20s. The frontal cortex of the brain is still under development—in particular, the sections involving reasoning and impulse control. The introduction of alcohol or other drugs into the normal and healthy development of adolescents can severely affect choices and most certainly healthy development (Brooks & McHenry, 2015). Figure 4.4 shows a picture of an addicted brain on the right where the receptor availability is significantly lessened and affects the neurotransmitter transmissions across the synaptic clefts, thus affecting sleep, energy, and depression.

The earlier adolescents use alcohol or drugs, the more significant their impairment and potential for addiction exists. Research supports early drug and alcohol use as a precursor to developing addictive disorders in life (Brooks & McHenry, 2015).

The combination of familial issues with mental illness and/or substance abuse, lack of support, impairment in normal brain development due to substance use, and the potential for other mental issues all contribute to the adolescent's decision making and potential involvement in the justice system. Therefore, the probation officer is in

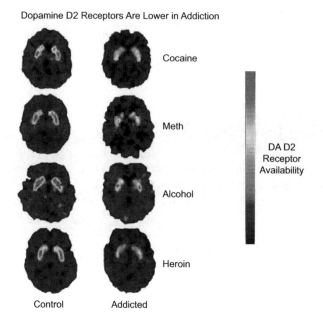

Figure 4.4

Images of Brain Development and Addiction

Source: Drugabuse.gov (2007)

need of basic assessment skills so as to refer for services. Unfortunately, for many juveniles, motivation and follow-through (despite the consequences) is quite high, making treatment compliance difficult—ultimately, contributing to reoffending. The use of *Motivational Interviewing (MI)* has been found to increase therapeutic movement with resistant populations (Miller & Rollnick, 2002).

Motivational Interviewing was developed by William Miller in the mid-1980s as an approach to client change utilizing the therapeutic aspects of the client/counselor relationship and by reducing resistance through active listening, thoughtful probes, open-ended questions, reflections and summarizations. The idea is to help the clients identify where they were in the change process and what aspects were they open to addressing. The acronym OARS (open ended questions, affirmations, reflections, and summarizations) reflects the skills utilized in the initial stages of the process (Miller & Rollnick, 2002). Training and certification can be found on their website: http://motivationalinterviewing.org/.

In assessing adolescent substance abuse, a number of questions can be asked: Has the adolescent's behavior changed significantly over time, particularly in a school setting? Has the adolescent's attitude changed toward school, peers, and other teachers? Is there a change in physical appearance or attire? What kinds of activities is the adolescent involved in and with whom? Have activities, interests, or grades changed significantly or declined? This, along with a thorough drug and alcohol assessment and a drug screen, can determine the need for treatment or counseling. A thorough assessment of mental health disorders is also necessary; in particular, one that specifically focuses on disorders that present early in adolescence, including conduct disorders, attention deficit disorder, anxiety and depression, and substance use disorders.

PRACTITIONER'S CORNER 4.1

Diagnosing Mental Health Disorders in Criminal Justice Settings: Challenges and Critical Issues with Juveniles

Contributor: Ms. Sarah Zucca, MA, LPC, CDAC

Corey is a 15-year-old African American male who was admitted to the detention center the previous evening due to his third public intoxication charge. He also has charges of petty larceny and truancy that are pending. When the counselor arrives to complete her screening/intake process, Corey greets her with a sullen mood, arms crossed, and little to no eye contact. The counselor has 20 minutes to accurately assess for suicidality, possible mental health/substance abuse diagnosis, and appropriate referrals to the community.

Working as a mental health/substance abuse clinician in a juvenile detention center forces the clinician to quickly connect and build rapport with the juveniles. Because most of the adolescents have had very little control in their lives, it is paramount to remind them of what control they do have. This can be achieved by accurately presenting confidentiality and especially limits thereof. It is also vital to remind them that you are not another adult trying to tell them what to do with their lives, but rather are interested in hearing what has been going on for them and assisting them with finding solutions to problems they would like to focus on. Acknowledging that it is hard to trust someone and share personal information after just meeting can help ease the possible discomfort. If proper rapport is not built, the clinician cannot appropriately assess for mental health/substance abuse needs. Once rapport is created, it is beneficial to utilize a quick screening inventory, such as the Massachusetts Youth Screening Inventory (MAYSI-3), that can help narrow down areas of clinical focus. Unless done on the computer, it is also helpful to ask residents whether or not they wish to read the MAYSI or have it read to them. This helps the resident "save face," gives critical information on their ability to read, and assists in determining possible referrals for additional educational services or assessments. Lastly,

continued

after determining which further services are needed, the clinician has to be comfortable with providing case management care and be knowledgeable of resources offered in the community and contacts to help link juveniles to upon release. It is also crucial to assess and keep in mind basic needs such as transportation, financial concerns, and parental involvement.

Case Study II: 17-year-old Caucasian male

A therapist begins running his group with the daily topic centering on personal responsibility and choice. During the discussion, a 17-year-old Caucasian male, who is turning 18 the next day, brings up his impending sentence of three years in the state system once he turns 18. He expresses his hopelessness that he will never be able to better his situation. To prove his point, he gives examples of how residents in the state system often continue to receive charges in order to survive. Knowing that this young man has a history of being in and out of the foster system, has been physically and sexually abused, and has a learning disorder, the therapist honors his situation by acknowledging the difficult experiences he has survived. The therapist also reminds him that he has several options when he gets to the state system: he could continue on the same path and receive additional charges, or he could choose to keep his head down, focus on his studies, and make something of his life. The therapist did not give much thought to the discussion after group. Two years later, he receives a letter from the resident thanking him for taking the time to encourage him to better himself. He has managed to stay out of trouble in the state system, is set to receive his GED, and is planning to become a probation officer.

This is a true example of an interaction I had with a resident that left a lasting impression on me. It taught me that despite not always getting immediate feedback of change I may be facilitating, it is important to never give up despite the high recidivism rate.

Medication Management

For both adolescents and adults, the evaluation for psychotropic medications and the use in treatment is critical. In 2006, almost 10 years ago, the Bureau of Justice Statistics found one-half of all jail and prison inmates have mental health issues and that suicide is the number-one cause of death among inmates. Those incarcerated in state or federal institutions have access to medical evaluation and supervision. Of growing concern and attention are those committing or attempting suicide, resulting in deaths and subsequent lawsuits by family members. More and more institutions are contracting with telepsychiatrists and implementing protocols and staff who regularly (in some cases, daily) monitor and provide suicide evaluation and medications. All staff and counselors are trained in suicide prevention and intervention. Those at risk or who have attempted suicide are placed in single cells with minimal clothing and are observed continuously so as to prevent suicide. This may draw an already overwhelmed staff to one area and leave sections in the facility with less coverage. As stated earlier in the chapter, jails and prisons are taking the place of mental health institutions; PwMI are being treated alongside offenders in the general population.

Telepsychiatry: A form of psychiatry that utilizes technology to deliver services to the patient whose mobility or ability to access services may be restricted for a variety of reasons. Physicians typically render services via teleconferencing technology.

Source: Crane (2015)

PSYCHOTROPIC MEDICATIONS

Only physicians can prescribe psychotropic medications to treat clients suffering from mental and emotional disorders. These medications are used to minimize or eliminate symptoms and have minimal or nonaddictive qualities. Those with co-occurring disorders will need both alcohol/drug treatment and medication management to treat and stabilize the mental disorder.

Mood stabilizers, such as Zoloft, Prozac, and Effexor, can be used to treat depression and, in some cases, depression and anxiety. An individual who has addiction issues will need to be evaluated for a nonaddicting medication if anxiety or PTSD symptoms are concurrently diagnosed. These will need to be monitored closely by the physician and treatment providers.

Anxiety disorders typically are treated short term with Klonopin, Ativan, or BuSpar. Those with addictive potential, such as Ativan and Klonopin, are not the best medications to treat anxiety. Physicians with experience in addiction typically do not prescribe addictive medications to an individual suffering from addiction. Clients with bipolar disorder may be put on Depakote or lithium, and those with psychotic disorders may be put on Haldol, Risperdal, or Zyprexa.

Those clients who suffer from ADHD or ADD will be evaluated for medication and may be placed on Ritalin or Cylert. Again, those clients with addiction issues will need to be evaluated for alternative nonpotentially addicting substances.

The use of over-the-counter (OTC) medication has become popular with those in adolescence due to the sedating qualities of the medications. Large quantities used with alcohol and other drugs potentially increase the risk for problems (Figure 4.5).

For many of those incarcerated and on probation or parole, follow-up with treatment and psychiatric visits is challenging. As is common, the wait time to see a psychiatrist is two to three months and in some cases longer. Those individuals released from prison may have a gap in mental health services due to nonpayment by insurance. If the wait is too long for a medication review, the client may discontinue or not engage in services.

Figure 4.5
Suffering and Substance Abuse
Source: Lillie Hawkins (2016)

Case Examples

The following scenarios provide criminal justice professionals with an application of the chapter information in hopes of bringing mental health and criminal justice systems together.

Correctional Issues: Initial Period of Detention

Bianca has just been incarcerated for the past two months for an outstanding warrant and her current arrest of drunk driving. Her family history is significant for addiction, and she has experienced an unstable family life. She grew up in the city and eventually started using alcohol and pot at the age of 9. She was arrested multiple times as a juvenile and spent time in a juvenile detention facility. Bianca is 24 years old, biracial (Hispanic and African American), has dropped out of high school, and has no formal training or military experience.

Bianca's use of alcohol has escalated over the past five years to the point now that her daily consumption of alcohol is at least 8 and 10 beers and marijuana. Bianca has experienced episodes of using pain killers, and at the age of 21, she started using heroin because it was less expensive. Her last use of all drugs was the day she was arrested two months ago. The first week in jail she underwent a mild to moderate withdrawal, including night sweats, agitation, vomiting, dizziness, shakiness with flulike symptoms, and severe headaches. Bianca did not alert staff to her discomfort, as this was the first time she ever stopped using alcohol and drugs other than previous brief stints in juvenile hall.

In addition to her alcohol and drug use, Bianca suffers from anxiety and depressive issues, nightmares, hypervigilance, and has a history of trauma in her family after having witnessed her father shoot and kill her brother. Her father is serving a life term for first-degree murder.

By her report, she is easily startled, has horrible nightmares at least three nights a week, has unstable mood most days, and has times where she contemplates suicide. Although she has never made an attempt, she has the means (Bianca owns two unregistered pistols). Bianca is going to be released in two weeks to the community and will be assigned a probation officer.

Community Corrections: Probation

In this scenario we walk through what the probation officer wants to be aware of in the post-jail discharge meeting and recommendations to be made to the judge for the court order.

Depending on local mental health resources, Bianca could be referred to a drug and alcohol counselor for assessment and recommendations. In some cases the county will pick up the cost of assessment and subsequent sessions while the insurance/medical assistance becomes active or reactivated. If there isn't *stopgap funding* then the discharging inmate needs to wait until funding becomes available, which means time without treatment or therapy and the potential to reoffend. In addition to a drug and alcohol assessment is the referral for a psychiatric evaluation. In some cases, the inmate has already been evaluated by the jail psychiatrist/counselor. However, if this has not occurred, it needs to be noted by the probation officer for consideration in probation orders. This chapter in particular, but this book in general, is helpful in educating and preparing the probation officer for basic assessment procedures. The probation officer may not be providing therapy; however, a general set of questions would reveal the symptoms of PTSD and a referral for psychiatric care and medication protocol.

The probation officer meets with Bianca and determines, based on a short interview, that Bianca's main issue and arrests have all been alcohol or drug related. Moreover, if she wasn't using or didn't have an alcohol and drug issue, she would not be in the criminal justice system. Her brand of trouble with her addiction involves the courts and is symptomatic of how out of control she is with her use. Therefore, an immediate referral is made to the county alcohol and drug office for assessment and to mental health for a psychiatric evaluation; a referral to a psychiatrist is also made for medication review. It is helpful to note if the clinician providing the assessment is both an alcohol and drug specialist and one who is knowledgeable and comfortable using the DSM; it will help with multiple referrals.

In an ideal referral world, Bianca makes an appointment with the drug and alcohol counselor that week, is seen by the mental health counselor the same week, they get releases of information and talk with each other and the probation officer, and set Bianca up for a medication review. The recommendations would be collective, collaborative, and informed based on the assessments. Again, this would be reflective of an ideal system of care.

The reality is that Bianca may not get an appointment for a month with either counselor, that the probation officer has 400 people on his or her respective caseload, that the funding for the year at the county has dried up, and that the inmate/client's insurance will not activate/reactivate for three months. The client is out of jail where she has been watched constantly and is now on her own again with thoughts of using and cravings to use, knowing that if she gets caught again, she has five years that she will serve for violating her probation order with the court (Figure 4.6).

Unfortunately, this is where we are in many cities and towns around the country. Relapse occurs, reoffending occurs, and the client ends up back in jail, this time for a longer period, and continues to suffer from addiction and PTSD. Most importantly, the client is not, in the truest sense, a criminal, but rather, acts to obtain/use drugs or alcohol, which helps with symptoms of untreated mental health disorders.

Although a familiar scenario, there are places around the country that offer treatment and counseling in the jails, alcohol and drug groups, assessment by psychiatrists for medication post-discharge, and a seamless transition from a therapeutic community in jail to treatment services in the "free" community. Bianca, if in that system, would be released to the community setting with an assigned case manager, and at least one month's worth of medication until she is able to meet with a psychiatrist for medication management. She would be referred to a clinician with experience in PTSD, and she would immediately enter some type of group treatment for her addiction. Her family would somehow be part of the reintegration into the community and her support network.

This all sounds great; however, it doesn't typically happen as presented here. Big caseloads for probation officers, unmotivated clients, gaps in mental health and substance abuse treatment, and, of course, significant gaps in funding resources are all issues that must be addressed.

Figure 4.6
Feelings of Loneliness and Isolation
Source: Alexa DeFrancesco (2016)

Local and Regional Police

Mary is an on again/off again homeless city resident. She was diagnosed with schizophrenia at the age of 17 and has been in and out of the mental health system since that time. She is 42 years old and is white. She lives most of her time in supervised living; however, there are times when she disappears for months on end to different towns within hitchhiking distance. In her life she has known substantial heroin addiction and subsidized her use with prostitution. She is HIV positive and has contracted hepatitis C. Most of the long-time regional law enforcement know Mary and have done what they could to help her at different points in her life to obtain housing and transportation so that she was able to make it to medical appointments. On some occasions, officers would arrest Mary just so that she might have a warm place to sleep and food to eat.

Local and regional law enforcement have learned quite a bit from her with regard to the mental health system, her disorder, and her medical status. Although they may not identify themselves as such, they are part of Mary's informal mental health treatment team. They listen to her, they understand about her disorder through her fits of yelling at walls and tearing at her skin to get the bugs off when in heroin withdrawal, and help facilitate transportation and housing for medical issues. She is part of the community, just as law enforcement is an integral aspect of the community's safety.

More and more, jail staff and law enforcement are providing triage assessment and referral and formal/informal treatment to those individuals who 30 or 40 years ago would have been placed in an acute and possibly long-term state facility for treatment and maintenance. Prevailing issues and the role and training of correctional staff and law enforcement are discussed in more detail in Chapters 5 through 8. Deinstitutionalization has put an increasing amount of responsibility on the criminal justice system to take care of persons with mental illness with little to no training or preparation other than on the job. This book has been written with this in mind.

Sidebar: My Experience

I started as a drug and alcohol counselor in 1984 with my first internship at a halfway house for recovering women. I then moved to working in a hospital setting in the detoxification unit. From there I worked for almost five years in a community-based mental health/substance abuse program, was a liaison with the state mental hospital, and provided evaluations in the jail and for the courts regarding alcohol and drug treatment. I then worked for the remaining seven years in private practice and outpatient treatment programs. Additionally, I provided licensure supervision to a federal probation officer and worked extensively with the courts. A majority of my 30-year career as a teacher and counselor has continuously interfaced with the criminal justice system. Even our international association for addiction, the American Counseling Association, is a combined title: addiction and offender counselors, indicating the close connection with the criminal justice system and addiction treatment/counseling.

In my first job I carried an average caseload of 60 to 65 clients in the outpatient agency, 90 percent of whom were involved in the criminal justice system. As a counselor, I was not prepared for my daily interactions with probation officers, court letters, and evaluations for services at the local jail and the differences in philosophy from criminal justice with respect to treatment. I found my work with probation and parole to be very rewarding and helpful to clients in that the "leverage" by probation helped motivate my clients, who were mainly addicts and alcoholics. The continuous support of probation and our treatment services allowed for therapeutic work to be done for the benefit of the client and the prevention for reoffense. When I worked in the jails, however, that staff sentiment changed in that all too many times when I assessed an inmate for detoxification services, the inmate had been in withdrawal for longer than needed and more than once I heard disparaging remarks about their mental health status. Their perspective was to utilize punishment vs. rehabilitation. Overall, though, many of my letters and appearances in court allowed for collaboration and recommendation for services and the benefit of the client.

As a counselor, what I found most helpful was the attitude of most criminal justice professionals: "What can we do to work together here to get this person help?" The second most helpful aspect was the willingness of probation and the courts to be the "heavy" when there was noncompliance. Rather than taking the person back to court, we would have a meeting with the client to explain the importance of compliance and that noncompliance would result in a consequence. Usually only one meeting was needed to get the client to at least comply with services and hopefully take responsibility and initiative and move forward.

Take-Home Message

In the counseling profession, one of the biggest areas of growth is in addiction services. With the resurgence of heroin use in epidemic proportions, the need for services has only increased. With that increase is the need for collaborative work between criminal justice and mental health and addiction counseling. As supported by current trends in corrections, some effective examples may include the use of street/crisis triage prevention teams, therapeutic communities/tiers in jail, seamless treatment from incarceration to outpatient services, halfway houses for ongoing support, and a merging of corrections and counseling. The future jobs in counseling will be in addiction, corrections, and mental health. The collaborative efforts of each will not only help to "deinstitutionalize" the jail/prison population, but will use the community to provide resources, as was done with the mental health population over 50 years ago. It will take cooperation and funding discussions within mental health and substance abuse as well as corrections—and, perhaps most importantly, a restructuring of cooperative programming.

An area needing mental health attention and support pertains to the needs of children with incarcerated parents. Services must be provided to children who have witnessed horrendous crimes and have watched a parent or family member be arrested; it can affect a child in terms of his or her development. The child who watches five police officers take down his father who is high on crack and out of control can be traumatized and creates a situation where that child is potentially destined to repeat similar behavior in adulthood. Trauma and trauma-informed care are referenced throughout and discussed in more detail in the final chapter of this textbook.

This chapter has outlined the criteria for the major mental health disorders and substance use disorders, the symptoms of the disorders that criminal justice professionals need to be aware of, the plight of the chronically mentally ill in our society, the work that is needed with juvenile probation and detention facilities, and medication compliance and the importance for client well-being.

QUESTIONS FOR CLASSROOM DISCUSSION

1. How do you think mental health and criminal justice practitioners and institutions should respond to individuals with various types of mental disorders?
2. What are your thoughts on addiction? How do you differentiate criminal behavior from addictive behavior?
3. What are your thoughts on those who suffer from a chronic mental illness and those who are afflicted by addiction?

KEY TERMS & ACRONYMS

- Anhedonia
- Assessment
- Beck Depression Scale
- Bipolar disorder
- CAGE
- Co-occurring disorders
- Diagnostic and Statistical Manual of Mental Disorders, fifth edition (DSM-5)
- DSM-IV-TR
- Flat affect

- Genetic loading
- Grandiosity
- Habilitation
- Michigan Alcoholism Screening Test (MAST)
- Minnesota Multiphasic Personality Inventory (MMPI)
- Motivational Interviewing (MI)
- Rorschach Inkblot Test
- Self-medicating

- Social learning
- Stopgap funding
- Substance Abuse Subtle Screening Inventory (SASSI)
- Suicidal ideation
- Suicide watch
- Telepsychiatrists/telepsychiatry
- Thematic Apperception Test (TAT)
- Triggers

Bibliography

American Psychiatric Association. (2013). *Diagnostic and Statistical Manual of Mental Disorders* (5th Ed.). Washington, DC: Author.

American Sociological Association (ASA). (January 16, 2013). Study Examines Link between Incarceration and Psychiatric Disorders. *ScienceDaily*. Retrieved June 23, 2016 from www.sciencedaily.com/releases/2013/01/130116085947.htm.

Brooks, F., & McHenry, B. (2015). *A Contemporary Approach to Substance Use Disorders and Addiction Counseling* (2nd Ed.). Alexandria, VA: ACA Press.

Bureau of Justice Statistics. (2006). *Mental Health Problems of Prison and Jail Inmates* (NCJ-213600) was written by BJS statisticians Doris J. James and Lauren E. Glaze. Following publication, the report can be found at http://bjs.ojp.usdoj.gov/index.cfm?ty=pbdetail&iid=789.

Cloud, D., & Davis, C. (February, 2013). *Treatment Alternatives to Incarceration for People with Mental Health Needs in the Criminal Justice System: The Cost-Savings Implications.* (pp. 1–6). New York, NY: Vera Institute of Justice.

Correia, K. M. (2000). Suicide Assessment in a Prison Environment: A Proposed Protocol. *Criminal Justice and Behavior, 27*(5), 581–599.

Cox, G. (2003). Screening Inmates for Suicide using Static Risk Factors. *The Behavior Therapist, 26,* 212–214.

Crane, K. (2015, January 15). Telepsychiatry: The new frontier in mental health. *U.S. News and World Report.* Retrieved from http://health.usnews.com on January 3, 2017.

Daniel, D. L. (2008). *Post-Traumatic Stress Disorder and the Causal Link to Crime: A Looming National Tragedy* (AY 2007–2009). Leavenworth, KS: School of Advanced Military Studies, U.S. Army Command and General Staff College.

Definition of anhedonia. (2016, May 13). Retrieved from http://www.medicinenet.com/script/main/art.asp?articlekey=17900

Ewing, J. A., & Rouse, B. A. (February, 1970). *Identifying the Hidden Alcoholic.* Paper presented at the 29th International Congress on Alcoholism and Drug Dependence, Sydney, Australia.

Federal Bureau of Prisons. (2014). *Management of Major Depressive Disorder: Federal Bureau of Prisons Clinical Practice Guidelines.* Retrieved June 23, 2016 from https://www.bop.gov/resources/pdfs/depression.pdf.

Geary, B. B. (2001). Assessment in Ericksonian Hypnotherapy and Psychotherapy. In Geary, B. B., & Zeig, J. K. (Eds.), *The Handbook or Ericksonian Psychotherapy* (pp. 1–17). Phoenix, AZ: The Milton Erickson Foundation.

Gorski, T. (1989). *Passages through Recovery: An Action Plan for Preventing Relapse.* Center City, MN: Hazelden Press.

Hayes, L. M. (1995). *Prison Suicide: An Overview and Guide to Prevention.* Alexandria, VA: National Center on Institutions and Alternatives.

Henrichson, C., & Delany, R. (2012). *The Price of Prisons: What Incarceration Costs Taxpayers.* New York, NY: Vera Institute of Justice.

James, D. J., & Glaze, L. E. (2006). *Mental Health Problems of Prison and Jail Inmates.* (pp. 1–16). Washington, DC: Bureau of Justice Statistics Special Report.

Miller, W. R., & Rollnick, S. (2002). *Motivational Interviewing: Preparing People to Change Addictive Behavior* (2nd Ed.). New York: Guilford Press.

Mumola, C. (2005). *Suicide and Homicide in State Prisons and Local Jails.* Washington, DC: U.S. Department of Justice, (NSJ No. 210036).

National Council for Behavioral Health. (2015). Community Mental Health Act. Retrieved from http://www.thenationalcouncil.org/about/national-mental-health-association/overview/community-mental-health-act/.

Noonan, M. E. (2012). The Price of Prisons: What Incarceration Costs Taxpayers. *US Department of Justice,* 1–33. Retrieved from http://archive.vera.org/sites/default/files/resources/downloads/price-of-prisons-updated-version-021914.pdf.

Piper, K. (2011). Retrieved from http://www.piperreport.com/blog/2011/06/25/hospitalizations-for-mental-health-and-substance-abuse-disorders-costs-length-of-stay-patient-mix-and-payor-mix/.

Slate, R. M., Buffington-Vollum, J. K., & Johnson, W. W. (2013). *The Criminalization of Mental Illness: Crisis and Opportunity for the Justice System* (2nd Ed.). Durham, NC: Carolina Academic Press.

Smith, B. A. (2014). *Juror Preference for Curative Alternative Verdicts for Veterans with PTSD.* Unpublished manuscript.

Tataro, C., & Lester, D. (2005). An Application to Durkheim's Theory of Suicide to Prison Suicide Rates in the United States. *Death Studies, 29,* 413–422.

Tripodi, S. J., & Bender, K. (2007). Inmate Suicide: Prevalence, Assessment, and Protocols. *Brief Treatment and Crisis Intervention*, 7(1), 40.

Vail, L. (2015). Various stories and parent's shout out. Meridian Behavioral Healthcare, Inc., Gainsville, FL.

Way, B. B., Miraglia, R., Sawyer, D. A., Beer, R., & Eddy, J. (2005). Factors Related to Suicide in New York State Prisons. *International Journal of Law and Psychiatry*, *28*, 207–221.

Wilson, J. K., Brodsky, S. L., Neal, T. M.-S., & Cramer, R. J. (2011). Prosecutor Pre-Trial Attitudes and Plea-Bargaining Behavior toward Veterans with Posttraumatic Stress Disorder. *Psychological Services*, *8*, 319–331. doi:10.1037/a0025330.

CHAPTER 5 **Intercept One**
Police–Citizen Encounters

About 4:25 a.m. "male caller said someone is threating his life . . . said they are at the house . . . asked his name he is Q . . . will not tell where he is . . . caller refuses to answer questions . . . caller hung up . . . not a good number . . . nfi."

[NFI stands for "no further information."]

Another 911 call was placed about 30 seconds later and that prompted a second entry reading:

"C/S 19YO SON BANGING ON HIS BEDROOM DOOR WITH A BB BAT, NFI."

[C/S stands for "Caller states."]

Foutris, Antonio LeGrier's lawyer, said that "as far as I know" his client made just one 911 call. It's not clear whether Antonio or another person made the other 911 call.

About a minute after the second call, a dispatcher who handled West Side 911 calls assigned an 11th District squadrol to a call she described as a "well-being check" and a domestic disturbance.

"72 Robert," she said, identifying the squadrol by its beat number, according to a recording of the dispatch. "We gotta check the well-being at 4710 West Erie, 4710 West Erie. The male caller said someone is threatening his life. It's also coming in as a domestic. The 19-year-old son [is] banging on his bedroom door with a baseball bat."

An officer assigned to the squadrol responded a few seconds later: "10–4."

Twelve minutes passed before officers assigned to the call on Erie pushed the talk button on their radios.

"Shots fired out here, shots fired, shots fired, shots . . ."—another officer cut the first officer out—"two shots fired."[1]

Introduction

Although it has been reported that about 7 to 10 percent of police encounters involve PwMI, statistics also clearly indicate that a disproportionate number of PwMI are involved in critical police encounters resulting in arrest, and at the most extreme end of the spectrum, police shootings (Franz & Borum, 2011; Ogloff, et al., 2013). For example, the *Washington Post* collected data on every fatal shooting by police of a person with mental illness in 2015 (Lowery, Kindy, Alexander, Tate, Jenkins, & Rich, 2015). According to Epperson (2016), the *Washington Post* data suggest that of the approximately 1,000 people who were shot and killed by police officers in 2015, ". . . 25 percent displayed signs of mental illness" (A21). Likewise, Morabito and Socia (2015) published the results of their research conducted in Portland, Oregon. They examined all use of force cases reported by city police departments between the years 2008 and 2011 and found a significant relationship between subjects' mental health and likelihood of injury to either subjects or the responding police officers when force was employed—but only when substance abuse was also a factor.

Recently, the intersection between the mental health and criminal justice systems has been emphasized as evidenced by media reports of police brutality toward PwMI (see, e.g., Borrelli, 2015; McLaughlin, 2015) and mistreatment of inmates with mental illness by correctional staff and contracted mental health providers in jails and prisons (e.g., Fellner, 2015). Simultaneously, the paucity of literature on effective responses to justice-involved offenders with severe and persistent mental illness (i.e., psychotic and major mood disorders) also has been documented. The need for further research is particularly necessary in policing and corrections—the components of the system facing the greatest challenges in terms of responding effectively in crisis situations involving PwMI in their care (Cross, Mulvey, Schubert, Griffin, Filone, Winckworth-Prejsnar, DeMatteo, & Heilbrun, 2014; DeMatteo, LaDuke, Locklair, & Heilbrum, 2013).

Public safety officials, including security agents and emergency medical personnel, firefighters, and law enforcement officers (LEOs), are often the first to respond when a person is experiencing a mental health crisis. Unfortunately, some first responders may feel ill prepared to handle these types of encounters given a general lack of knowledge as to signs and symptoms of mental illness and a number of other factors that present themselves in a crisis situation. In fact, despite an increase in police encounters with persons in crisis, it appears that only minimal attention is directed in police training to dealing with individuals who might be experiencing mental health issues. According to research by the Police Executive Research Forum (PERF), training academies allot approximately 60 hours of training on how to use a gun, but only 8 hours of training for strategies to address persons with mental illness (Lowery, et al., 2015).

This chapter closely examines the first point of intercept within the original SIM, which includes diversion opportunities more typically available during encounters with law enforcement and emergency services personnel (Munetz & Griffin, 2006). Considering that the intended audience for this text is future criminal justice professionals such as police, emphasis is placed on police–citizen encounters and pre-booking diversion strategies. Additional challenges facing law enforcement and the consumers they serve are also presented and discussed. Again, it should be noted that the SIM has very recently been updated to include an additional intercept point—that is, "Intercept 0" (Vincent-Roller, 2016); the reader is asked to consider that some of the pre-arrest/ pre-booking diversion strategies presented in this chapter (e.g. CIT and MHFA) are designed to prevent a crisis that would require police-intervention from occurring in the first place.

SNAPSHOT, 2014: POLICE-PWMI ENCOUNTERS THAT MADE NATIONAL HEADLINES

Elliot Rodger (Santa Barbara)
As reported by *Reuters* (Feldman, 2014), deputies with the Santa Barbara County Sheriff's Office had encountered Rodger three times previously, most recently responding to a *welfare check* call at his residence that had been placed by a county mental health worker. The deputies found Rodger outside of his apartment, and at that time had asked him about disturbing videos he had reportedly posted online; however, law enforcement never checked the videos, nor did they perform a weapons sweep. The sheriff's report from that incident stated:

> *Sheriff's deputies concluded that Rodger was not an immediate threat to himself or others, and that they did not have cause to place him on an involuntary mental health hold, or to enter or search his residence . . . The sheriff's office has determined that the deputies who responded handled the call in a professional manner consistent with state law and department policy.*

One month after this encounter, Rodger made national headlines after he opened fire on the campus of the University of California-Santa Barbara and had been found to have fatally shot 6 people (injuring 14 others, 7 of whom were struck with his vehicle) before turning the weapon on himself in an apparent suicide. The media frenzy continued after a final YouTube video and Rodger's 140-page manifesto promising to exact vengeance upon the women who spurned him were released for public consumption. According to *The Los Angeles Times* (Mather, Winton, Ceasar, & Flores, 2014), Rodger had been prescribed risperidone, an antipsychotic, but evidently had refused to take it.

continued

Army Specialist, Isaac Sims (Kansas City)

In Kansas City, a police standoff emerged over Memorial Day weekend from the home of Sims who was ultimately shot and killed by police. Sims, a veteran who served in Iraq, had been diagnosed with post-traumatic stress disorder (PTSD) since his return to the States. It was reported that he sought help from a local veterans' hospital a week prior to the incident for his paranoia; staff told him that there was no bed space and to check back in 30 days. Police had been called to his family's home after Sims fired shots, although he injured nobody. After a five-hour standoff with police, Sims emerged from the house brandishing a rifle and was shot down by police (Von Drehle, 2014).

James Boyd (Albuquerque)

Police in Albuquerque, New Mexico, shot and killed James Boyd, 38, a homeless man who they had encountered illegally camping in the Sandia Mountains. The shooting was preceded by a four-hour standoff, which, according to attorneys for the police, culminated in Boyd brandishing two knives (one in each hand), thereby invoking the use of deadly force by two of the responding officers (Ohlheiser & Izadi, 2015). Helmet cameras captured the incident on video, which was ultimately released to the media. In the video, Boyd, reportedly suffering with paranoid delusions (Heild, 2016), appears to be complying with police orders at the time he was shot. In January 2015, two officers were charged with open murder charges in this case.

Author's Note: These and other related incidents often invoke a great deal of pressure and criticism on police response—in particular, police use of force. Ironically, the typical police academy training dedicated to disability issues (including physical and mental disabilities) is about 8 hours at best.

Police as First Responders

The gate-keeping function police serve for PwMI in crisis situations has become more pronounced since deinstitutionalization of state hospitals throughout communities in the United States (Lamb & Weinberger, 2014; Wallace, Mullen, & Burgess, 2004) and the subsequent inability of community-based treatment providers to service the growing population of PwMI (International Association of Chiefs of Police, 2010; Slate, et al., 2013). Another development that has increased the visibility of PwMI in the community is state statutes that prescribe more rigid criteria for civil commitment to state hospitals. Lack of community support for PwMI and stigma, coupled with inadequate dispatch training and policies on best practices for navigating police encounters with PwMI, can result in increased incarceration for PwMI for minor offenses (International Association of Chiefs of Police, 2010; Slate, et al., 2013). The following section provides an introduction and discussion to diversion strategies at Intercept One (police–citizen encounters), which are designed to minimize further penetration into the justice system.

Specialized Police Responses to Crisis Events

With the number of encounters between police and PwMI increasing, *specialized policing responses (SPRs)* have been designed and implemented by police departments nationwide (and abroad) to provide pre-booking diversion options that may more effectively address any underlying issues and/or needs related to this particular population. SPRs prioritize treatment over incarceration, when possible. Depending on available resources, extent of community support, and department culture/philosophy, one of three primary types of response "teams" are utilized for dispatch during a crisis event: police-based specialized police response (sworn officers with special mental health training), police-based specialized mental health response (mental health consultants employed by the law enforcement agency), and mental health–based specialized mental health response (individuals who work directly for providers/agents in the community mental health system) (Compton & Kotwicki, 2007). As outlined in Chapter 3, examples of these programs can be broadly placed under three categories: (a) crisis intervention teams (CITs), (b) co-responder teams, and (c) follow-up teams (Reuland & Yasuhara, 2015). Each of these is explained in some detail next.

The term "welfare check" or "wellness check" (Siegel, 2013) refers to an act by police to seek out persons in the community and ascertain their well-being in a variety of circumstances (NAMI, 2016). It should be noted, however, that a police welfare check should not replace an assessment by a clinician who is more appropriately trained in mental health disorders.

Crisis Intervention Teams

To promote the safety of officers, consumers, and the general public during crisis encounters, first responders should be properly trained in mental health crisis intervention. The CIT model is one of the most well-known SPRs. In fact, it is the most widely adopted police-based specialized police response program in the United States (Gostomski, 2012; Watson, Ottati, Draine, & Morabito, 2011) and has gained popularity and been implemented outside the United States in countries such as Australia, New Zealand, Canada, and the United Kingdom (Hartford, Carey, & Mendonca, 2006; NSW Police Force, 2014). The CIT model was originally conceived following a 1987 incident in Memphis, Tennessee, that resulted in Joseph Dewayne Robinson—a man with a history of mental health and substance abuse issues—being fatally shot during a crisis encounter. When Memphis police arrived at the scene, Robinson was wielding a knife and appeared to be cutting himself. After failing to desist and release the weapon, Robinson allegedly began to approach police and was subsequently shot eight times (Heilbrun, DeMatteo, Yasuhara, Brooks-Holliday, Shah, King . . . & Laduke, 2012). As a direct response to this incident, a community task force composed of law enforcement, community mental health providers, addiction professionals, and consumer advocates was established. This task force collaborated and designed the CIT model (Heilbrun, et al., 2012, Watson, et al., 2011). Prior to the implementation of CIT, most police departments, including the Memphis Police Department, were offering a few hours of academy-based training in crisis intervention (Gostomski, 2012; Hails & Borum, 2003; Pearson, 2014).

As of 2015, there were close to 3,000 CIT programs throughout the United States, with the exception of Alabama, Arkansas, Rhode Island, and West Virginia (University of Memphis, n.d.). Primary objectives of the Memphis model[2] include (a) advanced training, (b) immediate crisis response, (c) safety of officer and consumer, and (d) proper care for persons in crisis (Pennsylvania Mental Health & Justice Center for Excellence, 2013).

Under the Memphis model, trainees receive a one-time, 40-hour, week-long training in how to respond to citizens in crisis (Pennsylvania Mental Health & Justice Center for Excellence, 2013). Depending on the needs of the community and the size of any given jurisdiction and available resources, training may take place multiple times throughout the year. Various training modules are facilitated by law enforcement personnel, community mental health professionals, educators, family and consumer advocates, and other professionals in related fields. Training sessions cover a variety of topics, including (a) signs and symptoms of mental illness, (b) types of psychotropic medications, (c) deescalation techniques, and (d) community resources. Two essential elements of the model are officer training and the development and maintenance of criminal justice–mental health partnerships. Training elements that are implemented successfully are expected to produce change in officers' attitudes, knowledge, and skills (i.e., learning outcomes) and subsequent behavior when encountering PwMI (i.e., behavior outcomes) (Cross, Mulvey, Schubert, Griffin, Filone, Winckworth-Prejsnar, . . . & Heilbrun, K., 2014).

In the majority of communities where CIT is implemented, persons who have attended are a diverse group of first responders, including (a) corrections officers, (b) school resource officers, (c) police and deputy sheriffs, (d) public safety dispatchers, (e) 911 operators, and (f) medical and mental health professionals ("What is CIT?," 2016). Most of the trainees are self-selected law enforcement volunteers who also come highly recommended by their respective departments (Thompson & Borum, 2006); this presents an issue for research evaluations. It should be noted, however, that in an increasing number of jurisdictions, new recruits and veterans are required to complete the full 40 hours of CIT training, making more comparative observations possible in future analyses of the program (Cross, et al., 2014; Pennsylvania Mental Health & Justice Center for Excellence, 2013).

Like with other types of training and development, the primary determinant with regard to availability is financial and then time restrictions. Given the 40-hour time commitment, departments have been reluctant to "give up" their officers, which results in only a minimum number of CIT-trained officers in many municipalities, and in some, none at all. Unfortunately, the number of police calls for services that are related to mental health issues continues to overwhelm departments across the United States (see, for example, Figure 5.1), and the trend is only moving upward (Smydo & Lord, 2016). For this reason, several jurisdictions have made accessible abbreviated CIT programs that provide a basic understanding of signs and symptoms of mental illness so to more effectively respond to a crisis event.

Figure 5.1

Police Cruiser

Source: By User: Victorgrigas (Own work). [CC BY-SA 3.0 (http://creativecommons.org/licenses/by-sa/3.0)] via Wikimedia Commons

Empirical Evidence

Law enforcement agencies that have implemented CIT report positive results (DeMatteo, LaDuke, Locklair, & Heilbrum, 2013; Pearson, 2014; Steadman, Deane, Borum, & Morrissey, 2000). In particular, CIT programs have been successful in (a) improving understanding of signs and symptoms of mental illness, (b) reducing stigma and negative attitudes toward PwMI, and (c) increasing the number of positive police interactions with PwMI overall (e.g., Compton, et al., 2006; Wells & Schafer, 2006). For example, Compton and colleagues (2006) reported results of surveys completed by 159 officers following a 40-hour block of CIT training. Findings revealed that there was a reduction in officers' stigmatizing attitudes related to mental illness (particularly schizophrenia), including improved attitudes regarding aggressiveness of PwMI (i.e., less likely to view PwMI as having an increased potential for violence). Trained officers also reported (a) enhanced knowledge about mental disorders, (b) better attitudes in support of working with local treatment programs, and (c) decreased desire for social distance from PwMI.

The extent to which the knowledge translates into behaviors, however, is much less known at this juncture, and more research is needed to draw any conclusions in this regard. For example, one long-term benefit of crisis intervention training should be a reduction in the number of violent interactions between PwMI and the police. Some evaluation of CIT effectiveness in reducing police officers' use of force against persons with mental illness has been conducted. For instance, Skeem and Bibeau (2008) found that CIT officers used force in only 15 percent of encounters against highly resistant subjects (i.e., high risk of violence). More recently, Compton, Broussard, Hankerson-Dyson, Krishan, and Stewart-Hutto (2011) collected data from 135 police officers belonging to urban police departments in the southern United States. Participants in the sample included 48 CIT-trained and 87 non–CIT-trained police officers. Officers were given three scenario-based vignettes depicting escalating situations involving a PwMI. Results revealed CIT-trained officers were less likely to use force to gain compliance from a PwMI. Additionally, when compared with their nontrained counterparts, CIT-trained officers selected actions related to lower use of force. Morabito, Kerr, Watson, Draine, Ottati, and Angell (2012) corroborated these earlier findings in a comparative study of CIT-trained police officers and police officers who had not been trained in CIT in the city of Chicago (n = 91 vs. n = 125, respectively). Results indicated that, when compared to their untrained counterparts, CIT officers used less force as subject resistance increased.

In a more recent study of the same city department, Morabito and Socia (2015) examined the relationship between suspects' mental illness and the likelihood of injury for both officers and suspects during use-of-force encounters in Portland, Oregon, from 2008–2011. Of all use-of-force incidents over that reporting period,

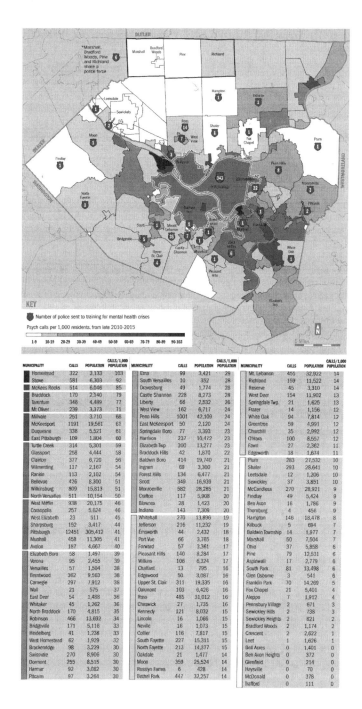

MUNICIPALITY	CALLS	POPULATION	CALLS/1,000 POPULATION	MUNICIPALITY	CALLS	POPULATION	CALLS/1,000 POPULATION	MUNICIPALITY	CALLS	POPULATION	CALLS/1,000 POPULATION
Homestead	322	3,133	103	Etna	99	3,421	29	Mt. Lebanon	455	32,922	14
Stowe	581	6,303	92	South Versailles	10	352	28	Richland	159	11,522	14
McKees Rocks	514	6,046	85	Dravosburg	49	1,774	28	Reserve	45	3,310	14
Braddock	170	2,140	79	Castle Shannon	228	8,273	28	West Deer	154	11,902	13
Tarentum	346	4,489	77	Liberty	66	2,532	26	Springdale Twp.	21	1,625	13
Mt Oliver	239	3,373	71	West View	162	6,717	24	Frazer	14	1,156	12
Millvale	251	3,710	68	Penn Hills	1001	42,109	24	White Oak	94	7,814	12
McKeesport	1191	19,561	61	East McKeesport	50	2,120	24	Greentree	59	4,991	12
Duquesne	336	5,521	61	Springdale Boro	77	3,393	23	Churchill	35	2,992	12
East Pittsburgh	109	1,804	60	Harrison	237	10,472	23	O'Hara	100	8,557	12
Turtle Creek	314	5,301	59	Elizabeth Twp	300	13,277	23	Fawn	27	2,362	11
Glassport	258	4,444	58	Braddock Hills	42	1,870	22	Edgeworth	18	1,674	11
Clairton	377	6,720	56	Baldwin Boro	414	19,740	21	Plum	283	27,532	10
Wilmerding	117	2,167	54	Ingram	69	3,300	21	Shaler	293	28,641	10
Rankin	113	2,102	54	Forest Hills	134	6,477	21	Leetsdale	12	1,206	10
Bellevue	426	8,300	51	Scott	349	16,939	21	Sewickley	37	3,851	10
Wilkinsburg	809	15,813	51	Monroeville	582	28,285	21	McCandless	270	28,921	9
North Versailles	511	10,154	50	Crafton	117	5,908	20	Findlay	49	5,424	9
West Mifflin	938	20,175	46	Blawnox	28	1,423	20	Ben Avon	16	1,786	9
Coraopolis	257	5,624	46	Indiana	143	7,309	20	Thornburg	4	456	9
West Elizabeth	23	511	45	Whitehall	270	13,896	19	Hampton	146	18,478	8
Sharpsburg	152	3,417	44	Jefferson	216	11,232	19	Kilbuck	5	694	7
Pittsburgh	12451	305,412	41	Emsworth	44	2,432	18	Baldwin Township	14	1,977	7
Munhall	458	11,305	41	Port Vue	66	3,765	18	Marshall	50	7,504	7
Avalon	187	4,667	40	Forward	57	3,361	17	Ohio	37	5,858	6
Elizabeth Boro	58	1,497	39	Pleasant Hills	140	8,284	17	Pine	79	12,531	6
Verona	95	2,455	39	Wilkins	106	6,324	17	Aspinwall	17	2,779	6
Versailles	57	1,504	38	Chalfant	13	795	16	South Park	81	13,498	6
Brentwood	362	9,563	38	Edgewood	50	3,087	16	Glen Osborne	3	541	6
Carnegie	297	7,912	38	Upper St. Clair	311	19,335	16	Franklin Park	70	14,269	5
Wall	21	575	37	Oakmont	103	6,426	16	Fox Chapel	21	5,401	4
East Deer	54	1,488	36	Ross	485	31,012	16	Aleppo	7	1,912	4
Whitaker	45	1,262	36	Cheswick	27	1,735	16	Pennsbury Village	2	671	3
North Braddock	170	4,815	35	Kennedy	121	8,032	15	Sewickley Hills	2	738	3
Robinson	466	13,692	34	Lincoln	16	1,066	15	Sewickley Heights	2	821	2
Bridgeville	171	5,116	33	Neville	16	1,073	15	Bradford Woods	2	1,174	2
Heidelberg	41	1,238	33	Collier	116	7,817	15	Crescent	2	2,622	1
West Homestead	62	1,929	32	South Fayette	227	15,311	15	Leet	1	1,626	1
Brackenridge	98	3,229	30	North Fayette	213	14,377	15	Bell Acres	0	1,401	0
Swissvale	270	8,906	30	Oakdale	21	1,477	14	Ben Avon Heights	0	372	0
Dormont	255	8,515	30	Moon	359	25,524	14	Glenfield	0	214	0
Harmar	92	3,082	30	Rosslyn Farms	6	428	14	Haysville	0	70	0
Pitcairn	97	3,264	30	Bethel Park	447	32,257	14	McDonald	0	378	0
								Trafford	0	111	0

Figure 5.2

Mental Health Calls Dispatched to Police in Pittsburgh, Pennsylvania

11.5 percent involved suspects with mental illness (n = 6,131). It should be noted that CIT training in Portland was universal during the reporting period, so all responding officers in the data set were CIT trained. Findings revealed that, in corroboration with previous studies on use of force overall, incidents in which force is employed are most likely to result in the injury of officers rather than subjects, and further, there are situational characteristics that significantly influence outcomes in both contexts, including race, sex, subject resistance, and the presence of weapons. With regard to mental illness specifically, Morabito and Socia (2015) found that it alone was not a significant predictor of injury; rather, the perceived co-occurrence of substance abuse with mental illness increased the likelihood of injury to both suspect and officer in their sample. This finding corroborates research reported by Dr. Brooks in the preceding chapter and is important considering misperceptions of the mental illness–violence relationship.

PRACTITIONER'S CORNER 5.1

Interactions between the Police and Persons with Mental Illness

Contributor: Jim Ruiz, PhD

Sometimes, incidents involving persons with mental illness can involve violence. But the vast majority of the time, they do not. When I was assigned to the French Quarter, I came to know "Ruthie the Duck Lady." She was known as an "eccentric" that could be found at all hours of the day and night walking the streets in a bridal gown followed by one more ducks. Sometimes, she would leave the ducks at home, and could be seen skating down Bourbon Street, her bridal veil trailing after her. Early one morning we were having breakfast in a bar and restaurant at Bourbon and Toulouse Sts., Ruthie came in with one of her ducks, and placed the duck on the bar. As Ruthie was a regular, the bartender immediately set up a beer with numerous cherries in it, and a small bowl. She shared her beer with the duck, and it quickly became intoxicated. It was obvious to us that Ruthie was afflicted with some form of mental illness, but we never had to worry about violent behavior from her. She died in 2008. http://www.eccentricneworleans.com/ruthie.htm

What comes to mind when you hear the phrase, "A person with mental illness?" Does it conjure up an image of a person sitting quietly in a corner shunning all contact with others, or does your mind's eye visualize an individual acting out franticly? For those who have not experienced a person with mental illness in the near or extended family, it's probably the latter. When a police officer receives a call for service, s/he usually consults his/her mental log of previous calls of this type, and begins to gird his-herself for the encounter. Usually, the most memorable for police will be those cases involving uncooperative persons with mental illness, and how s/he handled that encounter. What is more, police have been given the obligation of managing persons with mental illness with precious little education and/or training in that area.

Mental Health First Aid

Mental Health First Aid (MHFA) was developed and implemented first in Australia in 2001. By the end of 2007, there were over 600 instructors and 55 people trained in MHFA in that country (Kitchener & Jorm, 2008). The original curriculum can be delivered over the course of one or two days, and is facilitated by certified instructors; revisions have been made to the number of hours, depending on the version and the needs of the community in which it is being offered. The goal of MHFA is to promote a philosophy of resilience and recovery. Consequently, the original MHFA training program revolves around a five-step action plan referred to as ALGEE: **A**ssess risk of suicide or harm; **L**isten nonjudgmentally; **G**ive reassurance and information; **E**ncourage the person to get appropriate professional help; and, **E**ncourage self-help strategies. The program is typically offered to police officers, emergency personnel, students, school administration, and primary care professionals with a collective goal of reducing stigma associated with PwMI, helping those in danger of suicide or self-harm, and making referrals to appropriate treatment services (mentalhealthfirstaid.org; National Council for Behavioral Health, 2015). Training modules (topics) include anxiety, depression and mood disorders, psychosis, substance abuse disorders, and trauma (mentahealthfirstaid. org). In 2006, the need for a youth MHFA program was recognized, and one was developed in Australia with the same general foundation as the adult program, but with revisions including the addition of modules on topics such as deliberate self-harm and eating disorders (Kitchener & Jorm, 2008).

Interested in getting trained in MHFA? What about becoming a certified trainer? Visit the following website for more information as to the history and development of the program and for training opportunities in your area: http://www.mentalhealthfirstaid.org/cs/

Subsequent Adaptation and Adoption: Australia and Beyond

In Australia, mental health community leaders developed a special adaptation of the program for Aboriginal tribes within the nation. These tribal programs were more sensitive to different cultural beliefs, but were closely guided by mental health first aid experts. After some time, other countries began to take a more progressive stance with regard to mental health education and first aid training, and the program was adapted with appropriate cultural and content modifications in Australia and New Zealand, as well as internationally in Cambodia, Canada, China, England, Finland, Hong Kong, Ireland, Japan, Scotland, Singapore, Sweden, Thailand, the United States, and Wales

(Kitchener & Jorm, 2008); some of these countries are presently in the beginning stages of adaptation.

In the United States, implementation of the program began in 2007. The Mental Health First Aid Act of 2015 authorized 20 million dollars toward the development of the MHFA course (National Council for Behavioral Health, 2015). Reflective of the original model, participants are trained in recognizing the symptoms of substance abuse and common mental illnesses, initiating referrals to mental health resources, and deescalation techniques. Statistics show that over 600,000 people across the United States have been trained in the program and that there are approximately 9,000 instructors nationwide (mentalhealthfirstaid.org). The top five states that have the most people trained include California (52,637), Pennsylvania (44,704), Texas (33,468), Michigan (27,728), and Missouri (25,391) (National Council for Behavioral Health, 2015).

Empirical Evidence

Of the scant number of studies that have examined the effects of MHFA on behavioral change, the majority have been conducted outside of the United States and primarily in Australia. Both controlled and uncontrolled studies of the MHFA course (youth, teen, and adult versions) have been undertaken to examine the feasibility of providing the program in schools, at work, and in other community venues; to test relevant measures of student knowledge, attitudes, and behaviors; and to provide initial evidence of program effects. Across varied studies, participants completed a baseline questionnaire and then received the program; many participants also completed a post-test and between a 3- and 6-month follow-up. Statistically significant direct increases have been found in mental health literacy, confidence in providing Mental Health First Aid, knowledge of mental health and substance abuse resources and the confidence to provide help/make referrals, and indirect improvements in help-seeking intentions and student mental health. Furthermore, stigmatizing attitudes have been significantly reduced (see, for example, Hart, Mason, Kelly, Cvetkovski, & Jorm, 2016 [Teen MHFA in Australian secondary schools]; Kitchener & Jorm, 2002, 2004 [Workplace setting in Australia]; Jorm, Kitchener, O'Kearney, & Dear, 2004 [Public, rural setting in Australia]). Similar to CIT research, the extent to which direct knowledge has translated into behavior is a highly understudied outcome and one with limited support (e.g., see Kitchener & Jorm, 2006: Positive effects related to improvements in helping-behavior reported by recipients of MHFA after a 5 to 6 month post-training follow-up; as compared with Jorm, Kitchener, Sawyer, Scales, & Cvetkovski, 2010: Findings revealed that there were no effects on teachers' support of students with mental health needs in Southern Australia, nor were there improvements in students' mental health). The essential inquiry that has yet to be extensively tested is whether recipients of MHFA perceive their mental health needs have been met.

THINKING CRITICALLY: CIT IN ACTION

Consider the following case scenario; how might CIT-trained officers respond during the encounter?

Dispatch receives a call from two citizens to report a "homeless man who has been living on a park bench." According to one of the callers, the man has not moved for hours. When officers arrive, he does not respond. Officers prod him and he jumps up. He appears disoriented, brandishing a hanger and holding it like a rifle.[3]

Co-responder Teams

As the available research indicates, the existence and success of pre-booking diversion programs depend on successful and resourceful collaboration between individuals from multiple systems of care. In particular, when successful community partnerships are formed between mental health professionals and practitioners and law enforcement officers, the deployment of police–clinician SPRs can be an effective strategy during a crisis event at Intercept One. Several of these partnerships have been developed with an array of structural components and names, including, for example, a Behavioral Health Response Team (BHRT) (Portland, Oregon), Crisis Intervention Response Team (CIRT) (Houston, Texas), Mental Health Officer team (MHO) (Madison, Wisconsin), Mental Evaluation Unit (MEU) (Los Angeles, California), and Psychiatric Emergency Response Team (PERT) (San Diego, California). Research on this approach has produced positive results—in particular, a reduction in injuries to officers and an improvement in consumer mental health services linkages (International Association Chiefs of Police [IACP], 2010). A modified co-responder model appears to involve a pairing between CIT-trained police officers and *Mobile Crisis Units or Teams (MCUs or MCTs)* (IACP, 2010; Slate, et al., 2013) (see Figure 5.3). As a police-based specialized response, the primary role of CIT officers is to employ deescalation techniques and to minimize public safety risk and injury to officer or consumer. Since CIT has been discussed earlier in this chapter, the following section describes MCUs in some detail.

Mobile Crisis Outreach Teams or Units

The advent of MCTs or MCUs began shortly after the passage of the Mental Health Act in 1963 as one response to rapid deinstitutionalization and the philosophical shift away from a reliance on inpatient care to a more community-based approach (Casey, 2015). The MCT is considered a mental health–based specialized response (Compton & Kotwicki, 2007), and thus, a "team" generally consists of case managers, social workers, psychiatrists, psychologists, and registered nurses who have extensive training on mental health disorders and related treatment options (IACP, 2010; Slate, et al.,

Figure 5.3
Emergency Services
Source: By Mario Beauregard. Adobe Stock Images [Standard License]

2013). The primary goal of MCTs has historically been a "gatekeeping" function—in essence, to more effectively stabilize vulnerable persons who are experiencing an acute crisis event in a community setting, and consequently, reduce the number and duration of inpatient admissions (Carpenter, Falkenburg, White, and Tracy, 2013). With this in mind, cases in which an MCU was dispatched alongside police are reportedly more complex, more time consuming, and oftentimes, the consumers require transportation to a mental health facility or crisis center (Griffin, Heilbrun, Mulvey, DeMatteo, & Schubert, 2015).

The primary functions of the MCU are to assist in deescalation; perform crisis stabilization; assess the mental health (and possible substance abuse) status of the consumer; provide education, psychological support, and medication management and administration when needed; and, to link the consumer with local community mental health and substance abuse services. Further, whenever possible, MCUs have also provided follow-up care (Lord & Bjerregaard, 2014), which is discussed in some detail later. Ideally, the MCT is available seven days per week, 24 hours a day, and consumers needing assistance will have the ability to call the MCT directly for a nonthreatening mental health emergency, just as they would call 911 for other emergencies requiring the police (National Alliance on Mental Illness, 2016). Unfortunately, due to budgetary and other constraints governing counties, municipalities, cities, and towns, mobile crisis units may be understaffed and underutilized; availability may be limited to certain times, days, and also by procedural restrictions.

In some jurisdictions, the MCU cannot be dispatched unless accompanied by law enforcement (or until after the arrival of law enforcement). This presents a problem in some cases, however. In particular, some consumers/cases do not involve a public safety risk, and the presence of law enforcement can sometimes increase rather than minimize trauma. For this reason, recommendations have been made to dispatch an MCU as an alternative to police in situations where no crime or violence has occurred (IACP, 2010).

Formal evaluations of MCUs are scant, and most of the current research appears to be descriptive in nature. However, available data indicate that Mobile Crisis Teams are cost effective in terms of reducing the need for emergency medical services and the use of arrest. Furthermore, law enforcement and consumers alike have been notably positive about their encounters with the MCU (see IACP, 2010 and Lord & Bjerregaard, 2014 for a review of the relevant literature).

In review, diversion strategies available at Intercept One of the original SIM may include pre-arrest diversion programs, such as Crisis Intervention Teams (CITs), and Mobile Crisis Teams (MCTs), which typically involve the collaboration of first responders from the mental health system and law enforcement agencies (Slate, et al., 2013). CIT and MCT are the most practiced programs at this inception point. As presented and discussed here, Crisis Intervention Teams are comprised primarily by law enforcement officers who are trained in mental health and on how to use their skills to deescalate a situation if and when there is a need (Slate, et al., 2013). Mobile Crisis Teams can consist of case managers, social workers, psychiatrists, psychologists, and a variety of other persons working in helping, human service-oriented professions; these individuals are most likely to have significant training with regard to substance use and mental health disorders (and related crisis events), so if there is a situation that needs to be deescalated they can also assist (Slate, et al., 2013). CITs and MCTs are becoming increasingly important because the numbers of persons with mental illnesses are growing in the jail/prison population. According to the American Psychological Association (APA). 10 to 25 percent of U.S. prisoners have a serious mental illness, which includes schizophrenia, schizoaffective disorder, bipolar disorder, or major depressive disorder (Collier, 2014). As stated several times throughout this book, with the increased population, prisons are becoming known as the state hospitals for PwMIs (Slate, et al., 2013). Law enforcement agencies are now trying to use preventative programs like Crisis Intervention Teams to lower the rate of PwMIs going into jails/prisons, especially since it is recognized that they are not likely to receive the adequate treatments and medications that are needed for their mental illnesses (Slate, et al., 2013). Because persons with mental health diagnoses are often incarcerated instead of receiving the appropriate psychiatric care, crisis intervention should be utilized to prevent even further decompensation of individuals with a mental illness, to avoid entry into the prison system if possible, and to expedite recovery.

Police–Clinician Follow-Up

Despite community participation in SPR programs such as CIT and successful collaborative efforts at crisis response and intervention (MHFA and MCU), persons with mental health diagnoses are sometimes arrested and subsequently incarcerated. Furthermore, even individuals who are successfully stabilized and who remain in the community may not have knowledge of or access to the services they need to independently function in daily life. As such, follow-up care should be utilized to prevent *decompensation* of PwMI to avoid rearrest/reentry into the prison system, if possible, and to expedite recovery.

A follow-up team is a group of individuals, most often led by law enforcement officers, who are specially trained in mental health crisis intervention (e.g., CIT). It is important to note that follow-up programs are often a natural extension of the duties assigned to CIT-trained officers and/or Mobile Crisis Units; this type of program/level of care and support is usually reserved for persons with serious mental illness who are frequently encountering the criminal justice system (i.e., "frequent flyers"). There is no formal model of what a team should look like; rather, the needs of a community will dictate its clientele, composition, and primary tasks. Again, in some communities, follow-up teams involve the collaboration of police and MCUs or just police; in other communities, there may be follow-up teams with specific clientele, such as for adults or juveniles. Furthermore, depending on the jurisdiction, team members may also include community corrections officials (e.g., a probation officer) and behavioral health representatives (e.g., social workers, peer support staff, and nurses) (see Slate, Buffington-Vollum, & Johnson, 2013 for a comprehensive review of crisis intervention and follow-up teams in varied jurisdictions). Generally speaking, the primary function of the team is to evaluate a consumer's engagement in services (mental health and substance abuse) after a crisis event has occurred, and to and, if necessary, to educate the consumer(s) as to available resources. It is anticipated that this will reduce the number of repeat 911 calls as well as rearrests. As revealed by the research on CIT, and corroborated by individuals working in the field, a referral for follow-up is usually made by responding officers after a crisis event. At that point, members of the team perform community-based outreach, whereby they visit with consumers face to face to evaluate service engagement and mental health status. They will then provide periodic updates to other members of the team. Given these goals, the need for thorough documentation of PwMI–police encounters (information tracking) and sharing across systems of care is evident.

Studies that focus specifically on follow-up teams are difficult to find in a search of the literature; however, there is a growing body of research on multidisciplinary mental health crisis teams in general. Based on overall findings, it is possible to deduce positive effects when follow-up evaluation and referral are connected to crisis intervention. In particular, the evidence reveals that effective follow-up care after a crisis event may reduce the rate of suicide, reduce the likelihood of future contact with LEOs, and improve treatment engagement to some extent (e.g., Malone, Marriott, Newton-Howes, Simmonds, & Tyrer, 2007).

Police Discretion during a Crisis Encounter

Police are given the primary responsibility of responding to, resolving conflict of, and ensuring the safety of PwMI who cannot care for themselves under the doctrine of *parens patriae* (Latin for "the state as parent") (Curtis, 1976; Slate, et al., 2013). Thus, regardless of the community/jurisdiction and type of diversion strategies available, police generally have discretion to invoke five to six possible outcomes during a mental health crisis: do nothing, arrest, request the dispatch of a Mobile Crisis Unit, provide community-based information/referrals, refer and possibly transport a willing consumer to a *crisis stabilization unit (CSU)*, or initiate an involuntary emergency commitment for evaluation (i.e., see Figure 5.4). Of these options, the involuntary commitment option is the most controversial, and hence, it is discussed in more detail next.

Suicide-by-Cop (SbC) or police-provoked shooting: A term used to describe incidents involving police contact with citizens who are suicidal; in particular, these are incidents in which a citizen in crisis successfully attempted to provoke police into using deadly force (Pillay & Thomas, 2015).**Suicide-by-Cop**

By The Numbers
   Characteristics of citizens involved in 708 police-provoked suicide incidents[4]:

   95 percent involved male citizens

   29 percent were homeless

   35 = Mean age for men

   40 = Mean age for women

   Among males and females . . .

   41 percent were Caucasian

   26 percent were Hispanic

   16 percent were African American

---

continued on page 125

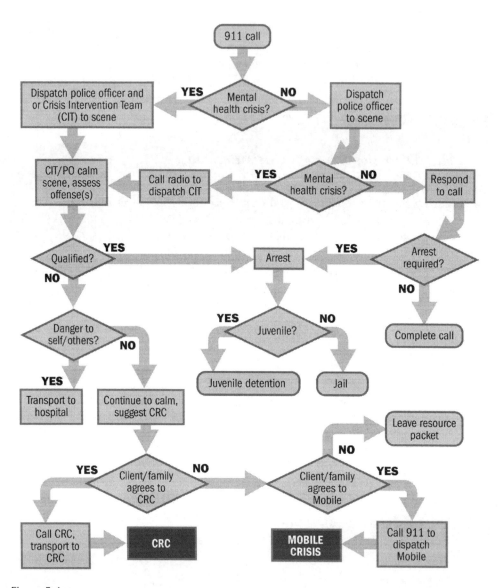

Figure 5.4

CIT Flowchart

62 percent of the men had confirmed or probable history of mental health issues

100 percent of the women had confirmed or probable mental health issues

80 percent of men were armed (60 percent with a firearm)

100 percent of women were armed (50 percent with a firearm, 50 percent with a knife)

In 87 percent of all cases, the individual had suicidal ideations prior to and/or during the incident, and . . .

36 percent were under the influence of alcohol at the time of the incident

PRACTITIONER'S CORNER 5.2

The Dangerousness Standard

Contributor: Jim Ruiz, PhD

There are also those infrequent instances when danger is present. We responded to a call in the Garden District of New Orleans regarding a person with mental illness manifesting violent behavior. When we arrived, the wife and neighbors were in front of the residence. They advised that the husband had been acting out all morning, and had threatened the wife with a knife. It was also learned that he was boiling water in the kitchen. Boiling water is a common weapon in New Orleans. It is more dangerous when grits are prepared in the boiling water as it has a thick consistency that remains in place once poured. It has also garnered the name "Cajun Napalm." Despite his behavior, there were complications. First, the house was in both his and his wife's names. If he wanted to tear the house up, that was his right as it was community property. We turned off the natural gas to the house so the stove would be inoperable, and waited about 30 minutes to allow any water that he may have been boiling to cool down. We made entry into the house without incident, but we could see he had a butcher's knife in his right hand. We created a barrier between him and us so in the event that he charged at us, we would have room to retreat. As we were trying to talk him into submission, the right hand holding the knife appeared from in the kitchen and it was thrown. It struck me handle first in my lower abdomen. I was frozen momentarily waiting for the pain when I heard the knife hit the floor. He finally surrendered without incident as we negotiated with him to be taken from the house on a gurney and placed into an ambulance so the neighbors would think he was sick, and being transported to the hospital. This gave us the opportunity to restrain him to the gurney, and transport him from the scene with no one injured.

Because police have little knowledge of the causes of mental illness, and usually conjure up the most violent cases from their past experiences, they arrive on the scene mentally geared up for, and in most cases, expecting a physical encounter. They also tend to want to handle the call quickly as rapid resolution of the call will reduce the possibility of violence. This approach can easily turn into a self-fulfilling prophecy. In many cases, police officers are given a commitment order from a coroner or medical examiner directing them to "present the body of Joe Smith at" some hospital. To the police, this amounts to an arrest warrant. When a person decides not to go with the police peacefully, that creates a "resisting arrest" scenario, and from there the situation tends to spin out of control.

From the perspective of the person with mental illness, s/he may or may not be aware of what is going on. In the vast majority of cases, they are aware, and they are not violent. These calls for

continued

service are usually the result of the person refusing to take or lying about whether they have taken their medication, thus causing the symptoms of the illness to manifest. In many cases, persons with mental illness report that the effects of the drugs are worse than the mental illness.

When the police arrive, and attempt to take the person, usually from their home to a hospital, the person refuses to go because s/he has either been to the hospital and has bad memories, and/or they are just afraid. As for the police, they, too, are afraid, and are interested in resolving the call as quickly as possible. This is a very volatile mix that usually leads to use of force, injuries, and at times death.

Commitment Statutes and the Role of Police

Under the authority of state statute, police in every state across the nation have the authority to initiate an involuntary commitment order requiring a person who presents as a danger to self or others to be transported to a mental health facility for an emergency evaluation. Depending on the structure of the community-based mental health system and the clientele served (children or adults, persons with physical health needs, males or females), the facility could be a hospital emergency room, a separate crisis stabilization unit (CSU), or some other designated receiving facility (Figure 5.5: Local emergency room). Two things should be noted here: First, if the circumstances allow, a PwMI in crisis will be given the opportunity to go for an evaluation voluntarily; should the individual refuse to go willingly and/or if the situation is such that it prevents this option (e.g., escalating violence toward self or others), a LEO may initiate an involuntary order and transport that person for the evaluation. The time for which the individual can be held involuntarily for evaluation is usually between 48 and 72 hours in most states, after which time a designated individual (most likely, a physician) may request a longer period of hospitalization if appropriate. It is also possible that a civil commitment process will be initiated. Examples of involuntary emergency commitment statutes are presented in the following box.

Emergency Evaluation Commitment Laws in the United States (2015)

Alaska
(ALASKA STAT. § 47.30.705 (a). If probable cause exists to believe that a person is gravely disabled or suffering from mental illness and is likely to cause serious harm to self or others, the person [may] be taken into custody and delivered to the nearest evaluation facility.

continued

District of Columbia

(D.C. CODE ANN. § 21–521.) An accredited officer or agent of the Department of Mental Health of the District of Columbia, or an officer authorized to make arrests in the District of Columbia, or a physician or qualified psychologist of the person in question, who has reason to believe that a person is mentally ill and, because of the illness, is likely to injure themselves or others if not immediately detained, may, without a warrant, take that person into custody.

Florida

FLA. STAT. § 394.463(1). [A] person may be taken to a receiving facility for involuntary examination if there is reason to believe that the person has mental illness and because of this (a) 1. the person has refused voluntary examination after conscientious explanation and disclosure of the purpose of the examination; 2. the person is unable to determine for him/herself whether examination is necessary; (b) 1. without care/treatment, the person is likely to suffer from neglect or refuse to care for him/herself; due to this his/her well-being is at risk; 2. there is substantial likelihood that without care/treatment the person will cause harm to him/herself or others through recent behavior.

Hawaii

HAW. REV. STAT. § 334–59 (d). If a law enforcement officer has reason to believe that a person is imminently dangerous to self or others, the officer shall call for assistance from mental health emergency workers designated by the director . . . (d) emergency hospitalization. if the physician or the psychologist who performs the emergency examination has reason to believe that the patient is: (1) mentally ill or suffering from substance abuse; (2) imminently dangerous to self or others; (3) in need of care or treatment, or both; the physician or the psychologist may direct [the] patient be hospitalized on an emergency basis or cause [the] patient to be transferred to another psychiatric facility for emergency hospitalization, or both.

Source: State Standards for Assisted Treatment. (2014, October 1). Retrieved July 23, 2015, from http://www.treatmentadvocacy center.org/storage/documents/state-standards-for-treatment.pdf

Police transport of a PwMI to a crisis or receiving center for a mental health assessment is viewed as a preferred diversion strategy at Intercept One (Figure 5.6). Unfortunately, however, officers are sometimes faced with constraints that prevent optimal diversion outcomes. In the case of emergency evaluation options, these constraints largely revolve around the manner of reception by mental health service providers at the receiving point. In particular, officers indicate that the outcome of a mental health crisis call, including those involving criminal behaviors and/or violence, are sometimes dependent on the officer's perception of the level of difficulty that will be encountered at a crisis receiving center or stabilization unit. In fact, police have reported that the arrest decision may take less time and provide a better outcome for the consumer (easier and immediate access to treatment/medication). Furthermore, for LEOs who are not trained in CIT or some other model of crisis intervention, the reluctance is based on discomfort with a lack of knowledge on what constitutes mental illness and

Figure 5.5

As a diversion strategy at Intercept One, police will often transport individuals in crisis to a local emergency room for mental health evaluation and crisis stabilization

Source: Bratina (2016)

on the logistics involved in the process of initiating an emergency evaluation. In other words, the officer's decision often rests on the amount of time that will be consumed navigating through the mental health system of care.

Oftentimes, choosing to arrest a PwMI will require less time—and perhaps may lead to consistent engagement in mental health and/or substance abuse treatment, something that many consumers will not receive (willingly or otherwise) in a community setting (Morabito, 2007). As a result of these and other obstacles previously discussed, research reveals that police are reluctant to initiate commitment paperwork and instead have developed informal decisions to manage PwMI whom they encounter in the field (Deane, Steadman, Borum, Veysey, & Morrissey, 1998; Morabito, 2007). Moreover, despite the increasing amount of training that LEOs are exposed to on the identification of mental health and substance abuse disorders and their training on proper deescalation techniques, the lack of resources available in the communities in which they serve creates obstacles that are difficult to overcome in the successful management of PwMI.

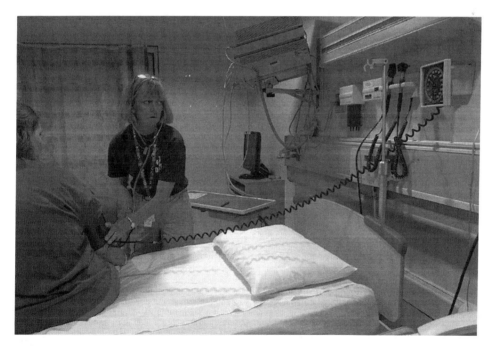

Figure 5.6

Woman Taking Blood Pressure of a Female Patient

Source: Jocelyn Augustino (2015) (FEMA Photo Library). [Public domain] via Wikimedia Commons

Additional Complexities of LEO–Citizen Encounters: Responding to Special Populations

The challenges presented so far in this chapter are becoming salient topics for research and policy exploration. The discussion, however, has revolved around general crisis calls involving adults with mental illness, and no particular emphasis has been placed on additional individual-level characteristics or circumstances of the persons whom first responders will encounter. In this section, the discussion turns toward additional complexities and challenges that may emerge, first, during a crisis event, but also at any other point throughout the criminal justice system. After the presentation of another case study, the chapter concludes with a brief introduction to police-specific mental health concerns.

Veterans

According to reports by the Substance Abuse and Mental Health Services Administration (SAMHSA) (2014) and the National Council for Behavioral Health (2012), there are approximately 25 million veterans living in the United States, many of whom have been exposed to traumatic events during combat which render them unable to easily reintegrate back into civilian society. In particular,

> since 2001, 2.4 million active duty and reserve military personnel were deployed to the wars in Iraq and Afghanistan. Of this group, 30% [or] nearly 730,000 men and women will have a mental health condition requiring treatment. Studies have shown that 18.5% of all OEF/OIF veterans[5] have post-traumatic stress disorder, Major Depression, or both PTSD and Major Depression. Other Mental Health Disorders are estimated to affect 11.6% of those without PTSD or Major Depression.
>
> ("Meeting the behavioral health needs of veterans," 2012, p. 3)

In addition to trauma and generalized mental health problems, other critical (and often related) issues faced by veterans include high rates of suicide, substance abuse, homelessness, and involvement in the criminal justice system (SAMHSA, 2014). In fact, PTSD (discussed in Chapter 4), suicide, and substance abuse are among the most significant issues facing military personnel and their family members. In 2014, an average of 20 veterans (women and men) committed suicide each day—a statistic that reveals a rate double that of the overall U.S. civilian population (Zoroya, 2016). Unfortunately, for many veterans, the wait list to be seen for any medical condition (including mental health) can take months (U.S. Department of Veteran Affairs [VA], Veterans Health Administration, 2016).

To reiterate the discussion in the preceding chapter, PTSD is short for post-traumatic stress disorder. It is a potentially serious mental health condition that often develops after a person has experienced a traumatic event or lived through significant trauma over a span of time (National Institute of Mental Health [NIMH], 2016). Typically occurring after a trigger in their environment, those suffering with the disorder may experience stress or fear, even when they are not in any danger. Other symptoms include flashbacks, bad dreams, lack of emotion, depression, tension, being easily startled, and difficulty sleeping (NIMH, 2016). Again, these factors may lead to *suicidal ideation*, or worse, a suicide attempt (Kopacz, Currier, Drescher, & Pigeon, 2016). Additionally, research indicates that although female veterans may be exposed less to traumatic combat situations, they are more likely to experience other kinds of traumatic events, including sexual harassment, sexual assault, and an overall lack of peer support from their fellow soldiers (Tsai, Rosenheck, Decker, Desai, & Harpaz-Rotem, 2012). Most importantly, all of these circumstances increase their likelihood for substance use or abuse, victimization, possible justice involvement, and suicide.

Many veterans with PTSD are given medications once they are finally seen by medical care providers; oftentimes, this further contributes to their issues. Some become addicted or begin to self-medicate—either because they develop a *tolerance* to the prescription medications and are seeking the perfect "cocktail" to relieve their symptoms, or they are unable to continue the prescription for a variety of reasons (e.g., lack of access to transportation, stable housing, and community-based services). Consequently, these individuals may begin to experience additional high-risk situations, such as loss of employment and personal relationships, and sometimes, homelessness (Figure 5.7). An increasing number of programs that specifically target homeless veterans have been conducted by the VA, and case outcomes have improved greatly when homeless programs (employment, healthcare, and housing services) are paired with mental health services (Tsai, et al., 2012).

Despite reports that an estimated 30 to 50 percent of homeless men have served in the military (Tessler, Rosenheck, & Gamache, 2001), data released by the U.S. Department of Housing and Urban Development (HUD) reveal that the proportion of homeless veterans has decreased in recent years. In fact, on a single night in January 2015, there were fewer than 48,000 homeless veterans and only 34 percent of this group living in unsheltered conditions—estimates that are down from previous years (U.S. Department of Housing and Urban Development [HUD], 2015). Of course, it must be noted that homeless at-risk veterans are a difficult population to track, and therefore, the data should be interpreted conservatively.

Across the United States, recent efforts have focused on expanding capacity inside the VA system. In particular, President Obama issued an executive order in 2012 titled Access to Mental Health Services for Veterans, Service Members, and Military Families. This order called for the VA to hire 800 peer-to-peer counselors and 1,600 mental

Figure 5.7

Broken American Hero—Harlem, New York City, United States

Source: By primeeyefab. Adobe Stock [Standard License]

health professionals, and to establish a small number of pilot projects involving community-based care providers, with the goal of overall improvement in the mental health
system (nationalcouncil.org, 2012). Moreover, a number of jurisdictions have established
Veterans' Treatment Courts, which will be discussed in more detail later in Chapter 7
of this text.

Despite attempts to provide different types of medical care through "Vet Centers"
that are scattered throughout cities in each state, not all veterans are eligible to use

these services because supply is limited and many consumers choose not to use these programs (allegedly, only 33 percent reported ever using VA services). Homeless veterans—in particular, those with multiple diagnoses—are much less likely to have ever used VA services or to obtain access should they attempt to use them (Tessler, Rosenheck, & Gamache, 2001). And further, research findings (in particular, those involving individuals with PTSD) can only reveal information related to individuals who are actively seeking/receiving services. It is safe to assume that many more soldiers, sailors, airmen, and marines have PTSD who have not come forward. The problem with gaps in service or an overall lack of engagement is that there is a significant proportion of individuals who are suffering with co-occurring PTSD or other mental health disorders and substance abuse who are not seeking help. Such individuals are at risk to themselves and others, and a combination of symptoms and maladaptive behaviors may lead to critical encounters with police. Although CIT programs and modified versions of CIT and MHFA do incorporate modules on veterans, PTSD, homelessness and supportive housing needs, and co-occurring substance abuse with this population, the brevity with which the information is delivered is probably insufficient, and continuing education related to these issues should be considered. Furthermore, police and other first responders who are not selected for or able to attend specialized training programs such as CIT may not have enough knowledge as to the prime issues facing this population of citizens. Finally, in the context of self-care among first responders, many of whom are veterans themselves, there is a tremendous amount of stigma that prevents this group from seeking services; as discussed briefly later, this presents a host of additional issues for departments and their officers.

Juveniles

Youth with emotional, mental, and behavioral health disabilities are more likely to be arrested and incarcerated when compared to their peer counterparts without disabilities (Holmquist, 2013). In fact, research has confirmed that youth offenders experience a significantly higher rate of diagnosable mental and behavioral health disorders in relation to the general youth population. (50 to 70 percent vs. 9 to 13 percent; see Schubert & Mulvey, 2014). Based upon these trends, there is an increased need for attention on challenges in relation to police encounters with juveniles who have mental and behavioral health disorders.

School-Related Concerns

The most substantial challenges related to police encounters with this population rise from what has been referred to as the *school-to-prison pipeline (STPP)*, which refers to policies and practices that appear to be used to push students out of the classroom and into the juvenile justice system ("School-to-Prison Pipeline," 2016). It is important to address this phenomenon when discussing police encounters with such juveniles because the pipeline reflects the prioritization of incarceration over education. Sadly, "twenty percent of youth offenders with emotional or behavioral health problems reported that they were arrested while in secondary schools" (Holmquist, 2013, p. 3).

The majority of negative outcomes related to STPP are a product of the heightened use of zero-tolerance policies that automatically impose severe punishments on students, regardless of any circumstances surrounding an offense (ACLU, 2008). Such policies have had a detrimental effect on rates of detention, suspension, expulsion, and even arrests among youth (Amurao, 2013). For example, student suspension rates have increased from 1.7 million in 1974 to 3.1 million in 2000—the most dramatic increases being among minorities and those students who have a history of abuse and neglect, poverty, and physical or mental health disabilities. Statistics reveal that rates of out-of-school suspension among students with behavioral and mental health disorders are slightly more than double that of students without disabilities (13 percent vs. 6 percent). Even more unsettling are reports that 92,000 youth were arrested or referred to law enforcement during the 2011–2012 school year; of these youth, "those with mental and behavioral health disorders represented a quarter of the population, while they were only 12% of the overall student body" (ACLU, 2008, p. 1).

The school-to-prison pipeline has led to more school districts increasing the use of police officers or school resource officers (SROs) as first responders to discipline disruptive students. According to the Center for Problem-Oriented Policing (2017), these sworn officers are expected to maintain three significant roles within schools: law enforcement, law-related counselors, and law-related educators. Current emphasis relies on their role as law enforcement, forcing them to deal with disruptive youth struggling with mental and behavioral health issues and referring them directly to the juvenile justice system. Controversy has emerged in regard to the use of SROs in an educational environment for juveniles with mental and behavioral health disorders. The competing missions between schools and the justice system create significant challenges for dealing with youth in general. Many of these challenges are linked to a lack of resources, training, and education related to student behavior as it relates to mental and behavioral health. In short, law enforcement, education professionals, and emergency personnel are not receiving adequate training and knowledge on how to manage students with mental and behavioral health issues.

Solutions

The most useful solutions for the current issue include the development of crisis intervention–based training and diversion programs geared toward decriminalization of youth. For example, some improvements in police–youth encounters have been seen when first responders are trained in *Crisis Intervention Training for Youths (CIT-Y)*, a modified version of CIT. Not only can this effective pre-arrest diversion technique be utilized for law enforcement, but it also works with schools, SROs, emergency response services, youth mental health providers, and parents to accomplish various goals (NAMI, 2009). CIT-Y training ranges from 8 to 40 hours, depending upon the jurisdiction, and provides a strict curriculum that embraces early intervention by merging with mental health services to prevent youth from becoming involved in the juvenile justice system. Aside from CIT-Y, other diversion programs have been developed and have revealed successful outcomes; examples include Children in Crisis (CIC) and Children's Crisis Intervention Training (CCIT) (NAMI, 2009); in the very recently updated SIM, such programs would fall under the newly introduced "Intercept 0", as early-intervention community diversion strategies (Vincent-Roller, 2016). Scholars recommend that diverting youth into community-based services at the earliest point of contact is the most influential and cost efficient. Similar to the SPRs discussed earlier, through partnerships with local mental health resources, youth-based diversion programs provide youth with necessary treatment while preventing crime and keeping the community safe (Vanderloo & Butters, 2012).

CIT-Y and other youth crisis intervention training programs are relatively new; thus, research on their outcomes is extremely limited. Not surprising, existing research suggests that programs that partner mental health and juvenile justice providers show successful outcomes. In particular, there is a decrease in the number of youth who are placed in residential and secure juvenile placement facilities and also significant support for mental health and recidivism outcomes (Vanderloo & Butters, 2012). Findings also show a significant reduction of symptoms and risk behaviors, improvement in functioning, and a decrease in recidivism rates; however, comparison groups were not matched on demographics or historical data, indicating once more the need for more research in this area. To produce meaningful results, it is essential that programs provide pre- and post-tests on training participants, construct program evaluations outside of training evaluations, and collect baseline data prior to implementing the program in order to collect supportive empirical evidence (NAMI, 2009).

Another diversion strategy is the use of *civil citations* as means of providing youth with the opportunity to change their behavior and avoid a felony record. The Florida Department of Juvenile Justice civil citation initiative represents a shift in managing first-time, nonviolent juvenile offenders (Florida Department of Juvenile Justice, 2015). The Civil Citation Program (CCP) allows police officers to issue citations rather than arrest youth ages 8 to 17 who commit misdemeanor offenses. Once cited, youth undergo two psychological assessments to determine criminogenic risk factors. The results of these assessments are then used to create an individualized treatment plan that embraces restorative justice elements, as well as community-based services. If the youth fails to complete their plan, they are then arrested and processed through the traditional juvenile justice system. According to program statistics, CCP has been a successful diversion measure, in that it has improved access to treatment services and provided many youth the opportunity to avoid arrest and further processing through the justice system, with a recidivism rate of only 3 percent. Furthermore, reports indicate that CCP is more cost effective, saving taxpayers more than 50 million dollars since its implementation in 2007 (National Criminal Justice Association, n.d.).

Key Points Thus Far

Consistent with the traditional funnel framework, the SIM can serve as a roadmap to effectively divert PwMI out of the criminal justice system to achieve the greatest impact on recidivism with this population; diversion strategies are available at the first interception. In fact, the research indicates that public safety risks are reduced when police and other first responders are trained in deescalation techniques, have an improved understanding of mental health and substance abuse disorders, and have the resources to provide appropriate service linkage to those in need. Conversely, current polices, programs, and practices in many jurisdictions do not properly identify and prioritize the mental health needs of police and other criminal justice actors who, in the course of their work, are subjected to trauma and stress on a regular basis. The remainder of this chapter provides an introductory discussion of issues pertaining to the mental health and wellness of the police.

The Mental Health and Well-Being of Police

Historically, little attention has been paid to the mental health maintenance of police officers and other first responders who are charged with resolving many of the social problems just set forth in the preceding sections (e.g., homelessness, PTSD, suicide risk, substance abuse, and co-occurring substance abuse and mental health disorders). What we do know, however, is that police undergo an enormous amount of stress (Ruiz, 1993), and due to the nature of the stress and the intervening trauma they encounter in the field, they are subject to their own mental health and substance abuse problems (O'Hara, Violanti, Levenson, & Clark, 2013). The most concerning issue is that police are even more resistant to seeking help/services than the general population. A great deal of the resistance can be attributed to stigma and role expectations. Stigma related to mental illness, such as presumptions of dangerousness and instability, were discussed in Chapter 1. With regard to role expectations of police, public perceptions revolve around this ideal moral being who is physically strong, mentally healthy, and emotionally balanced. Any sign of weakness in terms of mental or physical problems may render them incapable of properly doing the job. Public criticism (sometimes accompanied by violence) and fatigue due to the hours and on-the-job expectations, as well as dealing with untreated psychiatric conditions, follow them in both their professional and personal lives.

Compassion Fatigue: A phenomenon that is directly related to feelings of exhaustion and burnout that helping professionals experience after meeting the physical and emotional needs of the clients they serve (C. Lane, personal communication, June 11, 2016). Negative effects of compassion fatigue may include anger and irritability, increased cynicism, intimacy problems and problems in personal relationships, and suicidal thoughts.

Police Stress

Everyone experiences stress at some time. In fact, some levels of stress may actually benefit an individual—with regard to policing in particular, in helping to avoid dangerous situations and to motivate problem-solving responses under a variety of conditions and circumstances. The problem arises, however, when the levels of stress reach beyond what is considered "normal"; in other words, when they increase in frequency and intensity and persist without help or treatment support. For reasons discussed previously (e.g., stigma), this is often the case with police work. Clearly, police officers encounter stress-provoking situations on a day-to-day basis—some involving the exposure to traumatic events. In fact, there is a growing body of research related to the effects of *secondary traumatic stress (STS)* or *vicarious trauma* and burnout on police, mental health and social workers, and other human services and emergency medical response personnel (e.g., see Cieslak, Shoji, Douglas, Melville, Luszczynska, & Benight, 2014 for a review of the research).

Secondary traumatic stress (STS) may occur when an individual is indirectly exposed to at least one single traumatic event as recounted by another. The affected individual will experience symptoms that mimic post-traumatic stress disorder (PTSD).

Although the concept is often used interchangeably with vicarious trauma, they are not the same. Rather, vicarious trauma refers to the cognitive changes that may occur as a result of empathy from cumulative exposure to the traumatic event of another.

Burnout refers to work-related emotional exhaustion, which results from occupational stress. It is not to be used interchangeably with STS or vicarious trauma.

Source: National Child Traumatic Stress Network, Secondary Traumatic Stress Committee (2011).

The literature suggests that there are two types of stress associated with police work: organizational and operational. Organizational stress relates to factors such as rotating shift work, department culture, and interpersonal conflicts with other officers. Operational stress refers to the nature of police work and includes factors such as extended periods of boredom that are sharply contrasted with extreme traumatic events that provoke fear and unpredictability (Chae & Boyle, 2013). Unfortunately, untreated or delayed treatment for stress may lead to an increased susceptibility to other behavioral disorders, including anxiety, depression, and substance abuse. A continued failure to recognize stress and its effects (mental and physical), and to find a legitimate and safe stress-relief outlet to express feelings of frustration and disappointment at end of shift or any other time, can lead to problems with personal relationships, particularly when substance abuse (usually alcohol) is also used as a coping strategy. As a result, police and other first responders are susceptible to other psychological consequences which may include, *compassion fatigue*, self-rejection, and self-directed violence, including the risk of suicide (Chae & Boyle, 2013; O'Hara, et al., 2013).

Police Suicide

A national suicide fact sheet for the general population of adults reported that in 2013, there were approximately 41,149 suicides committed in the United States (a rate of 12.6 per 100,000, or 113 each day) (Centers for Disease Control [CDC], 2015). According to the report, 9.3 million adults (aged 18 and older) thought about suicide in the past year, 2.7 million people made a plan, and an estimated 1.3 million attempted suicide. Although existing comparative data on police-specific suicides are inconsistent in terms of reported risk compared with that of the general population, national data on occupational comparisons do consistently report increased risk for suicide among "protective services" or "service" workers, a category that includes police officers (Milner, Spittal, Pirkis, & La Montagne, 2013). In fact, in one study that examined workplace vs. nonworkplace national suicide rates between the period of 2003–2010, findings indicated that the workplace suicide rate for those in "protective services" occupations was 3.5 times greater than that of U.S. workers overall (Tiesman, Konda, Hartley, Menéndez, Ridenour, & Hendricks, 2015).

In a recent study based on web surveillance of suicides among LEOs between 2009 and 2013, findings revealed the following demographic trends related to completed suicides: a higher proportion of male LEOs between the ages of 40 and 44 complete suicide (92 vs. 6 percent, on average across all three years under examination); the average number of years of service among completers is about 15 to 19 years and, most often, among LEOs ranking below sergeant (O'Hara, et al., 2013). In corroboration with other research, the O'Hara et al. study revealed that the weapon of choice is a firearm. Of the web reports where a perceived reason was stated, personal problems of the officer was most commonly cited. Most concerning is that many departments stated that they did not notice any signs of suicidal ideation or possible imminent attempt.

Regardless of any inconsistencies in research and reported statistics, an officer taking his or her life has a significant impact on all parties involved—including the department.

Consequently, programming and policy must continue to be forthcoming with regard to critical-incident stress debriefing and ongoing mandatory periodic psychological assessments of officers. Effective strategies have included confidential peer-counseling programs, psychoeducation, and prevention training programs (Chae & Boyle, 2013).

Take-Home Message

Law enforcement has played an increasingly predominant role in the management of persons experiencing mental health disorders, with roughly 7 to 10 percent of encounters involving persons with mental illness (Franz & Borum, 2011). Thus, their role as first responders is crucial, in that they have the most discretion in resolving disputes involving persons with mental illness and have the best chance of diverting them from the justice system (Franz & Borum, 2011). In the past, mental health and law enforcement have not worked closely together, causing various challenges when dealing with persons with mental illness. Unfortunately, empirical and some anecdotal evidence suggests that police quite often become frustrated with the process of accessing crisis and emergency treatment services. In particular, police have reported encounters with treatment providers who are antagonistic toward them, making efficient consumer linkages and engagement in services difficult, if not impossible (Cross, et al., 2014; Franz & Borum, 2011; Ogloff, et al., 2013). Consequently, when diversion seems unlikely, police may feel compelled to arrest a citizen in crisis just to ensure imminent safety and access to treatment, albeit in a jail setting. This practice has been termed *mercy booking* (Reisig & Kane, 2014). Limited training and knowledge about mental illness, as well as the inability to obtain adequate resources and alternatives, have also contributed to current problems. The overarching theme of combined perceptions is that budgetary constraints in mental health services have created an overreliance on law enforcement when a mental health crisis occurs. Programs such as CIT and MHFA are extremely beneficial in terms of diverting a consumer in crisis to mental health services/treatment. Existing research indicates that these training programs increase knowledge among participants, thereby increasing empathy and reducing much of the stigma associated with mental health and substance abuse disorders at the most crucial point in time—before an individual case penetrates the criminal or juvenile justice system (e.g., see Compton, Esterberg, McGee, Kotwicki, & Oliva, 2006; Jorm, Kitchener, Sawyer, Scales, & Cvetkovski, 2010).

Unfortunately, at the same time, police and other first responders are struggling with job-related stress, which oftentimes leads to their own mental health–related issues. Given the stigma associated with mental illness and recovery, criminal justice officials neglect to engage in treatment services, which presents a number of issues that are only exacerbated during the course of their work. For so many reasons, it is essential that we continue to devise training programs that educate and improve responses to mental illness and co-occurring substance abuse. It is only when communities improve attitudes and access to services that we can effectively divert PwMI out of the criminal justice system and make significant reductions in the criminalization of mental illness.

Many of these challenges are not new, yet further research is needed to test the ways that crisis responders should continue to build on multidisciplinary collaborations, in particular those that involve diversion from further penetration into the criminal justice system. We must continue to train key personnel on how to deescalate crises and transport consumers to places other than jail for assessment, stabilization, and treatment. Furthermore, process and outcome data must be collected and analyzed and utilized to improve programs. Finally, with regard to the mental health maintenance of police and other gatekeepers, department supervisors should be trained in recognizing burnout or compassion fatigue, and policies should be developed and implemented with regard to addressing it. As a related measure, agencies should engage in mandatory critical-incident stress debriefing periods, whether after a traumatic event or at the close of each shift, where officers have the opportunity to safely discuss their concerns and frustrations in a supportive environment and develop useful coping strategies in dealing with both operational and organizational stressors.

QUESTIONS FOR CLASSROOM DISCUSSION

1. What are some of the challenges and needs of LEOs who come into contact with PwMI who are experiencing a mental health–related crisis? What are some of the challenges and needs of PwMI who come into contact with LEOs during a mental health crisis? Are these challenges and needs complementary or conflicting?
2. It has often been said that "CIT is not just training." What do you think is meant by this statement? How else might communities need to respond so that programs such as CIT and MHFA are successful at diverting PwMI and maintaining safety for first responders, consumers, and community members?
3. How might stigma play a role in the school-to-prison pipeline?

KEY TERMS & ACRONYMS

- Burnout
- Civil citation
- Compassion fatigue
- Crisis Intervention Training for Youths (CIT-Y)
- Crisis Stabilization Unit (CSU)
- Decompensation
- Mercy booking

- Mobile Crisis Unit or Team (MCU or MCT)
- Operation Enduring Freedom (OEF)
- Operation Iraqi Freedom (OIF)
- Parens patriae
- School-to-prison pipeline (STPP)

- Secondary traumatic stress (STS)
- Specialized policing responses (SPRs)
- Suicide by cop
- Suicidal ideation
- Tolerance
- Trigger
- Vicarious trauma
- Welfare check

Notes

1. Transcript is from audio related to a fatal police shooting that occurred on December 26, 2015, in West Garfield Park, a section of the city of Chicago. As transcribed, the audio covers the dispatch of units and the eventual call of "shots fired" during the minutes between about 4:26 and 4:41 a.m. Taken and slightly adapted from Nickeas (2016), *Chicago Tribune* (Jeremy Gorner contributed).
2. The "Memphis model" of CIT training, although the original format and the most replicated, is not the only model used across the United States (Cross, Mulvey, Schubert, Griffin, Filone, Winckworth-Prejsnar, DeMatteo, & Heilbrun, 2014).
3. Scenario taken and adapted from a CIT training program in Southeastern Florida.
4. Summary of statistics retrieved from American Association of Suicidology (2014), as reported from the following two studies: Mohandie, K., Meloy, J.R., & Collins, P.I. (2009). Suicide by cop among officer involved shooting cases. *Journal of Forensic Science, 54*(2), 456–462 and Mohandie, K., & Meloy, J.R. (2011). Suicide by cop among female subjects in officer involved shooting cases. *Journal of Forensic Science, 56*(3), 664–668.
5. Operation Enduring Freedom (OEF) and Operation Iraqi Freedom (OIF) (Publichealh.va.gov).

Bibliography

American Association of Suicidology. (2014). *Suicide by Cop.* Washington, DC: American Association of Suicidology.

Amurao, C. (2013). *Fact Sheet: How Bad is the School-to-Prison Pipeline.* PBS: Tavis Smiley Reports [website]. Retrieved from http://www. pbs. org/wnet/tavissmiley/tsr/education-underarrest/school-to-prison-pipeline-fact-sheet.

Bond, K. S., Jorm, A. F., Kitchener, B. A., & Reavley, N. J. (2015). Mental Health First Aid Training for Australian Medical and Nursing Students: An Evaluation Study. *BMC Psychology, 3*(1), 1.

Borrelli, A. (May 12, 2015). Vestal Man's Police Brutality Lawsuit Goes to Jury Trial. *Press and Sun-Bulletin.* Retrieved from http://www.pressconnects.com/story/news/local/2015/05/12/vestal-mans-police-brutality-lawsuit-goes-jury-trial/27189879/.

Brady, K., Back, S., & Coffey, S. (2004). Substance Abuse and Posttraumatic Stress Disorder. *Current Directions in Psychological Science, 13*(5), 206–209. Retrieved April 22, 2015, from JSOTR.

Carpenter, R. A., Falkenburg, J., White, T. P., & Tracy, D. K. (2013). Crisis Teams: Systematic Review of Their Effectiveness in Practice. *Psychiatrist, 37*, 232–237.

Casey, K. A. (2015). The Effectiveness of Mobile Crisis Outreach Model (Unpublished Doctoral Dissertation). The University of Texas at Austin, Austin, TX.

Center for Problem-Oriented Policing. (2017). Common roles for school resource officers. Retrieved from http://www.popcenter.org/responses/school_police/2

Centers for Disease Control [CDC]. (2015). Suicide: Facts at a glance [Fact sheet]. Retrieved from https://www.cdc.gov/violenceprevention/pdf/suicide-datasheet-a.pdf

Chae, M. H., & Boyle, D. J. (2013). Police Suicide: Prevalence, Risk, and Protective Factors. *Policing, 36*(1), 91–118.

Cieslak, R., Shoji, K., Douglas, A., Melville, E., Luszczynska, A., & Benight, C. C. (2014). A Meta-Analysis of the Relationship between Job Burnout and Secondary Traumatic Stress among Workers with Indirect Exposure to Trauma. *Psychological Services, 11*(1), 75–86.

Compton, M. T., Broussard, B., Hankerson-Dyson, D., Krishan, S., & Stewart-Hutto, T. (2011). Do Empathy and Psychological Mindedness Affect Police Officers' Decision to Enter Crisis Intervention Team Training? *Psychiatric Services*, *62*(6), 632–638.

Compton, M. T., Esterberg, M. L., McGee, R., Kotwicki, R. J., & Oliva, J. R. (2006). Brief Reports: Crisis Intervention Team Training: Changes in Knowledge, Attitudes, and Stigma Related to Schizophrenia. *Psychiatric Services*, *57*(8), 1199–1202.

Compton, M. T., & Kotwicki, R. J. (2007). *Responding to Individuals with Mental Illnesses*. Sudbury, MA: Jones & Bartlett Learning.

Cross, A. B., Mulvey, E. P., Schubert, C. A., Griffin, P. A., Filone, S., Winckworth-Prejsnar, K., DeMatteo, D., & Heilbrun, K. (2014). An Agenda for Advancing Research on Crisis Intervention Teams for Mental Health Emergencies. *Psychiatric Services*, *65*(4), 530–536.

Curtis, G. B. (1976). The Checkered Career of Parens Patriae: The State as Parent or Tyrant? *DePaul Law Review*, *25*(4), 895–915.

Deane, M., Steadman, H., Borum, R., Veysey, B., & Morrissey, J. (1998). Police Mental Health System Interactions: Program Types and Needed Research. *Psychiatric Services*, *50*(1), 99–101.

DeMatteo, D., LaDuke, C., Locklair, B. R., & Heilbrun, K. (2013). Community-Based Alternatives for Justice-Involved Individuals with Severe Mental Illness: Diversion, Problem-Solving Courts, and Reentry. *Journal of Criminal Justice*, *41*, 64–71.

Ellis, H. A. (2014). Effects of a Crisis Intervention Team (CIT) Training Program Upon Police Officers before and after Crisis Intervention Team Training. *Archives of Psychiatric Nursing*, *28*, 10–16.

Epperson, M. (2016, January 13). Where police violence encounters mental illness. *The New York Times*. Retrieved from http://www.nytimes.com on January 3, 2017.

Farmer, C., Vaughan, C., Garnett, J., & Weinick, R. (2014). *Pre-Deployment Stress, Mental Health, and Help-Seeking Behaviors among Marines* (pp. 1–73). Santa Monica, CA: Rand Corporation.

Feldman, D. (2014, May 24). Gunman kills six in drive-by shooting in California college town. *Reuters*. Retrieved from http://www.reuters.com on January 3, 2017.

Fellner, J. (May, 2015). Callous and Cruel: Use of Force against Inmates with Mental Disabilities in US Jails and Prisons. *Human Rights Watch* [Report]. Retrieved from https://www.hrw.org/report/2015/05/12/callous-and-cruel/use-force-against-inmates-mental-disabilities-us-jails-and.

Florida Department of Juvenile Justice (October, 2015). *Civil Citation Model Plan: A Guide to Implementation* (Florida Civil Citation Initiative, Section 985.12). Tallahassee, FL: Department of Juvenile Justice.

Franz, S., & Borum, R. (2011). Crisis Intervention Teams May Prevent Arrests of People with Mental Illnesses. *Police Practice and Research*, *12*, 265–272.

Gostomski, A. (2012). Vancouver Police Department: Police Officers' Assessment of the Effectiveness of the Crisis Intervention Training Program and Its Impact on their Attitudes towards their Interactions with Persons Living with Serious Mental Illness (Doctoral Dissertation) Arts & Social Sciences: School of Criminology.

Greenberg, J. (2013). *Comprehensive Stress Management* (13th Ed., pp. 61–64). Boston: McGraw-Hill.

Griffin, P. A., Heilbrun, K., Mulvey, E. P., DeMatteo, D., & Schubert, C. A. (2015). *Sequential Intercept Model and Criminal Justice: Promoting Community Alternatives for Individuals with Serious Mental Illness*. New York, NY: Oxford University Press.

Hails, J., & Borum, R. (2003). Police Training and Specialized Approaches to Respond to People with Mental Illnesses. *Crime & Delinquency*, *49*(1), 52–61.

Hart, L. M., Mason, R. J., Kelly, C. M., Cvetkovski, S., & Jorm, A. F. (2016). 'Teen Mental Health First Aid': A Description of the Program and an Initial Evaluation. *International Journal of Mental Health Systems, 10*(1), 1.

Hartford, K, Carey, R., & Mendonca, J. (2006). Pre-Arrest Diversion of People with Mental Illness: Literature Review and International Survey. *Behavioral Sciences & the Law, 24*, 845–856. doi: 10.1002/bsl.738NS.

Heilbrun, K., DeMatteo, D., Yasuhara, K., Brooks-Holliday, S., Shah, S., King, C., . . . & Laduke, C. (2012). Community-Based Alternatives for Justice-Involved Individuals with Severe Mental Illness Review of the Relevant Research. *Criminal Justice and Behavior, 39*(4), 351–419.

Heild, C. (2016, September 20). Police expert: Officers in Boyd shooting were 'reckless'. *Albuquerque Journal*. Retrieved from https://www.abqjournal.com on January 3, 2017.

Holmquist, J. (2013). *Students with Disabilities & the Juvenile Justice System: What Parents Need to Know*. Minneapolis, MN: PACER Center.

International Association of Chiefs of Police (IACP). (2010). *Building Safer Communities: Improving Police Response to Persons with Mental Illness* [Recommendations from the IACP National Policy Summit]. Retrieved from http://www.theiacp.org/portals/0/pdfs/ImprovingPoliceResponsetoPersonsWith-MentalIllnessSummit.pdf.

Jensen, K. B., Morthorst, B. R., Vendsborg, P. B., Hjorthøj, C. R., & Nordentoft, M. (2015). The Effect of the Mental Health First-Aid Training Course Offered Employees in Denmark: Study Protocol for a Randomized Waitlist-Controlled Superiority Trial Mixed with a Qualitative Study. *BMC Psychiatry, 15*(1), 1.

Jha, A., Kitchener, B. A., Pradhan, P. K., Shyangwa, P., & Nakarmi, B. (2012). Mental Health First Aid Programme in Nepal. *Journal of Nepal Health Research Council, 10*(22), 258–260.

Jorm, A. F., Kitchener, B. A., O'Kearney, R., & Dear, K. B. (2004). Mental health first aid training of the public in a rural area: a cluster randomized trial [ISRCTN53887541]. *BMC psychiatry, 4*(1), 1.

Jorm, A. F., Kitchener, B. A., Sawyer, M. G., Scales, H., & Cvetkovski, S. (2010). Mental Health First Aid Training for High School Teachers: A Cluster Randomized Trial. *BMC Psychiatry, 10*(1), 1.

Justiceforvets.org. (2015). *What Is a Veterans Treatment Court?* Retrieved April 25, 2015 from http://justiceforvets.org/what-is-a-veterans-treatment-court.

Kelly, C. M., Mithen, J. M., Fischer, J. A., Kitchener, B. A., Jorm, A. F., Lowe, A., & Scanlan, C. (2011). Youth Mental Health First Aid: A Description of the Program and an Initial Evaluation. *International Journal of Mental Health Systems, 5*(4), 1–9.

Kitchener, B. A. & Jorm, A. F. (2006). Mental Health First Aid Training: Review of Evaluation Studies. *Australian and New Zealand Journal of Psychiatry, 40*, 6–8.

Kopacz, M. S., Currier, J. M., Drescher, K. D., & Pigeon, W. R. (2016). Suicidal Behavior and Spiritual Functioning in a Sample of Veterans Diagnosed with PTSD. *Journal of Injury and Violence Research, 8*(1), 6.

Lamb, H. R., & Weinberger, L. E. (2014). Decarceration of US jails and prisons: where will persons with serious mental illness go? *Journal of the American Academy of Psychiatry and the Law Online, 42*(4), 489–494.

Lord, V. B., & Bjerregaard, B. (2014). Helping Persons with Mental Illness: Partnerships between Police and Mobile Crisis Units. *Victims and Offenders, 9*, 455–474.

Lowery, W., Kindy, K., Alexander, K. L., Tate, J., Jenkins, J., & Rich, S. (June 30, 2015). Distraught People, Deadly Results. *The Washington Post*. Retrieved from http://www.washingtonpost.com/sf/investigative/2015/06/30/distraught-people-deadly-results/.

Malone, D., Marriott, S., Newton-Howes, G., Simmonds, S., & Tyrer, P. (2007). Community mental health teams (CMHTs) for people with severe mental illnesses and disordered personality. *Cochrane Database of Systematic Reviews* 2007, Issue 3. Art. No.: CD000270. DOI: 10.1002/14651858.CD000270. pub2.

Mather, K., Winton, R., Ceasar, S., & Flores, A. (2014, May 24). Isla Vista shootings: Source names suspect in shooting rampage. *Los Angeles Times*. Retrieved from http://www.latimes.com on January 3, 2017.

McLaughlin, E. C. (March 19, 2015). Video: Dallas Police Open Fire on Schizophrenic Man with Screwdriver. *CNN*. Retrieved from http://www.cnn.com/2015/03/18/us/dallas-police-fatal-shooting-mentally-ill-man-video/.

Milner, A., Spittal, M. J., Pirkis, J., & LaMontagne, A. D. (2013). Suicide by Occupation: Systematic Review and Meta-Analysis. *British Journal of Psychiatry, 203*, 409–416.

Morabito, M. S. (2007). Horizons of Context: Understanding the Police Decision to Arrest People with Mental Illness. *Psychiatric Services, 58*(12), 1582–1587.

Morabito, M. S., Kerr, A. N., Watson, A., Draine, J., Ottati, V., & Angell, B. (2012). Crisis Intervention Teams and People with Mental Illness Exploring the Factors That Influence the Use of Force. *Crime & Delinquency, 58*(1), 57–77.

Morabito, M. S., & Socia, K. M. (2015). Is Dangerousness a Myth? Injuries and Police Encounters with People with Mental Illnesses. *Criminology & Public Policy, 14*(2), 253–276.

Munetz, M. R., & Griffin, P. A. (2006). Use of the sequential intercept model as an approach to decriminalization of people with serious mental illness. *Psychiatric Services, 57*(4), 544–549.

NAMI Minnesota. (n.d.) *Mental Health Mobile Crisis Response Teams*. St. Paul, MN: NAMI Minnesota. Retrieved from www.namihelps.org.

National Alliance on Mental Illness [NAMI] (2016). Calling 911 and talking with police [Webpage]. Retrieved at https://www.nami.org/Find-Support/Family-Members-and-Caregivers/Calling-911-and-Talking-with-Police.

National Child Traumatic Stress Network, Secondary Traumatic Stress Committee. (2011). *Secondary Traumatic Stress: A Fact Sheet for Child-Serving Professionals*. Los Angeles, CA, and Durham, NC: National Center for Child Traumatic Stress.

National Council for Behavioral Health. (November, 2012). Meeting the Behavioral Health Needs of Veterans: Operation Enduring Freedom & Operation Iraqi Freedom. Retrieved from http://www.thenationalcouncil.org/wp-content/uploads/2013/02/Veterans-BH-Needs-Report.pdf.

National Council for Behavioral Health. (2015). Community Mental Health Act. Retrieved from http://www.thenationalcouncil.org/about/national-mental-health-association/overview/community-mental-health-act/.

Nationalcouncil.org. (2012). *Meeting the Behavioral Needs of Veterans*. Retrieved April 25, 2015 from http://www.thenationalcouncil.org/wp-content/uploads/2013/02/Veterans-BH-Needs-Report.pdf.

National Institute of Mental Health. (November 3, 2016). Retrieved from https://www.nimh.nih.gov/health/topics/post-traumatic-stress-disorder-ptsd/index.shtml.

New South Wales Government. (2014). NSW Police Force: Community Issues, Mental Health. *NSWPF Mental Health Intervention Team*. Retrieved from http://www.police.nsw.gov.au/community_issues/mental_health.

Ogloff, J. R., Thomas, S. D., Luebbers, S., Baksheev, G., Elliott, I., Godfredson, J., . . . & Clough, J. (2013). Policing Services with Mentally Ill People: Developing Greater Understanding and Best Practice. *Australian Psychologist, 48*(1), 57–68.

O'Hara, A. F., Violanti, J. M., Levenson, R. L., & Clark, R. G. (2013). National Police Suicide Estimates: Web Surveillance Study III. *International Journal of Emergency Mental Health and Human Resilience, 15*(1), 31–38.

Ohlheiser, A. & Izadi, E. (2015, August 18). Judge: N.M. police officers will stand trial for 2014 fatal shooting of a homeless man. *The Washington Post.* Retrieved from https://www.washingtonpost.com on January 3, 2017.

Pearson, V. N. (2014). Police Officers on the Front Line as Mental Health Workers. *The Police Chief, 81,* 18–19.

Pennsylvania Mental Health & Justice Center for Excellence. (July 25, 2013). *Specialized Police Response in Pennsylvania: Moving toward Statewide Implementation.* Philadelphia, PA: Drexel University.

Pillay, P., & Thomas, S. D. M. (2015). Police Contact with Suicidal Individuals: A Comparison of Self-In flicted Suicidal Behavior and Potential Police Provoked Shooting Incidents. *International Journal of Emergency Mental Health and Human Resilience, 17*(2), 555–562.

Possis, E., Thao, B., Gavian, M., Leskela, J., Linardatos, E., Loughlin, J., & Strom, T. (2014). Driving Difficulties among Military Veterans: Clinical Needs and Current Intervention Status. *Military Medicine, 179*(6), 633–639. doi:10.7205/MlLMED-D-13–00327.

Reisig, M. D., & Kane, R. J. (2014). *The Oxford Handbook of Police and Policing.* New York, NY: Oxford University Press.

Ruiz, J. M. (1993). An Interactive Analysis between Uniformed Law Enforcement Officers and the Mentally Ill. *American Journal of Police, 12*(4), 149–162.

Ruiz, J. M. (2002). *Policing Persons with Mental Illness: The Pennsylvania Experience.* Harrisburg, PA: Pennsylvania State Data Center, Institute of State and Regional Affairs, Penn State Harrisburg.

Ruiz, J. M., & Miller, C. (2004). An Exploratory Study of Pennsylvania Police Officers' Perceptions of Dangerousness and Their Ability to Manage Persons with Mental Illness. *Police Quarterly, 7*(3), 359–371.

School-to-Prison Pipeline. (2016). American Civil Liberties Union Retrieved from https://www.aclu.org/issues/juvenile-justice/school-prison-pipeline.

Schubert, C. A., & Mulvey, E. P. (2014). Behavioral Health Problems, Treatment, and Outcomes in Serious Youthful Offenders. *Juvenile Justice Bulletin.* Retrieved from https://www.ojjdp.gov/pubs/242440.pdf.

Siegel, S. J. (2013). Capacity, Confidentiality and Consequences: Balancing Responsible Medical Care With Mental Health Law. *Current psychiatry reports, 15*(8), 380.

Simpson, J., & Morairty, G. (2013). *PTSD and Panic Disorder. Multimodal Treatment of Acute Psychiatric Illness: A Guide for Hospital Diversion* (pp. 106–128). Retrieved April 22, 2015 from JSTOR.

Skeem, J., & Bibeau, L. (2008). How Does Violence Potential Relate to Crisis Intervention Team Responses to Emergencies? *Psychiatric Services, 59*(2), 201–204.

Slate, R. N., Buffington-Vollum, J. K., & Johnson, W. W. (2013). *The criminalization of mental illness: Crisis and opportunity for the justice system.* Durham, NC: Carolina Academic Press.

Smydo, J., & Lord, R. (March 6, 2016). Data Shows Police Lack Crisis Intervention Team Training to Deal with Mentally Ill. *The Pittsburgh Post-Gazette.* Retrieved from http://www.post-gazette.com/news/health/2016/03/06/Pittsburgh-police-lack-Crisis-Intervention-Team-training-to-deal-with-mentally-ill/stories/201603060029.

Steadman, H. J., Deane, M. W., Borum, R., & Morrissey, J. P. (2000). Comparing Outcomes of Major Models of Police Responses to Mental Health Emergencies. *Psychiatric Services, 51*(5), 645–649.

Substance Abuse and Mental Health Service Administration [SAMHSA]. (2014). Veterans and Military Families Retrieved from http://www.samhsa.gov/veterans-military-families.

Svensson, B., & Hansson, L. (2014). Effectiveness of Mental Health First Aid Training in Sweden: A Randomized Controlled Trial with a Six-Month and Two-Year Follow-Up. *PLoS ONE, 9*(6), 1–8.

Tessler, R., Rosenheck, R., & Gamache, G. (2001). Gender Differences in Self-Reported Reasons for Homelessness. *Journal of Social Distress and the Homeless, 10*(3), 243–254.

The National Criminal Justice Association Center for Justice Planning. (n.d.). The Miami-Dade civil citation program: Diverting youth from system involvement. Retrieved from http://www.ncjp.org/index.php?q=content/miami-dade-civil-citation-program-diverting-youth-system-involvement.

Thompson, L., & Borum, R. (2006). Crisis Intervention Teams (CIT): considerations for knowledge transfer. In *Law Enforcement Executive Forum*. Paper 548.

Tiesman, H. M., Konda, S., Hartley, D., Menendez, C. C., Ridenour, M., & Hendricks, S. (2015). Suicide in U.S. Workplaces 2003–2010: A Comparison with Non-Workplace Suicides. *American Journal of Preventative Medicine, 48*(6), 674–682.

Tsai, J., Rosenheck, R. A., Decker, S. E., Desai, R. A., & Harpaz-Rotem, I. (2012). Trauma Experience among Homeless Female Veterans: Correlates and Impact on Housing, Clinical, and Psychosocial Outcomes. *Journal of Traumatic Stress, 25*(6), 624–632.

U.S. Department of Housing and Urban Development. (2015). HUD Reports Homelessness Continues to Decline Nationally: Progress Uneven as Some Communities Combat a Housing Affordability Crisis (HUD Press Release No. 15–149). Retrieved from http://portal.hud.gov/hudportal/HUD?src=/press/press_releases_media_advisories/2015/HUDNo_15–149.

U.S. Department of Veterans Affairs. (2016). Patient Access Data Retrieved from http://www.va.gov/health/access-audit.asp.

Vanderloo, M. J., & Butters, R. P. (2012). *Treating Offenders with Mental Illness: A Review of the Literature.* Utah: Utah Criminal Justice Center, University of Utah.

Von Drehle, D. (2014, May 27). Iraq vet killed in gunfire with police was turned away by VA hospital. *Time.* Retrieved from http://time.com on January 3, 2017.

Vincent-Roller, N. (2016, November 23). Introducing "intercept 0". [Web log post]. Retrieved January 10, 2017, from https://www.prainc.com.

Wallace, C., Mullen, P. E., & Burgess, P. (2004). Criminal Offending in Schizophrenia Over a 25-Year Period Marked by Deinstitutionalization and Increasing Prevalence of Comorbid Substance Use Disorders. *American Journal of Psychiatry, 161*(4), 716–727.

Watson, A. C., Ottati, V. C., Draine, J., & Morabito, M. (2011). CIT in Context: The Impact of Mental Health Resource Availability and District Saturation on Call Dispositions. *International Journal of Law and Psychiatry, 34*(4), 287–294.

Weaver, C. M., Joseph, D., Dongon, S. N., & Fairweather, A. (2013). Enhancing Services Response to Crisis Incidents Involving Veterans: A Role for Law Enforcement and Mental Health Collaboration. *Psychological Services, 10*(1), 66–72.

Wells, W., & Schafer, J. A. (2006). Officer Perceptions of Police Responses to Persons with a Mental Illness. *Policing: An International Journal of Police Strategies & Management, 29*(4), 578–601.

What Is CIT? (2016). National Alliance on Mental Illness [NAMI] Retrieved from http://www.nami.org/Get-Involved/Law-Enforcement-and-Mental-Health/What-Is-CIT.

Zoroya, G. (April 2, 2016). U.S. Military Suicides Remain High for the 7th Year. *Military Times.* Retrieved from http://www.militarytimes.com/story/military/2016/04/02/us-military-suicides-remain-high-7th-year/82550720/.

CHAPTER 6 **Intercept Two**
Pretrial Issues, Adjudication, and Sentencing/Jail

Meghan Kozlowski and Michele P. Bratina

Dave is a 32-year-old white male who was arrested for aggravated stalking on June 13, 2013. He had only been in California less than one year and was struggling to get on his feet. The arrest report read: "Dave states that he was tired of being homeless and hungry. Dave stated that he would rather stay in jail than have to worry about stealing food to survive." It also noted that he complained to the arresting officer about "nagging voices in his head" and that he purposely violated an injunction to go to jail. Upon intake at the county jail, Dave was screened for potential mental health issues and risk for suicide; the results indicated that he may have some history of treatment for mental illness, but that he did not pose a risk of self-harm at present. While in jail, Dave was further assessed by mental health staff, and after meeting with a public defender, was evaluated for competency. After two weeks of incarceration (and with no record of the competency evaluation results), correctional staff reported that Dave was agitated, pacing, and "gibbering" to himself. One correctional staff member reported that Dave seemed convinced that "the government" is recording every move he makes because they are planning on killing him when staff are not present. Dave has been neglecting his hygiene, and he refuses to eat any of his food, as he claims it is "probably poisoned." Recently, staff observed him to be extremely paranoid, constantly pacing in his cell, and screaming obscenities. Because of the paranoia, Dave has lost close to 10 pounds (case taken and adapted from Vail, 2015).

Introduction

Like "Dave" from the above case, offenders with mental health issues are often not diverted after their initial encounter with law enforcement, emergency medical personnel, or Mobile Crisis Teams. There are many reasons for this, and they may include the severity of offense, prior record, lack of police training in crisis intervention, and lack of community-based resources or other pre-booking diversion programs (Compton & Kotwicki, 2007). In such cases, the individual may be transported by police to the local jail or detention center, where he or she will be officially booked or processed and subsequently screened by correctional intake staff for custody issues, which may include mental health status, risk of self-harm/suicide, substance use/abuse, and propensity for violence (Compton & Kotwicki, 2007; Fagan & Ax, 2011; Osher, D'Amora, Plotkin, Jarrett, & Eggleston, 2012). Although this course of events certainly places a person with mental illness (PwMI) at risk for further penetration in the traditional justice system, it also moves the individual further along in the Sequential Intercept Model (SIM), thereby presenting opportunities for post-booking diversion strategies—the subject of this chapter.

Post-booking diversion at Intercept Two can occur after an arrest, during initial detention, during initial hearings, or during assistance by pre-trial services (DeMatteo, et al., 2013). A substantial part of diversion involves the availability and quality of resources related to the screening and assessment of offenders for mental health and co-occurring substance abuse after they have been arrested and subsequently charged with an offense. It also includes the screening and assessment for the risk of suicide/self-harm in secure confinement (Fagan & Ax, 2011).

Diversion programs allow the complex needs of PwMI to be managed in a community-based setting and remove the burden from correctional professionals who likely have minimal, if any, training in mental health intervention (Ryan, et al., 2010). This chapter provides some detail with regard to the application and evaluation of several diversion strategies, such as screening and assessment by correctional staff and the effectiveness of system integration in the development of effective jail diversion programming.

THERAPEUTIC INTERVENTION: MENTAL HEALTH SERVICES IN JAIL

In the community, mental health services are most likely provided by professional and/or licensed individuals who hold titles such as psychologist, licensed mental health counselor, and clinical social worker.

By comparison, in a correctional setting, mental health services are sometimes provided by paraprofessionals; this includes individuals who are employees of the correctional facility or persons who work for private companies who are contracted by the county, state, or government to work with correctional populations. Some of the positions held by these individuals include correctional counselor, drug treatment specialist, mental health technician, and inmate peer counselor (Fagan & Ax, 2011). Primary duties may include:

continued

- Crisis and suicide intervention services
- Development and review of individual treatment plans
- Mental health screening, evaluation, and assessment
- Maintenance of legible documentation

FAST FACT: IN THE UNITED STATES . . .

10 to 20 percent of police calls for service involve a mental health issue.

15 percent of males and 30 percent of females booked in jails each year have a serious mental illness.

20 to 24 percent of state prisoners and approximately 20 percent of local jail prisoners report a recent history of a mental health condition.

Source: National Alliance on Mental Illness [NAMI, 2016]; Treatment Advocacy Center [TAC, 2016]

Post-Booking Diversion: An Overview

Post-booking diversion programs are commonly categorized into three tiers, depending on an offender's stage in the legal process: pre-arraignment, post-arraignment, and mixed (Steadman, et al., 1995). Pre-arraignment programs involve the collaboration of jail and pre-trial services staff who work to negotiate client entry into mental health and other support services, secure client compliance, and obtain court concurrence. The goal at this level is the immediate identification and engagement of individuals needing mental health and/or substance abuse services before invoking the formal court process. Furthermore, pre-arraignment strategies save time and financial resources for the community and prevent criminalization and serious decompensation of a PwMI who would be more effectively served by another system of care (Griffin, Heilbrun, Mulvey, DeMatteo, & Schubert, 2015). Post-arraignment programs involve the collaboration of staff working in jails, community mental health centers, courts, and probation/pre-trial services. Programs at this stage focus on obtaining necessary mental health evaluations, negotiating treatment plans, obtaining program and client agreement, and obtaining satisfactory community supervision mechanisms for the court. A mixed program constitutes a combination of pre- and post-arraignment program organizations, staff, and issues as listed earlier. It is imperative to mention that even the most successful diversion strategies will require compliance from program participants.

THE CONCEPT OF PERCEIVED CHOICE

Imagine your professor assigns a group project. Consider these two scenarios: 1) Immediately, one student in your group begins to take charge and assigns each group member a task. 2) You and your fellow members have a discussion about who would like to complete each task. In which scenario are you more likely to effectively complete your assigned task?

Perceived choice measures a person's feelings and attitudes toward their involvement in treatment. Earlier, we used the example of a group project. In the context of this chapter, perceived choice refers to a participant's feelings and attitudes toward their involvement in diversion programming/mental health treatment. If a person has a high level of perceived choice, they believe that they have a say in choosing to participate in treatment or diversion programming. Broner and colleagues (2004) reported that participants with high levels of perceived choice were more likely to stay in treatment/stay involved with diversion programming.

Perceived choice is an important factor in determining diversion program effectiveness because diversion programs can only be successful if participants remain in the program. Therefore, making sure participants play an active role in the conversation about treatment is important.

As might be expected, diversion staff are a diverse mix of individuals and may include varied criminal justice and mental health professionals, including correctional staff, substance abuse and mental health counselors, physicians, probation officers, police, public defenders and states' attorneys, pre-trial services coordinators, court officials, and clergy or other ministerial representatives. Consequently, the ability to establish and maintain community partnerships across multiple systems of care cannot be overstated.

Like diversion staff, individuals served by post-booking diversion programs (i.e., consumers) are diverse in terms of demographic and clinical characteristics, criminal history, and specific mental health needs (Ryan, et al., 2010). In particular, diversion programs typically include participants who 1) are diagnosed with a severe and persistent mental illness, most frequently schizophrenia or other mood disorder; 2) have been hospitalized, visited the ER, or received medication for mental health problems or symptoms of mental illness in the 3 months prior to criminal justice contact; 3) are first-time offenders, have fewer prior arrests, and/or fewer felony charges than those not chosen for diversion; and/or 4) have spent a significant amount of time in jail within the 12 months preceding the current criminal justice contact (Broner, et al., 2004).

In Chapter 4, you read about the key symptoms associated with psychotic disorders: delusions, hallucinations, and disorganized speech/behavior.

Due to symptoms of their illnesses, PwMI often display behaviors that draw police attention, like in the case of Mr. H.M.:

H.M. is a 50-year-old homeless man, living on the streets of Washington, D.C. He is diagnosed with schizophrenia and experiences severe hallucinations and paranoid delusions. H.M. believes that outreach workers are actually trying to harm him, rather than help him. Because of these symptoms, H.M. does not utilize the city's many homeless shelters or cooperate with homeless outreach workers or mental health case managers.

During the winter, temperatures reach well below freezing on the streets. One particular night, the city declared a hypothermia emergency. Outreach workers patrolled the city looking for individuals in need of shelter. Workers found H.M. lying on the sidewalk wearing nothing but a t-shirt, jeans, shoes, and holding a thin blanket. When they approached him, H.M. attempted to strike them repeatedly and ran through the streets and into businesses screaming that the workers were trying to "kill him." Police witnessed the ordeal and began to intervene, making H.M. even more paranoid. After a 20-minute struggle, H.M. was ultimately arrested and taken to the police station for psychiatric evaluation.

Diversion Strategies

Because institutions, offenders, and communities are different, there is no preferred strategy or successful package of strategies that will be utilized across all cases. Some approaches suggested by Ryan and colleagues (2010) include assertive community treatment (ACT), intensive case management, intensive psychiatric probation and parole, mental health courts, and residential supports. Each of these programs is discussed in more detail in the remaining chapters of the text; however, they merit a brief introduction here.

Assertive community treatment (ACT) uses a team–based, community approach to supporting PwMI by focusing on continuity of treatment, decreasing hospitalizations, and enhancing social and emotional functioning. Similar to ACT, intensive case management is a community-based treatment that seeks to facilitate linkage to services and support normal functioning outside of frequent hospitalizations through enhanced community integration. Intensive psychiatric probation and parole are typically enforced by a parole or probation officer who is in charge of monitoring a PwMI's compliance with conditions of the court, which, in some cases, influences the likelihood of a client's hospitalization or incarceration.

Evidence–Based Practices: the integration of the best available research with clinical expertise in the context of patient characteristics, culture, and preferences.

Intensive psychiatric probation/parole may be mandated by mental health courts: specialized judicial entities made up of criminal justice staff and mental health treatment providers with the goal of benefiting court-involved PwMI. Though less common than the other diversion strategies described, residential support is a developing approach that provides specialized housing for justice-involved PwMI. Given the emphasis placed on utilizing *evidence-based practices* (EBPs) in the provision of mental health and substance abuse services in recent years, research and evaluation into program effectiveness is clearly necessary to determine similarities, differences, and efficacy of approaches.

Determining Diversion Program Effectiveness

Post-booking diversion programs are associated with improved criminal justice outcomes (fewer arrests and fewer days incarcerated) and improved clinical outcomes (access to benefits, usage of psychiatric services, and improved clinical functioning) (DeMatteo, et al., 2013). As previously stated, they may also provide modest savings or be cost neutral (Broner, et al., 2004). Ryan and colleagues (2010) suggest that post-booking diversion programs result in fewer criminal justice contacts, increased life satisfaction, reduced psychiatric symptoms, reduced psychiatric hospitalizations, reduced alcohol consumption, and increased work stability. Individuals who participate in diversion programs have shown improvement through increases in service-seeking behaviors for mental health counseling and psychiatric medication management and decreases in mental health hospitalizations (Broner, 2004). The benefits and successes discussed could not be achieved without proper processing and disposition.

Processing and Disposition

Processing and disposition of PwMI in the criminal justice system at Intercept Two can be categorized into two parts: screening and assessment, and system collaboration. Proper screening and assessment is crucial in identifying those currently diagnosed with a severe and persistent mental illness, those exhibiting symptoms of psychosis that have not yet been diagnosed, and those at risk for behaviors such as suicide or deliberate self-harm (Figure 6.1). System collaboration illustrates effective practices to aid in the integration of criminal justice and mental health systems as suggested by the Sequential Intercept Model. Each component is explained in more detail in the remaining sections of the chapter.

Figure 6.1

PwMI who enter a jail setting for the first time are at risk of isolation, victimization and other traumatic events; self-harm; and rapid decompensation

Source: Jagendorf (2011); *Cellblock* (2011) [Licensed under Creative Commons License 4.0: https://creativecommons.org/licenses/by-nc/4.0/]

Screening and Assessment

As discussed in Chapter 1, in comparison to the general public, mental illness is reported at consistently higher rates in correctional facilities. Specifically, in October 2014, the National Research Council (NRC) reported that 64 percent of jail inmates, 54 percent of state prisoners, and 45 percent of federal prisoners reported mental health concerns. Again, prevalence rates may differ across reports, depending on the way by which the researcher is measuring mental illness or mental health disorders, and due to a myriad of additional reasons related to data collection. Regardless, in order to benefit from diversion programs, PwMI must first be appropriately identified within the criminal justice system—primarily during the intake process at the jail. Unfortunately, not all incarcerated PwMI are identified in this way. For example, a study by Birmingham and colleagues (2000) found that only 23 percent of inmates with a current mental illness were identified by correctional staff at intake.

Screening and assessment procedures are designed to examine overall mental health, specific disorders, or specific risky behaviors associated with mental health such as suicide or self-harm. It is important to note that there are differences between these procedures, and Table 6.1 attempts to distinguish these in a concise manner. At Intercept Two, a screening is typically conducted by staff at the jail or juvenile assessment or catchment center. The tools used are relatively brief (e.g., 10 to 15 questions) and are mostly used to alert staff as to whether there are any significant mental health or substance abuse issues at intake ("red flags"). Although Ford Brooks explains comprehensive assessment procedures in Chapter 4, the subject merits some additional discussion here in the context of its use in a jail setting. During an assessment, professionals use multiple approaches to collect significant information about an inmate's mental health profile to complete a thorough psychiatric evaluation. Most commonly, clinicians and

---

TABLE 6.1　**Screening and assessment: What's the difference?**

Screening and assessment are both essential components of identifying PwMI in the criminal justice system; however, they each serve different purposes.

	Screening	Assessment
Definition	Process for evaluating the possible presence of a particular symptom or problem.	Process for defining the nature of symptoms or problems, determining a diagnosis, and developing treatment recommendations for addressing the problem or diagnosis.
Administration	Many screening tools require little to no special training to administer.	Assessment tools should only be administered by a qualified mental health professional.
Example	When screening for potential presence of schizophrenia, a question might be: "Do you ever see or hear things that other people can't see or hear?" This question is describing hallucinations, a major symptom of schizophrenia.	An assessment for schizophrenia would include more specific questions about the presenting symptom(s), i.e., hallucinations. For example, a question might be: "How long have you been hearing and seeing things that others don't see?" or "What kind of things do you hear or see that others don't?"

Source: http://www.ncbi.nlm.nih.gov/books/NBK83253/ and DSM-5

other mental health staff use a combination of inmate self-report and staff observations, and any interviews are typically conducted in a relatively private setting. Both types of assessments are used to examine the type and severity of any current symptoms as well as to construct treatment history, including all psychiatric treatment, medication, and mental health performance. By considering current symptomatology along with mental health history, conclusions can be made about current levels of cognitive, social, behavioral, and emotional functioning (Lurigio, 2006).

A significant concern regarding the screening and assessment of inmates in criminal justice institutions stems from the fact that these agencies frequently use measures that are developed in house by correctional or administrative staff in the facility. Although screening and assessment are crucial in identifying PwMI, there is no "gold standard" tool that is appropriate for all circumstances in all facilities. Although it is important that assessment not add unnecessary work to the already overflowing workload of criminal justice and mental health professionals, it is equally as important that PwMI are accurately identified and diagnosed using tools that are reliable and valid (Lurigio, 2006). In order to overcome barriers associated with implementing evidence-based screening and assessment tools (especially where budgets may be limited), tools must be quick; free or low cost; validated for use in multiple populations; straightforward; and easy to administer, score, and interpret.

RELIABILITY VS. VALIDITY

Reliability refers to consistency or stability of a measurement. Using the same assessment tool, would I get the same results twice?

Validity refers to the accuracy of results drawn from a measurement. Does the assessment tool measure what it is supposed to measure?

Source: http://ocw.jhsph.edu/courses/hsre/pdfs/hsre_lect7_weiner.pdf

---

Eliminating False Positives

A false positive refers to a situation where a person is identified as having a mental health need when there is no actual mental health need present. Also referred to as malingering (feigning symptoms of mental illness) in some contexts, it is important to be aware of false positives especially in a correctional setting. Inmates who do not have a mental illness may believe that reporting symptoms could provide them with an advantage in sentencing, cell or block assignment, or treatment within the facility (Martin, et al., 2013).

Table 6.2 identifies seven screening and assessment tools appropriate for use with adult offender populations (Lurigio, et al., 2006; Martin, et al., 2013). The first column states what tool is being used followed by its characteristics in the second column. The last column indicates which assessments and screenings are evidence based.

In contrast with the information pertaining to screening and assessment tools used with adult offender populations, Table 6.3 includes juvenile mental health assessments and screenings as found in the literature.

Suicide Screening and Assessment

Due to the high rates of suicide in forensic settings, especially among individuals with severe and persistent mental illness, a systematic assessment of suicide risk is necessary in all correctional institutions to comply with prevention efforts. Shea (2002) provided a list of elements that should be included in a systematic suicide risk assessment for individuals involved in the criminal justice system:

1. General clinical evaluation (mental health status exam)

2. Review of relevant records

3. Gathering necessary collateral information

4. Careful exploration of suicidal ideation, behavior, planning, desire, and intent

5. Identifying risk-enhancing factors

6. Synthesizing all of this material

7. Using clinical judgment to assess overall risk level

8. Crafting a risk reduction plan that targets modifiable factors

---

FAST FACT: IN THE UNITED STATES . . .

Suicide has been the *leading cause of death* in local jails since the year 2000.

    34 percent of all jail deaths in 2013 were due to suicide
    3,807 jail inmates died from suicide from 2001–2012

Source: Noonan, Rohloff, & Ginder, 2015

TABLE 6.2 Mental health screening and assessment tools for correctional populations

Tool	Characteristics	Evidence Based?
Brief Jail Mental Health Screen (BJMHS)	Eight questions for inmates in jail; developed to aid in the early identification of severe mental illnesses and other acute psychiatric problems during the jail intake process; administered by correctional officers, mental health, or medical professionals; yes/no questions; result options include not referred or referred	Yes
Correctional Mental Health Screen for Men (CMHS-M)	Twelve questions for male inmates in jail; developed to aid in the early detection of psychiatric illness during jail intake process; can be administered by correctional officers, mental health, or medical professionals; yes/no questions; result options include not referred, urgent referral, or routine referrals	Yes
Correctional Mental Health Screen for Women (CMHS-W)	Eight questions for female inmates in jail; developed to aid in the early detection of psychiatric illness during jail intake process; can be administered by correctional officers, mental health, or medical professionals; yes/no questions; result options include not referred, urgent referral, or routine referrals	Yes
England Mental Health Screen (EMHS)	Administration time 5 to 10 minutes for jail inmates; can be administered by correctional officers, mental health, or medical professionals	Yes
Jail Screening and Assessment Tool (JSAT)	Administration involves a 20-minute interview covering 10 content areas; for jail inmates; most typically administered by a psychiatric nurse, a psychologist, or an intern with clinical training	Yes
Kessler Psychological Distress Scale (K-6 Scale)	Six questions; used when screening for mood or anxiety disorders; self-administered	Yes
Kessler Psychological Distress Scale (K-10 Scale)	Ten questions; used to measure distress based on questions about anxiety and depressive symptoms; self-administered	Yes

Source: Information extracted from Martin et al. (2013)

TABLE 6.3 Juvenile mental health assessment/screening tools

Tool	Characteristics	Evidence Based
Massachusetts Youth Screening Instrument Version 2	Fifty-two questions for youth; assess mental health needs; not gender specific; three ways to administer; ages 12 to 17	Yes
Westerman Aboriginal Symptoms Checklist-Youth	Fifty-two-item questionnaire; assesses mental health needs; two ways to administer; measures specific risks; culturally diverse	Yes
Life Attitudes Schedule	Screens for suicide proneness; four subscales	No
Diagnostic Interview Schedule for Children	Short assessment; only predictive factors of suicide are measured	No
Drug Abuse Screening Test for Adolescents	Internally consistent; juveniles 13 to 19; more detailed assessment; self-report with pencil and paper	Yes
Structured Assessment of Violence Risk in Youth	Thirty-item rating; 24 risk factors; three domains; administered to youth	Yes
Adolescent Alcohol Involvement Scale	Fourteen items; pencil and paper report; self-report; tendency for higher scores	Yes

Source: Bureau of Justice Statistics (2013)

Forensic suicide assessments should include a standardized screening instrument (evidence based, as discussed earlier) and a clinical interview, allowing the offender to elaborate on his or her own subjective experiences. In addition to inmate self-reporting, institutional staff should be aware of clinical factors associated with suicide risk, such as impulsive behavior, severe agitation, increased distress, recent suicide attempts, hopelessness, rage, reckless behavior, social withdrawal, anxiety, dramatic mood changes, and lack of sense of purpose (Knoll, 2010).

Characteristics unique to correctional suicide risk factors have also been identified and divided into the following categories: historical factors, clinical factors, social factors, environmental factors, and acute items. Specific risk factors for each category are detailed in Table 6.4

TABLE 6.4 **Correctional suicide risk factors, as taken and adapted from Knoll (2010)**

Historical Factors
- Past suicide attempts
- History of psych treatment/mental illness, substance abuse, traumatic life events
- Family history of suicide
- Chronic physical illness
- Conviction of a violent crime against a person
- First incarceration

Clinical Factors
- Depression
- Suicidal ideation
- Hopelessness
- Irritation/rage, aggression
- Psychosis
- Personality disorder

Social Factors
- Recent life crisis
- Lengthy sentence
- Recent harassment/bullying
- Loneliness

Environmental Factors
- Secure housing/unit/isolation/single cell
- First two months secured placement
- Ligature points accessible

Acute Items
- Suicidal plan/intent
- Available means
- Acts of anticipation
- Recent substance use
- Insomnia

Source: Knoll (2010), pp. 191–192

Similar to mental health screening procedures, suicide screening and assessment is also highly variable across institutions and programs. Although there is no "gold standard" for assessing and preventing inmate suicides, best practices have been developed for prevention of inmate suicide in jails (Hayes, 1999, 2010, 2011, 2013). Criteria for these best practices include assessment/screening frequency and procedures, behavioral observation, examination of history, interaction and effective staff communication, employee training, attention to individual clinical needs, discharge determination, and limiting barriers to treatment.

IN THE NEWS: TANA LEKIN'S STORY

Tana Lekin was arrested for burglary, impersonating an officer, and public intoxication, among other charges, after she and a male friend broke into an elderly woman's home in search of drugs.

When police arrived on scene, they found Lekin in the basement of the home. She was visibly intoxicated and was displaying irrational, disorganized behaviors and speech. When confronted by officers, Lekin claimed that she, herself, was a police officer and suggested that she was in the house to collect the belongings of her mother who had recently been committed. Lekin spoke into an imaginary radio and would rapidly count from one to six out loud without apparent reason. During her transport to jail, Lekin was reportedly combative toward officers, kicking and flailing violently. Due to her lack of cooperation, officers did not complete the appropriate booking procedure. Lekin was placed in a cell where she continued to yell, kick, and pound on the door and walls.

The morning after her arrest, Lekin did not respond to a cell check. Fourteen minutes later, Tana Lekin was found asphyxiated in her cell after using an article of clothing to hang herself.

The Lekin family filed a lawsuit against the employees at the Jones County Jail for failing to recognize signs that Tana Lekin was suicidal.

Source: http://www.desmoinesregister.com/story/news/crime-and-courts/2016/02/18/family-files-lawsuit-iowa-jail-inmate-suicide/80547624/, http://www.desmoinesregister.com/story/news/investigations/2016/05/28/death-behind-bars-inmate-suicides-overdoses-among-causes/83671656/

ASSESSMENT/SCREENING TIMELINESS AND FREQUENCY

Hayes (2011) describes the initial intake suicide assessment as similar to taking someone's temperature. By taking someone's temperature, one can determine if the person currently has a fever but cannot determine if the person will have a cold in the future. Behavior and self-reported expressions at intake are time limited. These limitations do not undermine the importance of initial suicide screening, but do illuminate the management of continuously changing inmate mental health needs. Suicide screening must be an ongoing process beginning when the inmate is first arrested and brought to jail and ending when the inmate is released from the institution. Close attention should be paid to inmates who have been placed on suicide watch in the past; even after discharge from suicide watch, specialized mental health services should be ongoing. Special attention is also warranted during times of increased stress such as admittance to specialized housing units or around parole hearings.

A CORONER'S INQUEST: ASHLEY SMITH

For a case similar to Ms. Lekin's (earlier), though involving a 19-year-old female detained in a women's correctional facility in Canada, visit the following links:

https://youtu.be/tP-k47rIIyA

https://youtu.be/_oMRgHG2OvM

https://youtu.be/4rplCV3vRN8

Warning: Some of the materials contained in the videos may be disturbing (the last documents a completed suicide), and therefore, viewer discretion is advised.

BEHAVIORAL OBSERVATION

Consistent with the importance of continued assessment and screening is the examination of behavior expressed and displayed by an inmate, even if the inmate denies suicidal ideation at the time of assessment. Successful suicide prevention efforts will encourage behavioral analysis that is indicative of suicide risk such as suicidal statements, plans, gestures, or actions.

EXAMINATION OF HISTORY

Examination of history refers to the identification of and/or attention to prior risk of suicide and/or prior suicide attempts. Prior suicide attempts are one of the strongest predictors of future suicide attempts. Inmates' mental health histories should be available to all direct care staff, most usefully in an electronic mental health record.

Program Spotlight: Montgomery County, Maryland: Criminal Justice Behavioral Initiative

Founded in 2001, the Criminal Justice Behavioral Initiative in Montgomery County, Maryland, is a joint effort between the county police department, Department of Correction and Rehabilitation, and Department of Health and Human Services. Montgomery County's model consists of 1) a police Crisis Intervention Team (CIT) and Health and Human Services Mobile Crisis Team, 2) Clinical Assessment and Triage Services (CATS), 3) a Crisis Intervention Unit (CIU) within the jail, and 4) community reentry case management and discharge planning. Points 2 and 3 are most relevant for our discussion on Intercept Two of the SIM.

continued

PwMI who come in contact with the justice system in Montgomery County are subject to a comprehensive assessment by CATS therapists. The assessment includes crisis and suicide screening, full psychological evaluation, and medication and treatment history. Individuals who are not diverted are continually screened and assessed throughout their jail time and prior to release.

The jail's CIU houses individuals who require stabilization and treatment until they are able to be placed in general-population housing. The CIU is made up of male and female units. Staff include officers with specialized mental health training and master's-level therapists. Inmates on the unit have access to individualized therapy and the first jail-based dialectical behavior therapy (DBT) program in the nation.

Implementation of the Criminal Justice Behavioral Initiative from July 2011 to June 2015 has shown that the number of people who have received intensive and comprehensive mental health treatment on the CIU increased by 6.5 percent. The number of CIU therapy groups held has increased 143 percent, and the number of people who participated in CIU group therapy increased 159 percent.

Source: http://www.naco.org/resources/addressing-mental-illness-and-medical-conditions-county-jails-montgomery-county-md

INTERACTION AND COMMUNICATION

Best practices suggest that there should be frequent interaction between inmates and correctional, medical, and mental health staff, especially in specialized housing units. In addition, there should be increased interaction for inmates placed on suicide precautions. Communication and interaction between staff members is another crucial contributor to limiting inmate suicide. Multidisciplinary plans and approaches to care and communication between direct care staff (medical, mental health, custody) should be devised and maintained.

STAFF COPING AND SUICIDE PREVENTION EFFORTS

The following two examples illustrate programs/procedures that have been utilized in correctional settings with staff after a suicide or other crisis event.

Critical-Incident Stress Debriefing (CISD): One step in a series of critical stress management phases; offers psychological education and support for small, relatively homogenous groups that have been affected in some way by a traumatic event. The primary purpose of CISD is the reduction of distress and the promotion of recovery and group cohesion.

Psychological Autopsy: A direct technique for determining the key risk factors leading to a suicide so as to build upon knowledge in future prevention efforts; includes a thorough collection of data pertaining to the deceased derived from a combination of interviews and an examination of historical records (medical, criminal history, case notes, social work reports, etc.).

Source: Mitchell (n.d.), retrieved at http://www.info-trauma.org/flash/media-f/mitchellCriticalIncidentStressDebriefing.pdf; Cavanagh, Carson, Sharpe, and Lawrie (2003).

Employee Training

Extremely important to the success of suicide screening, assessment, and prevention is correctional staff/employee training. Suicide prevention training should be meaningful, long lasting, and contain information that is reflective of the current knowledge of suicide in confinement and forensic mental health. Employee training should not be limited to direct care staff, but available for all employees institution wide.

For suicide prevention and recommended practices as they relate to prisoners in the United States visit: https://www.usmarshals.gov/prisoner/suicide_prevention.htm.

Attention to Individual Clinical Needs

During screening, assessment, and continued observation, clinical needs of individual inmates should be considered when making decisions about watch status, discharge, and treatment planning. For example, security cameras may be efficient for temporarily monitoring an inmate who is at low risk for suicide; however, an inmate who is high risk would most likely benefit from person-to-person interaction. Although consistent policies should be enforced, it is also important to include recommendations on a case-by-case basis.

INSTITUTIONAL PROCEDURE RELATED TO INMATE SUICIDE: AN EXCERPT OF A DEPARTMENT ORDER TAKEN FROM THE ARIZONA DEPARTMENT OF CORRECTIONS

1.4 Inmates on a Continuous Watch, One Officer to Multiple Inmate Continuous Watch and Ten Minute Watch shall be provided with a minimum of two safety blankets, a safety smock, a suicide-resistant mattress and a small supply of toilet paper (i.e., a strand no longer 12 inches or approximately three squares) minus the cardboard roll.

    1.4.1 Whenever clothing is removed from a suicidal inmate, a safety smock shall be issued. No inmate shall ever be placed or kept in a cell naked at any time.

    1.4.2 Any additional items provided to the inmate shall be pre-approved by mental health staff.

        1.4.2.1 The maximum allowed items for a Continuous Watch, One Officer to Multiple Inmate Continuous Watch and Ten Minute Watch include:

            1.4.2.1.1 Jumpsuit.

            1.4.2.1.2 Undergarments.

---

continued

1.4.2.1.3 Unlaced footwear.

1.4.2.1.4 Writing and reading materials.

1.4.2.1.5 Spork.

1.4.2.1.6 Personal hygiene items (i.e., soap, tooth paste, tooth brush).

1.4.2.2 Razors, razor blades, towels, sheets, belts, shoe laces, and electronic appliances shall not be approved for a Continuous Watch, One Officer to Multiple Inmate Continuous Watch or Ten Minute Watch.

1.4.2.3 Mental health staff shall approve additional items only when deemed safe and clinically appropriate

Source: Arizona State Department of Corrections. (2009, September 16). Department Order 807: INMATE SUICIDE PREVENTION, PRECAUTIONARY WATCHES, AND MAXIMUM BEHAVIORAL CONTROL RESTRAINT, Pages 8–9. Retrieved from https://corrections.az.gov/sites/default/files/policies/800/0807.pdf

DISCHARGE DETERMINATION

The determination to discharge an inmate from suicide watch must only be made by a qualified mental health professional (MHP). Before discharge, the MHP should conduct a comprehensive suicide risk assessment to ensure an inmate has received effective care and is no longer at risk for suicide. In addition, following discharge, inmates should be kept on a "mental health caseload" for continued monitoring.

MINIMIZATION OF BARRIERS TO TREATMENT

When working with incarcerated populations, there are unique barriers to mental health treatment. It is critical that these barriers are minimized when screening and assessing for suicide risk. Professionals should avoid procedures that make suicide precautions seem punitive while still taking appropriate precautions to identify suicide risk, diminish the risk of suicide, and maintain safety of all inmates and staff.

SPOTLIGHT ON MATTERS OF THE LAW: SELECT COURT CASES RELATED TO TREATMENT OF PWMI

The General Population

Under current laws, those suffering from mental illness have the right to seek and continue medical and other therapeutic measures to treat symptoms at their own discretion. Studies have shown that allowing patients to control and determine what type of treatment they receive is more successful than forced treatment (see Rosenthal & Rogers, 2014 for a brief review of the literature); in particular, forced medication has been found to make the patient feel as if they

continued

have little control over their own lives and may cause low self-esteem, and ultimately, self-harm. Contemporary commitment laws are indicative of a converse viewpoint—one that is based upon a concern for public safety. As previous examples set forth in Chapter 5 have shown, if patients are regarded as a threat to themselves or others, treatment can in fact be forced upon them by an order of the court.

Incarcerated Populations

Generally speaking, prisoners have no constitutional right to treatment. For justice-involved PwMI, however, constitutional protections may be found under the Eighth Amendment—assuring freedom from cruel and unusual punishment. This protection has been extended to an individual's right to access adequate medical care, which includes psychological or psychiatric services (*Estelle v. Gamble*, 1976). A judge may also exercise authority to require correctional treatment plans are implemented to ensure the administration of prescribed medications, the timely response to inmate medical service requests, the provision of individual and group therapy, and the proper facilitation of a number of other mental healthcare treatment provisions. The following are highlights derived from seminal cases regarding access to treatment, as well as the right to refuse it, in institutional settings.

Wyatt v. Stickney (1972)

Issue: Do patients in public mental institutions have a constitutional right to treatment?

Held: Yes, people who are involuntarily committed to state institutions because of mental illness or developmental disabilities have a constitutional right to treatment that will afford them a realistic opportunity to return to society.

The Court articulated that the following three conditions must be present for treatment programs in public mental health institutions to be considered "adequate and effective" under the Constitution:

A humane psychological and physical environment, qualified staff in numbers sufficient to administer adequate treatment; and individualized treatment plans.

Estelle v. Gamble (1976)

Issue: Do prisoners have a constitutional right to healthcare?

An inmate in a state correctional institution brought a civil rights action under 42 U.S.C. § 1983 against the state corrections department medical director and two correctional officials, claiming that he was subjected to cruel and unusual punishment in violation of the Eighth Amendment for inadequate treatment of a back injury he claimed to have sustained while he was engaged in prison work.

Held: Yes. Deliberate indifference by prison personnel to a prisoner's serious illness or injury constitutes cruel and unusual punishment contravening the Eighth Amendment.

continued

Washington v. Harper (1990)

Issue: Do inmates have a constitutional right to refuse treatment?

Held: The Court established that in correctional settings defendants can refuse medication until they become a danger to themselves or others or become gravely disabled.

Defendants can refuse medications in the state hospital setting, but because the setting is more therapeutic than correctional institution per se, it seems to be easier to obtain judicial authorization to medicate involuntarily in a treatment setting.

Sell v. U.S. (2003)

Issue: Does the U.S. Constitution permit the forced administration of an antipsychotic drug to a mentally ill but nonviolent inmate for the sole purpose of rendering that inmate competent to proceed to trial, even for charges that were serious but did not involve a violent offense?

Held: The involuntary administration of medication for purposes of restoring competence to stand trial was constitutionally permissible only under the following conditions:

If the defendant is a danger to him- or herself or others;

If the defendant is facing a "serious" charge;

If treatment is medically appropriate and is substantially unlikely to have side effects that could undermine the fairness of the trial; and

If treatment is the least restrictive alternative available to further important governmental interests.

Systems Collaboration

A successful diversion strategy at Intercept Two is one that effectively determines the mental and behavioral health and social needs of the offender and, if possible, minimizes any further penetration in the traditional justice system by allowing for the provision of services to be rendered in a community setting. In order to achieve this, there must be systemic collaborations—professionals from the fields of criminal justice and mental health working together for a common goal that benefits both systems of care and PwMI.

Steadman and colleagues (1995) found that four components of systems collaboration appeared consistently in the most effective jail diversion programs: integrated services, regular meetings, boundary spanners, and strong leadership. The remainder of this chapter will briefly introduce and explain these key components.

Integrated services are potentially the most crucial component of all when following the SIM. Integrated services require criminal justice and mental health agencies to regularly coordinate their interactions. The establishment of multidisciplinary groups is also crucial to the success of integrated service models. For example, services may be provided by mental health workers, but they are informed by a collaboration of judges, public defenders' offices, district attorneys, probation offices, and jail services. Assertive community treatment (ACT) and forensic assertive community treatment (FACT), discussed later, are two programs that exemplify integrated services.

Assertive Community Treatment

As explained in the beginning of this chapter, the ACT model of care uses a team-based community approach to supporting PwMI by focusing on continuity of treatment, decreasing hospitalizations, and enhancing social and emotional functioning. Notable elements of ACT include low client-to-staff ratios, high-intensity services, assertive outreach efforts, and 24/7 access to care, all in a community-based setting. ACT utilization with forensic populations has shown a decrease in psychiatric hospitalizations and chronic homelessness (Beach, et al., 2013).

Forensic Assertive Community Treatment

PwMI present unique risks and challenges. FACT, or *forensic assertive community treatment*, is a specialized variation of the ACT model for PwMI who are involved with the criminal justice system (Lamberti, et al., 2004). The FACT model targets various strategies designed to interface with criminal justice processes at key intercept points in order to prevent future criminal justice involvement. Evidence suggests that FACT supports diversion efforts, as FACT participants had significantly fewer jail bookings, greater outpatient contacts, and fewer hospital days than did non-FACT participants (Cusack, et al., 2010).

Key Staff Meetings

Regular meetings of key treatment providers and criminal justice professionals are useful for keeping all key stakeholders (justice and behavioral health staff) informed about protocols, recently admitted and released offenders from the jail, and what services are needed. Participants at these meetings may include pre-trial or probation officers, drug/alcohol specialists, mental health caseworkers, judges, and psychiatrists. Agendas for these meetings can incorporate discussions of newly screened inmates, evaluation procedures, and information sharing about client progress.

Program Leadership

It is important that the diversion program administrator/director has a thorough understanding of all system components and informational networks involved in the program. He or she should have strong communication and networking skills because program leaders essentially advocate for diversion. An effective leader in this role must have the ability to demonstrate the importance of the agency or organization's specific diversion program, and diversion in general, to a variety of people.

Boundary Spanners

A *boundary spanner*, also known as a forensic liaison, serves as the direct manager of interactions between the correctional, mental health, and judicial staff participating in the diversion program. Boundary spanners act as a link to PwMI who are incarcerated, share information with other parties, hold meetings to develop discharge plans, and/ or coordinate with the mental health system, psychiatric hospitals, and the probation office to move PwMI through the system. Essentially, boundary spanners are the "glue" that holds all components of diversion together (Steadman, et al., 1995). Because of this, a boundary spanner should be someone who has the trust and recognition of people from each of the collaborating systems. The concept of boundary spanners is reintroduced in Chapter 8, where roles related to reentry are examined and discussed.

THINKING CRITICALLY: SCREENING AND ASSESSMENT OF PWMI

Charlotte was arrested for the first time in her mid-fifties after shoplifting from a Wal-Mart. She was married, held a master's degree in special education, and had a respectable job working for an addictions agency. Charlotte and her husband had recently moved to a new area from their long-time home, and she was having a difficult time coping with the change. Charlotte was led to the criminal justice system by her own secret battle with addiction and depression.

After the first shoplifting incident, Charlotte was given a six-month sentence of probation. Soon after, she lost her job, continued to drink heavily, and the symptoms of her depression worsened. She began to make a "career" out of shoplifting from other grocery stores and was quickly rearrested and given a jail sentence for violation of her parole.

Protocol at the county jail called for each inmate to receive extensive mental health screening as part of the booking process. First, Charlotte met with a correctional staff person who screened her for potential mental health symptoms and suicide risk. The screening was brief, and the staff person was well trained. Charlotte was cooperative and willing to respond to most of the questions she was asked. She screened positive for symptoms of depression and substance use disorder. Because of her depressive symptoms, alcohol use, and reportedly low self-esteem, Charlotte also scored high on the suicide risk screen.

Charlotte was then appropriately referred to the jail's psychological support services specialist for further evaluation. A licensed therapist met with Charlotte to complete a comprehensive assessment. The therapist asked Charlotte questions about her experiences with alcohol and depression. She was able to get a clearer picture of Charlotte's specific needs, possible diagnoses, and potential

---

continued

risk factors. After the assessment was over, Charlotte was assigned to a cell in the Crisis Intervention Unit, where she would be continually monitored and screened for suicidal ideation until she was released or diverted.

Then the therapist who met with Charlotte had a meeting with additional jail therapists, correctional officers, and community mental health providers. Charlotte was identified as being eligible for a diversion program with the city's behavioral health center. The behavioral health center would provide Charlotte with individual and group counseling services to help her get healthy and stay sober.

Charlotte's experience with mental health screening and assessment in jail was a positive one. She was appropriately screened, assessed, identified, and referred for diversion. Charlotte is a "success story."

What factors made Charlotte's identification possible? What might have happened differently if these factors were not in place?

Take-Home Message

Intercept Two is important because it is where the course of an individual is to be determined, immediately after being detained by the police. For example, if an officer arrests an individual who is assumed to have a mental health issue, initial detention is where one may be able to determine whether an individual is eligible for diversionary programs so to avoid further penetration into the criminal justice system at the early stages. As described in Chapter 5, during the process, "mercy bookings" may occur, whereby someone is detained in order to provide shelter and temporary aid for an individual with mental illnesses who has been arrested (Lamb, et al., 2002). It is important that an individual has been properly screened for mental illness, competency, substance abuse, trauma, or any other factors that may be related to the offense committed or risk for criminal propensity. Proper screening allows for the possibility of pre-trial diversion and allocation of medical services, if need be, assuming there is a strong service linkage to comprehensive services (SAMHSA, 2015).

PwMI are rearrested and reconvicted at an alarming rate, and their incarceration is not the answer. This problem can be addressed through a collective effort involving correctional personnel, law enforcement, and community health providers and diversion strategies, when effectively utilized at this inception point, can save the criminal justice system time and resources (money) by keeping persons with mental illness out of the system and in their respective communities for as long as possible.

Unfortunately, not all PwMI are identified at Intercept Two, or some may be ineligible for post-booking diversion. Chapter 7 introduces diversion strategies that may be available beyond the initial period of detention, including competency evaluations, the insanity test, potential placement in forensic hospitals, and mental health courts.

QUESTIONS FOR CLASSROOM DISCUSSION

1. What are the key components of a post-booking diversion program? Which of these components do you think is the most important? Why?
2. What are some foreseeable challenges that could arise for correctional or mental health staff during the screening and assessment process for PwMI? Can you identify some potential solutions to avoid or address these challenges?
3. Choose a career opportunity available within a post-booking diversion program that you would like to have (i.e., probation/parole officer, correctional officer, mental health counselor, boundary spanner). Explain why you chose the position. Describe in detail what you think a typical work day would look like. Include potential challenges and successes.

KEY TERMS & ACRONYMS

- Assertive community treatment (ACT)
- Boundary spanners
- Evidence-based practices (EBPs)
- Forensic assertive community treatment (FACT)
- Malingering
- Perceived choice
- Post-booking diversion
- Reliability
- Validity

Bibliography

Arizona State Department of Corrections. (2009, September 16). Department Order 807: INMATE SUICIDE PREVENTION, PRECAUTIONARY WATCHES, AND MAXIMUM BEHAVIORAL CONTROL RESTRAINT, Pages 8–9. Retrieved from https://corrections.az.gov/sites/default/files/policies/800/0807.pdf.

Beach, C., Dykema, L., Appelbaum, P. S., Deng, L., Leckman-Westin, E., Manuel, J. I., . . . & Finnerty, M. T. (2013). Forensic and Nonforensic Clients in Assertive Community Treatment: A Longitudinal Study. *Psychiatric Service, 64*(5), 437–444.

Birmingham, L., Gray, J., Mason, D., & Grubin, D. (2000). Mental Illness at Reception into Prison. *Criminal Behavior and Mental Health, 10,* 77–87.

Blue-Howells, J. H., Clark, S. C., Berk-Clark, C., & McGuire, J. F. (2013). The U.S. Department of Veterans Affairs Veterans Justice Programs and the Sequential Intercept Model: Case Examples in National Dissemination of Intervention for Justice-Involved Veterans. *Psychological Services, 10*(1), 48–53.

Broner, N., Lattimore, P. K., Cowell, A. J., & Schlenger, W. E. (2004). Effects of Diversion on Adults with Co-Occurring Mental Illness and Substance Use: Outcomes from a National Multi-Site Study. *Behavioral Sciences and the Law, 22,* 519–541.

Cavanagh, J. T. O., Carson, A. J., Sharpe, M., & Lawrie, S. M. (2003). Psychological Autopsy Studies of Suicide: A Systematic Review. *Psychological Medicine, 33,* 395–405.

Compton, M. T., & Kotwicki, R. J. (2007). *Responding to individuals with mental illnesses.* Sudbury, MA: Jones & Bartlett Publishers.

Cusack, K. J., Morrissey, J. P., Cuddeback, G. S., Prins, A., & Williams, D. M. (2010). Criminal Justice Involvement, Behavioral Health Service Use, and Costs of Forensic Assertive Community Treatment: A Randomized Trial. *Community Mental Health Journal, 46*(4), 356–363.

DeMatteo, D., LaDuke, C., Locklair, B. R., & Heilbrum, K. (2013). Community-Based Alternatives for Justice Involved Individuals with Severe Mental Illness: Diversion, Problem-Solving Courts, and Reentry. *Journal of Criminal Justice, 41*, 64–71.

Fagan, T. J., & Ax, R. K. (Eds.) (2011). *Correctional Mental Health: From Theory to Practice.* Thousand Oaks, CA: Sage Publications, Inc.

Feinstein, B. (2013). Saving the Deific Decree Exception to the Insanity Defense in Illinois: How a Broad Interpretation of Religious Command May Cue Establishment Clause Concerns, *John Marshall Law Review, 46*(2), 561–582.

Griffin, P. A., Heilbrun, K., Mulvey, E. P., DeMatteo, D., & Schubert, C. A. (2015). *Sequential Intercept Model and Criminal Justice: Promoting Community Alternatives for Individuals with Serious Mental Illness.* New York, NY: Oxford University Press.

Hayes, L. M. (1999). Suicide in Adult Correctional Facilities: Key Ingredients to Prevention and Overcoming the Obstacles. *Journal of Law, Medicine, and Ethics, 27*(3), 260–268.

Hayes, L. M. (2010). *National Study of Jail Suicide: 20 Years Later.* Washington, DC: U.S. Department of Justice, National Institute of Corrections.

Hayes, L. M. (2011). *Guiding Principles to Suicide Prevention in Correctional Facilities.* Baltimore, MD: National Center on Institutions and Alternatives (NCIA).

Hayes, L. M. (2013). Suicide Prevention in Correctional Facilities: Reflections and Next Steps. *International Journal of Law and Psychiatry, 36*, 188–194.

Jagendorf. (2011). Cell Block. [CC BY 2.0 (Retrieved from http://creativecommons.org/licenses/by/2.0)], via Wikimedia Commons.

Knoll, J. L. (2010). Suicide in Correctional Settings: Assessment, Prevention, and Professional Liability. *Journal of Correctional Health Care, 16*(1), 188–204.

Lamb, H. R., Weinberger, L. E., & DeCuir Jr., W. J. (2002). The Police and Mental Health. *Psychiatric Services, 53*(10), 1266–1271.

Lamberti, J. S., Weisman, R., & Faden, D. I. (2004). Forensic Assertive Community Treatment: Preventing Incarceration of Adults with Severe Mental Illness. *Psychiatric Services, 55*(11), 1285–1293.

Lurigio, A. J., & Swartz, J. A. (2006). Mental Illness in Correctional Populations: The Use of Standardized Screening Tools for Further Evaluation or Treatment. *Federal Probation, 70*(2), 29–35.

Martin, M. S., Colman, I., Simpson, A. I. F., & McKenzie, K. (2013). Mental Health Screening Tools in Correctional Institutions: A Systematic Review. *BMC Psychiatry, 13*, 275–285.

Mitchell, J. T. (n.d.). *Critical Incident Stress Debriefing (CISD).* Retrieved from www.info-trauma.org.

National Alliance on Mental Illness [NAMI]. (2016). Jailing People with Mental Illness Retrieved at http://www.nami.org/Learn-More/Public-Policy/Jailing-People-with-Mental-Illness.

National Coalition for Mental Health Recovery. (2014). *Involuntary Outpatient Commitment Myths and Facts.* Washington, DC: National Coalition for Mental Health Recovery.

Noonan, M., Rohloff, H., & Ginder, S. (2015, August). *Mortality in local jails and state prisons, 2000-2013-statistical tables.* Retrieved January 4, 2017, from https://www.bjs.gov/content/pub/pdf/mljsp0013st.pdf.

Osher, F., D'Amora, D. A., Plotkin, M., Jarrett, N., & Eggleston, A. (2012). *Adults with Behavioral Health Needs under Correctional Supervision: A Shared Framework for Reducing Recidivism and Promoting Recovery.* New York: Council of State Governments Justice Center.

Rosenthal, H. & Rogers, S. (2014). National Coalition for Mental Health Recovery. *Involuntary outpatient commitment myths and facts* [Fact sheet]. Retrieved from http://www.ncmhr.org/downloads/NCMHR-Fact-Sheet-on-Involuntary-Outpatient-Commitment-4.3.14.pdf.

Ryan, S., Brown, C. K., & Watanabe-Galloway, S. (2010). Toward Successful Postbooking Diversion: What Are the Next Steps? *Psychiatric Services, 61*(5), 469–477.

Shea, S. C. (2002). *The Practical Art of Suicide Assessment: A Guide for Mental Health Professionals and Substance Abuse Counselors.* New York, NY: Chinchester.

Steadman, H. J., Morris, S. M., & Dennis, D. L. (1995). The Diversion of Mentally Ill Persons from Jails to Community-Based Services: A Profile of Programs. *American Journal of Public Health, 85*(12), 1630–1635.

Torrey, E. F., Zdanowicz, M. T., Kennard, A. D., Lamb, H. R., Eslinger, D. F., Biasotti, M. C., & Fuller, D. A. (2014). *The Treatment of Persons with Mental Illness in Prisons and Jails: A State Survey.* Arlington, VA: Treatment Advocacy Center.

Vail, L. (2015). Meridian Behavioral Health Services [Case study].

CHAPTER 7 **Intercept Three**
Secure Confinement and Court

". . . deliberate indifference to serious medical needs of prisoners constitutes the 'unnecessary and wanton infliction of pain' . . . proscribed by the Eighth Amendment."
—Estelle v. Gamble (1976)

Introduction

The two preceding chapters presented a number of possible diversion strategies available at the intercept points of arrest, pre-booking, and initial detention in a jail setting. Interwoven throughout the discussions were some of the barriers and challenges related to implementing these strategies, such as the lack of funding, community "buy-in," or prevailing agency philosophies that seem to prefer punishment over treatment. Because of such challenges, it is possible that a person with mental illness (PwMI) will not be diverted before or during the initial stages of the criminal or juvenile justice process. Moreover, it may be that the actions or behaviors of the individual during an encounter with police or other first responders may have been serious enough (or violent enough) to warrant an arrest and subsequent detainment (Massaro, 2005). At that point, it is essential that correctional staff properly identify mental health issues and related service needs.

As we have learned in Chapter 6, however, it is possible that jail personnel will not have the proper training or tools to effectively screen, assess, and manage PwMI in that setting. If that is the case and the consumer penetrates further into the criminal justice system, additional strategies can be used at Intercept Three prior to conviction and sentencing. Consider the case of R.C.

R.C. was released from jail more than one year ago after spending about six months at the state hospital under a *forensic commitment*. He has a long history of schizophrenia with several state hospital admissions and *CSU* admissions. Mr. R.C. was released under a *conditional release order (CRO)* as *not guilty by reason of insanity* in Div.V court.[1] His charges were violent, and he has violent tendencies when he is off his medications. His release was carefully coordinated by the *forensic specialist* to ensure that he had secured appropriate housing with his family. She made sure he was not going to miss any medication dosages by scheduling a medication management appointment the day after his release. She also preplanned for his days to begin by him attending groups specifically designed for individuals with chronic illnesses; he started these two days after his release. The forensic specialist also secured his social security and medical benefits. Mr. R.C. receives the most intensive forensic services from the team, which he needs to help him remain in the community. He is seen at the office at least three times per week, calls the team weekly, and receives a home visit at least twice per month. Mr. R.C. reports that this is the best he has ever done and now he has friends.

(Taken and adapted from Vail, 2015)

R.C.'s case illustrates that successful diversion can take place beyond arrest and after a period of incarceration—especially when two key conditions are present: the resources are available and the client is actively engaged in services and treatment. Oftentimes, for reasons just discussed throughout the preceding chapters (e.g., stigma, fear of violence, public safety, and lack of community-based resources or cooperation of service providers), PwMI at Intercept Three find themselves spending a considerable amount of time in secure detention. In fact, reports indicate that PwMI spend more time incarcerated (about 15 months longer, on average) than persons without mental illness for the same, if not less serious, charges such as misdemeanor disorderly conduct, trespassing, and panhandling; they also return to jail more often (Kim, Becker-Cohen, & Serakos, 2015; Torrey, Kennard, Eslinger, Lamb, & Pavle, 2010). Considering that correctional institutions have historically operated as a means to deliver punishment first and not treatment, the representation of PwMI incarcerated is concerning.

This chapter is divided into two parts. Part one presents and discusses some of the challenges faced by inmates and correctional staff during a prolonged period of incarceration for PwMI. In part two, solutions to these challenges are introduced, as the chapter outlines key diversion strategy options available at Intercept Three, prior to their release, trial, or conviction, including correctional treatment, forensic services, forensic commitment or conditional community release, evaluation for competency and/or insanity, and transfer of a case to specialized mental health courts.

Part One: Beyond Initial Detention—PwMI Incarcerated

Correctional and behavioral health system administrators at the state level are aware of the large amount of individuals with mental health and substance abuse disorders who are funneling simultaneously through theirs and other public health and welfare-related systems of care (Osher, Amora, Plotkin, Jarrett, & Eggleston, 2012). Unfortunately, as previously stated, most jails, prisons, and juvenile detention centers are not fully equipped to meet the needs of this population of offenders. Overcrowding of PwMI and shrinking treatment and programming budgets continue to plague departments of correction in most locations—challenging administration and staff to treat those who may have a serious mental health condition (and co-occurring substance abuse problems) with limited resources and expertise. As a result, there have been patterns of neglect, mistreatment, and even disregard for the well-being of vulnerable PwMI (Human Rights Watch, 2003) (Figure 7.1).

Figure 7.1

Crazy

Source: By Ankihoglund. Standard License; Adobe stock library

---

Excerpt of Letter from Inmate R.U., Nevada, June 4, 2002

At one point [and] time in my life here in prison I wanted to just take my own life away. Why? Everything in prison that's wrong is right, and everything that's right is wrong. I've been jump[ed], beat, kick[ed] and punch[ed] in full restraint four times . . . Two times I've been put into nude four point as punishment and personal harassment . . . During the time I wanted to just end my life there was no counseling, no programs to attend. I was told if I didn't take my psych meds I was "sol." Three times I [attempted suicide] by way [of hanging] myself. I had no help whatsoever days and week[s] and months I had to deal with myself. Depression, not eating, weight loss, everyday, overwhelmed by the burdens of life. I shift between feeling powerless and unworthy to feeling angry and victimized. I would think about death or killing myself daily. For eight months or a year I was not myself. From Oct 2000 to like Sept or Nov of 2001 . . . I was just kept into a lock[ed] cell ready to end my life at any given time. Each [time] I would try to hang myself it never work[ed] out. I cut my arms. I really was going thru my emotions and depression . . . I would rather live inside a zoo. The way I've been treated here at this prison I couldn't do a dog this way.

Source: Abramsky (2003) [Human Rights Watch]

General Adjustment Issues

As discussed previously, a substantial number of inmates suffer from major depression, mood disorders, anxiety, and trauma. For some, psychotic symptoms may also be observed, including delusions, disorganized thinking, hallucinations, and bizarre behaviors (some of which are the result of taking psychotropic medications). Moreover, other specialized populations (e.g., geriatric, females, or inmates with developmental disorders and/or substance abuse) may have mental health and multiple other medical issues, which results in the increased necessity for screenings, diagnostic exams, and follow-up services. Aside from the complexities associated with these conditions, the most commonly reported issues for PwMI in a correctional setting revolve around barriers to accessing mental healthcare and difficulty in navigating the challenging prison environment (Figure 7.2). The following discussion provides a brief introduction to some of the more common concerns.

Victimization

Due to the nature of their illnesses and symptoms which render them vulnerable, PwMI overall (but especially geriatric inmates) are increasingly exposed to violence and victimization in a jail or prison setting (McLearen & Magaletta, 2011). In particular, multiple reports indicate that females and males with mental illness are

Figure 7.2

Berlin-Hohenschonhausen Memoria

Source: By Matyas Rehak. Standard License; Adobe stock library

disproportionately represented among victims of sexual and other forms of physical violence while incarcerated (Listwan, Daigle, Hartman, & Guastaferro, 2014; Torrey, et al., 2014; Wood & Buttaro, 2013). Staggering rates of financial, physical, and self-victimization (self-harm, discussed later) have also been found among geriatric inmates with mental health concerns (McLearen & Magaletta, 2011). Although they report increased fear of victimization, PwMI will not often reach out for help; perhaps that is because they have been discouraged from doing so or they fear stigmatization or retaliation.

Disciplinary Issues and Segregation

The primary goal of corrections is to manage inmates efficiently and effectively. To accomplish this, staff are trained in the use of techniques designed to maximize control and institutional safety (Carlson, 2011; Compton & Kotwicki, 2007; Fellner, 2015; Osher, et al., 2012). The response to rule-violating behavior, therefore, is often based on traditional principles of punishment rather than therapeutic intervention (Fellner, 2015). In many cases, correctional officers will interpret behavior symptomatic to an inmate's illness as disruptive, dangerous, annoying, provocative, or disrespectful, and therefore, will initiate disciplinary procedures by charging infractions (Carlson, 2011; Compton & Kotwicki, 2007). Disciplinary infractions require disciplinary hearings, which almost always result in some type of punishment or sanction prevailed upon the inmate or inmates involved. Sanctions usually come in the form of administrative segregation or additional criminal charges, which may lead to an inmate spending more time incarcerated, thereby contributing to overcrowding issues, further decompensation of mental health conditions, and an increase in the costs associated with care and confinement of this population (Carlson, 2011; Torrey, Zdanowicz, Kennard, Lamb, Eslinger, Biasotti, & Fuller, 2014).

FAST FACT

In Broward County, Florida, it costs $80 a day to house a regular inmate but $130 a day for an inmate with mental illness.

In New York's Rikers Island Jail, the average stay for all inmates is 42 days; for mentally ill inmates, it is 215 days.

Source: Torrey, Kennard, Eslinger, Lamb, & Pavle (2010, p. 10)

Solitary Confinement and Use of Force

Use of force (including chemical and physical restraints or physical punishment) and solitary confinement (segregation from the general population) are often utilized by prison officials as a means of controlling or punishing "problematic" inmates who have psychiatric problems. Aside from the forced administration of medication, these correctional strategies have possibly invoked the most controversy; at the same time, however, they have produced the most policy changes with regard to the treatment of PwMI who are incarcerated. There is also a substantial literature base as to the subject matter (e.g., Carlson, 2011; Fellner, 2015; Glowa-Kollisch, Kaba, Waters, Leung, Ford, & Venters, 2016; Metzner & Fellner, 2010).

USE OF FORCE

As prescribed by policy and under limited circumstances, corrections officers are authorized to use chemical agents (e.g., "pepper spray"), electric stun devices, arm and leg restraints, and sometimes "hands on" tactics to control aggressive, unresponsive, and unruly inmates to gain their compliance. Policy typically requires, however, that staff attempt to secure compliance first by using other, less restrictive, means (e.g., deescalation techniques) (Fellner, 2015). Although statistics on correctional use of force are not readily available, existing reports and anecdotal evidence suggest that staff often respond with excessive violence—in particular, when inmates engage in nonthreatening behavior that could be symptomatic of mental illness, such as screaming or muttering obscenities and urinating in one's cell (Torrey, et al., 2014). Furthermore, incidents have also been reported where corrections staff continued to use physical force on inmates with mental illness beyond what was needed to gain compliance (see, e.g., Fellner, 2015; Winerip & Schwirtz, 2014). The case of Jermaine Padilla in California is instructive as to these reports.

CASE SNAPSHOT: JERMAINE PADILLA IN CALIFORNIA

Padilla had been sentenced to a 10-month period of incarceration for a probation violation. Records released later indicate that Padilla had a history of serious mental illness and had been decompensating over the course of about four to five weeks after being transferred to an administrative segregation unit; some of his behaviors as observed by staff included refusing to eat, urinating and defecating in the cell and smearing feces all over his body, and responding to internal stimuli (auditory hallucinations and delusions). After he refused to voluntarily comply with his treatment regimen (the administration of psychotropic medication), and to protect Padilla from further self-injury, corrections staff were forced to perform a cell extraction so that they could administer medication to stabilize him. A recording of the incident was made by staff per procedural guidelines, but it was later used as evidence in a class action suit filed in the district court (*Coleman* v. *Brown*, 2013; Fellner, 2015). At the time of this writing, the video, which is approximately 30 minutes long and shows correctional staff using pepper spray to get Padilla to "cuff up" so that he could be medicated, can be found on YouTube: https://www.youtube.com/watch?v=Sxp8jUWqVP4

Researchers have argued that some of the reasons for the increasing misuse of force against prisoners with serious mental illness include a lack of efficient mental health treatment in correctional settings, inadequate use-of-force policies they relate to PwMI, and a lack of sufficient training and supervision (Fellner, 2015). Again, there is a concerning lack of data on use-of-force incidents in U.S. prisons and jails; however, several egregious incidents have made their way into the mainstream media—in particular, those occurring at the jail complex at Rikers Island, New York. We examine a few of these case studies next.

USE OF FORCE AT RIKERS ISLAND JAIL COMPLEX, NEW YORK, NEW YORK

Luis Rosario

Rosario got into a verbal altercation with correctional staff in a mental health solitary unit. According to a report filed by the inmate, staff drug him from the cell and one held him by his handcuffs and one beat him while their captain watched. The bones in Rosario's face were broken, and his jaw needed to be wired shut.

Mr. Dixon and Mr. Lane

Both inmates, each with unique histories of serious mental health problems and periods of solitary confinement at the jail, had allegedly splashed guards with liquid. According to the accounts of clinical staff, a group of correction officers took the men individually into an examination area, where, against the inmates' cries for help and for desistence, continued to physically and brutally beat them while superiors looked on.

Excerpts taken and adapted from Michael Winerip and Michael Schwirtz, "Rikers: Where Mental Illness Meets Brutality in Jail," *New York Times*.

SOLITARY CONFINEMENT

Referred to as "administrative segregation" by prison staff (Metzner & Fellner, 2010), isolation has also been used for disciplinary or administrative reasons—sometimes in conjunction with or after an incident when force was used—to control the behaviors (or noncompliance) of PwMI in correctional settings. *Specialized housing units (SHUs)* have been designed and utilized by correctional staff to segregate and isolate inmates from the general population and to ensure the safety of inmates and staff. The use of SHUs to confine inmates with mental illness has grown as the number and proportion of PwMI in the correctional setting has grown (Metzner & Fellner, 2010).

Once segregated from the general population—for days, months, or even years—inmates in solitary cells are isolated for about 23 to 24 hours a day (under surveillance with no social interaction), with about 4 to 5 hours a week allotted for recreation (Fellner, 2015). In some jurisdictions, correctional facilities have entire mental health buildings or housing units that only house inmates with serious mental afflictions or other classes of offenders (e.g., sexual predators); inmates who are classified and placed in these units may have access to treatment programs and specialized staff; however, they are still isolated, segregated, and confined (Carlson, 2011).

Research observations have indicated that solitary confinement may provoke some of the following psychological effects: anger, anxiety, depression, cognitive disturbances, perceptual distortions, obsessive thoughts, paranoia, and psychosis. It is important to note that these maladaptive outcomes have also been observed among inmates with no remarkable history of mental illness as a result of the psychological trauma invoked by the incarceration experience (Metzner & Fellner, 2010). Aside from psychological consequences, the unfortunate circumstances of this level of care include a lack of educational or vocational activities and a higher likelihood of self-harming behaviors. For these and other reasons, the use of solitary confinement with inmates who have serious mental health issues has been restricted, if not banned altogether, in some jurisdictions (Torrey, et al., 2014).

Self-Harm

For people with serious mental illness, the combination of solitary confinement and lack of access to proper treatment and/or medication to control psychiatric symptoms is a futile mix. In this state of isolation, stress, and acute psychiatric crisis, PwMI may often resort to *self-injurious behavior (SIB)*, which may include acts of fatal and non-fatal self-harm, ranging from cutting/lacerations, head banging, ingestion of a foreign body, insertion of items in bodily orifices (including genitals), smearing feces, setting fire to a cell or to oneself, mutilation, overdose, hanging/trauma from ligature, and other suicide attempts (Helfand, 2011; Kaba, Lewis, Glowa-Kollisch, Hadler, Lee, Alper, Selling, MacDonald, Solimo, Parsons, & Venters, 2014).

FAST FACT

Correctional staff view SIB as more disruptive to the operation of a jail/prison than having to observe an inmate who is under suicide watch. In fact, when inmates engage in injurious behaviors, staff are at an increased risk for stress and burnout.

Source: (Helfand, 2011)

Research has indicated that solitary confinement is a strong indicator of SIB. Without access to other coping strategies (e.g. substance abuse, social interaction), inmates self-injure as a means to express their desire to escape conditions of extreme isolation (Helfand, 2011; Kaba, et al. 2014). Self-mutilation and suicidal behavior has also been found to be quite common among juveniles who are placed in detention facilities (DePrato & Phillippi, 2011). For both juveniles and adults, SIB has been associated with borderline personality disorder/traits, major depression, and a history of suicidal behavior (DePrato & Phillippi, 2011; Helfand, 2011).

THINKING CRITICALLY

Do you think that inmates who display symptoms of serious mental illness should always be subject to disciplinary infractions for erratic behaviors or for breaking the rules? What do you suppose a problem might be if exceptions are made by staff? What about if no exceptions are made—does that pose a problem?

SUICIDE

The topic of suicide has been introduced and discussed in preceding chapters of this book. In the context of Intercept Three, however, it remains a salient concern with respect to the continued correctional management of PwMI who are already at high risk for self-injury. Suicide has been the leading cause of death in local jails each year since 2000. In the context of state and federal prisons, suicide was the third leading cause of death in 2007 (preceded only by natural causes and AIDS) (Daniel, 2007; Hayes, 2010). Although the rates of prison suicide are lower than that of inmates in a jail setting, both comparatively exceed the rates found among members of the general population.

Some of the contributory factors found to be related to suicide among incarcerated PwMI in jails and prisons include new legal issues, relationship difficulties, isolation, and other stress factors related to the correctional setting (e.g., fear of victimization, violence, and stigmatization); there are also predisposing factors, including substance abuse that immediately preceded the most recent incarceration, "recent loss of stabilizing resources, severe guilt or shame over the alleged offense, current mental illness, prior history of suicidal behavior, and approaching court date" (Hayes, 2010, p. 1). Ironically, institutional directives that are designed to prevent suicidal and self-injurious behaviors require that officials employ isolation options, including administrative segregation (solitary confinement) and *suicide watch* (Kaba, et al., 2014). Clearly, correction officials and staff should collaborate and discuss options that may be more effective in meeting the needs of inmates and preventing them from further self-harm and possible death.

Inmates who have expressed suicidal ideation or have previously attempted suicide are often required to undergo one or more of the following suicide prevention measures:

- The removal of all clothing, and possibly, the wearing of a smock ("turtle suit") or other antisuicide protective garment or item (e.g., mattress, pillow, blanket)

- The removal of all bedding and other "anchoring" items that could be used as a hanging device

- Suicide watch, which may include close observation (10- to 15-minute intervals) or constant observation (no interruption)

Hayes (2010 & 2013)

Summary of Part One

Due to a host of adjustment issues, including those just described, outcomes for justice-involved PwMI often reflect a tragic chain of events that involve relapse and a perpetual failure to comply with conditions of incarceration or community release programs (Massaro, 2005). Reentry concerns are discussed in the next chapter. The good news is that things have been improving in some jurisdictions with regard to the training of correctional staff and court personnel (Carlson, 2011), the proper classification and placement of inmates with mental health issues, and the implementation of specialized housing units and innovative programming in order to accommodate the needs of special populations (Kim, Becker-Cohen, & Serakos, 2015).

Part Two: Diversion Strategies at Intercept Three

Jail-Based Treatment

With so many PwMI who are now incarcerated, efforts must be made to either divert inmates into community-based mental health settings (if possible) or to provide best practices in relation to the provision of treatment in prison and jail settings. Aside from initial mental health screenings and evaluations upon intake (discussed in Chapters 4 and 6), optimal treatment strategies may include ongoing and consistent observation, screening, and evaluation for short-term crisis events; therapeutic interventions; medication management; and other support programs related to recovery and reentry (e.g., job skills, education, housing, daily living) (Lamb & Weinberger, 1998; Shankar, 2011; Torrey, et al., 2014). Furthermore, screening, assessment, and therapeutic interventions should be performed by well-trained and educated mental health professionals who are employed with or contracted for by the department of corrections. These individuals would comprise a multidisciplinary psychiatric team that could also make referrals to inpatient psychiatric hospitals when necessary (Lamb & Weinberger, 1998).

Therapeutic intervention in jails or prisons has historically been pharmacologically based. In short, when hospitalization for sick inmates is not an option, staff rely on psychotropic medications to keep inmates calm and under control (Shankar, 2011). The complexities associated with administering medication in correctional settings include overt inmate refusal of treatment, a general distrust of correctional staff, and unpleasant side effects associated with some medications. Moreover, the costs for some psychotropic medications are taxing on correctional budgets, and they generally increase between 15 and 20 percent each year (Daniel, 2007). To control costs in this regard, *restricted formularies* (older-generation psychotropic medications and generic versions) have been used with incarcerated PwMI. This has been a concerning issue, in particular, because the chemical composition of these formularies may not have the same positive effect on the symptoms as did prior more progressive medication(s) and, in fact, may exacerbate the mental health condition of the patient because of multiple side effects (Daniel, 2007).

As with individuals receiving mental health treatment in the community, optimal outcomes with incarcerated PwMI usually involve a combination of pharmacological and psychotherapeutic interventions. In some jurisdictions, departments of correction have identified specific treatment needs and have been allotted resources to implement programming and therapeutic interventions to meet those needs. For example, recognizing the high rates of victimization and trauma among females in correctional settings, cognitive behavioral approaches, such as *dialetical behavior therapy (DBT)*, have been used with some success. *Therapeutic communities (TCs)* have also been adapted for use in correctional settings. TCs emphasize successful trauma intervention and the promotion/development of peer support and counseling. Results have been mixed as to the effectiveness of TCs—in particular, in the ability to effectively serve the needs of diverse clientele (Loper & Levitt, 2011).

Peer-Based Services

One of the most effective strategies in engaging PwMI in mental health treatment and programs is by offering peer services or peer support programs. Peer support programs are available in all 50 states and have been designated as a best practice by the Substance Abuse and Mental Health Services Administration (SAMHSA) due to the empirical evidence as to their effectiveness in reducing symptoms and hospitalizations and in improving treatment engagement, social functioning, and well-being/self-esteem among consumers (Daniels, Cate, Bergeson, Forquer, Niewenhous, & Epps, 2013; "Peer Services," 2016).

Peer-based programs entail the employment of peer support specialists (or recovery specialists)—individuals who have attained their own significant recovery and who have also been trained to work in a variety of roles, such as counselor, crisis worker, case manager, wellness coach, and educator. Figure 7.3 shows an example of one training program in action. The primary objective is to promote long-lasting recovery by helping people stay out of the hospital and live independently. Peer support professionals

Figure 7.3
Veterans' Initiative Trains Peer Mentors
Source: By Traci Patterson, Mental Health of America Greater Houston. http://www.mhahouston.org/photos/457/in/18/

are stationed in jails, hospitals, crisis stabilization units, and drop-in centers and are available to provide support and help locate additional resources in a variety of clinical settings for whatever services are needed ("Peer Services," 2016). Through their collaborative partnerships with local agencies (e.g., social services, criminal and juvenile justice, veterans' affairs), support specialists can make sure that justice-involved clients are compliant in their treatment and help them meet the challenges of daily life in tasks ranging from developing and maintaining relationships, grocery shopping, and managing money to taking medication and keeping doctor appointments. Although there has been financial support for peer-based programming and empirical evidence of positive outcomes, the statistical findings are still moderate, and more rigorous methodology is needed to draw consistent conclusions (Chinman, George, Dougherty, Daniels, Ghose, Swift, & Delphin-Rittmon, 2014).

Forensic Services

Another diversion strategy available at Intercept Three, is the implementation of forensic services, which may include evaluations, case management, and placement in a community outpatient setting or a state hospital. Forensic case management and court-ordered treatment can occur in a secure (inpatient) or community-based (outpatient) setting. Forensic clients released from state hospitals or from jail and ordered to receive community-based care are usually monitored by the court under a conditional release order (CRO, discussed later) (Manguno-Mire, Coffman, DeLand, Thompson, & Myers, 2014). The state allots a select number of "forensic beds" to a county or jurisdiction (Torrey, et al., 2010); these beds are located in a secure (forensic) hospital and are reserved for seriously mentally ill felony offenders who have been committed to the state under the doctrine of *parens patriae* and evaluated by a legally defined "expert" examiner under a court order for competence and/or sanity ("About Adult Forensic Mental Health," 2014; "Forensic Services: Program Overview," 2016; New York State Office of Mental Health, 2016; Roesch, Zapf, Golding, & Skeem, 1999). Evaluations and legal concepts pertaining to competency and sanity are discussed in more detail later in the chapter; for now, forensic case management and state forensic hospitals are introduced and discussed in some detail.

Case Management

A forensic case manager (sometimes referred to as a *forensic liaison* or forensic specialist) is an individual who is most likely employed by a community mental health provider under contract with the county, region, or state to provide an array of services to justice-involved individuals with serious mental illness (forensic clients) in both secure and community settings (Slate, et al., 2013; Steadman, Morris, & Dennis, 1995).

Knowledge Check

Under state statute, forensic clients are "accused" individuals who have received an order for evaluation of competency or sanity, have been adjudicated as incompetent to stand trial (IST)/incompetent to proceed (ITP), *or found* not guilty by reason of insanity (NGI) *due to serious mental illness.*

CAREER OPTIONS

For the position of forensic case manager (juvenile and adult), the following qualifications have been sought:

continued

A BA/BS degree in a human service field from an accredited college or university

One or more years of full-time experience working with adults with mental health disorders

Good organizational skills and the ability to develop partnerships with other service agencies in the community

Excellent communication skills, both verbal and in writing; ability to maintain records

A valid driver's license, current auto insurance, a reliable vehicle, and a good driving record

If you have experience working in the criminal justice system in some capacity, employers see that as an extra bonus (hence, why internships are excellent opportunities)

Source: Glassdoor.com; "Position Description," retrieved at http://www.nwcsb.com/pds/Juvenile_Forensic_Case_Manager.pdf

Forensic case managers are considered liaisons or boundary spanners (discussed in Chapters 6, 8, and 10), as they are generally responsible for the coordination of services between two or more systems of care. In particular, services provided by forensic case managers may include the coordination of mental health evaluations, service planning, service linkage, service coordination, monitoring of service delivery, and evaluation of service effectiveness (Steadman, et al., 1995). Case managers assigned to forensic clients who are living in the community are responsible for monitoring compliance with the court-ordered release plan, providing early intervention to avoid revocation of *conditional release* (discussed shortly), and reporting to the court on progress/compliance. Whether a client is suitable for community placement or secure placement in a forensic hospital will depend on recommendations made by a forensic evaluator, and by order of the court.

Forensic Hospitals

Forensic hospitals are secure treatment facilities that are geared toward housing persons with serious mental illness who have most likely been court ordered and committed to a state department that oversees mental health services (Powitsky, 2011). Depending on the jurisdiction and/or the mission of the lead agency, organizational differences may be observed across facilities. When offenders are admitted into a forensic treatment center, they are expected to follow a treatment plan that may include competency training, medication management, group and individual therapy, and participation in a variety of programs tailored to the individual's specific needs. For IST or ITP patients, the primary goal is to restore competency; for NGI patients, it is to secure, stabilize, and treat ("Forensic Facilities," 2014).

Given the various types of clients served, forensic facilities generally have three levels of security: minimum/nonsecure, medium, and maximum. Minimum-security state hospitals are under secured access with locked doors and 24/7 supervision. These facilities are typically used for forensic patients with misdemeanors, nonviolent offenses, and those with low risk of elopement. Medium-security state hospitals are under secured access by way of electronic fences, controlled access, and limitations on personal items allowed in the facility. Maximum-security state hospitals are normally operated under restricted movement, specialized monitoring, and continuous observation; these facilities are reserved for patients who are charged with felonious crimes and who have been determined to present a risk of violence ("Forensic Mental Health Services," 2013; "Forensic Services: Program Overview," n.d.).

Commonly, defendants found incompetent or not guilty by reason of insanity are indefinitely committed to the state department, which controls mental health services, and are then placed in one of several hospitals across the state. State statutes outline the process of forensic commitment; the time in which placement must occur is also prescribed by state statute and ranges anywhere from 14 to 30 days. A major issue with

Figure 7.4

Aerial View of the Treasure Coast Forensic Treatment Center, Indiantown, Florida

Source: Courtesy of Jim Cheney at Prufrock Communications

forensic secure placement is the lack of available beds and lengthy waitlists. Given the legal mandate on the limit for which an individual with mental illness can be held in jail after commitment to a treatment facility, there is an enormous amount of pressure on the facilities to effectively manage the waitlists—which can be as long as four months (Fuller, Sinclair, Geller, Quanbeck, & Snook, 2016). Once a person is transported to a forensic facility (usually from jail by the sheriff's office), the length of stay depends completely on the individual's participation and response to treatment (Slate, et al., 2013). Some reports have indicated that, on average, ITP patients are discharged within a four-month period (Wasserman, 2014); this is in stark contrast with the average length of stay for NGI patients, which is a little over four years (Fuller, et al., 2016).

As long as criminal charges are pending or prosecution deferred, a periodic status report must be given to the courts to determine their length of stay or if conditional release becomes an option. Discharge from a forensic hospital does not necessarily mean an individual will be released into the community; in fact, if hospital staff find that some ITP and NGI clients need continued treatment in a secure setting beyond that which can be rendered in the forensic facility, civil commitment is an option that might be considered (Wasserman, 2014). Figure 7.4 provides one example of a forensic hospital in the state of Florida.

CAREER SPOTLIGHT

Contributor: Cymantha Bryce, MS
Position: Resident Advocate (RA) — Treasure Coast Forensic Treatment Center

Employer:

Correct Care, LLC
Treasure Coast Forensic Treatment Center
96 Allapattah Rd.
Indiantown, FL 34956

The Treasure Coast Forensic Treatment Center (TCFTC) located in Central Florida is a 224-bed, all-male treatment center. TCFTC provides recovery services for individuals who are deemed incompetent to proceed and not guilty by reason of insanity.

The resident advocate is a liaison between TCFTC administration, TCFTC residents, and the residents' family members. The RA position ensures that TCFTC has not violated the rights of the resident or his family. This position investigates and provides follow-through for grievances submitted by the resident or the resident's family. The RA is a member of several administrative committees and is the chairperson for the Resident Governance Council as well as the Ethics Committee.

In addition, TCFTC participated in the evidence-based diversion program Crisis Intervention Team (CIT) training. CIT is a training for first responders, correctional officers, LEOs, probation

continued

officers, and other community partners with the focus on diverting individuals with mental illness out of the criminal justice system and into the most appropriate service network. As the current RA, I am a certified CIT coordinator. I coordinate as well as provide instructional sessions for the Treasure Coast CIT quarterly.

Qualifications for the RA position are as follows (from job description):

Minimum Requirements

- Master's degree in psychology, social work, criminal justice, or a related field with two years of practical experience; or
- Bachelor's degree with a minimum of three years of direct service experience in a correctional/mental health setting; and
- A high level of familiarity with the medical and mental healthcare systems at the local, state, and federal levels is desirable.

Conditional Release

A justice-involved PwMI who is detained, whether in a jail, prison, or forensic hospital, and who has demonstrated a low public safety risk may be given the opportunity for release into the community with conditions—otherwise referred to as conditional release or "mental health probation" (Slate, et al., 2013). The individual will continue to be committed under the designated state department of mental health services, and the department will contract with providers to oversee the client's progress. Factors that judges consider in their decision to grant conditional release include the seriousness of the offense committed, the individual's behavior while held in jail, the amount of time between the last reported unlawful act and the hearing, whether there are family or friends in the community who are willing to support the individual, and other factors (Dirks-Lindhorst & Linhorst, 2012). Once approved by a treatment team and the state and reviewed and accepted by the client, a judge will sign a CRO, that will be accompanied by a conditional release plan (CRP)—a document that sets forth all of the conditions the client is expected to follow (see the following example from the state of Florida).

An Excerpt of a Conditional Release Plan, as Taken from a Model Order Adjudicating Defendant Not Guilty by Reason of Insanity and Placing the Defendant on Conditional Release

(a)   The Defendant will remain in outpatient treatment for his mental illness during his conditional release period. Such treatment will be provided by the _____

---

continued

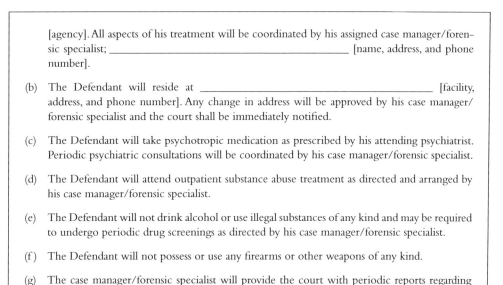

[agency]. All aspects of his treatment will be coordinated by his assigned case manager/forensic specialist; _____ [name, address, and phone number].

(b)   The Defendant will reside at _____ [facility, address, and phone number]. Any change in address will be approved by his case manager/forensic specialist and the court shall be immediately notified.

(c)   The Defendant will take psychotropic medication as prescribed by his attending psychiatrist. Periodic psychiatric consultations will be coordinated by his case manager/forensic specialist.

(d)   The Defendant will attend outpatient substance abuse treatment as directed and arranged by his case manager/forensic specialist.

(e)   The Defendant will not drink alcohol or use illegal substances of any kind and may be required to undergo periodic drug screenings as directed by his case manager/forensic specialist.

(f)   The Defendant will not possess or use any firearms or other weapons of any kind.

(g)   The case manager/forensic specialist will provide the court with periodic reports regarding compliance with the conditions of release and his progress in treatment. These reports will be submitted every six months or as required by the court.

(h)   The conditional release plan has been reviewed by the Defendant. The Defendant understands the conditions of release listed and agrees to comply with them.

Source: Florida Department of Children and Families, AFMH Model Court Orders and Motions

Persons in the community under a CRO are usually monitored by a forensic liaison or case manager who provides periodic updates to the court with regard to the client's status. The majority of clients on conditional release are persons who have been acquitted as NGI; however, in some cases, if the court determines that an individual adjudicated ITP presents a low public safety risk and may be effectively managed in the community, it is possible that the individual will be granted conditional release, with community-based competency restoration included as one of the conditions, in addition to mental health treatment and monitoring by the court (Manguno-Mire, et al., 2014). The most common methods of monitoring are monthly face-to-face visits with the client, telephone contact, and the development of relationships with community support workers and others who have regular contact with the individual on conditional release. Forensic case managers may also attend programs with their clients and make random visits to the community in which the client resides and/or works.

In contrast to traditional community supervision of criminal defendants who are under probation and parole, the vast majority of conditional release revocations are a product of CRP violations rather than the commission of a new crime or violent behavior. For example, CROs have been revoked for the client's failure to take prescribed medications or to attend scheduled treatment appointments as set forth in the CRP. Recent research has revealed that conditional release programs have reduced recidivism and minimized the number of arrests and revocations over longer durations than indicated previously (Manguno-Mire, et al., 2014). To be successful, treatment programs for substance abuse issues must be provided, as well as close monitoring of mental health symptoms and very intensive supervision for individuals who have history of failure and rule violations (Hayes, Kemp, Large, & Nielssen, 2013; Manguno-Mire, et al., 2014).

Therapeutic Jurisprudence (Courts and Court Services)

Therapeutic jurisprudence refers to a multidisciplinary study of therapeutic and antitherapeutic consequences in relation to the application of the law (Wexler, 2000). Traditionally, the criminal justice system has utilized legal sanctions, including incarceration, both to punish offenders and to deter them from further criminal activity. Conversely, the treatment community emphasizes the development and maintenance of therapeutic relationships to help motivate individuals to reduce their dependence on drugs, change their behavior, and take control of their lives. Specialty or problem-solving courts have emerged in recent years as evolving agents of the therapeutic jurisprudence philosophy, offering competing perspectives on the causes of substance abuse and addiction, family violence, and mental health and trauma. The following sections offer an introductory discussion of problem-solving courts that cater to the needs of justice-involved PwMI, including drug and mental health treatment court programs. A brief discussion of veterans' court is also provided at the end of the section.

Drug Treatment Court

The first drug court was established in 1989 in Dade County, Miami, Florida, and at the end of 2014, there were close to 3,000 drug treatment courts (DTCs) of all types operating across the United States (e.g., adult, juvenile, family, and DWI) (National Institute of Justice [NIJ], 2006). Drug courts combine intensive supervision, mandatory drug testing, treatment, and incentives to help offenders with substance abuse problems. Among other conditions (described later), drug court involvement requires a client to undergo intensive supervision and mandatory drug testing over a certain period of time, to be determined by the drug court program team. If any violations are discovered, the prompt utilization of sanctions is imposed in an attempt to correct the behavior. Alternatively, incentives are used to reward program compliance, as encouragement and support are essential components of a successful outcome and a full recovery for clients (Marlowe, 2012).

A drug court "workgroup" or "team" is typically composed of a judge, prosecutor (district or state attorney), defense counsel, treatment provider(s), probation officer(s), law enforcement, and a court coordinator. All of these people communicate and work together to come up with a treatment plan for the participant and monitor them to ensure they are staying on their route to recovery (Griffin, Heilbrun, Mulvey, DeMatteo, & Schubert, 2015). Typically, offenders will elect to enter a drug court program as a diversion from the traditional court process or as a condition of probation. Goals, rules, and expectations are explained early in the process; the offender must appear in treatment court on a regular basis to be assessed by the team and to report progress to the Court. A program usually consists of individual and group counseling and mandatory drug testing. Clients are provided help with employment, education, healthcare services, and housing services. After the client has successfully completed the program (12 to 18 months, on average), they will likely participate in a graduation and their charges may be dismissed, reduced, or set-aside (Office of National Drug Court Policy [ONDCP] "Fact Sheet: Drug Courts," 2011). Studies have produced positive results with regard to reduction in recidivism and prevention of drug use/abuse; however, because of poorly designed research methodologies and an overall lack of rigor, many have failed to produce generalizable results (Griffin, Heilbrun, Mulvey, DeMatteo, & Schubert, 2015; Wilson, Mitchell, & Mackenzie, 2006). According to the literature, more recent methodologies have shown improvement in this regard, and preliminary results continue to be quite promising (Griffin, et al., 2015; Rossman, Roman, Zweig, Rempel, & Linquist, 2011).

Mental Health Treatment Court

Modeled after drug treatment courts, mental health courts (MHCs) emerged in 1997, with the first one implemented in Broward County, Florida (Slate, et al., 2013). There are now over 300 MHCs in various states throughout the United States (Burns, Hiday, & Ray, 2012). Along with the traditional goals of meting out justice and keeping the public safe, the central (and nontraditional) goals of MHC include connecting individuals with behavioral health services and providing access to quality treatment, improving psychiatric symptoms, improving overall quality of life, and reducing recidivism rates (Odegaard, 2007). Participation in an MHC program is voluntary, but clients can be referred by police officers, judges, attorneys, probation officers, case managers, prison staff, family members, and other agencies or individuals who come in contact with an offender. MHC programs typically last between 12 and 18 months, during which time clients are expected to be involved in supervision/probation appointments, regular drug testing, judicial review hearings, community service or other pro-social activities, and any additional services needed such as drug and alcohol treatment or support with job placement.

> **FAST FACT**
>
> *Role of Gender in Mental Health Courts*
>   Males with mental illness are more likely to be involved in violent crimes and exhibit violent behavior than women (Ennis, McLeod, Watt, Campbell, & Adams-Quackenbush, 2016). Despite similar recidivism rates, however, women are more likely to be referred to mental health court than men (Ennis, et al., 2016).

In most cases, criteria for participation in an MHC require that the defendant must have a current primary diagnosis of a major mental health disorder within the last two years as defined by the DSM. The most frequently cited disorders among MHC clients have included schizophrenia, major mood disorder (bipolar disorder, major depressive disorder), and psychotic disorder (schizoaffective disorder) (Odegaard, 2007). The defendant must be assessed by a psychiatrist or psychologist if there is not a current diagnosis to determine that the defendant has a serious mental illness. Although MHC programs accept most misdemeanor clients on the docket, some do not allow felony forensic clients to participate (Griffin, Steadman, & Petrilla, 2002). Additionally, like DTCs, MHCs follow a behavioral modification–based model of sanctions and rewards; however, procedural guidelines as to the content and process may differ across programs (Griffin, et al., 2012, 2015; Odegaard, 2007). For these and other reasons, MHCs and other problem-solving court programs have been criticized for failing to comply with more formal and consistent procedural guidelines and potentially violating client due-process rights. There have also been concerns raised as to process efficiency, in that research findings indicate a lack of support for swift diversion, which was the original intention of MHC implementation (Griffin, et al., 2015).

By and large, the research reveals that participation in MHC programs has reduced recidivism and violence among persons with mental illness; it has also been shown to increase engagement in mental health and other treatment services (Burns, Hiday, & Ray, 2012; Hiday, Wales, & Ray, 2013; Keator, Callahan, Steadman, & Vesselinov, 2013; McNiel, Sadeh, Delucci, & Binder, 2015). Completion of the program has been a determining factor related to recidivism in some studies (e.g., Moore & Hiday, 2006). In terms of improvements in psychiatric and substance abuse symptoms, the research is conflicting; however, it seems that mental health service delivery depends on the services available and the collaboration among provider agencies in the jurisdiction that delivers the services (Honegger, 2015).

Veterans' Treatment Court

Given the success of specialized mental health and drug court programs in reducing the population of PwMI incarcerated and improving recidivism rates, veterans' treatment courts (VTCs) were developed to meet the needs of the veteran population increasingly coming into contact with the criminal justice system—in particular, for nonviolent offenses that are largely attributable to post-traumatic stress disorder (PTSD) acquired during deployment and exposure to combat-related situations (Knudsen & Wingenfeld, 2015).

VTC programs focus on underlying causes of criminal behavior, and members of the treatment team collaborate to wrap veterans in an array of services so that they can engage in treatment (including trauma-based treatment and proper medications), but also get help with needs such as housing, transportation, and obtaining medical services and other veterans' benefits (Knudsen & Wingenfeld, 2015). In order to be eligible for the VTC, individuals must have committed a nonviolent felony or misdemeanor; qualify for Veterans' Administration (VA) benefits; and have PTSD, substance abuse, or some other psychological problem. Participation in VTC is completely voluntary. Participants will come before judges on a regular basis to discuss their progress, and they will receive support and guidance from veteran mentors, which has been proven to be the most essential, and successful, component of the program (Russell, 2009).

Given the relative youth of veteran court programs, empirical evidence of program effectiveness is available, though sparse. Table 7.1 provides a snapshot of existing research as it relates to the implementation of veterans' court at the county level, including program characteristics as well as any outcome data, where available.

TABLE 7.1 Intercept Three: A Sample of Veterans' Court Programs in the United States

State	Year Implemented	No. Clients Served	Felony or Misdemeanor	Program Evaluations
California (Orange County)	2008	Program currently has 50 participants; specific population served unknown	Both (must be first offense)	No
Colorado (El Paso County)	2009	140+ served, with 99 in evaluation as of 2013; can be referred from anywhere	Both	Yes: community spent 161k compared to 3+mil for prison; 33 program graduates; over 25% of participants experience positive benefits across all factors (drug use, employment, etc.)

State	Year Implemented	No. Clients Served	Felony or Misdemeanor	Program Evaluations
Texas (40 counties in North Texas)	2011	Currently serving 37 veterans	Both, but felony must be nonviolent	No
Pennsylvania (Lancaster County)	2012	N/A	Both, excluding homicide and Megan's Law charges	Yes, but unavailable
Kentucky (115 counties)	2012	N/A	N/A	Yes, but unavailable

Source: California, retrieved at http://www.courts.ca.gov/13955.htm; Colorado, retrieved at http://www.courts.state.co.us/Courts/County/Custom.cfm?County_ID=6&Page_ID=501; Texas, retrieved at http://www.northtexas.va.gov/features/VetTxCourtProgram.asp; Pennsylvania, retrieved at http://www.pacourts.us/judicial-administration/court-programs/veterans-courts; Kentucky, retrieved at http://courts.ky.gov/courtprograms/vtc/Pages/default.aspx.

Matters of the Law: Competency and Insanity

The diversion options just presented are highly salient at Intercept Three for identifying custody and treatment strategies with justice-involved PwMI. There are additional legal issues to consider during the period between an initial encounter with law enforcement and adjudication. If properly trained in behavioral health and crisis intervention, first responders and correctional staff (including mental health workers) might observe behaviors that, upon further examination, could delay and/or prevent the further processing of an individual through the legal system. Specifically, there are important concerns in relation to two legal concepts: competency to stand trial and the insanity defense. These concepts are defined and contrasted next in terms of their primary differences. Case examples are also provided for further clarification.

Competency to Stand Trial

Basic constitutional rights pertaining to due process make it crucial that a criminal defendant is capable of knowingly, intelligently, and voluntarily participating in the legal process, which particularly entails his or her own defense. The authority for this rule of law, which pertains to a defendant's mental state, can be found in the case of *Dusky v. U.S.*, 32 U.S. 402 (1960). Under *Dusky*, the U.S. Supreme Court held that the basic standard for determining competency is whether "the Defendant has a sufficient present ability to consult with his attorney with a reasonable degree of rational understanding, and whether he has a rational as well as factual understanding of the proceedings against him" (*Dusky v. U.S.*, 402, 1960). The requirement of a rational and factual understanding should be underscored here, for a defendant could have a factual understanding of the purpose of a judge and jury, yet believe that both have been given orders by Satan to punish him severely.

Competency refers to the mental state of the defendant at the present time—not at the time of the offense. Thus, "present" may include any point after the offense has been allegedly committed and during the legal process from initial police custody and interrogation to the expected time of trial and sentencing. The issue as to a defendant's competency may be raised multiple times during the processing of a case if the defendant's mental condition changes; the intent is to determine the ability of a defendant to perform a specific function throughout proceedings (Andrews, 2003). Competency is most likely to be determined prior to a trial; however, issues of competency have also been found to surface after sentencing and conviction phases due to capital punishment cases (Slate, et al., 2013). If a defendant is found to be incompetent (incompetent to proceed to trial or ITP), the criminal justice process should be temporarily halted, and proceedings should resume only when competency is determined or restored, if at all.

Psychiatric Advance Directive: Like in case of a medical emergency that renders a person incompetent to make important medical decisions, a psychiatric advance directive can be utilized to determine the mental health treatment options for a consumer when that person is in a mental health crisis situation and is found to be too sick to make decisions related to psychiatric care. Unfortunately, advance directives in this regard are underutilized.

Source: "Psychiatric Advance Directive" (2016), Retrieved at http://www.mentalhealthamerica.net/psychiatric-advance-directive.

State legislation differs slightly with respect to some of the procedural aspects of competency and competency examinations in particular; however, some generalizations can be made. For example, the need for a competency examination is typically initiated by several individuals who have contact with the defendant and, hence, the opportunity for direct observation. Such individuals may include police, correctional staff, the warden of a correctional facility, and forensic mental health staff. More often, however, the issue is raised by counsel—in particular, the defendant's attorney or public defender (Mental Health Procedures Act [Pennsylvania], 1976). A court may also initiate an examination on its own motion. The burden of proof with regard to the defendant's status is that of the party who raised the issue, and that party will order that evaluations be conducted. The defendant has a right to have counsel represented during a competency examination, as well as any subsequent hearings pertaining to competency status. Further, the defendant has the right to remain silent and to not participate or answer any of the questions asked by the examiner (Andrews, 2003). The competency examiner may also be ordered by the court to assess a defendant for mental status at the time of the offense or insanity, a concept that is discussed in more detail next.

Depending on a number of factors related to the client and the charges, as well as available resources in a jurisdiction (e.g., available hospital beds and costs associated with the service), competency restoration may occur in one of three different settings:

- Jail

- Community

- Forensic treatment center (hospital)

Competency training is much less costly when delivered in a jail setting, according to the literature; however, given the infancy of jail-based programming and the lack of available data, no conclusion has been drawn as to differences in effectiveness as related to outcome (competency restored) and place of delivery (Kapoor, 2011).

Insanity as a Defense

In contrast with competency, which requires an evaluation of one's mental capacity at present state, a determination that a defendant is not guilty by reason of insanity (NGRI) is made based on a defendant's mental state at the time the offense was committed. Insanity is an affirmative defense, it does not result in a stay of criminal proceedings. Rather, it is introduced later during a trial as a means to attain an acquittal for the defendant, hence, dismissing or ending any prosecution in the criminal court. The following case study may offer some clarification through the application of both constructs to a fictional account.

COMPETENCY VS. SANITY: THE CASE OF SALLY AND MAC

Imagine for a moment that Sally hears voices in her head that tell her to hurt Mac. Let's say that she ignores them for as long as possible, but then is compelled to listen to them and finally hurts Mac—pretty badly, actually. She is quite vocal about the incident, and suddenly the district attorney (DA) builds a pretty strong case against her. Seems like an open and shut case, right?

Well, not necessarily. Once detained in the local jail, some guards notice Sally arguing and carrying on with individuals who are not present, and so they inform the warden that she "just isn't right." At this point, it seems there may be an issue regarding her competency to stand trial for the

---

continued

current charges. In fact, in order to move forward and prosecute someone like Sally, the DA, her defense counsel, or the court will have to order that she be evaluated by a psychologist to determine whether or not she is competent to stand trial. What does this mean? In short, it means that Sally must express a basic understanding of the nature of the charges against her and the adversary nature of the judicial system. She must also be able to cooperate with her defense lawyers.

Why is this important? Well, consider this: Imagine that Sally's defense lawyer explained the charges against her and what might happen if she's found guilty. Her defense counsel may tell her she is facing assault charges and could possibly be sentenced to 15 to 20 years in prison. Now imagine that after all the explanation, Sally still does not understand what is going on and instead keeps insisting that she be able to watch her favorite programs at home on her television and from her own bed. It's possible that Sally is so lost in her own world of visions and voices that she is unable to distinguish hallucinations from reality anymore. For these reasons, she might be found incompetent to stand trial.

What does this mean for Sally and her criminal case? Well, we should keep in mind that state law will vary slightly, but it is not uncommon for violent offenders deemed incompetent to proceed (ITP) to be committed to state mental institutions and be subjected to periodic reevaluations which are sent to the court. Sometimes, a person may be deemed nonrestorable, and therefore, the charges must be dismissed. Other times, a reevaluation will indicate that the defendant has become competent; in that case, the defendant will be tried on the original charges.

There are several ways that a person may be found ITP with regard to mental health. One reason is that they are not able to tell the difference between reality and hallucinations or delusions. Another reason is that a person may have a severe intellectual disability, which renders it impossible for them to function at a normal level intellectually. Learning disabilities and dementia may also contribute to a person being found ITP.

Competency to stand trial involves an inquiry as to the defendant's current state of mind. What if we determined that Sally was completely sane during the assault on Mac? What if the circumstances here were that Sally had a psychotic break soon after she committed the crime and now was not competent to stand trial? The point is that Sally would still be ITP even though she was not psychologically impaired at the time of the crime.

Insanity Defense

How would the situation be different if Sally was not functioning normally at the time of the offense against Mac? Imagine that Sally comprehends the charges against her and has been able to assist her public defender in preparation for trial; however, at the time of the crime, she was hearing voices and did not really know what she was doing. In that case, Sally's defense attorney might argue that she is not guilty by reason of insanity (NGI or NGRI).

Insanity can be a complex concept to explain and, worse yet, to understand. Here is the (very) basic premise: In order to find a person guilty of a crime, the state has to prove that the person committed the crime and that they had criminal intent; in other words, *mens rea*, or a guilty mind. In other words, if a person steals his co-worker's bicycle because it is exactly the same as his and, therefore, he truly believes it is his, then he cannot be convicted of theft, which is a crime, because he did not have the necessary intent to commit a crime.

In the context of describing how the insanity defense works, this means that a person like Sally, who has a mental illness and lacked awareness of her behavior and the wrongfulness of it, can certainly plead NGRI. This is the insanity defense.

During pre-trial examination, and upon a motion by the court, an evaluator will be charged with determining the defendant's criminal responsibility by conducting a *mental status at the time of the offense (MSO) evaluation*. From a legal standpoint, there are three tests related to making a determination of insanity: the M'Naghten "right or wrong" cognitive test, the irresistible impulse volitional prong test, and the model penal code test (Feinstein, 2013; Moriarty, 2014). Under M'Naghten and irresistible impulse rulings, burden is placed on the defense to prove by a preponderance of the evidence that the defendant, at the time of the offense, was operating under a defect of reason from disease of the mind and was unaware of the wrongful nature of the act committed (Feinstein, 2013; Slate, et al., 2013). Over the years, criticism has circulated around M'Naghten/irresistible impulse rulings, due to the fact that they may not take full consideration of the true impact mental illnesses may have on impairing judgment and impulse control. With the 1954 case of *Durham v. U.S.*, a reformed "product" test for insanity was brought about, which disregarded both the M'Naghten and irresistible impulse tests (Moriarty, 2014). The Durham product test set out a ruling that stated "an accused is not criminally responsible if his unlawful act was the product of mental disease or mental defect" (Moriarty, 2014, p. 12); however, due to the broad nature of this ruling, both state and federal courts rejected it. In 1955, the American Law Institute (ALI) formulated a model penal code test known as the "ALI standard" that essentially combined and rephrased the M'Naghten/irresistible impulse tests (Feinstein, 2013; Moriarty, 2014).

Although the ALI standard was favored throughout the courts for many years, the very high-profile John Hinckley case in 1981[2] prompted yet another reform, known as the Insanity Defense Reform Act (IDRA). IDRA demanded an affirmative defense and burden of proof (Moriarty, 2014). By the early 1990s, attention was shifted back toward the M'Naghten and ALI standards, which eventually had become, and continue to be, the predominant methodologies for evaluating insanity defenses throughout the United States (Slate, et al., 2013).

An MSO evaluation is designed to determine whether, because of a mental disease or defect, a defendant experienced cognitive impairment at the time of the commission of an offense that renders him or her unable to be held criminally liable. The evaluation consists of three parts:

1. Historical information related to the defendant
2. The mental state of the defendant at the time of the offense
3. The present mental state of the defendant

Source: http://www.psychwest.com/forensicsanity.html

State laws are instructive as to criteria regarding an MSO evaluation or examination. In regard to what specifically constitutes a mental disease or defect, it is when there is a significant impairment to the capacity of the defendant to understand what they have done (Andrews, 2003). In Pennsylvania, for example, if the defendant disagrees with the conclusion of the MSO report conducted by the court-appointed psychiatrist, the court must allow reasonable compensation for the defendant to retain another psychiatrist. Further, in the instance that the court makes a pre-trial determination that the defendant is criminally responsible, the defendant may raise the issue again later to the jury assigned to hear the case (Mental Health Procedures Act, MHPA, 50 P.S. §7402(e) & §7402(f)).

The insanity defense has not been well received by the public, and this is reflective in jury decisions when it is used. In fact, in the United States, it is invoked in only about 1 percent of all felony cases, and is successful in only a small proportion of those (Feinstein, 2013). There is a considerable amount of controversy surrounding the idea of acquittal based upon a criminal defendant's mental state, and there have been ongoing debates and legislative changes designed to ameliorate public concerns of malingering and unjust acquittals. In some jurisdictions, juries have the option of invoking a verdict of guilty but mentally ill (GBMI), which attaches criminal liability and periods of continued incarceration, but acknowledges the defendant's need for mental health treatment (McGraw, Farthing-Capowich, & Keilitz, 1985).

Challenges

In regard to the longevity of sentencing and placement, some scholars have found various scenarios where defendants who received NGRI verdicts actually spent more time in confined psychiatric treatment than individuals who were sentenced to a traditional correctional institution (Fellner, 2006). Current screening and assessment practices present weak areas that need improvement in order to help retain the offender's due-process rights and to reduce correctional concerns, and ultimately, recidivism rates. Presented as the global theme throughout this textbook, behavioral health and criminal justice officials often neglect to communicate with each other, which makes it difficult for them to work collaboratively as a team to help those with serious mental illness avoid penetration into the traditional criminal justice system. Unfortunately, this failure to integrate and to share pertinent information has resulted in pretty severe consequences for some individuals. The case of Ralph Tortorici is presented as illustrative of this point in the chapter's "snapshot" feature.

CASE SNAPSHOT: RALPH TORTORICI

When an Incompetent Defendant Is Allowed to Stand Trial

At 9:10 a.m. on December 14, 1994, Ralph Tortorici opened fire with a .270- caliber Remington rifle on a group of students gathered in Lecture Center 5 of the State University of New York at Albany, uptown campus. The 26-year-old psychology student held the class of 35 hostage as he nervously paced around, demanding to speak to various university and government officials. As a scuffle ensued between he and one male student, 19-year-old Jason McEnaney, Tortorici's gun went off, and a single bullet shot and seriously wounded McEnaney. Tortorici was ultimately charged with 14 counts of aggravated assault, kidnapping, and attempted murder; his lawyer subsequently entered a plea of not guilty by reason of insanity.

After the shooting, Tortorici's history of physical and mental illness was uncovered and indicated prior episodes of paranoia, auditory hallucinations, and delusional thinking. When he was evaluated for competency after the shooting, he was deemed incompetent to stand trial and was sent to a secure facility for treatment. During his brief treatment, Tortorici refused to take medications and was still reportedly delusional, but was shortly reassessed and found competent to stand trial. Tortorici was quickly sent back to jail to await his trial date. Later, a separate expert for the prosecution concluded that Tortorici was, once again, not competent to stand trial; however, although the report suggested hearings on the matter and deference to a sanity assessment until Tortorici could fully participate in the process, the Court denied the request and the trial ensued with Tortorici in absentia. The jury rejected the insanity defense, and Tortorici was convicted on all counts and was sentenced to prison for 20 to 47 years, the maximum sentence permissible under law. Just three weeks after Tortorici was sent to prison, he attempted suicide, and over the course of the next few years, was shuttled back and forth between the prison and a secure psychiatric facility.

In the end, Tortorici managed a successful suicide attempt; on August 10, 1999, he hanged himself with a sheet in his prison cell.

Source: *Frontline: A Crime of Insanity* (2002)

Situations like what happened to Ralph Tortorici are all too common for justice-involved PwMI. It is hoped that in the future, these situations can be avoided through the successful integration of criminal justice and mental health systems.

Practitioner's Corner 7.1
Determinations of Competency to Stand Trial in Juvenile Court as Contrasted with Adult Court

Contributor: Taylor P. Andrews, Esquire

I share my observations from my 44 years of criminal defense practice in Pennsylvania. For 35 of those years I was the chief public defender of a suburban-rural county with approximately 225,000 residents and five judges.

continued

One of those judges was assigned to juvenile court. I would characterize our juvenile court as being very protective of children and reluctant to adjudicate delinquency unless it was necessary. Our juvenile court judges have been sensitive that the creation of even a juvenile record may stigmatize a child when he or she becomes an adult. My observations may not be shared by practitioners from jurisdictions where the juvenile court is more readily punitive in its approach.

With the increased involvement of adults with serious mental illness in the criminal justice system, I have seen an increase in the number of cases in adult court where there is an issue raised as to competency to stand trial. The most common reason for the incompetency is due to psychosis related to mental illness. I have not seen the same increase in juvenile court.

The standard for competency is the same in juvenile court as it is in adult court. The Pennsylvania statute addressing competency states:

> Whenever a person who has been charged with a crime is found to be substantially unable to understand the nature or object of the proceedings against him or to participate and assist in his defense, he shall be deemed incompetent to be tried, convicted or sentenced so long as such incapacity continues.

> *(50 Pa. C. S. A. § 7402)*

Furthermore, the U.S. Supreme Court holding in Dusky v. U.S. also applies. It states:

> The test must be whether the Defendant has a sufficient present ability to consult with his attorney with a reasonable degree of rational understanding—and whether he has a rational as well as factual understanding of the proceedings against him.

> *(Dusky v. U.S. 362 U.S. 402, 1960)*

An "ability to assist in his defense" and to "consult with his attorney" and to have a "rational as well as factual understanding of the proceedings" are the critical elements of competency. In juvenile Court most juveniles must rely on their attorney even more than most adults due to their immaturity and lack of experience. Disagreements between client and attorney are less frequent in juvenile Court than in adult Court. It is, therefore, less likely that a juvenile would be found to be unable to consult with his attorney than is the case in adult Court. This is one reason why there are fewer trial competency issues raised.

There is also a difference in the objective of juvenile Court as opposed to adult Court that impacts the frequency of trial competency issues. The object in adult Court is punitive. The object in juvenile Court is rehabilitative and restorative. If there is an issue of incapacity in a juvenile Court proceeding, that problem may be addressed in the process without a trial competency determination but with an outcome that is designed to address the capacity issue. This is often of benefit to the juvenile because delays are avoided. The alternative would be to first adjudicate whether the incapacity rose to the level of rendering the juvenile incompetent to stand trial. If so, treatments or education would be provided to address the incapacity so that competency could be restored and then the action would proceed to probably address many of the same issues.

There are, of course, times when a juvenile is incompetent to proceed, even in the juvenile process. Severe developmental disabilities may deprive a juvenile of sufficient understanding of the process so that a case could not proceed. A youngster may be psychotic due to a mental illness or physical condition. Attention would be given to whether sufficient capacity could be gained by training and/or treatment to bring the juvenile to sufficient understanding that he/she was competent.

In such cases the process would be similar to adult Court. There would first be a ruling on the question of competency, and the case would not move forward until there was a finding that the juvenile was competent. The issue of competency could be renewed during the process if the juvenile's condition deteriorated. The determination of incompetency would not *terminate the process, but would suspend the process until competency was established. If competency could not be established, then the juvenile process would be dismissed without prejudice. This means it could be renewed if competency were established at a later time.*

Another reason why there are fewer trial competency claims raised in juvenile Court is that many of the serious mental illnesses that compromise competency do not have an onset until very late adolescence or early adulthood. Through there are cases of childhood schizophrenia and bipolar disorder, these mental illnesses that can have psychotic symptoms typically more often have their onset in the late teenage years. Most adult cases where trial competency is an issue involve mental illnesses with psychotic symptoms.

Take-Home Message

From a philosophical viewpoint, the primary role of state correctional agencies is to maintain institutional safety through proper functioning and management of the population. The increase in the number of people with serious mental illnesses in jails and prisons over recent decades, however, has transformed these facilities into de facto psychiatric institutions. This transformation can be attributed in part to insufficient funding and support by community mental health systems. Regardless of the reasons for the change, it has become clear that corrections staff must be better prepared to interact with detainees who have serious mental health needs. As discussed in Chapter 6, all detainees should be screened and assessed at intake for mental health and substance abuse history and prior treatment regimens, including medication management. Detainees with a history or current presentation of behavioral health symptoms should always be observed for competency and sanity issues. When competency is in question, a criminal defendant may be subjected to a series of evaluations that will render a decision as to whether the case should move forward (competent) or should pause until treatment occurs (incompetent). Inmates should also be screened for suicidal ideation, and proper management and care should be followed continuously for those found to be at risk for self-harm. It is also essential that staff be trained in proper response strategies when encountering PwMI who are experiencing adjustment issues related to their illnesses and symptomology. Strategies to combat stigma and to facilitate respect toward PwMI must be implemented. In some cases, diversion options can be used to filter PwMI out of the traditional criminal justice setting or to more effectively manage their care while incarcerated. For example, forensic case management and peer-based programming have been shown to be effective at minimizing adjustment difficulties and increasing treatment compliance. In some instances, detainees may be transferred to secure forensic hospitals, where they are more likely to receive the level of care needed to manage their illness. Finally, problem-solving, treatment-focused courts are used as a means to divert some offenders into a community-based care setting, while integrated into an array of services that are closely managed by a team of criminal justice and behavioral health professionals.

Most importantly, successful outcomes rely largely on effective collaboration and partnerships between criminal justice professionals and behavioral health providers and other cross-systems efforts designed to address complex needs of individuals—needs that cannot be effectively addressed by a single system of care. This subject is further addressed in the remaining chapters of the text.

QUESTIONS FOR CLASSROOM DISCUSSION

1. A variety of problem-solving courts have been implemented for individuals suffering from mental illness and addiction. Why are these courts necessary?
2. What kind of materials would help you better communicate with a person with a mental health disorder? Make a list of tools you think would assist you in better responding to or protecting persons with mental illness.
3. What clues might suggest that a person behaving inappropriately in a jail or prison setting may be either decompensating or contemplating suicide?
4. How does competency affect the criminal justice process? Compare and contrast this with sanity.

KEY TERMS & ACRONYMS

- Conditional release order (CRO)
- Conditional release plan (CRP)
- CSU
- Dialetical behavior therapy (DBT)
- Forensic commitment
- Forensic liaison

- Forensic specialist
- Incompetent to proceed (ITP) or incompetent to stand trial (IST)
- Mental status at the time of the offense (MSO) evaluation
- Not guilty by reason of insanity (NGRI or NGI)
- Parens patriae

- Restricted formularies (prescription psychotropic medications)
- Self-injurious behavior (SIB)
- Specialized housing units (SHUs)
- Suicide watch
- Therapeutic communities (TCs)

Notes

1. Div. V Court (Division V Court) refers to felony mental health court in that jurisdiction.
2. In 1981 Hinckley attempted to assassinate then U.S. President Ronald Regan and was ultimately acquitted under a NGRI verdict. This outcome caused a great deal of controversy and was the impetus for restrictions on (and in some states abolition of) the insanity defense (Feinstein, 2013).

Bibliography

Andrews, T. (2003). *Mental Health Procedures and Criminal Law.* Notes presented at the meeting of the Pennsylvania Bar Institute, Montour County, PA.

Benson, M. L., Alarid, L. F., Burton, V. S., & Cullen, F. T. (2011). Reintegration or stigmatization? Offenders' expectations of community re-entry. *Journal of Criminal Justice, 39*(5), 385–393.

Bauer, R. L., Morgan, R. D., & Mandracchia, J. T., (2010). Offenders with severe and persistent mental illness. In T. J. Fagan & R. K. Ax (Eds.), *Correctional Mental Health: From theory to best practice* (pp. 189–212). Thousand Oaks, CA: Sage Publications.

Burns, P. J., Hiday, V. A., & Ray, B. (2012). Effectiveness 2 Years Postexit of a Recently Established Mental Health Court. *American Behavioral Scientist, 20*(10), 1–20.

Canada, K. E., Angell, B., & Watson, A. C. (2010). Crisis Intervention Teams in Chicago: Successes on the Ground. *Journal of Police Crisis Negotiations, 10*, 86–100.

Carlson, P. M. (2011). Managing the Mentally Ill from a Correctional Administrator's Perspective. In Fagan, T. J., & Ax, R. K. (Eds.), *Correctional Mental Health: From Theory to Best Practice* (pp. 57–75). Thousand Oaks, CA: Sage Publications Inc.

Center for Public Policy Priorities. (2014). Mental Health Screening and Intake in County Jails. Retrieved from HYPERLINK "http://www.legis.state.tx.us/tlodocs/83R/handouts/C2102014 050510001/719abd7c-9cd9–4092-aae9–46d5765f52cf.PDF" http://www.legis.state.tx.us/tlodocs/83R/handouts/C2102014050510001/719abd7c-9cd9–4092-aae9–46d5765f52cf.PDF.

Chinman, M., George, P., Dougherty, R. H., Daniels, A. S., Ghose, S. S., Swift, A., & Delphin-Rittmon, M. E. (2014). Peer Support Services for Individuals with Serious Mental Illnesses: Assessing the Evidence. *Psychiatric Services, 65*(4), 429–441.

Colorado Judicial Branch. (2015). Veterans Trauma Court. Retrieved from http://www.courts.state.co.us/Courts/County/Custom.cfm?County_ID=6&Page_ID=50.

Compton, M. T., & Kotwicki, R. J. (2007). *Responding to individuals with mental illnesses.* Sudbury, MA: Jones & Bartlett Publishers.

Correctional Service Canada. (2012). Review of Mental Health Screening at Intake. Retrieved from HYPERLINK "http://www.csc-scc.gc.ca/publications/005007–2514-eng.shtml" http://www.csc-scc.gc.ca/publications/005007–2514-eng.shtml.

Daniel, A. E. (2007). Care of the Mentally Ill in Prisons: Challenges and Solutions. *Journal of the American Academy of Psychiatry and the Law, 35*, 406–410.

Daniels, A. S., Cate, R., Bergeson, S., Forquer, S., Niewenhous, G., & Epps, B. (2013). Best Practices: Level-of-Care Criteria for Peer Support Services: A Best-Practice Guide. *Psychiatric Services, 64*(12), 1190–1192.

DePrato, D., & Phillippi, S. (2011). Juvenile Offenders. In Fagan, T. J., & Ax, R. K. (Eds.), *Correctional Mental Health: From Theory to Practice* (pp. 281–308). Thousand Oaks, CA: Sage Publications, Inc.

Dirks-Linhorst, P. A., & Linhorst, D. M. (2012). Recidivism outcomes for suburban mental health court defendants. *American Journal of Criminal Justice, 37*(1), 76–91.

Ennis, A. R., McLeod, P., Watt, M. C., Campbell, M. A., & Adams-Quackenbush, N. (2016). The Role of Gender in Mental Health Court Admission and Completion. *Canadian Journal of Criminology and Criminal Justice, 58*(1), 1–30.

Feinstein, B. (2013). Saving the Deific Decree Exception to the Insanity Defense in Illinois: How a Broad Interpretation of Religious Command May Cue Establishment Clause Concerns, *John Marshall Law Review, 46*(2), 561–582.

Fellner, J. (2006). Corrections Quandary: Mental Illness and Prison Rules. *Harvard Civil Rights-Civil Liberties Law Review, 41*, 391.

Fellner, J. (2015). Human Rights Watch. Callous and cruel: Use of force against inmates with mental disabilities in US jails and prisons [Report].   Retrieved from https://www.hrw.org/report/2015/05/12/callous-and-cruel/use-force-against-inmates-mental-disabilities-us-jails-and#406663.

Florida Department of Children and Families. (2014). About Adult Forensic Health (AFMH) Retrieved from http://www.myflfamilies.com/service- programs/mental-health/about-adult-forensic-mental-health.

Florida Department of Children and Families, Office of Substance Abuse and Mental Health. (November, 2014). *State Mental Health Treatment Facility: Forensic Waitlist Review.* Tallahassee, FL: Florida Department of Children and Families.

Forensic Facilities. (2014). Retrieved July 26, 2016 from http://www.myflfamilies.com/service-programs/mental-health/forensic-facilities.

Franz, S., & Borum, R. (2011). Crisis Intervention Teams May Prevent Arrests of People with Mental Illnesses. *Police Practice and Research, 12*, 265–272.

Fuller, D. A., Sinclair, E., Geller, J., Quanbeck, C., & Snook, J. (2016). *Going, Going, Gone: Trends and Consequences of Eliminating State Psychiatric Beds.* Arlington, VA: Treatment Advocacy Center, Office of Research & Public Affairs. Retrieved from TACReports.org/going-going-gone.

Glowa-Kollisch, S., Kaba, F., Waters, A., Leung, Y. J., Ford, E., & Venters, H. (2016). From Punishment to Treatment: The "Clinical Alternative to Punitive Segregation" (CAPS) Program in New York City Jails. *International Journal of Environmental Research and Public Health, 13*, 182–192.

Gonzales, A. R., Schofield, R. B., & Hagy, D. W. (2007). Mental Health Screens for Corrections. *National Institute of Justice.* Retrieved from https://www.ncjrs.gov/pdffiles1/nij/216152.pdf.

Griffin, P. A., Heilbrun, K., Mulvey, E. P., DeMatteo, D., & Schubert, C. A. (Eds.). (2015). *The Sequential Intercept Model and Criminal Justice: Promoting Community Alternatives for Individuals with Serious Mental Illness.* New York, NY: Oxford University Press, USA.

Griffin, P. A., Steadman, H. J., & Petrila, J. (2002). The use of criminal charges and sanctions in mental health courts. *Psychiatric Services, 53*(10), 1285–1289.

Hayes, H., Kemp, R. I., Large, M. M., & Nielssen, O. B. (2013). A 21 Year Retrospective Outcome Study of New South Wales Forensic Patients Granted Conditional and Unconditional Release. *Australian and New Zealand Journal of Psychiatry, 48*(3), 259–282.

Hayes, L. M. (2013). Suicide Prevention in Correctional Facilities: Reflections and Next Steps. *International Journal of Law and Psychiatry, 36*(3), 188–194.

Helfand, S. (2011). Managing Disruptive Offenders: A Behavioral Perspective. In Fagan, T. J., & Ax, R. K. (Eds.), *Correctional Mental Health: From Theory to Practice* (pp. 309–326). Thousand Oaks, CA: Sage Publications, Inc.

Hiday, V. A., Wales, H. W., & Ray, B. (2013). Effectiveness of a Short-Term Mental Health Court: Criminal Recidivism One Year Postexit. *Law and Human Behavior.* Advance online publication. doi: 10.1037/lhb0000030.

Honegger, L. N. (2015). Does the Evidence Support the Case for Mental Health Courts? A Review of the Literature. *Law and Human Behavior, 39*(5), 478.

Human Rights Watch. (2003). *Ill-Equipped: U.S. Prisons and Offenders with Mental Illness.* New York, NY: Human Rights Watch.

Illinois Department of Human Services. (n.d.). Forensic Services-Program Overview Retrieved from http://www.dhs.state.il.us/page.aspx?item=67499.

The Judicial Branch of California. (2011). Orange County Combat Veterans Court. Retrieved from http://www.courts.ca.gov/13955.htm.

Kaba, F., Lewis, A., Glowa-Kollisch, S., Hadler, J., Lee, D., Alper, H., ... & Venters, H. (2014). Solitary confinement and risk of self-harm among jail inmates. *American Journal of Public Health, 104*(3), 442–447.

Kapoor, R. (2011). Commentary: Jail-Based Competency Restoration. *Journal of the American Academy of Psychiatry and the Law, 39,* 311–315.

Keator, K. J., Callahan, L., Steadman, H. J., & Vesselinov, R. (2012). The Impact of Treatment on the Public Safety Outcomes of Mental Health Court Participants. *American Behavioral Scientist, 57*(2), 213–243.

Kentucky Court of Justice. (2015). Veterans Treatment Court. Retrieved from HYPERLINK http://courts.ky.gov/courtprograms/vtc/Pages/default.aspx.

Kim, K., Becker-Cohen, M., & Serakos, M. (2015). *The Processing and Treatment of Mentally Ill Persons in the Criminal Justice System: A Scan of Practice and Background Analysis.* Washington, DC: Urban Institute.

Knudsen, K. J., & Windgenfeld, S. (2014). A Specialized Treatment Court for Veterans with Trauma Exposure: Implications for the Field. *Community Mental Health Journal, 52*(2), 127–135.

Kohrt, B. A., Blasingame, E., Compton, M. T., Dakana, S. F., Dossen, B., Lang, F., Strode, P., & Cooper, J. (2015). Adapting the Crisis Intervention Team (cit) Model of Police—Mental Health Collaboration in a Low-Income, Post-Conflict Country: Curriculum Development in Liberia, West Africa. *American Journal of Public Health, 105,* e73–e80.

Lamb, R. H., & Weinberger, L. E. (1998). Persons with Severe Mental Illness in Jails and Prisons: A Review. *Psychiatric Services, 49*(4), 483–492.

Listwan, S. J., Daigle, L. E., Hartman, J. L., & Guastaferro, W. P. (2014). Poly-Victimization Risk in Prison: The Influence of Individual and Institutional Factors. *Journal of Interpersonal Violence, 28*(13), 258–281.

Loper, A. B., & Levitt, L. (2011). Mental Health Needs of Female Offenders. In Fagan, T. J., & Ax, R. K. (Eds.), *Correctional Mental Health: From Theory to Best Practice* (pp. 213–231). Thousand Oaks, CA: Sage Publications Inc.

Manguno-Mire, G. M., Coffman, K. L., DeLand, S. M., Thompson, J. W., & Myers, L. (2014). What Factors Are Related to Success on Conditional Release/ Discharge? Findings from the New Orleans Forensic Aftercare Clinic: 2002–2013. *Behavioral Sciences & the Law, 32*(5), 641–658.

Marlowe, D. B. (2012). *Behavior Modification 101 for Drug Courts: Making the Most of Incentives and Sanctions.* Alexandria, VA: National Drug Court Institute.

Massaro, J. (2005). *Overview of the Mental Health Service System for Criminal Justice Professionals.* Delmar, NY: GAINS Technical Assistance and Policy Analysis Center for Jail Diversion.

McGraw, B. D., Farthing-Capowich, D., & Keilitz, I. (1985). The Guilty but Mentally Ill Plea and Verdict: Current State of Knowledge. *Villanova Law Review, 30*(1), 118–191.

McLearen, A., & Magaletta, P. R. (2011). Understanding the Broad Corrections Environment: Responding to the Needs of Diverse Inmate Groups. In T. J. Fagan & R. K. Ax (Eds.), *Correctional Mental Health* (pp. 327–350). Thousand Oaks, CA: Sage Publications.

McNiel, D. E., Sadeh, N., Delucchi, K. L., & Binder, R. L. (2015). Prospective Study of Violence Risk Reduction by a Mental Health Court. *Psychiatric Services, 66*(6), 1–6.

Mental Health America. (2016). *Peers: Their Roles and the Research.* Retrieved from http://www.mentalhealthamerica.net/peer-services.

Metzner, J. L., & Fellner, J. (2010). Solitary Confinement and Mental Illness in U.S. Prisons: A Challenge for Medical Ethics. *Journal of the American Academy of Psychiatry and the Law, 38,* 4–8.

Moore, M. E., & Hiday, V. A. (2006). Mental Health Court Outcomes: A Comparison of Re-Arrest and Re-Arrest Severity between Mental Health Court and Traditional Court Participants. *Law and Human Behavior, 30*(6), 659–674.

Moriarty, J. (Ed.) (2014). *The Insanity Defense: American Developments: The Role of Mental Illness in Criminal Trials.* London: Routledge.

National Institute of Justice. (2006). *Drug Courts: The Second Decade* (An NIJ Special Report). Washington, DC: U.S. Department of Justice, Office of Justice Programs.

New York State Office of Mental Health. Division of Forensic Services (DFS). (2016). Retrieved from https://www.omh.ny.gov/omhweb/forensic/BFS.htm.

Odegaard, A. M. (2007). Therapeutic Jurisprudence: The Impact of Mental Health Courts on the Criminal Justice System. *North Dakota Law Review, 83*(1), 225–259.

Office of National Drug Control Policy. (2011). *Drug Courts: A Smart Approach to criminal Justice.* Washington, DC: Office of National Drug Control Policy.

Osher, F., D'Amora, D. A., Plotkin, M., Jarrett, N., & Eggleston, A. (2012). Adults with behavioral health needs under correctional supervision: A shared framework for reducing recidivism and promoting recovery. New York: Council of State Governments Justice Center. Pennsylvania State Legislature. (1976). *Mental Health Procedures Act* (P.L. 817, No. 143, Cl. 50). Harrisburg, PA.

Powitsky, R. J. (2011). Comparison of Correctional and Community Mental Health Service Delivery Models. In Fagan, T. J., & Ax, R. K. (Eds), *Correctional Mental Health: From Theory to Best Practice* (pp. 37–56). Thousand Oaks, CA: Sage Publications Inc.

Roesch, R., Zapf, P. A., Golding, S. L., & Skeem, J. (1999). Defining and assessing competency to stand trial. In I. B. Weiner, & A. K. Hess (Eds.), *Handbook of forensic psychology* (2nd ed., pp. 327–349). New York: John Wiley and Sons.

Rossman, S. B., Roman, J. K., Zweig, J. M., Rempel, M., & Lindquist, C. H. (2011). *The Multi-Site Adult Drug Court Evaluation: Executive Summary.* Washington, DC: Urban Institute.

Russell, R. T. (2009). Veterans Treatment Court: A Proactive Approach. *New England Journal on Criminal and Civil Confinement, 35*(2), 357–372.

Shankar, G. (2011). Clinical Psychopharmacology in Correctional Settings. In Fagan, T. J., & Ax, R. K. (Eds.), *Correctional Mental Health: From Theory to Best Practice.* Thousand Oaks, CA: Sage Publications Inc.

Slate, R. N., Buffington-Vollum, J. K., & Johnson, W. W. (2013). *The criminalization of mental illness: Crisis and opportunity for the justice system.* Durham, NC: Carolina Academic Press.

Steadman, H. J., Morris, S. M., & Dennis, D. L. (1995). The Diversion of Mentally Ill Persons from Jails to Community-Based Services: A Profile of Programs. *American Journal of Public Health, 85*(12), 1630–1635.

The Unified Judicial System of Pennsylvania. (2015). Veterans Courts. Retrieved from http://www.pacourts.us/judicial-administration/court-programs/veterans-courts.

Torrey, E. F., Kennard, A. D., Eslinger, D., Lamb, R., & Pavle, J. (2010). *More Mentally Ill Persons Are in Jails and Prisons Than Hospitals: A Survey of the States.* Arlington, VA: Treatment Advocacy Center.

Torrey, E. F., Zdanowicz, M. T., Kennard, A. D., Lamb, H. R., Eslinger, D. F., Biasotti, M. C., & Fuller, D. A. (2014). The treatment of persons with mental illness in prisons and jails: A state survey. Treatment Advocacy Center.

U.S. Department of Justice, Civil Rights Division. (2014). *Investigation of the Pennsylvania Department of Corrections' Use of Solitary Confinement on Prisoners with Serious Mental Illness and/or Intellectual Disabilities* (Communication with Governor Tom Corbett). Washington, DC: U.S. Department of Justice, Civil Rights Division.

U.S. Department of Justice, Office of Justice Programs. (2016). *Drug Courts*. Retrieved from https://www.ncjrs.gov/pdffiles1/nij/238527.pdf

U.S. Department of Veterans Affairs. (2011). Veterans Treatment Courts Offer Second Chance. Retrieved from http://www.northtexas.va.gov/features/VetTxCourtProgram.asp.

Vail, L. (2015). Various stories and parent's shout out. Meridian Behavioral Healthcare, Inc., Gainsville, FL Wasserman, A. L. (2014). Florida Department of Children and Families, Office of Substance Abuse and Mental Health. *State Mental Health Treatment Facility Forensic Waitlist Review*. Tallahassee, FL.

Wexler, D. B. (2000). Therapeutic Jurisprudence: An Overview. *Thomas M. Cooley Law Review, 17*, 125–134.

Wexler, D. B. (2011). *Therapeutic Jurisprudence: An Overview*. Retrieved from http://www.law.arizona.edu/depts/upr-intj/intj-o.html.

Wilson, D. B., Mitchell, O., & Mackenzie, D. L. (2004). A Systematic Review of Drug Court Effects on Recidivism. *Journal of Experimental Criminology, 2*, 459–487.

Winerip, M. & Schwirtz, M. (2014, July 14). Rikers: Where mental illness meets brutality in jail. *The New York Times*. Retrieved from https://www.nytimes.com on January 4, 2017.

Wisconsin State Legislature. (2010). *Involuntary Commitment for Treatment*. (WIS. STAT. ANN. § 51.20(1) (a)).

Wood, S. R., & Buttaro, A. (2013). Co-occurring Severe Mental Illnesses and Substance Abuse Disorders as Predictors of State Prison Inmate Assaults. *Crime & Delinquency, 59*(4), 510–535.

CHAPTER 8 **Intercept Four**
Reentry to the Community from Secure Detention

"There's a tremendous need to implode the myths of mental illness, to put a face on it, to show people that a diagnosis does not have to lead to a painful and oblique life. . . . We who struggle with these disorders can lead full, happy, productive lives, if we have the right resources."

— *Elyn R. Saks*

Introduction

Reentry is defined as the process of leaving jail and returning to society, and it can have a large impact on the individuals being released, as well as on the communities to which they are returning (Phillips & Spencer, 2013). Approximately 600,000 individuals are released from U.S. jails and prisons each year (Harrison & Karberg, 2003)—about one-sixth of whom have mental illness. The general goal of reentry is to manage the transition of previously incarcerated or incapacitated individuals back into the larger society ("Offender Reentry," 2015). For the individual offender, this proves to be a major change in status from that of "imprisoned offender" to "released ex-offender" (Travis, 2000). For individuals with behavioral health and substance use treatment needs, the transition becomes particularly daunting, and the extent to which they have received help identifying their needs and navigating support services in the community may have a profound impact on their likelihood of reoffending (Benson, Alarid, Burton & Cullen, 2011).

Similar to their relatively healthy counterparts, PwMI who are being discharged from correctional settings face a number of reintegration barriers upon release (e.g., stigma, limited access to treatment and other support services), making recidivism one of the primary concerns. In fact, comparable to other incarcerated populations, reincarceration rates are high among PwMI—particularly among those who also suffer from substance abuse and addiction (Draine & Herman, 2007). Consequently, as stated in Chapter 7, without access to proper treatment and support services that meet their social needs, many PwMI (both children and adults) may find themselves ensnared in a web of multiple encounters with the criminal justice system and, in particular, longer and more frequent periods of incarceration (Lurigio, Rollins, & Fallon, 2004).

Intercept Four of the Sequential Intercept Model, the foundation for this chapter, relates to reentry of individuals from state hospitals, jails, and prisons. It is the point at which previously incapacitated individuals are returning to their communities, and it represents another opportunity to connect them with diversion options. For instance, a number of social services, behavioral-based interventions, and life skills should be integrated into post-release plans in order to minimize risk and attain successful reentry. It is also important that available services/programs address the unique interpersonal and cultural needs of those being released (Skeem, Winter, Kennealy, Louden, & Tatar, 2013).

This chapter describes the process of reentry in the United States as it specifically relates to offenders with mental health issues. The content is divided into three key sections. The first section provides a general discussion of reentry with some emphasis on special challenges faced by persons with serious mental illness, including psychological and social needs and concerns, as well as needs pertaining to employment, housing, co-occurring substance abuse and dependency disorders, and access to public assistance benefits upon release. Reentry models are also presented and discussed. In section two, the institutions responsible for the implementation of reentry initiatives are then outlined briefly, including law enforcement, parole, and community treatment providers. Some legal implications regarding the right to treatment are also introduced. In the final section, specific reentry programs, most considered *best practices* in forensic mental health, are outlined with respect to their effectiveness. Although the emphasis is placed on the discharge of individuals from correctional institutions, most of the discussion can be applied in any context, and anything referring to hospital discharge specifically is noted.

What Is a "Best Practice"?

"Public health programs, interventions, and policies that have been evaluated, shown to be successful, and have the potential to be adapted and transformed by others working in the same field."

Source: http://library.umassmed.edu/ebpph/best_pract.cfm

Section One: Reentry for PwMI

To reiterate and summarize information presented in previous chapters, American prisons and jails house three times the amount of persons with mental illness than do our nation's psychiatric hospitals—a finding that suggests incarceration is replacing mental health treatment for many individuals in need of care for their illness (Satel, 2003; Slate, Buffington-Vollum, & Johnson, 2013). Moreover, research reveals that there are approximately 210,000 individuals with serious mental illnesses (SMIs) who are incarcerated in state and federal jails and prisons on any given day (Kondo, 2003). Although the "pains" of imprisonment and reintegration back into the community are certainly felt by offenders without mental health concerns, there are profound differences with respect to inmates with SMI—differences that are exponential by comparison (Slate, et al., 2013). Some of the challenges were discussed in Chapter 7, but nevertheless deserve reiteration here.

During their incarceration, persons with mental illness are oftentimes targets for cruelty and perpetual victimizations, such as physical and sexual abuse by other inmates (Crisanti & Frueh, 2011). Furthermore, their strange behaviors (e.g., muttering, pacing, proclaiming delusional beliefs) can cause them to be punished more often, mostly resulting in solitary confinement, causing their mental state to deteriorate further (Satel, 2003; Slate, et al., 2013). In fact, there have been numerous accounts—some presented throughout this text—that point to the detrimental failure of correctional staff to pay attention to clear symptoms of distress among inmates suffering with serious mental illness—symptoms that were predictive of acute crisis (see, e.g., Earley, 2007; "Mentally Ill Homeless Veteran," 2014; "The New Asylums," 2013).

As stated in the introduction, prior research has indicated that, post-release, offenders with mental illness (OMIs) recidivate (measured by arrest) at rates comparable to their counterparts who are relatively healthy; however, OMI are more likely to be reincarcerated (Bauer, Morgan, & Mandracchia, 2011; Lurigio, et al., 2004; Skeem, Hernandez, Kennealy, & Rich, 2012). Although research on offender reentry indicates that mental illness does not directly cause involvement in crime and delinquency, findings have suggested that mental health status may have an indirect effect. In particular, it is argued that having a serious mental health disorder may predispose an individual to risk factors, which predict general offending behaviors and high recidivism rates (Skeem, et al., 2012). Thus, although mental health needs should not be ignored, multiple other crime-provoking risk factors must be identified, addressed, and monitored throughout the course of incarceration and beyond.

SPOTLIGHT: FEMALES WITH SERIOUS MENTAL ILLNESS IN THE PRISON SYSTEM

The number of women coming into contact with the criminal justice system has been rapidly increasing in the past few decades (Chesney-Lind & Pasko, 2013). More specifically, women accounted for approximately 22 percent of annual arrests in the United States between 1990 and

continued

1998, and by 1998, the number of women incarcerated, on probation, and on parole increased by 88 percent, 40 percent, and 80 percent, respectively (Chesney-Lind, 2000). Further, although there seems to be a high prevalence of mental health issues among prison and jail inmates in general, such issues are more common among females. For instance, in 2005, about 73 percent of females in state prisons had a mental health problem, compared with 55 percent of males; in federal prisons, 61 percent of females vs. 44 percent of males; and in local jails, 75 percent of females vs. 63 percent of males. These statistics take on special importance for programming designed to assist female offenders with mental health issues.

Although the implementation of reentry programming seems promising for the offender population at large, the special needs of female offenders, especially those with mental health concerns, have not always been considered in the design of pre- and post-release reentry programs (Chesney-Lind, 2000; Chesney-Lind & Pasko, 2013). Particularly, female offenders often enter the criminal justice system having experienced physical and mental health issues related to their unique histories of violence that often involves sexual, emotional, or physical abuse and other victimizations. Furthermore, female offenders also face challenges with regard to child rearing and parenting or custodial concerns and substance use (Chesney-Lind, 2000; Chesney-Lind & Pasko, 2013). Although the crimes that women commit are not likely to be violent, but more often are related to drugs, alcohol, or property crimes, the return or recidivism of high-risk female offenders is imminent because of trauma or other gender-specific circumstances as just described (Bloom & McDiarmid, 2000; Chesney-Lind, 2000; Chesney-Lind & Pasko, 2013; Prichard, 2000). Thus, the importance of development and implementation of a reentry plan that will address the special mental health needs and concerns of female offenders is necessary to increase their ability to reintegrate into society and decrease their rates of recidivism.

Factors Related to Recidivism

Criminogenic Risk Factors

Research conducted with offender populations more generally has identified what has been referred to as the "central eight" criminogenic risk factors, which determine an individual's likelihood of reoffending (Osher, D'Amora, Plotkin, Jarrett, & Eggleston, 2012). Contrary to *static factors of offending risk*, such as age at first arrest and other demographic characteristics that are unchangeable, *dynamic risk factors* are those that are malleable and can change over time and include:

1) **Presence of antisocial behavior** (early and continuing engagement in antisocial acts)

2) **Antisocial personality pattern** (low self-control, seeking immediate gratification, aggressive)

3) **Antisocial cognition** (antisocial thinking patterns, including thoughts favorable toward law-breaking)

4) **Antisocial associates** (isolation from law-abiding friends, and strong associations with criminals)

5) Family and/or marital (poor/strained relations and relationship quality)

6) School and/or work (poor interpersonal relationships in these settings, and low performance and satisfaction)

7) Leisure and/or recreation (low levels of involvement in pro-social/law-abiding activities)

8) Substance abuse (tobacco excluded) (Osher, et al., 2012)

The top four factors (referred to in the literature as the "big four") are highlighted in bold because, from a treatment perspective, these must be successfully addressed before intervention with the remaining four factors will be effective. Research with offending populations, with or without mental illness, has revealed the predictive power of criminogenic risk factors on recidivism. In particular, findings have revealed that justice-involved PwMI are at risk for reoffending post-release due to the presence of generalized criminogenic risk/needs rather than factors unique to mental illness (e.g., lack of access to medication) (Barrenger & Draine, 2013; Skeem, et al., 2014). That is not to say that unmet mental health needs do not contribute to reoffending; rather, research indicates the relationship is more of an indirect one. It is possible that having mental illness indirectly exposes an individual to environments (physical and social) that are conducive to criminal offending—for example, associating with antisocial peers. Although an individual who is successfully managing psychotropic medication may be less likely to strike a police officer during an encounter, that individual may continue to have multiple encounters with law enforcement unless other general criminogenic needs are addressed—in this case, the development of pro-social relationships or involvement in more pro-social activities, such as spending more time at a community drop-in center during certain hours of the day. The influence of environment on successful reintegration of PwMI is discussed in more detail next.

Risk Environments

For many PwMI, reentry into the community after a period of incarceration can be a difficult transition. There are multiple risk environments to consider: physical, social, economic, and political (Barrenger & Draine, 2013). The physical environment is simply where the person returns to once released. It is often found that those returning go to concentrated areas within urban cities. The communities may lack treatment facilities, housing, employment, education, or social services—essentially any resource

for successful reentry (Barrenger & Draine, 2013). There may also be social disorganization in these areas as well. Stigma oftentimes complicates these social struggles, and a
combination of limited family support, perceived personal failings, and the realization
that few options are available, may make it easier to return back to old illegal habits
(Draine & Herman, 2007). For political and a host of other reasons (e.g., stigma and
policy restrictions on hiring those with a criminal record), there is a lack of financing
and employment opportunities for those leaving jails. There are also policies in place
that deny those with criminal histories from obtaining benefits such as Medicaid and
SSI. The main difference between PwMI and the general population is that the former
often need access to medications and treatment to help with the continued management of their illness. Unfortunately, however, these are often not provided for beyond
the first 30 days after release back into the community setting There is also a lack of
follow-up to determine if these persons are keeping up with medication and treatment
plans. Programs and planning have been put in place by the criminal justice and mental
health systems in response to these barriers; a few are presented later in the final section
of this chapter.

FAST FACT: MEASURING RISK FOR VIOLENCE

One of the most frequently used assessment tools among clinicians for determining the risk of
violence among forensic adult psychiatric patients is the HCR-20. The HCR-20 is a 20-item scale,
consisting of 10 past-oriented "historical" (H) items, including previous violent behavior and major
mental disorder diagnosis; 5 present-oriented "clinical" (C) items, such as impulsivity and/or active
symptoms of a disorder; and 5 future-oriented "risk management" (R) items, including factors like
stress and cost–benefit analysis of the criminal act. Responses are based on a 3-item Likert scale
and range from 0 (not at all) to 2 (definitely). Scores from items on each of the three scales are then
added to determine summative scores on each of the three scales as well as an overall (total) score.
The rater is asked to consider the risk factors in the context of their application on a case-by-case
basis before making a final clinical judgment of low, medium, or high risk (Skeem, Winter, Kennealy, Louden, & Tatar, 2014).

To address the needs related to recidivism, and to attain the most effective public
safety outcomes, correctional and behavioral health administrators draw from multiple
theoretical frameworks that conceptualize risks, needs, allocation of resources, and the
impact of programming on reoffending. In short, these models are useful for administrators seeking treatment strategies that can be empirically tested and are shown to be
effective at minimizing recidivism among offenders with mental illness. There are several existing models in this regard, each used by individuals working in distinct systems
of care (Osher, et al., 2012).

Models of Reentry

Risk-Need-Responsivity (RNR) Model

This is an evidence-based model that is most widely utilized by correctional administrators. The model was first developed in the 1980s, became formalized in 1990, and has been used with increasing success to assess risk of reoffending, determine criminogenic needs (crime-invoking dynamic risk factors), and design culturally specific reentry programming that will rehabilitate offenders in communities in the United States and abroad (Bauer, et al., 2011; Osher, et al., 2012). The model has three core principles that can be briefly outlined as follows:

- *Risk principle*: Level of services should be matched with the offender's risk of reoffending (determined using scientifically based assessment tools). Consequently, individuals who are at a high risk will receive the most intensive services (Bauer, et al., 2011).

- *Need principle*: Dynamic criminogenic needs must be assessed, and treatment and case planning should target these needs in particular.

- *Responsivity principle*: It is important to minimize interpersonal and cultural barriers that may prevent an offender from effectively receiving a rehabilitative intervention; individual learning style, cognitive ability, motivation, and physical abilities must be considered when planning and designing treatment options (Osher, et al., 2012).

Over the years, RNR has become the most influential model for planning related to the treatment and rehabilitation of offenders. It has been empirically tested numerous times, and because of its positive effects at reducing recidivism, has been distinguished as an effective evidence-based practice (Bauer, et al., 2011). It should be noted that the model has been criticized for its inability to work in multiple settings with employees and administrators who are diverse in terms of education, treatment and correctional philosophies, and management practices (Osher, et al., 2012). Furthermore, the model is designed for use with correctional goals in mind, and although more recent literature on RNR has promoted the idea of collaboration among criminal justice system actors, the model does not incorporate a framework for integrating goals from multiple systems of care, including the mental health system (Osher, et al., 2012).

System Integration/Reentry Services Approaches

There are additional reentry models specific to offenders with mental illness; in particular, in addition to mapping offender needs and service delivery, they are designed to encourage and support collaboration between multiple systems of care. These include shared responsibility and interdependence (SRI); critical time intervention (CTI); sensitizing providers to the effects of correctional incarceration on treatment (SPECTRM); and assess, plan, identify, and coordinate (APIC) models. The first three models are briefly outlined in the following text box. Given its popularity with OMI and the accumulated amount of evidence as to its effectiveness with reentry, APIC is discussed in more detail on its own in the following section.

Shared responsibility and interdependence (SRI) (formalized by Draine, Wolff, Jacoby, Hartwell, & Duclos, 2005): Focus on individual and community dynamics—not systems centric; ACTION approach, which is a training curriculum that focuses on establishing connections and networking opportunities between individuals from multiple criminal justice and behavioral health agencies; in short, it involves strengthening linkages and information sharing.

Critical time intervention (CTI) (formalized by Draine & Herman, 2007): Limited to the point of release; emphasis placed on strengthening ties between correctional staff and communities. Also provides for the inclusion of offender services, in particular, motivational coaching and advocacy and training in problem-solving strategies.

Sensitizing providers to the effects of correctional incarceration on treatment (SPECTRM) (formalized by Rotter, McQuistion, Broner, & Steinbacher, 2005): Basically cultural competency training for providers inexperienced about inmates'/criminogenic needs. It is narrowly designed to specifically address the ways in which the incarceration experience affects the attitudes and behaviors of justice-involved OMIs.

Source: Griffin, Heilbrun, Mulvey, DeMatteo, & Schubert, 2015.

APIC Model

The APIC model (assess, plan, identify, and coordinate) was designed by Osher and colleagues in 2003 as a means to organize the transition between jail programming and community-based services for offenders with mental health and/or co-occurring substance abuse disorders. It is considered a best practice model and has been utilized to accomplish effective transitions for consumers and the best possible strategic partnerships between providers of mental health, substance abuse, and an array of other services (Griffin, et al., 2015; Osher, et al., 2012).

APIC is a hierarchal model that requires first that the clinical and social needs of the consumer be *assessed*. These may include interviews or the examination of documentation related to the psychological, medical, and social needs of the consumer, as well as any strengths. An assessment of public safety risk is also of utmost importance. Next, the case manager and team must *plan* for different treatment programs and services that are needed for transitional success; ideally, programs will be available/offered during the period of incarceration (even if brief) and the inmate will willingly participate. In the context of community-based care, long-term needs, transportation, housing needs, medical regimens, and connections to medical providers are considered at this stage. Reentry personnel must also ensure that the consumer has proper identification and medical insurance, and any financial service barriers should be addressed at this time. In particular, there may be income and benefit entitlements (e.g., veterans' benefits, Social Security, food stamps), and the consumer may need help navigating through the application or facilitation process—a point discussed in a bit more detail later in the chapter. Following planning, the team must *identify* specific programs and resources for the consumer. In this stage, the RNR model (discussed earlier) is instructive, as the consumer's treatment and supervision should be matched with level of risk or need, and cultural, learning, and other differences must be considered when aligning services. Finally there must be *coordination* involved between the consumer, consumer's family, case managers, and treatment facilities to ensure that there are no gaps (Eno Louden, Manchak, O'Connor, & Skeem, 2015).

PRACTITIONER'S CORNER 8.1

The APIC Model in Action: The Case of Michael

Contributor: Brian D. Stubbs, CPS, Published Author, and Founder of Decide 2 Evolve (www.decide2evolve.com)

Michael has been arrested and has three charges: one misdemeanor trespassing, one misdemeanor possession of stolen property, and one felony destruction of government property. He pleads guilty to all three charges, using free counsel from a public defender. He will serve three to six months in the local county prison.

While in prison, Michael states to the prison's medical staff that he's become crazy. His present mental state is from two situations. First, Michael's prescribed psychiatric medicines are expensive—they aren't provided by the county prison. Thus, the medicines the prison provides Michael confuse him—they're a different color and different size. He cheeks them, spitting them into his cell toilet 15 minutes after leaving the prison psychiatrist. Second, in the community, Michael walked from his apartment complex to his 1:1 weekly counseling sessions with his trusted female counselor, Sharon, a licensed professional counselor. There are peer-led support groups in this prison and the prison's medical staff have invited Michael to attend them, but he refuses "I just talk with Sharon."

Due to state laws, Michael will lose his Supplemental Security Income (SSI) while incarcerated. Additionally he'll lose his room at the long-term structured residence (apartment complex), food stamps, clothing vouchers, and active county transportation.

continued

Michael's home plan can be developed due to him having that known three- to six-month sentence time. He's awarded good-time behavior, equaling five days a month, reduced toward his overall sentence time. He's isolated 23 hours a day in his own cell for his protection from the general population.

Here's Michael's home plan:

A scheduled appointment with a community-based psychiatrist within 30 to 60 days from prison release. He'll be provided three to seven days' worth of prison-approved generic medicines. Any physical doctor or community appointments are assigned to his forensic case manager. Also, Michael will have a parole officer, supported living worker, forensic peer support/mentor, and financial payee—all part of his court-committed community treatment plan. He'll be required to attend adult psychiatric and/or socialization courses at an adult community-run drop-in center. Or, he can work a paid or volunteer job during the week instead of drop-in center attendance. All while having his payee pay weekly financial restitution.

Author's Note: *The type of counseling Brian is referring to in Michael's case is referred to as 1:1 (one on one) crisis counseling. This type of counseling is appropriate for individuals who have experienced a crisis situation or traumatic event; the three primary goals of treatment are safety, stability, and connection (rapport) (American Psychological Association, 2011). Brian's reference to peer counseling and peer-led groups is indicative of the peer support model, which, as discussed briefly in* Chapter 7, *involves the development of linkages between persons who have common illnesses and the practice of sharing knowledge and experiences as part of the treatment modal. Peer support staff are most likely to be volunteers who are not compensated; it should also be noted that although certification is available and often attained, peer specialists are not required to hold a license or a degree. Consequently, peer support should not replace traditional therapy and services, but rather complement them; medical and mental healthcare should be sought when deemed appropriate and necessary (*What Is Peer Support, *2015).*

Legal Issues: The Right to Treatment Post-Release

As discussed in Chapter 6, generally speaking, prisoners have no constitutional right to treatment. However, over the past 30 to 40 years, there have been a number of Supreme Court decisions regarding inmates' lack of access to adequate medical care in prison, starting with the seminal case of *Estelle v. Gamble*, decided in 1976. Two primary areas of litigation have emerged in recent years with regard to mental health treatment in jails or prisons: access to adequate care and the right to refuse treatment, particularly the right to refuse the administration of certain types of psychotropic medications (see, e.g., *Ruiz v. Estelle*, 1980, *Washington v. Harper*, 1990, *Sell v. United States*, 2003). It should be noted that constitutional protection extends to having the capability to access psychological or psychiatric services both pre- and post-release (Courturer, Maue, & McVey, n.d.). In this context, a judge may exercise the authority to require that correctional treatment and discharge plans are implemented to ensure that inmates are administered prescribed medications, that patient medical service requests are timely responded to, that individual and group therapy are provided, and that a number of other mental healthcare treatment provisions are in place in anticipation of release back into the community (Fellner, 2006; Slate, et al., 2013).

THINKING CRITICALLY

Former U.S. President George W. Bush said: "America is the land of the second chance, and when the gates of the prison open, the path ahead should be a better life." Thoughts? To what extent do you believe the criminal justice system is responsible for providing mental health services to incarcerated populations? What about for juveniles in detention?

More generally, to what extent are correctional institutions responsible for offering offenders a better life after secure detention? (Figure 8.1 illustrates "secure detention" at Rikers Island, New York.)

Section Two: Effective Reintegration and the Role of Professional Service Providers

The importance of effective service coordination for individuals with serious mental illness—in correctional settings or otherwise—cannot be overstated. Though offenders have the right in most cases to refuse treatment during their incarceration, and especially once released in the community (Andrews, 2003), steps should still be taken to identify the most appropriate course of treatment and services, and discharge planning should begin immediately upon booking at the correctional institution (Osher & King, 2015). Oftentimes, individual treatment needs require a consumer of services to work

Figure 8.1

An Aerial Photo of Rikers Island, off Queens, New York

Source: Sfoskett (2004) at the English language Wikipedia [GFDL (http://www.gnu.org/copyleft/fdl.html), GFDL (http://www.gnu.org/copyleft/fdl.html), or CC-BY-SA-3.0 (http://creativecommons.org/licenses/by-sa/3.0/)] via Wikimedia Commons [Photograph]. Retrieved from https://commons.wikimedia.org/wiki/File%3ARikers_Island.jpg

with a multitude of providers, all of which may be funded through various sources and therefore required to meet conflicting contractual obligations. Consequently, for some, service coordination then becomes a major challenge to successful reintegration (Carlson, 2011). It is therefore essential that *continuity of care (COC)* is maintained through systems integration and collaboration so that critical information sharing among and between correctional staff and treatment providers can take place.

To accomplish positive transition, reentry programs should be designed to involve those in the community who can assist the offender in the process of social integration; in this way, reentry ideally results in the collaborative efforts of a diverse group of stakeholders composed of law enforcement, probation and parole, treatment providers, faith-based organizations, family members of offenders, and possibly victims or family members of victims (Yoon & Nickel, 2008). This bidirectionality is illustrated in Figure 8.2.

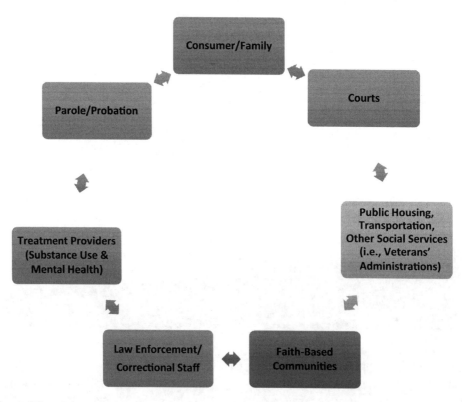

Figure 8.2

Multiple systems of care

Source: Author

LANGUAGE DECODER: WHAT IS CONTINUITY OF CARE?

In the context of mental health treatment, the phrase continuity of care (COC) is used to refer to a uniform or organized process of ongoing mental healthcare management aimed at supporting the ongoing treatment of patients without any significant breaks in service. It has been suggested that without continuity of care in the provision of mental health services, clients may become socially isolated and experience economic hardship and threats to their quality of life (Joyce, Wild, Adair, McDougall, Gordon, Costigan, Beckie, Kowalsky, Pasmeny, & Barnes, 2004).

Unfortunately, due to what is often viewed as competing interests, there has historically been a significant disjunction in the continuity and coordination of services between correctional staff and community service providers for individuals with mental illness who leave correctional settings (Fagan & Ax, 2003). In many jurisdictions, integration practices have been implemented quite recently to address and minimize *linkage blindness* and encourage systematic integration between multidisciplinary service providers, teams, and staff (Osher & King, 2015). In keeping with the theme of coordinated integration strategies, additional guidelines include incorporating risk assessment instruments into decision making, focusing attention on substance abuse, gathering data from multiple sources, and involving multiple parties in discharge and treatment plans (Dirks-Linhorst & Linhorst, 2012).

In sum, successful transition planning and reintegration requires that justice, mental health, and substance abuse system administrators develop a capacity to forge working partnerships with each other and with other community service providers. Effective partnerships have been evidenced in various localities and state systems through the development and maintenance of policies related to formal interagency agreements between public health and welfare and correctional authorities, often referred to as *memorandums of understanding (MOUs)* (Koyanagi & Blasingame, 2006); one example of a MOU between the Florida Departments of Children and Families and Corrections (DCF and DOC, respectively) was introduced in Chapter 3. In accordance with best practices, interagency agreements should include:

- Funding incentives

- Removal of barriers

- Provision of resources to learn and grow

- Utilization and sharing of fidelity scales or other evaluation measures

- Cross-systems mapping/information sharing (Koyanagi & Blasingame, 2006; Vail, n.d.)

Section Three: Best Practices in Reentry Programming for PwMI

Preventing reincarceration is a complex task that can be made nearly impossible if risks are not assessed or specialized needs ignored during reentry planning (Barrenger & Draine, 2013). As discussed previously, when it comes to offenders with mental illness, the main focus of reentry has been on connecting OMIs to community-based mental healthcare (and/or substance abuse providers) for treatment as soon as possible upon release. Unfortunately, many PwMI who return to the community fall into a crisis situation which may put them at risk for reoffending due to lack of employment, education, and housing opportunities—a predicament not unlike that of their counterparts who do not suffer from mental illness (Skeem, et al., 2014). Based on the principles of RNR (discussed earlier), reentry programming that caters specifically to the individual needs of females, males, juveniles, adults, seniors, and persons with serious mental health and/or substance abuse concerns that begins immediately upon intake should be occurring. The following section provides a summary review of varying local, state, and federal reentry initiatives outlined by identified offender needs.

Examples of Reentry Initiatives

Identified Need: Employment

According to the reentry literature, securing meaningful employment is a crucial factor related to post-release success for individuals preparing to discharge from a detention facility. Not only is having a job crucial to financial support for day-to-day life, but it is also an important determination of release eligibility (Baron, Draine, & Salzer, 2013). For PwMI who are transitioning from a correctional setting, the process of seeking employment appears to be more difficult, and the presence of additional barriers may hinder the ability to secure work. For example, the percentage of justice-involved PwMI working or looking for work before or after incarceration is the lowest rate among groups of persons with disabilities. Furthermore, job opportunities that are offered to PwMI are more likely to be entry-level minimum wage positions lacking any opportunities for ambitious pay raises or other career advancements/promotions. These findings may be attributable to a number of individual-level risk factors, such as psychiatric symptoms or addiction, which may prevent PwMI from obtaining or seeking a position, or to social-structural-level factors, such as restrictive policies and/or stigmatization or a combination of both (see Baron, et al., 2013).

SUPPORTED/SUPPORTIVE EMPLOYMENT

Supportive employment (SE) is a technique that is utilized to help integrate PwMI who have been discharged from state hospitals or correctional settings into the competitive workforce in order to promote individual well-being and, potentially, the risk for reoffending. The strategy of the program is to assist clients with immediate job placement in paid positions where they will receive intensive on-the-job training and constant support from a job coach (Wehman, 2012). This is unlike *vocational rehabilitation* programs, which require pre-employment training and the development of job skills first in order to be eligible for job placement services. Originally designed in the 1980s for individuals with learning disabilities, supported employment programs work well for people who face the most complex challenges—in particular, individuals who have no work history or an intermittent history; who have the dual stigmatization of a criminal record and serious, persistent issues that may include substance use, mental illness, and developmental disabilities; and those who are in need of ongoing supports (Baron, et al., 2013; Wehman, Lau, Molinelli, Brooke, Thompson, Moore, & West, 2012). Specific versions of supported housing have included individual placement and support (IPS) and augmented supported employment, which basically refers to the inclusion of immediate placement but with other interventions, such as skills training (Kinoshita, Furukawa, Omori, Watanabe, Marshall, Bond, Huxley, & Kingdon, 2010).

Research findings with respect to the effectiveness of SE with forensic clients repeatedly illustrate the effectiveness of IPS in terms of initial job placement (see Morgan, Flora, Kroner, Mills, Varghese, & Steffan, 2012), designating SE as an evidence-based practice (EBP); however, findings are mixed with regard to the maintenance of employment over time. For example, studies of IPS have indicated that, whereas 77 percent of consumers become gainfully employed, fewer than 45 percent remain in the same positions over an 18- to 24-month period (Baron, et al., 2013). This finding, however, may be explained by individual and structural-level factors or criminogenic needs (e.g., pro-criminal associations) that impede success in meeting program goals (Baron, et al., 2013).

Identified Need: Housing

As discussed in Chapter 2, individuals with severe mental illness once lived by the hundreds of thousands in state mental institutions; however, the deinstitutionalization movement that began during the 1960s reshaped the landscape and the challenges that PwMI confront in their lives (Slate, Buffington-Vollum, & Johnson, 2013). Appropriate and supportive housing for individuals with mental illness in community settings is generally not available, and if it is accessible, the living conditions are typically substandard and inadequate ("Homelessness and Housing," 2016). Consequently, persons with mental illness leave critical or habitual care services with insufficient necessities for their housing or support and end up descending into homeless shelters and/or the criminal justice system. Numerous others live nomadically, moving from place to place and with parents or other family members. Besides family, group homes become the foremost housing option for people with a mental illness (Culhane, Metraux & Hadley, 2002). Unfortunately, PwMI face harsh resistance from neighborhoods where *NIMBY (not-in-my-backyard)* movements occur due to developments or neighborhoods not wanting housing dedicated to rehabilitating justice-involved PwMI (Slate, et al., 2013). Thus, primary needs of homeless persons with serious mental illness include the need for decent, affordable housing and the need for supportive assistance.

Supported or Supportive Housing

Supported housing refers to programs in which there is a combination of housing and services intended as a cost-effective way to help people live more stable and productive lives in a community-based setting (Culhane, et al, 2002; Montgomery, Forchuk, Duncan, Rose, Bailey, & Veluri, 2008). The majority of individuals who qualify for supportive housing services have significant transitional issues and service needs, are typically homeless, with very little income, and tend to have serious mental health issues. An array of services are rendered in the program, ranging from medical and wellness, mental health, substance use management and recovery, vocational and employment, money management, coordinated support, life skills training, household establishment, and tenant advocacy (see, for example, "Supporting Pennsylvanians through Housing," 2016).

Though empirical research on the effectiveness of supportive housing programs with OMI is limited (Miller & Ngugi, 2009), findings generally support successful outcomes in terms of improving quality of life and cost savings (Culhane, et al., 2002; Montgomery, et al., 2008). For example, findings have indicated positive outcomes with regard to housing retention among veterans in a VA supportive housing program (Montgomery, Hill, Culhane, & Kane, 2014) and ex-offenders with mental health issues who were released from jail and diverted into a community transitional program in two major Canadian cities in Ontario (Cherner, Aubry, Ecker, Kerman, & Nandlal, 2014). Further, studies suggest that, on average, it is much cheaper to provide PwMI with supported housing services in the community rather than allowing them to remain living on the streets. For example, homeless individuals who are mentally ill expend, on average, about $40,000 a year in public services (Culhane, et al., 2002). Research has found the majority of these costs are centered in acute-care hospitals (emergency rooms or crisis units), homeless shelters, and incarceration. For each person in supportive housing under a combined city and state program, the average costs in public services were reduced by an average of $16,000 per housing unit (Culhane, et al., 2002).

Identified Need: Disability Benefits

As has been stated elsewhere in this text, a significant proportion of individuals incarcerated in jails, state penitentiaries, and federal prisons are reported to have a history of mental health issues; estimates further indicate that anywhere between 17 and 20 percent have a serious mental illness. It has been repeatedly argued that mental illness and ex-offender status have a dual stigmatization effect, making reintegration all the more complex to navigate. Barriers to housing, employment, and treatment needs may lead to chronic homelessness and recidivism, and individuals who are uninsured or underinsured are particularly vulnerable to negative outcomes in relation to their ability to access proper (effective) care for their illness and underlying symptoms. For these reasons, two programs are offered through the Social Security Administration (SSA) that can provide eligible PwMI income and other benefits to assist with the transition from a correctional to community setting; these programs are *Supplemental Security Income (SSI)* and *Social Security Disability Insurance (SSDI)*. There is, however, the matter of being able to effectively navigate the application process. Consequently, interagency planning programs have been implemented to help released inmates with program enrollments for which they are eligible—sometimes even before they leave the jail setting (Patel, Boutwell, Brockmann, & Rich, 2014).

SSI/SSDI, OUTREACH, ACCESS, AND RECOVERY (SOAR)

SOAR is a model that is used to help PwMI who are homeless determine eligibility requirements, complete enrollment, and receive disability benefits; it is currently available in 50 states. The target population for the program is people who are homeless or at risk for homelessness. Research related to the SOAR program has indicated that connecting people in jails and prisons with Medicaid enrollment upon release could significantly improve the reentry process. SOAR can be used as a tool to access Medicaid and Medicare, which can provide the foundation for reentry plans to succeed (Blandford & Osher, 2013).

The National Alliance on Mental Illness (NAMI) and Mental Health America (MHA) (formerly the National Mental Health Association) are two of the largest advocacy organizations for consumers, their friends, and family members. Please visit the following websites for more information: http://www.nami.org/, http://www.mentalhealthamerica.net/

Identified Need: Case Management and Transition Planning Teams/ACT and FACT

ASSERTIVE COMMUNITY TREATMENT (ACT)

As an attempt to provide more intensive case management to individuals with serious mental illness who are preparing for reentry from state hospitals or correctional settings, one diversion strategy that has been shown to be effective is the use of multidisciplinary transition teams—in particular, an EBP model known as assertive community treatment (ACT) (Lamberti, Weisman, & Faden, 2004). ACT was originally designed "to assist persons with severe mental illnesses to function in the community, while attempting to prevent homelessness and hospitalizations" (Slate, et al., 2013, p. 467). ACT is a mobile team-based outpatient service model for providing comprehensive psychiatric care and case management supports to people with serious mental illnesses (Slade, McCarthy, Valenstein, Visnic, & Dixon, 2013). Teams provide high-risk consumers treatment at their home/place of residence and are available 24 hours a day, seven days a week (Slate, et al., 2013). ACT is recognized as an effective treatment for persons with severe psychiatric conditions, bipolar disorder, or schizophrenia who are high users of inpatient hospital services and low utilizers of community-based mental health services. It is also a community-based treatment approach for outpatients with severe mental illness that causes difficulties in daily living activities and social functioning, often including problems with relationships, physical health, addiction, work, daytime activities, and living conditions (Stobbe, Wierdsma, Kok, Kroon, Roosenschoon, Depla, & Mulder, 2014).

The ACT model requires a clinician team leader, normally a social worker or psychologist, as well as one or more nurses, a psychiatrist, and a substance abuse specialist (Slade, et al., 2013). These teams work with individuals who are mentally ill to ensure the continuation of care from a hospital setting to an outpatient practice, ensure functionality in the community, and reduce future hospitalization. Most of the services that are provided occur in a patient's home, a shelter, or the streets and are not usually provided in a clinic (Weinstein, Henwood, Cody, Jordan, & Lelar, 2011).

Many forms of services are provided by assertive community treatment, such as planning and monitoring treatment; taking patients to medical appointments and dentist appointments; representing them at hearings; and helping them manage money, pay bills, and apply for services. Other services that are provided are help with housekeeping, shopping, cooking, transportation, finding and keeping jobs, and housing, while also educating patients about mental illness, drug abuse counseling, and coping with psychotic episodes or crises (Phillips, Burns, Edgar, Mueser, Linkins, Rosenheck, Drake, & McDonel-Herr, 2001). Considered to be one of the most effective methods for providing services to people with SPMI program services can cost annually from $6,000 to more than $12,000 per client, and clients may continue to receive these services indefinitely (Slade, et al., 2013); these costs are offset by savings associated with reduced hospitalization or incarceration (Phillips, et al., 2001).

Assertive community treatment is considered one of the most effective methods for providing services to people with severe and persistent mental illness, and in 2010, more than 65,000 persons with serious mental illness were enrolled in more than 800 assertive community treatment programs in 38 U.S. states (Slade, et al., 2013). As stated earlier, research evidence indicates that the program reduces the need for psychiatric hospitalization and emergency medical care, and patients in the program are more likely to find housing, are less likely to be jailed, and usually claim to be more satisfied with this program than with other forms of community treatment (Phillips, et al., 2001; Stull, McGrew, & Salyers, 2012). Some negative aspects of these programs that have been identified in the literature include interactions that are seen as intrusive, restricting, and encouraging dependency or practices that seem to produce conflicts over money and medications or that are viewed as authoritative (Stull, et al., 2012).

Forensic Assertive Community Treatment (FACT)

This program is an incorporation of the original ACT program, but the caseload will primarily consist of those with mental illnesses who have also been in contact with the law. It provides intensive and supportive care from multidisciplinary teams in the community. The focus is on the criminal history of the offender with mental illness (Davis, Fallon, Vogel, & Teachout, 2008). The FACT team also relies on a predominance of referrals from the criminal justice agencies while also engaging probation officers (Slate, et al., 2013). This program and the team provide rehab ilitation, counseling, and material support and help the consumer find a real sense of belonging in the community in which they return. It has been found that it is associated with better functioning in the community and fewer jail days (Davis, et al., 2008).

Critical Time Intervention (CTI)

CTI is a case management process that incorporates three different steps to support transitions into the community: transition, try-out, and transfer to care. It follows these steps to create a smoother transition from jail or prison into the community for PwMIs (Draine & Herman, 2010). The length of each stage oftentimes depends on the individual and their motivation for change and help. Linkage to effective community programs right out of incarceration is a great help to the consumers. The programs that they are connected to may include mental health programs or community supports such as family or different support groups. There is still a need, however, to incorporate more help with basic human needs such as housing and employment. It has been found that many recipients just go through the steps and do not learn anything due to the lack of motivation because of not receiving housing or employment once released (Draine & Herman, 2010).

PROGRAM SPOTLIGHT: JOURNEY FORWARD IN FLORIDA

This program is sponsored by the Office of the Public Defender, 19th Judicial Circuit, and facilitated by a team of reentry staff in a four-county area in southeastern Florida. The main goal of this program is to break the cycle of recidivism for offenders who are housed inside the four county jails in the judicial circuit. The program is designed for offenders with mental health and/or substance abuse disorders. Treatment is offered during the period of incarceration, and aftercare services are included post-release. It includes a 90-day treatment program that involves cognitive behavioral therapy (CBT), trauma-informed care, motivational interviewing, 12-step substance abuse programs, exercise and nutrition, and a voluntary spiritual component ("St. Lucie County's Journey Forward," 2010). In various workshops offered at the jail, inmates are able to work toward educational, financial, and employment goals. Once released, they are provided with housing, transportation, treatment and mental health providers, vocational testing, resume writing, food stamps, and relapse prevention ("St. Lucie County's Journey Forward," 2010). This program has been found to be successful in lowering the rates of recidivism.

Some examples of reentry programming have included pre-release education or vocational programs, drug rehabilitation, skill building or work training, supportive housing, and the implementation and use of reentry or specialty courts in which, as described in the preceding chapter, a courtroom workgroup or "team" creates a more therapeutic environment in order to facilitate the offender's journey through the criminal justice system and back into the larger society (Walters, 2013; Yoon & Nickel, 2008). Specific evidence-based reentry initiatives have proven to be effective for persons with serious mental illness.

LEAD BY EXAMPLE: THE CASE OF BRAD H.

The case of *Brad H. vs. City of New York* is the first class action suit in which the court ordered a correctional system to provide discharge planning for inmates with mental illness. In the 1999 lawsuit filed by the Urban Justice Center, the points of the complaint can be summarized as follows: Inmates with mental illness at the city's jails were being subjected to release during the middle of the night, when they were taken to the subway station with less than two dollars and two subway tokens. There was no discharge plan, and therefore, no provisions for the alignment of mental health and other social support services in the community (e.g., housing, transportation, substance abuse treatment, reinstatement of Medicaid and/or Social Security disability benefits) (Jones, 2007; Urban Justice Center, n.d.).

The 2003 settlement agreement mandated the city to provide discharge planning to the 15,000-plus inmates at the time confined in the jails who received or would receive psychiatric services (Urban Justice Center, n.d.). Discharge planning would begin during incarceration and would continue beyond release; services in this context include mental health treatment during confinement and continuity of care upon release in the form of continued treatment, housing assistance, and assistance with obtaining public benefits and other social services. The settlement also contained a stipulation requiring release during daytime hours and provisions for the continued monitoring of the city's compliance, which has been reinstated every two years (Jones, 2007; Urban Justice Center, n.d.). Although compliance has met with its challenges, the landmark decision has been heralded as most progressive in terms of shaping mental health services provided to inmates in New York and across the nation (Jones, 2007).

Barriers to Reintegration Efforts

However promising advancements might be from practical, treatment, and legal standpoints, most jails lack adequate treatment facilities for the number of mentally ill inmates entering the system—precluding their ability to effectively manage inmates experiencing acute and ongoing crisis (Slate, et al., 2013). Further, despite the watchful eye of the courts, mental health understaffing still persists throughout most correctional settings, which may oftentimes result in poor or nonexistent discharge planning. There is also a significant amount of stigma associated with mental illness, and thus, the general public tends to view PwMI as violent and uncontrollable, thereby expressing little sympathy for them (Corrigan & Watson, 2002; Davey, 2013). Ironically, this (mostly media-generated) societal rejection of persons with mental illness has resulted in laws that are detrimental to the well-being of incarcerated offenders with mental health issues—particularly as they prepare to return to larger society (Davey, 2013).

In contrast, mainstream news media has also uncovered some of the injustices facing persons with mental illness while incarcerated, and thus, strong advocacy and support for change have recently reemerged (see Chapter 2 for historical context). Given more exposure of the circumstances and a broader understanding of the goals of reentry, the future outlook appears relatively promising (Figure 8.3). For example, reform

Figure 8.3

A Photo of Signposts (Hope and Despair)

Source: Taken from: Pixabay.com; licensed for use under Creative Commons CCO.
[Photograph]. Retrieved from https://pixabay.com/en/directory-signposts-hope-466935/

efforts at the jail or prison level include the development of separate treatment units that segregate PwMI from the general population, and the development of jail-based reentry programs, such as Journey Forward in Florida, continues with effective results. These programs are multidimensional, and many focus on recovery from addiction, education, housing, and the development of job skills.

In the context of continuity of care for inmates with mental illness post-release (community-based care), there have also been developments that show promise moving forward. Initiatives such as ACT teams, intensive case management, crisis intervention teams (CITs), and supported housing are designed to emphasize post-release treatment for individuals with co-occurring substance abuse and mental health problems and other criminogenic needs (Heilbrum, DeMatteo, Strohmaier, & Galloway, 2015). Although all have been proven effective in reducing recidivism, these services are notoriously under-funded in the public health systems (Slate, et al., 2013). However, recent federal regulations regarding the use of money from Medicaid—the major money provider for persons with mental illness—will make a profound direct impact on post-release access to care for incarcerated persons (Rogers, 2014). The effects of expanded Medicaid eligibility in this regard, of course, are premature and therefore should be assessed at a later time.

Take-Home Message

The underlying theme of this chapter has been that discharge planning is an extremely valuable tool to provide for the mental health and other needs of justice-involved PwMI in the prevention of recidivism and subsequent recycling of individuals between the mental health and criminal justice systems of care. More research should be conducted on the effectiveness of discharge planning so that it may be improved and implemented as an evidence-based practice in multiple settings with forensic populations (e.g., in hospitals, jails, prisons).

The impact of incarceration and reentry is not confined to the offender and the prison walls. These things also affect the community as a whole. Lack of adequate housing, community and social supports, education, and employment are included in the threats to successful reentry into the community (Woods, Lanza, Dyson, & Gordon, 2013). Planning and communication are key to improving the reentry process for those with mental illness and keeping them out of the criminal justice system. In order to be effective (and to minimize recidivism and other possible negative outcomes), discharge planning should be a fluid process that ideally begins upon intake (whether in a hospital or correctional setting) and continues beyond community reentry. *Boundary spanners* should provide PwMI (youth and adults) with information that will assist them in making a more successful transition to the community. Depending on the needs of the individual, reintegration efforts may include focus on the development of skills related to gaining and maintaining employment, coping strategies, motivation, money management, substance abuse and mental health treatment, literacy and education, parenting, wellness education, and adult continuing education. Forensic liaisons can develop and maintain relationships with individuals from multiple systems of care (e.g., police, courts, probation/parole, public welfare, youth and family services, drug and alcohol and mental health services) to facilitate access to services that are needs based and culturally appropriate for the individual consumer.

QUESTIONS FOR CLASSROOM DISCUSSION

Read the following case study and consider the remaining discussion questions in light of the facts and what you have learned regarding discharge/transition planning.

According to her family, A.L. was an individual who always strived to succeed in all aspects of her life. They reported that she obtained her nursing license with lots of hard work and diligence. However, she struggled with mood swings but lacked the insight to seek any treatment. As time went on, A.L. became so manic that she began to experience delusions and ended up in the streets of Gainesville. She was involuntarily hospitalized several times but never followed up with treatment. Eventually, A.L. was arrested for practicing medicine without a license and incarcerated. She was evaluated for competency and subsequently committed to the Department of Children and Families as incompetent to proceed. She currently sits at the county jail awaiting placement to a state forensic hospital.[1]

1. Assess A.L.'s clinical and social needs and public safety risks.
2. Develop a plan for the treatment and services required to address A.L.'s needs, both while in custody and upon reentry.
3. Identify required community and correctional programs responsible for post-release services.
4. Coordinate the transition plan to ensure implementation and avoid gaps in care with community-based services.

KEY TERMS & ACRONYMS

- Best practices
- Boundary spanners
- Continuity of care (COC)
- Dynamic risk factors
- Linkage blindness
- Memorandums of understanding (MOUs)

- NIMBY (not in my backyard)
- Social Security Disability Insurance (SSDI)
- Static factors of offending risk

- Supplemental Security Income (SSI)
- Supportive/supported employment (SE)
- Vocational rehabilitation

Note

1. Case study taken and adapted from Vail (2015).

Bibliography

Andrews, T. (2003). *Mental Health Procedures and Criminal Law.* Notes presented at the meeting of the Pennsylvania Bar Institute, Montour County, PA.

Baron, R. C., Draine, J., & Salzer, M. S. (2013). "I'm Not Sure That I Can Figure Out How to Do That": Pursuit of Work among People with Mental Illnesses Leaving Jail. *American Journal of Psychiatric Rehabilitation, 16*, 115–135. doi:10.1080/15487768. 2013 .7 89696.

Barrenger, S. L., & Draine, J. (2013). "You Don't Get No Help": The Role of Community Context in Effectiveness of Evidence-Based Treatments for People with Mental Illness Leaving Prison for High

Risk Environments. *American Journal of Psychiatric Rehabilitation, 16*, 154–178. doi:10.1080/1548776 8.2013.789709.

Bauer, R. L., Morgan, R. D., & Mandracchia, J. T., (2010). Offenders with severe and persistent mental illness. In T. J. Fagan & R. K. Ax (Eds.), *Correctional Mental Health* (pp. 189–212). Thousand Oaks, CA: Sage Publications..

Benson, M. L., Alarid, L. F., Burton, V. S., & Cullen, F.T. (2011). Reintegration or stigmatization? Offenders' expectations of community re-entry. *Journal of Criminal Justice, 39*(5), 385–393.

Blandford, A. M., & Osher, F. (2013). *Guidelines for the Successful Transition of People with Behavioral Health Disorders from Jail and Prison.* United States Substance Abuse and Mental Health Services Administration, GAINS Center for Behavioral Health and Justice Transformation.

Bloom, B., & McDiarmid, A. (2000). Gender-responsive supervision and programming for women offenders in the community. *Topics in Community Corrections Annual*, 11–18.

Carlson, P. M. (2011). *Managing the Mentally Ill from a Correctional Administrator's Perspective.* In Fagan, T. J., & Ax, R. K. (Eds). *Correctional Mental Health: From Theory to Best Practice.* Thousand Oaks, CA: Sage Publications Inc.

CBS New York. (2014). *Mentally Ill Homeless Veteran.* Retrieved from http://newyork.cbslocal. com/2014/03/19/officials-mentally-ill-homeless-veteran-baked-to-death-in-overheated-jail-cell/.

Cherner, R., Aubry, T., Ecker, J., Kerman, N., & Nandlal, J. (2014). Transitioning into the Community: Outcomes of a Pilot Housing Program for Forensic Patients. *International Journal of Forensic Mental Health, 13*(1), 62–74. Retrieved from http://doi.org/10.1080/14999013.2014.885472.

Chesney-Lind, M. (2000). Women and the criminal justice system: Gender matters. *Topics in Community Corrections, 5*, 7–10.

Chesney-Lind, M., & Pasko, L. (2013). *The female offender: Girls, women, and crime.* Thousand Oaks, CA: Sage Publications.

Connecticut Reentry Program Reduces Recidivism of Mentally Ill Offenders. (2012). *Corrections Managers Report, 18*(3), 37.

Corrigan, Patrick W., & Watson, A. C. (2002). Understanding the Impact of Stigma on People with Mental Illness. *World Psychiatry, 1*(1), 16–20.

Crisanti, A. S., & Frueh, B. C. (2011). Risk of Trauma Exposure among Persons with Mental Illness in Jails and Prisons: What Do We Really Know? *Current Opinion in Psychiatry, 24*(5), 431–435.

Culhane, D. P., Metraux, S., & Hadley, T. (2002). Public Service Reductions Associated with Placement of Homeless Persons with Severe Mental Illness in Supportive Housing. *Housing Policy Debate, 13*(1), 107–163.

Davey (2013). Retrieved from https://www.psychologytoday.com/blog/why-we-worry/201308/mental-health-stigma.

Davis, K., Fallon, J., Vogel, S., & Teachout, A. (2008). Integrating into the Mental Health System from the Criminal Justice System: Jail Aftercare Services for Persons with a Severe Mental Illness. *Journal of Offender Rehabilitation, 46*(3/4), 217–231.

Dirks-Linhorst, P., & Linhorst, D. (2012). Monitoring Offenders with Mental Illness in the Community: Guidelines for Practice. *Best Practices in Mental Health, 8*(2), 47–70.

Draine, J., & Herman, D. B. (2007). Critical Time Intervention for Reentry from Prison for Persons with Mental Illness. *Psychiatric Services, 58*(12), 1577–1581.

Draine, J., & Herman, D. B. (2010). Critical Time Intervention. *Journal of Community Corrections, 20*(1), 11–18.

Draine, J., Wolff, N., Jacoby, J. E., Hartwell, S., & Duclos, C. (2005). Understanding community re-entry of former prisoners with mental illness: a conceptual model to guide new research. *Behavioral Sciences & the Law, 23*(5), 689–707.

Earley, P. (2007). *Crazy: A Father's Search through America's Mental Health Madness.* New York, NY: Penguin Group, Inc.

Eno Louden, J., Manchak, S., O'Connor, M., & Skeem, J. L. (2015). Applying the Sequential Intercept Model to Reduce Recidivism among Probationers and Parolees with Mental Illness. In Griffin, P. A., Heilbrun, K., Mulvey, E. P., DeMatteo, D., & Schubert, C. M. (Eds.), *The Sequential Intercept Model and Criminal Justice: Promoting Community Alternatives for Individuals with Serious Mental Illness,* (pp. 118–136). New York, NY: Oxford University Press.

Fagan, T. J., & Ax, R. K. (2003). *Correctional mental health handbook.* Thousand Oaks, CA: Sage Publications.

Fellner, J. (2006). Corrections Quandary: Mental Illness and Prison Rules, *Harvard Civil Rights-Civil Liberties Law Review, 41,* 391.

Frontline. (2005). The New Asylums [DVD]. Retrieved from http://www.shoppbs.org/product/index.jsp?productId=2000133.

Griffin, P. A., Heilbrun, K., Mulvey, E. P., DeMatteo, D., & Schubert, C. A. (2015). *Sequential Intercept Model and Criminal Justice: Promoting Community Alternatives for Individuals with Serious Mental Illness.* New York, NY: Oxford University Press.

Harrison, P. M., & Karberg, J. C. (2003). *Prison and Jail Inmates at Midyear 2002* [No. NCJ-198877]. Washington, DC: Bureau of Justice Statistics, US Dept. of Justice.

Heilbrun, K., DeMatteo, D., Strohmaier, H., & Galloway, M. (2015). The Movement toward Community-Based Alternatives to Criminal Justice Involvement and Incarceration for People with Severe Mental Illness. In Griffin, P. A., Heilbrun, K., Mulvey, E. P., DeMatteo, D., & Schubert, C. M. (Eds.), *The Sequential Intercept Model and Criminal Justice: Promoting Community Alternatives for Individuals with Serious Mental Illness* (pp. 1–20). New York, NY: Oxford University Press.

Homelessness and Housing. (2016). Retrieved from http://www.samhsa.gov/homelessness-housing.

Jones, D. (2006). Discharge planning for mentally ill inmates in New York City jails: A critical evaluation of the settlement agreement of Brad H. v. City of New York. *Pace Law Review 27,* 305.

Joyce, A. S., Wild, T. C., Adair, C. E., McDougall, G. M., Gordon, A., Costigan, N., ... & Barnes, F. (2004). Continuity of care in mental health services: Toward clarifying the construct. *The Canadian Journal of Psychiatry, 49*(8), 539–550.

Kinoshita, Y., Furukawa, T. A., Kinoshita, K., Honyashiki, M., Omori, I. M., Marshall, M., ... & Kingdon, D. (2013). Supported employment for adults with severe mental illness. *The Cochrane Database of Systematic Reviews,* 2010(1), CD008297. http://doi.org/10.1002/14651858.CD008297.

Kondo, L. (2003). Advocacy of the establishment of mental health specialty courts in the provision of therapeutic justice for mentally ill offenders. *American Journal of Criminal Law, 28,* 255–336.

Koyanagi, C., & Blasingame, K. (2006). *Best Practices: Access to Benefits for Prisoners with Mental Illness.* Issue Brief. Washington, DC: Judge David L. Bazelon Center for Mental Health Law.

Lamberti, J. S., Weisman, R., & Faden, D. I. (2004). Forensic Assertive Community Treatment: Preventing Incarceration of Adults with Severe Mental Illness. *Psychiatric Services, 55*(11), 1285–1293.

Lehman, A. F., Goldberg, R., Dixon, L. B., McNary, S., Postrado, L., Hackman, A., & McDonnell, K. (2002). Improving employment outcomes for persons with severe mental illnesses. *Archives of General Psychiatry, 59*(2), 165–172.

Lurigio, A. J., Rollins, A., & Fallon, J. (2004). Effects of Serious Mental Illness on Offender Reentry. *Federal Probation, 68,* 45.

Miller, M. G., & Ngugi, I. (2009). *Impacts of Housing Supports: Persons with Mental Illness and Ex-Offenders*. Olympia, WA: Washington State Institute for Public Policy.

Montgomery, E., Hill, L., Culhane, D., & Kane, V. (2014). *Housing First Implementation Brief*. Philadelphia, PA: VA National Center on Homelessness Among Veterans, US Department of Veterans Affairs.

Montgomery, P., Forchuk, C., Duncan, C., Rose, D., Bailey, P. H., & Veluri, R. (2008). Supported Housing Programs for Persons with Serious Mental Illness in Rural Northern Communities: A Mixed Method Evaluation. *BMC Health Services Research, 8*(1), 1.

Morgan, R. D., Flora, D. B., Kroner, D. G., Mills, J. F., Varghese, F., & Steffan, J. S. (2012). Treating Offenders with Mental Illness: A Research Synthesis. *Law and Human Behavior, 36*(1), 37.

Morrissey, J. P., & Goldman, H. H. (1986). Care and Treatment of the Mentally Ill in the United States: Historical Developments and Reforms. *The Annals of the American Academy of Political and Social Science, 484*(1), 12–27.

National Institute of Justice. Office of Justice Programs. Offender Reentry. (2015). Retrieved from http://www.nij.gov/topics/corrections/reentry/pages/welcome.aspx.

Osher, F., D'Amora, D. A., Plotkin, M., Jarrett, N., & Eggleston, A. (2012). Adults with behavioral health needs under correctional supervision: A shared framework for reducing recidivism and promoting recovery. New York: Council of State Governments Justice Center.

Osher, F., & King, C. (2015). Intercept 4: Reentry from jails and prisons. In Griffin, P. A., Heilbrun, K., Mulvey, E. P., DeMatteo, D., & Schubert, C. A. (Eds.), *The sequential intercept model and criminal justice: Promoting community alternatives for individuals with serious mental illness* (p. 95). New York, NY: New York, NY: Oxford University Press, USA.

Patel, K., Boutwell, A., Brockmann, B. W., & Rich, J. D. (2014). Integrating Correctional and Community Health Care for Formerly Incarcerated People Who Are Eligible for Medicaid. *Health Affairs, 33*(3), 468–473.

Peers for Progress. (2016). *What Is Peer Support?* Retrieved from http://peersforprogress.org/learn-about-peer-support/what-is-peer-support/.

Phillips, L. A., & Spencer, W. M. (2013). The Challenges of Reentry from Prison to Society. *Journal Of Current Issues In Crime, Law & Law Enforcement, 6*(2), 123–133.

Phillips, S. D., Burns, B. J., Edgar, E. R., Mueser, K. T., Linkins, K. W., Rosenheck, R. A., . . . & Herr, E. C. M. (2001). Moving Assertive Community Treatment into Standard Practice. *Psychiatric Services, 52*(6), 771–779.

Rogers (2014). Retrieved from http://csgjusticecenter.org/reentry/media-clips/medicaids-new-prisoner-population/.

Rotter, M., McQuistion, H. L., Broner, N., & Steinbacher, M. (2005). Best practices: The impact of the "incarceration culture" on reentry for adults with mental illness: A training and group treatment model. *Psychiatric Services, 56*(3), 265–267.

Satel, S. (2003). Out of the Asylum, into the Cell. *New York Times*, A-29.

Skeem, J. L., Hernandez, I., Kennealy, P., & Rich, J. (2012). *CA-YASI Reliability: How Adequately Do Staff in California's Division of Juvenile Justice Rate Youths' Risk of Recidivism*. Irvine, CA: University of California.

Skeem, J. L., Winter, E., Kennealy, P. J., Louden, J. E., & Tatar II, J. R. (2014). Offenders with Mental Illness have Criminogenic Needs, Too: Toward Recidivism Reduction. *Law and Human Behavior, 38*(3), 212.

Slade, E. P., McCarthy, J. F., Valenstein, M., Visnic, S., & Dixon, L. B. (2013). Cost Savings from Assertive Community Treatment Services in an Era of Declining Psychiatric Inpatient Use. *Health Services Research, 48*(1), 195–217.

Slate, R. M., Buffington-Vollum, J. K., & Johnson, W. W. (2013). *The Criminalization of Mental Illness: Crisis and Opportunity for the Justice System* (2nd Ed.). Durham, NC: Carolina Academic Press.

St. Lucie County's Journey Forward Sets Inmates on Path to Success. (2010). *Florida Partners in Crisis: Success Stories, 1–4*. Retrieved from http://www.stluciesheriff.com/pdf/Article_FL-Partners-in-Crisis_2010.pdf.

Stobbe, J., Wiersdma, A. I., Kok, R. M., Kroon, H., Roosenschoon, B. J., Depla, M., & Mulder, C. L. (2014). The Effectiveness of Assertive Community Treatment for Elderly Patients with Severe Mental Illness: A Randomized Controlled Trial. *BMC Psychiatry, 14*(1), 1.

Stull, L. G., McGrew, J. H., & Salyers, M. P. (2012). Processes Underlying Treatment Success and Failure in Assertive Community Treatment. *Journal of Mental Health, 21*(1), 49–56.

The Sentencing Project. (2002). Mentally ill offenders in the criminal justice system: An analysis and prescription. Retrieved from http://www.sentencingproject.org/wp-content/uploads/2016/01/Mentally-Ill-Offenders-in-the-Criminal-Justice-System.pdf

Travis, J. (2000). *But They All Come Back: Rethinking Prisoner Reentry*. Washington, DC: US Department of Justice, Office of Justice Programs, National Institute of Justice.

Urban Justice Center (n.d.). Mental Health Project. *Brad H. v City of New York*. Retrieved from https://mhp.urbanjustice.org/mhp-bradH.v.cityofnewyork.

Walters, J. H. (2013). The National Institute of Justice's Evaluation of Second Chance Act Adult Reentry Courts: Program Characteristics and Preliminary Themes from Year.

Wehman, P. (2012). Supported Employment: What is it? *Journal of Vocational Rehabilitation, 37*(3), 139–142.

Wehman, P., Lau, S., Molinelli, A., Brooke, V., Thompson, K., Moore, C., & West, M. (2012). Supported Employment for Young Adults with Autism Spectrum Disorder: Preliminary Data. *Research and Practice for Persons with Severe Disabilities, 37*(3), 160–169.

Weinstein, L. C., Henwood, B. F., Cody, J. W., Jordan, M., & Lelar, R. (2011). Transforming Assertive Community Treatment into an Integrated Care System: The Role of Nursing and Primary Care Partnerships. *Journal of the American Psychiatric Nurses Association, 17*(1), 64–71.

Woods, L. N., Lanza, A. S., Dyson, W., & Gordon, D. M. (2013). The Role of Prevention in Promoting Continuity of Health Care in Prisoner Reentry Initiatives. *American Journal of Public Health, 103*(5), 830–838. doi:10.2105/AJPH.2012.300961.

Yoon, J., & Nickel, J. (2008). *Reentry & Partnerships: A Guide for States & Faith-Based and Community Organizations*. New York, NY: Council of State Governments Justice Center.

CHAPTER 9 **Intercept Five**
Community-Based Corrections and Support Services

Charles G. Curie, former administrator of the U.S. Substance Abuse and Mental Health Services Administration (SAMHSA), on interviews he had with patients with mental illness who were about to be discharged from a state hospital:

> I asked them the question what they needed to make their transition success-ful and what they needed to deal with and manage their illness. They never spoke in terms of programs, they did not speak in terms of needing a psychi-atrist or even a social worker, but what they spoke of was that they needed a job, a home, and meaningful personal relationships—or, to use a direct quote, "I need a life, a real life; I need a job, a home, and a date on the weekend." They want a life, a real life with its rewards.
>
> (Recommendations to Improve Mental Health Care in America, 2003)

Introduction

Throughout the preceding chapters, challenges and potential diversion strategies have been introduced and discussed with respect to justice-involved persons with men-tal illness who enter the criminal justice system—from their initial encounter with law enforcement and subsequent arrest (Intercept One), to the point at which the indi-vidual is discharged from a period of incarceration and attempts to reintegrate into a community setting (Intercept Four). In line with the traditional criminal justice funnel, however, the journey through the forensic mental health system may not end there. In fact, consumers of mental health and substance abuse services who are justice-involved and under community supervision (usually probation) (Figure 9.1) represent another large group to consider for the purposes of community reintegration and the last inter-cept point in the Sequential Intercept Model ([SIM] Munetz & Griffin, 2006).

Figure 9.1

Photo of California Department of Corrections & Rehabilitation Uniform Badge

Source: California Department of Corrections & Rehabilitation, http://www.cdcr.ca.gov/img/carousel-home1.jpg

As was noted at the beginning of the text, the SIM is anchored by "community" at both ends, illustrating the importance of integrative partnerships between multiple agencies. In the context of Intercept Five, communities should be able to provide and encourage the proper utilization of resources, while simultaneously aiding in the reduction of recidivism (and quantifying effectiveness). However, for a number of reasons already described in preceding chapters, there is high likelihood that PwMI on community supervision will violate the conditions of probation or parole (Skeem & Louden, 2006). Not only does community supervision present a complicated host of conditions and restrictions to follow, but for many probationers and parolees who lack the ability to function due to the nature of their illness, or for those who are unable to access resources and necessary services because of financial, housing, or transportation restrictions, it presents more of a barrier to successful reintegration in the community. Consistent with RNR principles and the framework of APIC and other models presented in Chapter 8, individuals with serious mental health and/or substance abuse needs who are determined to be at a high risk for reoffending should receive more intensive (specialized) community-based supervision to include, among other services, the coordination of closer monitoring and more integrative treatment resources and prioritized housing and other service needs (Osher, D'Amora, Plotkin, Jarrett, & Eggleston, 2012).

This chapter presents a framework for reducing recidivism and behavioral health problems among individuals who are under correctional control or supervision in the community; in other words, individuals who are on probation or parole. Despite some of the overlap from the preceding chapters, it is meant to provide a description of consumer needs post-commitment (public health or criminal justice systems) and the potential for inter-agency collaboration, with the goal of identifying and overcoming barriers to adjusting successfully in the community. First, the chapter reviews the issues pertaining to PwMI who are under community-based correctional supervision and the circumstances that have led to the need for alternative responses.

Mental Health and Community Corrections

In 2014, there were an estimated 4,708,100 adults (1 of every 52 individuals) under the authority of community supervision in the form of probation and parole in the United States (Kaeble, Maruschak, & Bonczar, 2015). According to one report, offenders with any mental illness make up about 16 percent of all probationers and 5 to 10 percent of parolees (Dirks-Linhorst & Linhorst, 2013). When applied to the total number incarcerated, these percentages show that there are over 650,000 probationers with mental illness and between 42,000 and 84,000 parolees with mental illness (Dirks-Linhorst & Linhorst, 2013). Additional findings suggest that approximately 7 percent to 9 percent of male probationers and parolees have serious mental illness and that those with co-occurring SMI and substance abuse disorders have rates as high as 40 percent and 50 percent (Feucht & Gfroerer, 2011; as cited in Osher, D'Amora, Plotkin, Jarrett, & Eggleston, 2012).

The research also suggests that justice-involved persons with mental illness are more likely than those without mental illness to recidivate (commit a new offense) or violate terms of their release and to do so more quickly, resulting in their return to prison (Bailliargeon, et al., 2009; Skeem, Winter, Kennealy, Eno Louden, & Tatar, 2014). In particular, lack of treatment options and community integration strategies lead to a 60 to 80 percent increase in risk of one reincarceration incident and an 80 to 140 percent increase in risk of a second reincarceration for offenders with serious mental illness (Baillargeon, et al., 2009). With such a large number of probationers and parolees being reincarcerated for *technical violations* or the commission of new crimes, there is a need for necessary review of factors that lead to recidivism among this population, as well as an examination of relevant programs with empirical evidence of effective community reintegration. Again, some of this information may be overlapping that which has been presented in previous chapters; however, it will now be presented along with potential solutions in the context of Intercept Five.

The Case for Recidivism

As discussed in Chapter 8, previous research has shown that mental illness in itself has little direct correlation to recidivism (Skeem, Winter, Kennealy, Eno Louden, & Tatar, 2013). Rather, the presence of mental illness increases the likelihood for *other* factors that are directly associated with criminal activity (criminogenic risk factors, discussed in more detail in Chapter 8)—the most significant of which include the presence of antisocial personality traits and antisocial cognition (thinking styles conducive to law breaking) (Osher, D'Amora, Plotkin, Jarrett, & Eggleston, 2012). Four additional indicators that moderately predict recidivism among PwMI include substance abuse, employment instability, family problems, and low participation in pro-social leisure (Osher, et al., 2012; Skeem, et al., 2013). Homelessness is also a significant factor (Ostermann & Matejowkowski, 2014). Given the risk that having co-occurring mental health and substance abuse presents for offenders under community supervision—in particular, with respect to the potential for recidivism and, in some cases, the manifestation of violent behaviors—the following section provides a review of the literature related to this prevalent relationship.

Mental Illness and Substance Abuse

Previous research has shown that as high as 70 percent of individuals with serious mental illness also have a history of substance abuse (Hartwell, Deng, Fisher, Siegfriedt, Roy-Bujnowski, Johnson, & Fulweiler, 2013). In Figure 9.2, alcohol is depicted as the drug of choice. Offenders with mental illness are more likely to be under the influence of drugs or alcohol when taking part in criminal activity than those without serious mental illness, and a *dual diagnosis* of mental illness and substance abuse disorder consistently increases the likelihood of recidivism when compared with the presence of mental health or substance abuse independently

Figure 9.2

Photo of Man in Liquor Store

Source: By Tom Sodge. n.d. Retrieved from https://unsplash.com/tomsdg

(Hartwell, et al., 2013; Stephens, 2011). For example, in a study conducted by Balyakina, Mann, Ellison, Sivernell, Fulda, Sarai, & Cardarelli (2014) probationers with co-occurring substance abuse and mental health disorders were 22 times more likely to recidivate in comparison with those who only had substance abuse or mental health disorder alone (Balyakina, et al., 2014).

Despite a strong relationship between substance abuse and offending behaviors among PwMI, there has been little previous research examining the importance of access to substance abuse treatment among members of this population (Hartwell, et al., 2013). Results of existing research, however, indicate that a substantial proportion of offenders with PwMI successfully access substance abuse treatment within the two years following their release into the community (Hartwell, et al., 2013). However, the underlying success factors seem to pertain to whether treatment was court ordered as part of a release plan. In particular, only a small proportion of offenders are mandated to seek substance abuse treatment post-release (Hartwell, et al., 2013). This is problematic because it has been consistently shown that, due to a number of barriers (no transportation, lack of benefits/insurance, weak supervision, and poor additional community supports), PwMI fail to utilize community-based services with regularity. Another factor that can cause offenders to not seek substance abuse treatment relates to the stigma that results from having mental illness and being a substance abuser; this perception may cause PwMI to avoid taking part in a treatment program (Hartwell, et al,. 2013). In fact, many offenders who enter substance abuse treatment enter detox services, which shows that treatment is primarily sought when an individual is in complete crisis and in need of medical attention (Hartwell, et al., 2013). Based on these findings, researchers have concluded that information gained from the initial screening processes with offenders should be utilized to develop a multidisciplinary treatment plan, whereby substance abuse treatment for offenders with mental health disorders should be mandated as a stipulation of release through proper coordination and planning (Hartwell, et al., 2013; Stephens, 2011).

THINKING CRITICALLY: AN EXCERPT FROM A LAW JOURNAL ON PROBATION OFFICER DISCRETION REGARDING MENTAL HEALTH TREATMENT

Imagine that you have been convicted of a federal drug crime and you have a history of addiction and mental health issues. You are now in court to be sentenced. Once you hear that you will be spending the next five years in prison, you do not even give a second thought to everything else the judge is saying. You do your time, you are released from prison, and you meet your probation officer.

continued

At that point, the officer, not the judge, decides you need to spend more time confined—this time, in a restrictive inpatient facility. In fact, the judge, five years ago at sentencing, ordered the probation officer to make such a decision (Teitelbaum, 2012, p. 1554).

What if this were your brother, a parent, or you? In consideration of research discussed earlier, how might the court justify such discretion?

Legal Matters: Probation and Parole Officer Discretion

In many cases at the time of sentencing, judges give probation officers the discretion to decide whether an offender is released early, unconditionally, or with viable mandated treatment options (Teitelbaum, 2012). These practices have become so commonplace that many do not think twice about these proceedings. However, Article III of the United States Constitution limits judicial power to the courts (Teitelbaum, 2012). Probation and parole officers are granted the ability to mandate additional mental health treatment through sentencing guidelines only if the court has reason to believe that the defendant is in need of psychological or psychiatric treatment approved by the United States Probation Office. If there is no basis for mental health treatment or further supervision, the case can be thrown out (Teitelbaum, 2012). Probation is also granted the ability to extend sentencing through community supervision due to their dual status as district court employees and law enforcement officers within the federal system. Although probation officers are, in fact, delegates of the court, they are still not permitted to make decisions that are essentially considered to deprive defendants of their individual liberty interests under the U.S. Constitution (Teitelaum, 2012).

Possible solutions to maintain the legality of increased mental health supervision by probation officers include judges making final decisions at sentencing that are not indeterminate (flexible) (Teitelbaum, 2012). A more viable option would have the judge setting a sentence of maxim restriction in which the probation officer has the legal discretion to reduce, but not increase, the sentence as they see fit (Teitelbaum, 2012).

Additional Barriers to Success

Probation and parole service providers must be able to meet the specialized needs of persons with mental illness in order to reduce recidivism and promote successful community integration. One of the biggest problems observed at Intercept Five is the breach in communication between correctional administrators and officers, service providers, and other key stakeholders at various agencies (e.g., school personnel, courtroom case managers, attorneys). Also, there is a lack of knowledge with respect to services available for persons with mental illness. Thus, although research has shown that parole and probation supervision does reduce recidivism, specialized mental health and substance abuse training would further increase successful release into the community (Ostermann & Matejowkowski, 2014). Resource guides have been designed and used in some communities and made available to individuals working in multiple, but integrated, systems of care. For example, police officers may find it extremely useful to have referral information for local *respite care* or other crisis management services on hand during a crisis encounter, should diversion be an option (Compton & Kotwicki, 2007). In addition to the training of community release personnel and the dissemination of mental health and substance abuse (MH/SA) information to key actors, focus has been given to the development of more effective transition planning (and, as stated earlier, the implementation of multidisciplinary treatment plans)—in particular, that which utilizes an integrative approach to pre-release conditions (Stephens, 2011).

Summary of Post-Commitment Needs

It has been well established that offenders with mental illness who are released from a correctional or forensic hospital setting have an increased likelihood for recidivism when compared to offenders without mental illness (Osher, et al., 2012; Skeem & Louden, 2006; Stephens, 2011). As presented in the preceding sections and in Chapter 8 of this text, some of the following responses have been identified as post-commitment needs that may reduce recidivism with this population:

- Substance abuse screening and monitoring

- Guidelines for determining effective community mental health treatment and evidence-based practices

- Better understanding of offender risk level and the identification and continued observation of criminogenic needs (changeable risk factors) during the period of supervision

- Increased community supervision and information sharing across agencies

- An integrated system of transition planning for offenders with mental illness and provisions in place for unrestricted access to service needs

It is true that offenders without mental illness share many of the same needs as forensic clients; they also share many of the same restrictions to meeting their needs for success in the community setting (Osher & King, 2015). These restrictions have been reviewed throughout the course of the text, as have many of the ways in which they can be overcome. The most important strategies, and those that are essential in terms of the role of community corrections officials and service providers at Intercept Five, is that of interagency and intra-agency cooperation, ongoing assessment of risk and needs of the clients, and the seamless provision of integrated service needs (Louden, Manchak, O'Connor, & Skeem, 2015). Specific information as to what this may look like in any given community is reviewed next.

Agency Collaboration and Systems Integration

There are a number of ways by which a community can work to develop collaborative and multisystemic partnerships to accomplish the effective integration of probationers and parolees with mental illness and co-occurring substance abuse needs. Examples of strategies may include the creation of collaborative committees or teams and the facilitation of community partnership meetings with service providers and key agency leaders to include juvenile and/or adult probation officers, clients and families (depending on the needs at the time), and other stakeholders in community corrections. Meetings could revolve around practical matters, funding, new programs, research findings, or even the review of problematic cases for multidisciplinary perspectives/input and to engage in the discussion of potential solutions. Furthermore, various agencies involved in the care and supervision of this population should employ individuals who are capable of being trained as effective boundary spanners. The ongoing exchange of information between agencies and providers is also an essential strategy for positive change, as well as the timely handoff of such information (Osher, D'Amora, Plotkin, Jarrett, & Eggleston, 2012). With respect to information sharing, privacy concerns should be noted and respected in the context of successful and respectful provider–client relationships, but also under the provisions of federal, state, and local laws pertaining to sharing of medical records and other personal health information (Petrila, Fader-Towe, & Hill, 2015).

To best understand how justice officials can aid in the development of effective responses to PwMI entrenched in their system of care and promote practices in community corrections agencies to reduce the high rates of recidivism among this group, research findings with respect to best or evidence-based practices should be consulted and suggestions for positive changes noted. Existing literature provides support for the ongoing training of direct services staff across systems. For example, training related to problem-solving techniques and available resources for effective supervision could provide probation and parole officers with the skills needed to foster compliance and reduce risk of negative outcomes. Likewise, the system-wide training of law enforcement officers (including community corrections), public defenders, district attorneys, jail personnel, mental health workers and providers, and courtroom personnel on topics related to mental health and substance abuse signs and symptoms and barriers to reintegration is likely to foster interagency relations, the sharing of information and resources, and the reduction of stigmatizing beliefs about PwMI (Louden, et al., 2015).

Specialized Probation

The importance of supportive correctional transition planning cannot be overstated, as knowledge of resources and the ability to make community connections for one's clients contributes to the development of trustworthy and positive relationships through respect and adequate attention to their case (Dirks-Linhorst & Linhorst, 2012).

This can be achieved through the use of specialized personnel who have received adequate and ongoing training about mental health and co-occurring substance abuse disorders and treatment needs. The research informs that there are five key features of specialty probation (Skeem, Emke-Francis, & Eno Louden, 2006, pp. 121–122, as cited in Eno Louden, et al., 2015):

Caseloads that consist only of probationers with mental illness

Officers have reduced caseloads (M = 48 vs. M = 100 plus)

Officers are provided with ongoing training in mental health–related issues

Community resources are integrated, so officers may serve on multidisciplinary teams

Officers are trained to use problem-solving strategies as compared to punishment and sanctions used in a traditional probation setting

Specialization and emphasis on a rehabilitative model are ideal for community protection and adequate treatment (Dirks-Linhorst & Linhorst, 2012).

Practitioners are to address conditions of release violations on a case-by-case basis in order to avoid unnecessary violations that can result in a return to incarceration (Dirks-Linhorst & Linhorst, 2012). In particular, case managers should be cognizant of mental illness and decompensation triggers when considering whether or not to revoke parole and admit the offender back into the system (Dirks-Linhorst & Linhorst, 2012). Also, minor violations such as missing doctor's appointments or periodic absences from treatment programs should be viewed as treatment issues and not warranting of revocations (Dirks-Linhorst & Linhorst, 2012). Additional guidelines for community monitoring of mental illness include incorporating risk assessment instruments into decision making, focusing attention on substance abuse, gathering data from multiple sources, and involving multiple parties (Dirks-Linhorst & Linhorst, 2012).

LEARN BY EXAMPLE: SPECIALIZED COMMUNITY TRANSITION TEAMS FOR OFFENDERS WITH MENTAL ILLNESS (OMI)

As discussed in Chapter 8, transition planning involves the simple planning of community treatment services and coordination among prison personnel and community mental health providers. One example of transition planning is the Transition from Prison to Community (TPC) program in which correctional staff, law enforcement, and social service providers collaborate with a large

continued

focus on planning for the inmate's release into the community. Research findings have shown that participation in the TPC program reduces recidivism for all offenses.

FACT programs have also been implemented with success since the late 1970s. These specialty programs focus more on access to services than transition planning. Persons enrolled in a FACT program who have forensic involvement (criminal charges filed against them) are given 24/7 access to psychiatrists, nurses, social workers, and substance abuse counselors. Research evaluations on the effectiveness of FACT have shown that participation in the program has led to reduced recidivism and a reduction of days spent incarcerated.

Source: Kondrat, Rowe, & Sosinski (2013).

Program options have been examined for their ability to reduce offending behavior for PwMI in community corrections, but nevertheless, definitive results have not been produced on a consistent basis (Baillargeon, et al., 2009; Skeem & Eno Louden, 2006). Findings do show that specialized or specialty mental health probation does in fact increase mental health service access and reduce recidivism—which are its primary goals (Manchak, Skeem, Kennealy, & Louden, 2014). It is unclear, however, if the reduction in recidivism is due to the treatment programs or to the core principles of specialized probation programs such as FACT (discussed in Chapters 6 through 8), which incorporate boundary spanning, more intense supervision, and high-quality probation officer–client relationships (Skeem, Manchak, & Peterson, 2011).

Resistance to Treatment

Throughout the text attention has been focused on systematic barriers to access mental health and other services in the community. Although the idea has been briefly considered in one or two places in preceding chapters, a complete discussion of service utilization has not been offered. The most important point to communicate in this regard is that many justice-involved PwMI are resistant to treatment, and despite best efforts regarding cross-systems training, collaboration, integration, and funding of resources, a consumer may simply just not engage in services, and therefore, may decompensate, reoffend, and return to jail and/or prison. To accommodate the needs of consumers, any public safety concerns, and the management concerns of providers who collect and report data on utilization, some strategies have been implemented in various locales so to increase service engagement. For example, as presented earlier in the text, some jurisdictions have established MOUs (memorandums of understanding) between departments of corrections and community-based providers so to facilitate initial after-care appointments for inmates with mental health and/or substance abuse needs who are soon to be released from correctional facilities. In addition to the benefits of facilitating discharge planning prior to release, this type of system is quite useful if it is possible to record any missed appointments as "no shows" for data reporting purposes.

There have also been more controversial attempts at increasing access to and utilization of services for persons with mental illness who are considered at risk of harming themselves or someone else. For example, the use of *assisted outpatient treatment (AOT)* laws as a means of mandating that an offender engage in treatment in the community are instructive in this regard; this controversial legislation is discussed in the following section.

Effectiveness of Community Treatment Orders

Research has shown that recidivism among offenders with mental illness is a widespread problem in which many factors affect frequently negative outcomes. Swigger and Heinmiller (2014) explain the effectiveness of community treatment orders in which mental health patients are required to receive outpatient community mental health treatment, including forced medication (Swigger & Heinmiller, 2014).

Assisted Outpatient Treatment

Assisted outpatient treatment (AOT) legislation has already been passed in 45 states; at the time of this writing, the 5 states that do not have AOT are Connecticut, Maryland, Massachusetts, New Mexico, and Tennessee (see Figure 9.3) (Treatment Advocacy Center, 2011). Also called outpatient commitment, AOT is designed for consumers who have a poor history of treatment compliance, as it is court-ordered treatment (including medication management), which is often attached as a condition of release for justice-involved individuals with mental health and/or substance abuse needs who are remaining in a community setting.

AOT has been found to be effective in terms of success related to reducing the likelihood of hospitalization as well as the duration thereof. It has also been found to reduce chronic homelessness and the frequency of arrests and violent episodes, incarceration, victimization, and caregiver stress, and observed to increase treatment compliance (Treatment Advocacy Center, 2011). It should be noted that the implementation of AOT is often incomplete or inconsistent because of legal, clinical, official, or personal barriers to treatment.

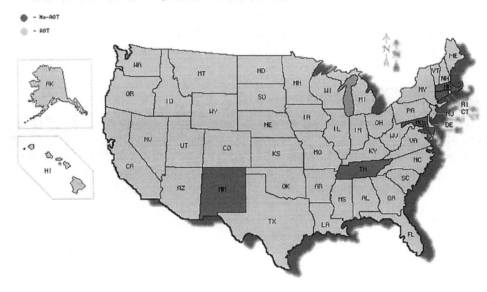

Figure 9.3

AOT in the United States, 2016

Source: Michele P. Bratina (own work) via http://diymaps.net

THINKING CRITICALLY: WHAT ARE THE BENEFITS OF AOT?

Reduces arrests
Increases medication compliance and access to other forms of treatment
Reduces homelessness
Reduces hospitalization
Reduces crime and violence
Reduces caregiver stress
Some would argue that AOT is used to prevent tragedies from occurring. Consider the following stories. Would you agree with that statement?

Policy Matters: The Cases of Kendra Webdale and Laura Wilcox

The usage of AOT has been hotly contested in the United States and abroad (Canada; see, e.g., Swigger & Heinmiller, 2014). New York Senate Bill S.7254, or "Kendra's Law," ushered in forced community treatment after journalist and photographer Kendra Webdale was shoved from the platform and into the path of a subway train in New York City by a man with schizophrenia, causing public uproar for reform in the mental health field (Swigger & Heinmiller, 2014). Similar to the New York legislation, Laura's Law (California) is named after a young woman by the name of Laura Wilcox, a California native, who was shot and killed at the age of 19 years old by a man who had untreated chronic mental illness.

Although both pieces of legislation have made it possible to mandate at-risk offenders to get the help they need, the media sensationalism surrounding these and other cases prompted negative stereotypes of persons with mental illness as violent and out of control, much like the cases of James Holmes (Aurora movie theater shooting) and Adam Lanza (Sandy Hook Elementary School shooting), presented in the opening chapter of this book.

The current programs are created with the goal to provide services to persons who need them in a much less restrictive manner than if they were detained in an inpatient psychiatric facility (Swigger & Heinmiller, 2014). Unlike in the U.S. justice system, where community mental health supervision is based on the recommendation of a judge or probation officer, community treatment orders are issued by a physician, in which the patient is compelled to comply. Patients who fail to comply will be issued an order for examination, which serves much like a warrant for the doctor in which police may take the patient into custody and return them to the physician for examination (Swigger & Heinmiller, 2014). Rigorous empirical research on the subject of community treatment orders is relatively limited; however, studies have yielded positive results as to their effectiveness on increasing service utilization, reductions in offending behaviors, and a host of other positive outcomes (see the "Thinking Critically" text box).

Take-Home Message

Released offenders with mental illness who are under community supervision have an increased likelihood for recidivism when compared to offenders without mental illness. Although there is some evidence of effectiveness with specialty probation and integrative approaches to training and the coordination of services, there is an immediate need for additional research on the effects of supervision and transition planning on a larger scale to institute change. Despite changes in policies and procedures at the agency level, justice-involved PwMI are still being rearrested and reconvicted at an alarming rate, and continued incarceration is not the answer. This problem can be addressed through a collective effort involving correctional personnel, law enforcement, and community health providers. Some examples of successful strategies include the continued use of probation officials who are trained in CIT or deescalation techniques and in trauma-informed care approaches to management and supervision of specialized populations of offenders. Supported and other housing programs should be prioritized, along with other methods to assist the consumer in maintaining a stable environment, including supported employment and consistent engagement in treatment programs. For juvenile offenders on probation, there are juvenile probation officers (JPOs) who have received specialized training and who manage a reduced number of specialized cases. Other programs found to be successful with youthful offenders who are being supervised in the community include mentoring and/or after-school programs (Big Brother/Big Sister), targeted case management, alternative and special education (development of an Individualized Education Plan [IEP]), student assistance teams (SATs), youth building programs (i.e., Boys and Girls Club, YMCA/YWCA), school-based prevention programs, community coalitions, and peer-based support services.

QUESTIONS FOR CLASSROOM DISCUSSION

1. What kinds of treatment options are available to offenders with mental health/substance abuse disorders who are under community supervision? Make a list of tools that you think would assist community corrections officials in better responding to or protecting persons with mental illness.
2. How does the community work to accomplish service engagement for persons with serious mental illness but who are not under criminal justice supervision?
3. Compare and contrast assisted outpatient treatment (AOT) with commitment to an inpatient psychiatric facility. Identify three pros and three cons with regard to AOT.

KEY TERMS & ACRONYMS

- Assisted outpatient treatment (AOT)
- Dual diagnosis
- Respite care
- Technical violations

Bibliography

Baillargeon, J., Williams, B. A., Mellow, J., Harzke, A. J., Hoge, S. K., Baillargeon, G., & Greifinger, R. B. (2009). Parole Revocation among Prison Inmates with Psychiatric and Substance Use Disorders. *Psychiatric Services*, *60*(11), 1516–1521.

Balyakina, E., Mann, C., Ellison, M., Sivernell, R., Fulda, K., Sarai, S., & Cardarelli, R. (2014). Risk of Future Offense among Probationers with Co-Occurring Substance Use and Mental Health Disorders. *Community Mental Health Journal*, *50*, 288–295.

Carr, A. (2012). The Impact of Personality Disorders on Legally Supervised Community Treatment: A Systematic Literature Review. *Community Mental Health Journal*, *50*, 664–672.

Cherner, R., Nandlal, J., Ecker, J., Aubry, T., & Pettey, D. (2013). Findings of a Formative Evaluation of a Transitional Housing Program for Forensic Patients Discharged into the Community. *Journal of Offender Rehabilitation*, *52*, 157–180.

Dirks-Linhorst, P., & Linhorst, D. (2012). Monitoring Offenders with Mental Illness in the Community: Guidelines for Practice. *Best Practices in Mental Health*, *8*(2), 47–70.

Hartwell, S., Deng, X., Fisher, W., Siegfreidt, J., Roy-Bujnowsi, K., Johnson, C., & Fulwiler, C. (2013). Predictors of Accessing Substance Abuse Services among Individuals with Mental Disorders Released from Correctional Custody. *Journal of Dual Diagnosis*, *9*(1), 11–22.

Kaeble, D., Maruschak, L. M., & Bonczar, T. P. (2015). *Probation and Parole in the United States, 2014.* Washington, DC: U.S. Department of Justice, Office of Justice Programs, Bureau of Justice Statistics.

Kondrat, D., Rowe, W., & Sosinski, M. (2013). An Exploration of Specialty Programs for Inmates with Severe Mental Illness: The United States and the United Kingdom. *Best Practices in Mental Health, 8*(2), 99–108.

Louden, J. E., Manchak, S., O'Connor, M., & Skeem, J. L. (2015). Applying the sequential intercept model to reduce recidivism among probationers and parolees with mental illness. In Griffin, P. A., Heilbrun, K., Mulvey, E. P., DeMatteo, D., & Schubert, C. A. (Eds.), *The sequential intercept model and criminal justice: Promoting community alternatives for individuals with serious mental illness* (pp. 113–131). New York, NY: Oxford University Press, USA.

Manchak, S. M., Skeem, J. L., Kennealy, P. J., & Eno, Louden, J. (2014). High Fidelity Specialty Mental Health Probation Improves Officer Practices, Treatment Access, and Rule Compliance. *Law and Human Behavior*, Advance Online Publication. Retrieved from Http://dx.doi.org/10.1037/hb0000076.

Munetz, M. R., & Griffin, P. A. (2006). Use of the sequential intercept model as an approach to decriminalization of people with serious mental illness. *Psychiatric Services, 57*(4), 544–549.

Osher, F., D'Amora, D. A., Plotkin, M., Jarrett, N., & Eggleston, A. (2012). *Adults with behavioral health needs under correctional supervision: A shared framework for reducing recidivism and promoting recovery.* New York: Council of State Governments Justice Center.

Osher, F., & King, C. (2015). Intercept 4: Reentry from jails and prisons. In Griffin, P. A., Heilbrun, K., Mulvey, E. P., DeMatteo, D., & Schubert, C. A. (Eds.), *The sequential intercept model and criminal justice: Promoting community alternatives for individuals with serious mental illness* (p. 95). New York, NY: Oxford University Press, USA.

Ostermann, M., & Matejowkowski, J. (2014). Exploring the Intersection of Mental Health and Release Status with Recidivism. *Justice Quarterly, 31*(4), 746–766.

Petrila, J., Fader-Towe, H., & Hill, A. B. (2015). Sequential intercept mapping, confidentiality, and the cross-system sharing of health-related information. In Griffin, P. A., Heilbrun, K., Mulvey, E. P., DeMatteo, D., & Schubert, C. A. (Eds.), *The sequential intercept model and criminal justice: Promoting community alternatives for individuals with serious mental illness (p. 257). New York, NY: Oxford University Press, USA.*

Petrila, J., Fader-Towe, H., & Hill, A. B. (2015). Sequential intercept mapping, confidentiality, and the cross-system sharing of health-related information. In Griffin, P. A., Heilbrun, K., Mulvey, E. P., DeMatteo, D., & Schubert, C. A. (Eds.), *The sequential intercept model and criminal justice: Promoting community alternatives for individuals with serious mental illness* (p. 257). New York, NY: Oxford University Press, USA.

Recommendations to Improve Mental Health Care in America: Report from the President's New Freedom Commission on Mental Health Constitution and Campaign Reform, Senate, 108th Cong. 9 (2003) (Testimony of Charles G. Curie).

Sharma, M., & Bennett, R. (2015). Substance Abuse and Mental Illness: Challenges for Interventions. *Journal of Alcohol & Drug Education, 59*(2), 3.

Skeem, J. L., & Louden, J. E. (2006). Toward evidence-based practice for probationers and parolees mandated to mental health treatment. *Psychiatric Services, 57*(3), 333–342.

Skeem, J. L., Winter, E., Kennealy, P. J., Louden, J. E., & Tatar II, J. R. (2013). Offenders with Mental Illness Have Criminogenic Needs, Too: Toward Recidivism Reduction. *Law and Human Behavior, 38*(3), 212–224.

Stephens, D. J. (2011). Substance Abuse and co-occurring disorders among criminal offenders. In T. J. Fagan & R. K. Ax (Eds.), *Correctional mental health: From theory to best practice (pp. 235–256)*. Thousand Oaks, CA: Sage Publications.

Swigger, A., & Heinmiller, B. (2014). Advocacy Coalitions and Mental Health Policy: The Adoption of Community Treatment Orders in Ontario. *Politics & Policy, 42*(2), 246–270.

Teitelbaum, A. (2012). Dubious Delegation: Article III Limits on Mental Health Treatment Decisions. *Michigan Law Review, 110*(8), 1553–1582.

Treatment Advocacy Center (2011). *Assisted Psychiatric Treatment: Inpatient and Outpatient Standards by State*. Retrieved January 6, 2017, from http://www.treatmentadvocacycenter.org/storage/documents/State_Standards_Charts_for_Assisted_Treatment_-_Civil_Commitment_Criteria_and_Initiation_Procedures.pdf

Weeks, R., & Widom, C. S. (1998). Self-Reports of Early Childhood Victimization among Incarcerated Adult Male Felons. *Journal of Interpersonal Violence, 13*(3), 346–361.

CHAPTER 10 **Conclusions and Suggestions for Change**

It is not every kind of frantic humour, or something unaccountable in a man's behavior, that points him out to be such a man as is exempted from punishment; it must be a man that is totally deprived of his understanding and memory, and doth not know what he is doing, no more than an infant, than a brute, or a wild beast, such a one is never the object of punishment.

—Articulation of the "Wild Beast Test" of 1723, one of the earliest tests used to assess criminal insanity
Source: Hamilton, 1986.

Introduction

This textbook was structured as a presentation of the five points of inception and diversion in the Sequential Intercept Model ([SIM] Munetz & Griffin, 2006), in its original form. Throughout the preceding chapters, it is hoped that three key implications were established. First, that there is an overrepresentation of persons with mental illness who are involved in the justice system as offenders. Second, the criminal (or juvenile) justice system has historically been ill equipped to respond to the needs of offenders with mental health needs—in particular, the complex needs of females and males and females with serious mental illness (SMI). Figure 10.1 illustrates the extreme isolation of the correctional setting, for example. Finally, to make positive changes, responses require effective cross-systems training, tolerance, creativity, and the development of unique partnerships between multiple agencies and systems of care. It also requires, at the very least, a basic understanding of mental health and substance abuse disorders and an open-minded approach to the underlying causes of behavior. This is

Figure 10.1

Prison Cell Block

Source: Taken from Pixabay.com [Photograph] [CCO Public Domain]. Retrieved from https://pixabay.com/en/prison-jail-cell-cell-block-crime-598851/

particularly true in the case of children's mental health issues, although the focus of the book is on adults in the forensic system.

The previous chapters presented a host of suggestions related to diversion and more positive interventions in the forensic mental health system. Because the primary undercurrent of this text has been cross-systems collaboration and information sharing, recommendations for practitioners moving forward revolve around this theme and include, first and foremost, the creation of a community stakeholders group that consists of individuals from varied disciplines and agencies who can effectuate change. An essential next step would be to conduct ongoing trainings that include programmatic needs, many of which are discussed in more detail throughout this text. These include systems mapping (Chapter 3), knowledge of signs and symptoms related to mental illness and substance use disorders (Chapter 4), other knowledge-building programs that reduce stigma and teach valuable deescalation techniques (e.g., Crisis Intervention Teams [CIT], Chapter 5), and an array of services that are grounded in *trauma-informed care (TIC)*, a subject reserved for this chapter.

The purpose of this chapter is two-fold: First, it is intended to highlight important points made in the previous nine chapters and to present suggestions related to systems integration for further reflection and evaluation. Second, the chapter is intended to provide a foundation against which generalizations can be made on the role of trauma as it relates to mental health and co-occurring substance abuse disorders and, ultimately, justice involvement for many individuals. It is recommended that the future use of the SIM as a conceptual guide to forensic mental health be expanded to incorporate trauma-informed approaches to the apprehension, care, and treatment of PwMI who enter the criminal or juvenile justice systems of care. It seems that positive change can only be made once the root causes of behavior are addressed. The remaining sections of the chapter are presented in the order just described, beginning with the review of primary issues.

Review of the Issues and Suggestions for Change

On any given day, roughly 17,000 youth (18 years of age or younger) are committed to and confined in juvenile detention facilities throughout the United States ("Key Facts: Youth in the Justice System," 2012), most for nonviolent offenses (Wagner & Rabuy, 2016). Among adults, approximately 2.3 million persons are confined to adult correctional facilities (jails and prisons, state and federal) (Wagner & Rabuy, 2016) at any point in recent history. According to an emergent (and methodologically robust) line of research, many of these individuals—both youth and adults—have been affected by trauma, poverty, violence, educational disadvantage, and substance abuse. As stated early in the text, some estimates have indicated that anywhere between 20 and

50 percent of adults and over 70 percent of juveniles in detention have at least one mental health disorder and that the majority are diagnosed with a co–occurring substance use disorder (see Ditton, 1999; Hayes, 2012; James & Glaze, 2006; NAMI, 2013; Shufelt & Cocozza, 2006; Teplin, Abram, McClelland, Mericle, Duncan, & Washburn, 2006).

Issues Presented

Some of the primary issues related to consumers of substance abuse and mental health services that have been identified thus far include an underfunded mental health system; chronic homelessness; an overreliance on the justice system to control and treat offenders with mental illness; compromised public safety; increased arrest; incarceration, criminalization, and mistreatment of PwMI in correctional settings; stigma; and a lack of training for criminal justice actors who work in policing and corrections. Some have argued that these problems can be traced to the declining use of commitment to state-run inpatient hospitals and the subsequent displacement of persons with chronic mental illnesses into poorly developed community-based mental health systems that are unprepared, and sometimes unwilling, to meet their needs (Griffin, Heilbrun, Mulvey, DeMatteo, & Schubert, 2015; Slate, Buffington-Vollum, & Johnson, 2013).

The Importance of Systems Integration

Although diversion options throughout the course of the justice system are available and have been discussed, significant gaps still affect treatment outcomes and the rates of recidivism; these gaps exist across multiple systems of care. Ultimately, the most comprehensive system of care that encompasses mental health and substance abuse services would incorporate the collaboration between stakeholders from multiple systems of care, and an array of treatment programs and services would be accessible, recovery oriented, evidence based, and driven by the needs of consumers (Council of State Governments, 2002; Griffin, et al., 2015). This idea of community collaboration is depicted in Figure 10.2.

Needs Assessment

Once community linkages have been established and collaborative teams developed, an informal needs assessment should be conducted with constant communication with providers, mental health and substance abuse committees in the community, case management, consumers, and representatives from any managed mental health and substance abuse care networks in the service area. Needs would then be addressed through consumer and provider surveys. In particular, relevant stakeholders from the locale should be asked to participate in a systems integration survey designed to determine accomplishments, gaps, and solutions to effective integration across systems working with the target populations.

Figure 10.2

Joining Hands

Source: Pixabay.com [Photograph] [CCO Public Domain]. Retrieved from https://pixabay.com/en/joining-hands-help-handshake-770559/

Information Sharing of Identified Service Needs

Public meetings consisting of providers, case managers, consumers, community representatives, and administrative personnel could meet at a single location to review and discuss the results from the survey, followed by suggestions for future endeavors. Aside from these meetings, areas of need will be identified through previous advisory board meetings, current discussions, and review of the data provided by provider annual reports. Many gaps in services and needs for funding/development have been identified throughout this text—several of which include:

- Budget concerns that may lead to cuts in services, less spending on medications (e.g., formularies), or more lengthy waiting lists for services/inpatient beds.

- Integrated training for mental health (MH), public welfare, substance abuse (SA), and justice workers that includes more in-depth information pertaining to SA/MH issues and services available in the locale and the use of deescalation techniques in MH crisis situations.

- Advocacy and creative solutions designed to keep children with MH/SA issues in school and out of juvenile justice facilities (school-to-prison pipeline).

- Successful integration of juveniles and adult forensic populations as they transition back into the community.

- Successful integration of state hospital civilly committed persons as they transition back into the community.

- Improve the data system to have better information on service utilization.

- Housing available for all individuals with mental health and substance abuse disabilities.

- Employment programs designed to assist PwMI in entering the competitive work environment and to build tenure in a meaningful position.

- Increase in effective communication across systems—particularly between law enforcement, consumers, and service providers (including educators).

- Training and support for workgroups formed to address the gaps in services.

Recommended Services and Supports

Although a plethora of needs are certainly paramount in terms of an effective system of care, the justice system is not and should not become the lead agency charged with the majority of these functions. Rather, jurisdictions/locales/communities across the nation must utilize a *systems of care (SOC)* approach to addressing forensic mental health needs of its consumers of related services. In brief, this relates to a cross-systems approach to recovery in which an array of services will be accessible to all partner agencies. In an SOC model, partnering agencies may include public welfare and children and youth services, Medicaid, juvenile justice, education, mental health and disability, substance use, and veterans' affairs. Depending on their presence in any given community, other agencies may become part of the SOC—in particular, those agencies that provide services related to housing, transportation, and employment.

THINKING CRITICALLY

By now, you have read multiple times about the gaps in services related to mental health in community and correctional settings. You have also been informed that PwMI without access to treatment (medication, in particular) and other primary needs such as housing and employment do not fare well and often end up in the criminal justice system. Over the past two to three years or more, however, the media has broadcast stories of PwMI who had violently attacked innocent persons in a movie theater, a kindergarten class, a navy yard, and at other random and seemingly safe locations. Moreover, the perpetrators have often been portrayed as educated, gainfully employed individuals who resided in regular housing, often with family members who appear to be relatively stable and concerned about their well-being. Research some of these cases, and identify common characteristics associated with the offenders, victims, and circumstances surrounding the traumatic event. What does the research say about the relationship between mental illness and violent offending? Identify characteristics of most justice-involved PwMI, and compare and contrast these with perpetrators whose stories reached mainstream media; how do they compare?

Policy Matters / Recommendations

Based on gaps and identified needs in the overall SOC as listed earlier, the following matrix outlines four specific policy goals that should be incorporated into the development of a comprehensive system of care. This information, as presented, can be used to more effectively identify persistent goals, objectives, and strategies that are reflective of the prioritized needs of the community.

These suggestions are presented to encourage the commitment to positive changes in forensic mental health. Although the effects of deinstitutionalization had started to present themselves decades ago, policy changes to improve the system have not been particularly forthcoming (Compton & Kotwicki, 2007; Slate, et al., 2013). Rather, it would seem that funding for mental health and substance abuse services is the first to be cut when states are seeking to minimize spending. What is often left are ineffective

TABLE 10.1 Integrative Solutions for a Comprehensive System of Care (SOC)

Goals	Objectives	Suggested Actions
Integration of services	Communities should identify strategies to enhance community-based resources and multiagency collaboration to improve outcomes for children and adults with mental health/substance abuse disorders.	Hold a series of meetings and trainings to enhance collaboration with the judiciary, child welfare, providers, school districts, law enforcement, and other state agencies who encounter MH/SA populations. Develop workgroups, committees, and subcommittees who are charged with the identification of strategies to enhance services and motivation for children and families involved in the system of care. Research and distribute best evidence-based practices for treatment and recovery. Develop improved data collection procedures and utilize multiple methodologies for data analysis with regard to measuring outcomes. Track results.
Early intervention and delinquency/crime prevention	County-specific children in crisis workgroups composed of multiagency personnel (e.g., DJJ, child welfare, MH/SA providers, law enforcement, school district, county commissioners) shall be developed and charged to work with K–12 exceptional student education (ESE) and mainstream personnel. Such groups will identify estimates of the number of children who will qualify for services and develop strategies for them to access the appropriate services when needed—particularly during periods of crisis and transition between behavioral health and community settings.	Distribute county-wide MH/SA services lists to local schools, law enforcement agencies, and state public health and human services agencies for widespread dissemination. Meet with school administrators and other personnel responsible for intervention at each of the schools in a region or locale to discuss the referral process. Meet with student resource officers to discuss community-based services and referrals and to advise them about training opportunities. Meet with families/parents to discuss community-based services and referrals and to advise them about the importance of early intervention, prevention, and treatment. Participate in Department of Juvenile Justice (DJJ) multidisciplinary staff meetings and local child welfare review teams and initiatives. Identify areas of need regarding children's mental health (CMH) and substance abuse (SA) services and transition from intensive services/inpatient/residential to community-based settings (school). Identify sound data collection methodologies to assess outcomes.

continued

Goals	Objectives	Suggested Actions
Promote cross-training opportunities	A multiagency steering committee should be developed to work with individuals to identify training interests and needs and assist them in accessing training opportunities, with the goal in mind of a more effective system-wide model of referrals and services.	Promote training opportunities in the community to specifically target: • Children and adults with disabilities currently receiving services. • Children and adults with disabilities not currently receiving services. • Judicial agents who order clients to seek/receive mental health and substance abuse services in the community or while detained in a facility. • Legal aid staff, public defenders, and state attorneys who advocate for outcomes related to civil liberties and public safety. • Public health personnel who provide medical services to at-risk children and adults. • Agents in the criminal justice system, particularly jail personnel and those responsible for law enforcement. • Child welfare personnel. • School personnel. Continue to support and forge relationships with persons leading existing training programs. The core group in any community is usually the Crisis Intervention Team (local or regional). Utilize agency staff and providers who have personal and professional skills related to best practices by allowing them the opportunities to design and facilitate evidence-based training programs. Continue to work with outside agencies at the local, state, and federal levels who specialize in training in several of the key areas related to MH and SA. Always consider cultural competency when developing training programs and/or assessing existing ones. Implement brief evaluations after training to assess motivation and positive and negative outcomes.

continued

Goals	Objectives	Suggested Actions
Reform and transform forensic mental health services	To keep people with serious mental illness who do not need to be in the criminal justice system in the community.	Contract with community-based care agencies to perform forensic oversight; includes hiring one person who will monitor forensic services for the region. Ensure that there are enough full-time forensic specialists/case managers employed in each region, along with peer-support staff in the community and correctional settings. Implement policy that mandates specialized probation and parole staff who are trained in best or evidence-based practices, and who, as mandated by law or policy, maintain a specialized case load of no more than 30 to 40 clients (fewer for juvenile probation officers). Develop a center of innovation for promising and evidence-based practices. Support community reintegration for forensic clients who have been in the state hospital. Implement an integrated system of services and supports for co-occurring mental health/drug and alcohol recovery. Implement housing and forensic workgroups to address the following: • Develop employment opportunities. • Structured housing options. • Access to Medicaid, medical services, and SSI/Disability. • Access to medication without breaks in treatment. Provide recommendations for educating judges and other professionals in the courts regarding competency, insanity, and commitment evaluations and requirements.

Source: Author

public policies which make life more difficult for PwMI and, at the same time, cause an increasing amount of stigma (Compton & Kotwicki, 2007). Taken together, such circumstances prevent PwMI from seeking and utilizing the necessary services to help address underlying trauma and a plethora of human service needs that place them at risk for repeat offending. Thus, as stated several times earlier in the text, the nature of serious mental illness makes it likely that people with a multitude of symptoms will have contact with law enforcement and the courts, often resulting in unnecessary arrest or incarceration/detention (Griffin, Heilbrun, Mulvey, DeMatteo, & Schubert, 2015).

On a positive note, practitioners who work with justice-involved PwMI with serious mental illness have noticed high levels of resilience among them, in spite of having untreated symptoms which may include the presence of hallucinations (e.g., hearing voices) and delusions (e.g. being convinced that the U.S. president is plotting to kill you). In fact, for many PwMI, maladaptive behaviors such as panhandling or self-medicating with illicit substances make perfect sense as practical adaptations to daunting environments (e.g., jail or prison) or as solutions to dealing with untreated trauma and symptoms that impair their ability to function in daily life (Compton & Kotwicki, 2007). After entering the justice system, PwMI who never had the opportunity to address the underlying trauma that led them to their present circumstances may be exposed to frequent retraumatization through violence and victimization as they cycle in and out of the system (Courtney & Maschi, 2013; Miller & Najavits, 2012; Weeks & Widom, 1998). At this point in the chapter, it makes sense to transition to a discussion about trauma and its role in the forensic mental health system.

Contemporary Issues in Forensic Mental Health: The Role of Trauma

What Is Trauma?

Trauma is broadly defined as experiences that produce intense emotional pain, fear, or distress, often resulting in long-term physiological and psychosocial consequences (Bowen & Murshid, 2016). Trauma can encompass a person's life in many ways, as it occurs in a number of forms, including physical, psychological, and emotional. In some cases—in particular, incidents of sexual violence—the trauma is repressed or shrouded in secrecy, and even when confronted, many victims deny it ever happening. Additionally, trauma can often be ignored despite victim reports, creating additional psychological strain (Rosenberg, 2011). Although in many cases the physiological and psychological damages may be severe, trauma is treatable, and those who have experienced it can overcome it through engagement in effective treatment and services facilitated by competent service providers (Read, van Os, Morrison, & Ross, 2005).

The remainder of this section presents an introduction and discussion related to the intersections of childhood traumatization, mental health issues, and involvement in the criminal justice system.

Adverse Childhood Experiences (ACE)

In 2011, an ACE study was completed by the Centers for Disease Control and Prevention (CDC) and Kaiser Permanente to assess childhood trauma and its effects on future health and well-being (Rosenberg, 2011). The results from the study indicated that there was a strong correlation between childhood abuse or dysfunction and risk factors for several of the leading causes of death in adults (Felitti, et al., 1998). Furthermore, subsequent research findings have concluded that trauma is the single greatest preventable cause of chronic mental illness, drug and alcohol abuse, suicide, and many other maladaptive outcomes (Felitti, et al, 1998; Levenson, Willis, & Prescott, 2014; Read, et al, 2005). The ACE pyramid presented in Figure 10.3 illustrates trauma outcomes.

Given these research findings, the relationship between early trauma and subsequent periods of incarceration for some individuals is not surprising. The literature suggests that the majority of people served by public mental health and substance abuse systems have experienced some form of trauma, which may include sexual assault, domestic violence, neglect, and child abuse (Rosenburg, 2011). Furthermore, research findings indicate that witnessing violence or being the victim of physical violence during childhood (especially at a very young age) places individuals at a higher risk for incarceration during adulthood (see, e.g., Driessen, Schroeder, Widman, von Schönfeld, & Schneider, 2006; Greene, Haney, & Hurtado, 2000; Kerig & Becker, 2015; Levenson, et al., 2014).

The more severe the trauma, the higher the risk for disorders such as alcoholism, depression, drug use, and suicide attempts, along with other negative aftermaths. In fact, approximately 50 percent of those who have been diagnosed with bipolar disorder and schizophrenia also meet the criteria for substance use disorder; they are referred to as *dual diagnosis* clients (Sharma & Bennett 2015). In the context of prevention related to institutional violence, the following interventions have been utilized with some success: psychoeducation and the development of coping skills to deal with post-traumatic stress disorder (PTSD) and substance abuse concerns (Miller & Najavits, 2012).

Trauma-Informed Care

A trauma-informed care approach recognizes the intersection of trauma with many health and social problems for which people seek services and treatment (Bowen & Murshid, 2016). Trauma-informed care is conceptualized as an organizational change process centered on a specialized framework intended to promote healing and reduce

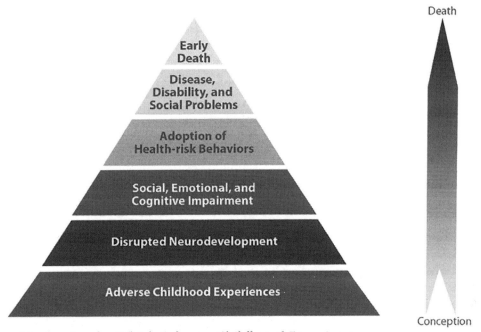

Mechanism by Which Adverse Childhood Experiences
Influence Health and Well-being Throughout the Lifespan

Figure 10.3

Adverse Childhood Experiences (ACE) Pyramid (ACE Presentation Graphics)

Source: Taken from Centers for Disease Control and Prevention, National Center for Injury Prevention and Control, Division of Violence Prevention [Graphic]. Retrieved from http://www.cdc.gov/violenceprevention/acestudy/ace_graphics.html

the risk of retraumatization for vulnerable individuals; components of the framework have been referred to as the "four Rs":

Realize the impact of trauma and also understand recovery.

Recognize symptoms in clients.

Respond to applying policy and procedure.

Resist the retraumatizing of individuals.

(Substance Abuse and Mental Health Services Administration [SAMHSA], 2016)

Within this framework, SAMHSA has outlined the core principles of trauma-informed care, which include safety, trust, transparency, collaboration and peer support, empowerment, choice, and the intersectionality of identity characteristics (Bowen & Murshid, 2016). Safety refers to treatment programs designed to keep the consumer out of danger and to prevent further trauma from occurring. Trust and transparency pertains to the extent to which the agency is transparent in its policies and procedures while maintaining the goal of building trust with staff, clients/consumers, and the community members. Collaboration consists of staff viewing clients/consumers as active partners, which is often done through peer support, such as peer mentoring (Bowen & Murshid, 2016). Empowerment refers to the agency allowing the client/consumer to have a voice in the decision-making process. The last principle has to deal with cultural differences that make an individual's treatment unique. The key to treatment involves compassion and support, and effective approaches will be racially, ethnically, and spiritually relevant, as well as gender specific (Rosenberg, 2011).

In the context of forensic mental health, trauma-informed programs operate on the belief that treatment—particularly that which is rendered in a correctional setting—can potentially revictimize individuals who are seeking help. In traditional justice system approaches to addressing mental health and trauma, a history of trauma in an individual's past is commonly viewed as an unimportant detail; offending behaviors are essentially viewed as deviance, and the offender is thereby viewed as a "deviant" or "criminal." Conversely, a TIC approach turns blame and stigmatization on its head. Instead of criminalizing mental health and substance abuse, the behaviors are viewed through a trauma lens, and the individual is viewed as a potential victim who may be self-medicating to cope with the underlying issues.

PRACTITIONER'S CORNER 10.1

Cross-System Collaboration in Practice: Juvenile Emotional Behavioral Disorders

Contributor: Kelly M. Carrero, PhD

Shawn is 13 years old and was just sent to a juvenile correctional facility. Shawn, his mother, and little sister have moved around quite a bit, staying with different friends and relatives after his father was incarcerated seven years ago. A little over three years ago, when Shawn was about to turn 10 years old, he began getting in trouble at his new school for being disrespectful and disruptive. In addition, Shawn was having a difficult time interacting with his peers and was academically about two grade levels below his peers. His teacher wanted to meet with Shawn's mom to discuss

continued

her concerns. Shawn's mom was working two jobs and had little time to spend with him, much less meet with the school regarding their concerns. Unfortunately, the few interactions Monica did have with the school were very short and, frankly, seemed rather unproductive to Monica—she did not understand why the school was unable to handle Shawn for the few hours they had him in their care. One afternoon, after an altercation with a peer, Shawn threw a tantrum that resulted in destroying the classroom and him purposely banging his head against a wall. Shawn was suspended from school for three days. During his "time off from school," Shawn was caught breaking into his neighbor's house and taking some video games. The judge placed Shawn on probation and advised Shawn's mom to pay careful attention to Shawn because he is "entertaining a dangerous path." Shawn's mother agreed and returned home with every intention to check in on him more frequently. Shawn's troubles continued and he got into more fights at school. His teacher made a referral for him to be tested by a multidisciplinary team to see if he qualified for special education—perhaps as a student with severe emotional disturbance. Unfortunately, the fights at school violated the terms of his probation, and he was sent to stand before the judge prior to the assessment being completed by the multidisciplinary team. While in court, the judge asked Shawn's mom if she was able to adequately supervise him or if he needed to be sent to a 90-day lock-up facility for juveniles. Through tears, Shawn's mom elected to have him go to the 90-day lock-up in hopes that he would learn his lesson, stay out of trouble, and allow her to get a peaceful night of sleep. Shawn's heart broke as he watched his mother walk out of the courtroom, surrendering him to the court. After 90 long days and sleepless nights and many altercations with fellow inmates, Shawn was released to his mother and placed back on probation. Shawn withdrew from his mother and became very difficult to deal with at home. His mother felt it would be best for Shawn to stay with his uncle across town so he could have a male role model and disciplinarian. Shawn started a new school and continued with his old behaviors. He was disrespectful to his teachers, disruptive during class, refused to do any academic work, and had many altercations with his peers. His teacher contacted his uncle and told him about Shawn's behaviors. That evening, his uncle hit him with a belt three times, gave him extra chores, and told him he was not to leave the house or play any video games. The next day, Shawn brought a knife to school with the intention of scaring his teacher and peers. He showed the knife to one of his classmates before school, and the classmate told the teacher, who informed the principal. Moments later, the school resource officer was in the classroom to escort Shawn out of the school building and to the police station. Shawn's probation officer was contacted, and Shawn was sent to a holding cell in the juvenile correctional facility.

Unfortunately, Shawn's story is not at all unique. Many children who are in crisis are living in chaotic situations that do not permit stability and adequate time for mental health screening, subsequent diagnostic testing, and individualized educational programming. Moreover, clear indicators of mental health concerns in young children, such as failure to make adequate academic progress and failure to develop and maintain friendships, are not easily detected when children move to several new schools in such a short amount of time. Children often demonstrate academic gaps when they first move to a new school with a new curriculum. In addition, developing friendships takes time, so it seems normal for there to be a period of adjustment, both academically and socially. However, Shawn appears to be an adolescent who is at risk for developing mental health concerns and court involvement that will only persist without proper treatment and overall opportunities to enhance his physical, academic, emotional, and behavioral

continued

wellness. Shawn, his family, and agencies providing services to Shawn could have benefited from a systems of care approach (Eber & Keenan, 2004). The goal of systems of care is to promote long-term success and positive outcomes through a "seamless" continuum of community-based services. Many stakeholders using the systems of care approach utilize the wraparound process (Burchard, Bruns, & Burchard, 2002; Eber, Sugai, Smith, & Scott, 2002). The wraparound process is a process to planning and implementing comprehensive child- and family-centered services and support (Bruns et al., 2005). It is a system-level intervention that aims to integrate existing services around children and youth with emotional and/or behavioral health needs and their families to address problems in a comprehensive way (Eber & Nelson, 1997). Eber, et al. (2002) consider the wraparound process a planning process that is to be used as a tool within a systems of care approach to facilitate collaboration among stakeholders. Finally, Shawn, and many others like Shawn, could have benefitted from attending a school that has comprehensive systematic screenings in place for academics, behavioral, and social domains (i.e., Fuchs & Fuchs, 2006; Lane, Kalberg, & Menzies, 2009; Sugai, et al., 2000). Initial screening would have likely identified Shawn as having academic, behavioral, and social concerns and he would have immediately received school-wide and classroom-wide interventions and supports to address his specific areas of concerns.

FAST FACT

An effective intervention strategy that has been used with juvenile populations in response to their behavioral health needs: **Positive Behavior Interventions and Supports (PBIS)**

Definition:
[A] broad range of culturally appropriate practices of systemic school-wide, classroom, and individualized strategies for achieving important social and learning outcomes while preventing challenging behaviors of all students.

Major Components:
Systematically preventing and addressing behaviors by linking outcomes, data, practices, and systems and supporting data-based decision making, student behavior, and staff behavior.

Source: Lewis, T. J., & Sugai, G. (1999). Effective behavior support: A systems approach to proactive schoolwide management. Focus on Exceptional Children, 31(6), 1–24.

Take-Home Message

Subjects reviewed and presented in this book have clearly indicated the increasing need for juvenile and criminal justice officials (police/first responders, court personnel, and correctional staff) who are trained specifically in crisis intervention and various mental health–related issues. Training is occurring in the United States and abroad, and is shown to be effective in terms of increasing awareness and knowledge pertaining to mental health and co-occurring substance abuse disorders. Notwithstanding positive feedback from both empirical and anecdotal observations, there is the need for more evaluation so that more of the progressive training programs, some of which were introduced in this text, can be categorized as evidence based. The overarching goals of programs such as MHFA, ACT or FACT, CIT, systems mapping, and trauma–informed care are public safety and the diversion of people with serious mental illness who do not need to be in the criminal justice system. Although there are a plethora of needs that are certainly paramount in terms of an effective system of care, the criminal justice system should not be the lead agency in meeting these needs. Instilling a vision of hope beyond a history of trauma and illness is vital to a successful recovery (Figure 10.4).

Figure 10.4

Person Joyfully Watching the Sunset

Source: Pixabay.com [Photograph]. [CC0 Public Domain]. Retrieved from https://pixabay.com/en/person-human-joy-sunset-sun-110305/

The Treatment Advocacy Center (TAC)

The TAC is a national nonprofit organization whose primary role is the dissemination of information pertaining to policy and practice related to effective treatment and recovery of PwMI. Their website hosts a searchable "Preventable Tragedies" database, where interested persons could conduct a search for cases of violent encounters with PwMI as victims or perpetrators that resulted in injury or death. The database can be found here: http://www.treatmentadvocacycenter.org/problem/preventable-tragedies-database

---

The SIM was used as a guide to illustrate each potential diversion point in the traditional criminal justice funnel. Thus, chapter by chapter, the text focused on ways to potentially funnel PwMI out of the juvenile and criminal justice systems. Points of interception are clearly quite important, but despite the best of intentions, poor symptom control and a fragmented network of care in the community frequently result in the criminalization and unnecessary arrest of PwMI. Quite often, PwMI have restricted access to medical care, yet experience increased rates of homelessness, exposure to trauma, and substance use, which presents challenges to the criminal justice professionals who encounter them; unfortunately, this interface of criminal justice and mental health is consistent from the cradle to the grave (Bloom, 2016; Courtney & Maschi, 2013).

PwMI have the burden of navigating through a seemingly fragmented system of care in search of services related to their overall well-being (Bloom, 2016). Various agencies who are sought out for assistance often have conflicting philosophies regarding treatment and recovery; consequently, consumers, in their struggle to get help, may show a lack of follow-through or compliance with programmatic requirements. Service utilization is even more difficult once justice involvement is part of the equation (Slate, et al., 2013). The message is clear: when we criminalize mental illness and resist the effects of traumatization, we dismiss violence as normal and minimize the impact of violence on victims. In short, we prioritize offending over victimization! Rather than blaming such individuals as being "treatment resistant," we must evaluate the true issues and collaborate across systems to create a more seamless path to obtaining the needed supports and services.

While completing this text, the mental health system in the U.S. observed a positive turn on the policy front, with the passage of a significant piece of mental health reform legislation. On December 13, 2016, President Obama signed into law HR 34, the 21st Century Cures Act. Among other reforms, the Act incorporates the following changes to the system of care: Increased funding support and expansion of CIT, MHFA, ACT and FACT, and AOT; mandates related to data collection as it pertains to police encounters with PwMI and the incarceration of forensic populations; clarification of information-sharing as it pertains to HIPAA restrictions; and, the expansion of efforts to decriminalize mental illness (Treatment Advocacy Center, 2017). Given its very recent passage, it is too soon to report outcomes, though it will be interesting to monitor developments over time.

QUESTIONS FOR CLASSROOM DISCUSSION

1. Of all five intercept points on the original SIM, which do you believe is the most important? How might you propose to fix any issues at this particular intercept point?
2. What does systems integration refer to? Why is it important? Consider an example of what you learned related to this topic. What value does this topic have for you?
3. What does trauma-informed care refer to? Why is it important? Consider an example of what you learned related to this topic. What value does this topic have for you?

KEY TERMS & ACRONYMS

- Dual diagnosis
- Positive behavior interventions and supports (PBIS)

- System of care (SOC)
- Trauma-informed care (TIC)

Bibliography

Bloom, S. L. (2016). Advancing a National Cradle-to-Grave-to-Cradle Public Health Agenda. *Journal of Trauma & Dissociation, 17*(4), 383–396.

Bowen, E. A. & Murshid, N. S. (2016). Trauma-informed social policy: A framework for analysis and advocacy, *American Journal of Public Health*, Advance online publication, doi: 10.2105/AJPH.2015.302970.

Burchard, J. D., Bruns, E. J., & Burchard, S. N. (2002). The Wraparound Approach. In Burns, B. J., & Hoagwood, K. (Eds.), *Community Treatment for Youth: Evidenced-Based Interventions for Severe Emotional and Behavioral Disorders* (pp. 69–90). New York: Oxford University Press.

Campaign for Youth Justice. (April, 2012). *Key Facts: Youth in the Justice System.* Washington, DC: Campaign for Youth Justice.

Compton, M. T., & Kotwicki, R. J. (2007). *Responding to individuals with mental illnesses.* Sudbury, MA: Jones & Bartlett Publishers.

Council of State Governments. (2002). *Criminal Justice/ Mental Health Consensus Project* (Doc. No 197103). Washington, DC: U.S. Department of Justice.

Courtney, D., & Maschi, T. (2013). Trauma and Stress among Older Adults in Prison: Breaking the Cycle of Silence. *Traumatology, 20*(10), 1–9.

Ditton, P. M. (1999). Special report: Mental health and treatment of inmates and probationers. Washington, DC: US Department of Justice, Bureau of Justice Statistics.

Driessen, M., Schroeder, T., Widmann, B., von Schönfeld, C. E., & Schneider, F. (2006). Childhood Trauma, Psychiatric Disorders, and Criminal Behavior in Prisoners in Germany: A Comparative Study in Incarcerated Women and Men. *Journal of Clinical Psychiatry, 67*(10), 1486–1492.

Eber, L., & Keenan, S. (2004). Collaboration with Other Agencies: Wraparound and Systems of Care for Children and Youths with Emotional and Behavioral Disorders. In Rutherford, Jr., B., Quinn, M.,(Eds.), Mathur, R. *Handbook of Research in Emotional and Behavioral Disorders* (pp. 502–516). New York: Guilford Press.

Eber, L., & Nelson, C. M. (1997). School-Based Wraparound planning: Integrating Services for Students with Emotional and Behavioral Needs. *American Journal of Orthopsychiatry, 67*(3), 385–395.

Eber, L., Sugai, G., Smith, C., & Scott, T. M. (2002). Wraparound and Positive Behavioral Interventions and Supports in the Schools. *Journal of Emotional and Behavioral Disorders, 10*(3), 171–180.

Felitti, V. J., Anda, R. F., Nordenberg, D., Williamson, D. F., Spitz, A. M., Edwards, V., . . . & Marks, J. S. (1998). Relationship of Childhood Abuse and Household Dysfunction to Many of the Leading Causes of Death in Adults: The Adverse Childhood Experiences Study (ACES). *American Journal of Preventative Medicine, 14*(4), 245–258.

Fuchs, D., & Fuchs, L. S. (2006). Introduction to Response to Intervention: What, Why, and How Valid Is It? *Reading Research Quarterly, 41*(1), 93–99. doi: 10.1598/RRQ.41.1.4.

Greene, S., Haney, C., & Hurtado, A. (2000). Cycles of Pain: Risk Factors in the Lives of Incarcerated Mothers and Their Children. *The Prison Journal, 80*(1), 3–23.

Griffin, P. A., Heilbrun, K., Mulvey, E. P., DeMatteo, D., & Schubert, C. A. (Eds.). (2015). *The Sequential Intercept Model and Criminal Justice: Promoting Community Alternatives for Individuals with Serious Mental Illness.* New York, NY: Oxford University Press, USA.

Hayes, L. M. (2012). National study of jail suicide 20 years later. *Journal of Correctional Health Care, 18*(3), 233–245.

Honberg, R. (2015). *Two Major Mental Health Bills Introduced in US Senate.* National Alliance on Mental Illness. Retrieved from https://www.nami.org/About-NAMI/NAMI-News/Two-Major-Mental-Health-Bills-Introduced-in-US-Sen.

James D. J., Glaze L. E. (2006). *Mental health problems of prison and jail inmates* (Bureau of Justice Statistics Special Report NCJ 213600). Washington, DC: U.S. Department of Justice, Office of Justice Programs.

Kerig, P. K., & Becker, S. P. (2015). Early Abuse and Neglect as Risk Facto rs for the Development of Criminal and Antisocial Behavior. In Morizot, J., & Kazemian, L. (Eds.), *The Development of Criminal and Antisocial Behavior* (pp. 181–199). Springer International Publishing Switzerland.

Lane, K. L., Kalberg, J. R., & Menzies, H. M. (2009). *Developing Schoolwide Programs to Prevent and Manage Problem Behaviors: A Step-by-Step approach.* New York, NY: Guilford Press.

Levenson, J. S., Willis, G. M., & Prescott, D. S. (2014). Adverse Childhood Experiences in the Lives of Male Sex Offenders: Implications for Trauma-Informed Care. *Sexual Abuse: A Journal of Research and Treatment, 28*(4), 340–359.

Lewis T. J., Sugai G. (1999). Effective behavior support: A systems approach to proactive schoolwide management. *Focus on Exceptional Children, 31*(6), 1–24.

Miller, N. A., & Najavits, L. M. (2012). Creating Trauma-Informed Correctional Care: A Balance of Goals and Environment. *European Journal of Psychotraumatology, 3,* 1–8.

National Alliance on Mental Illness (NAMI) (2013). *Mental illness facts and numbers.* Retrieved from https://www2.nami.org/factsheets/mentalillness_factsheet.pdf

National Alliance on Mental Illness(NAMI) (n.d.). *Understanding Health Insurance.* Retrieved from http://www.nami.org/Learn-More/Understanding-Health-Insurance.

Read, J., Van Os, J., Morrison, A. P., & Ross, C. A. (2005). Childhood Trauma, Psychosis, and Schizophrenia: A Literature Review with Theoretical and Clinical Implications. *Acta Psychiatra Scandinavica, 112,* 330–350.

Rosenberg, L. (2011). Addressing Trauma in Mental Health and Substance Use Treatment. *The Journal of Behavioral Health Services & Research, 38*(4), 428–431.

Rutherford, R. B., Quinn, M. M., & Mathur, S. R. (Eds.) (2004). *Handbook of Research in Emotional and Behavioral Disorders.* New York: Guilford Press.

Sharma, M. & Bennett, R. (2015). Substance abuse and mental illness: Challenges for interventions. *Journal of Alcohol & Drug Education, 59*(2), 3–6.

Shufelt, J. L., & Cocozza, J. J. (2006). *Youth with mental health disorders in the juvenile justice system: Results from a multi-state prevalence study* (pp. 1–6). Delmar, NY: National Center for Mental Health and Juvenile Justice.

Slate, R. N., Buffington-Vollum, J. K., & Johnson, W. W. (2013). *The criminalization of mental illness: Crisis and opportunity for the justice system.* Durham, NC: Carolina Academic Press.

Substance Abuse and Mental Health Service Administration [SAMHSA] (2016). SAMHSA's Efforts to Address Trauma and Violence [Webpage]. Retrieved on January 6, 2017, from https://www.samhsa.gov/topics/trauma-violence/samhsas-trauma-informed-approach

Sugai, G., Horner, R. H., Dunlap, G., Hieneman, M., Lewis, T. J., Nelson, C. M., Ruef, M. (2000). Applying Positive Behavior Support and Functional Behavioral Assessment in Schools. *Journal of Positive Behavior Interventions, 2*(3), 131–143. doi: 10.1177/109830070000200302.

Teplin, L., Abram, K., McClelland, G., Mericle, A., Dulcan, M., & Washburn, D. (2006, April). *Psychiatric disorders of youth in detention.* Washington, DC: Office of Juvenile Justice and Delinquency Prevention. Juvenile Justice Bulletin, Office of Justice Programs.

Treatment Advocacy Center [TAC] (2017). 21st Century Cures Act [Webpage]. Retrieved on January 13, 2017, from http://www.treatmentadvocacycenter.org/component/content/article/3715

Wagner, P., & Rabuy, B. (2016). *Mass Incarceration: The Whole Pie 2016.* Northampton, MA: Prison Policy Initiative.

Weeks, R., & Widom, C. S. (1998). Self-reports of early childhood victimization among incarcerated adult male felons. *Journal of Interpersonal Violence, 13,* 346–361.

INDEX